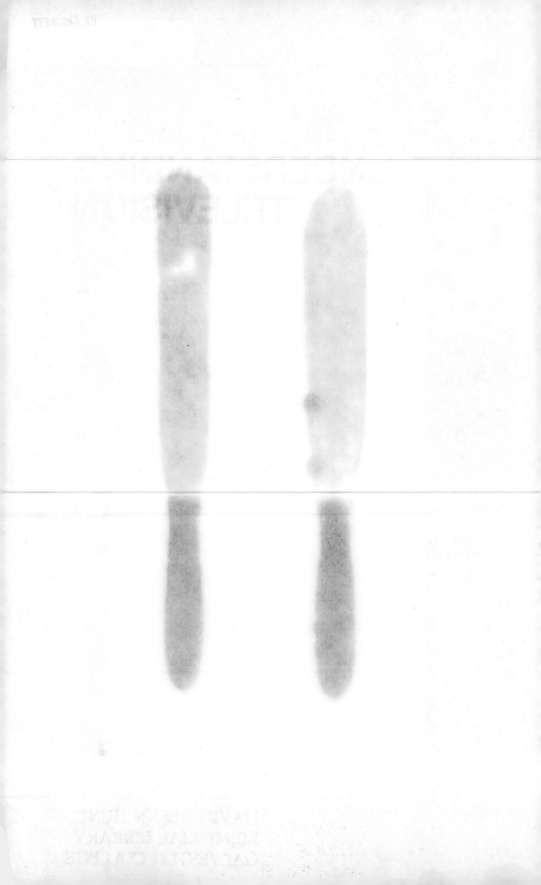

UNDERSTANDING TELEVISION

Essays on Television as a Social and Cultural Force

Edited by

Richard P. Adler

PRAEGER SPECIAL STUDIES • PRAEGER SCIENTIFIC

Library of Congress Cataloging in Publication Data
Main entry under title:

Understanding television.

   Includes essays from two earlier collections,
Television as a social force and Television as a
cultural force.
   "A Cambria Press book."
   Bibliography: p.
   Includes index.
   1. Television broadcasting--United States--
Addresses, essays, lectures. I. Adler, Richard.
II. Title. Television as a social and cultural
force.
PN1992.3.U5U5 1981   791.45'0973   81-47781
ISBN 0-03-055806-9   AACR2
ISBN 0-03-055801-8 (pbk.)

Published in 1981 by Praeger Publishers
CBS Educational and Professional Publishing
A Division of CBS, Inc.
521 Fifth Avenue, New York, New York 10175 U.S.A.

23456789   145   98765432

Acknowledgments

Arnheim, Rudolph. 1957. "A Forecast of Television." The article was written and first published in 1935. Reprinted in his book, *Film as Art*. Berkeley, California: University of California Press, pp. 188-198 Reprinted with permission. Copyright © by The Regents of the University of California.

Cater, Douglass. 1975. "Television and Thinking People." Published in *Television as a Social Force: New Approaches to TV Criticism*. New York: Praeger Publishers, pp. 1-7. Copyright © by the Aspen Institute Program on Communications & Society.

Novak, Michael. 1975. "Television Shapes the Soul." Published in *Television as a Social Force*. New York/ Praeger Publishers, pp. 9-21. Copyright © by the Aspen Institute Program on Communications & Society.

Comstock, George. 1978. "Televison and Human Behavior." Reprinted from *Television and Human /Behavior*. New York: Columbia University Press, pp. 1-17. Reprinted with permission. Copyright © by The Rand Corporation.

Wood, Peter H. 1976. "Televison as Dream." Published in *Television as a Cultural Force*. New York: Praeger Publishers, pp. 17-35. Copyright © by the Aspen Institute Program on Communications & Society.

Thorburn, David. 1976. "Television Melodrama." Published in *Television as a Cultural Force*. New York: Praeger Publishers, pp. 77-94. Copyright © by David Thorburn.

Berger, Arthur Asa. 1981. "Semiotics and TV." Published in *Understanding Television: Essays on Television as a Social and Cultural Force*. New York: Praeger Publishers. Copyright © by Arthur Asa Berger.

Zettl, Herbert. 1981. "Television Asthetics." Published in *Understanding Television*. New York: Praeger Publishers. Copyright © by Herbert Zettl.

Littlejohn, David. 1976. "Thoughts on Television Criticism." Published in *Television as a Cultural Force*. New York: Praeger Publishers, pp. 147-173. Copyright © by the Aspen Institute Program on Communications & Society.

Arlen, Michael. 1980. "Smooth Pebbles at Southfork." Reprinted from *The New Yorker*, March 24, 1980, pp. 112-121. Reprinted by permission. Copyright © 1980, The New Yorker Magazine, Inc..

Modleski, Tania. 1979. "Search for Tomorrow in Today's Soap Operas." Reprinted from *Film Quarterly*, Vol. 33, No. 1, pp. 12-21. Reprinted by permission. Copyright © by The Regents of the University of California.

Hough, Arthur. 1981. "Trials and Tribulations—Thirty Years of Sitcoms." Published in *Understanding Television*. New York: Praeger Publishers. Copyright © by Arthur Hough.

Preface

This volume grew out of two earlier anthologies published by Praeger. *Television as a Social Force* and *Television as a Cultural Force* contained essays which were written for a series of conferences sponsored by the Aspen Institute Workshop on Television. With support from the National Endowment for the Humanities and the John and Mary R. Markle Foundation, the Workshop was established to encourage leading humanists, scholars and critics from a variety of fields to give more attention to the significance of television in American life.

Understanding Television includes those essays from the earlier collections which have remained most relevant. They have been supplemented by a group of new essays commissioned especially for this volume, along with a number of valuable articles reprinted from elsewhere. While the earlier two books were essentially collections of conference papers, the contents of this volume were selected and arranged to provide a systematic introduction to the critical study of television as an institution and of its major program genres.

R. P. A.

Palo Alto
December 1980

Table of Contents

PART ONE: OVERVIEWS

PART TWO: CRITICAL APPROACHES

PART THREE: DRAMA

PART FOUR: NEWS

PART FIVE: THE FUTURE

Introduction

Richard P. Adler

"Of all the wonders of television," historian Daniel Boorstin has noted, "none is more remarkable than the speed with which it came." The printing press took five centuries to achieve its full impact. Television required less than a generation. While only one American household in one hundred had television in 1948, nearly nine out of ten had acquired TV sets by 1960. A decade later, television ownership in the U.S. had become virtually universal.

This most massive of mass media has thoroughly interwoven itself into the fabric of our daily lives. It has become an intimate companion, a part of the domestic scene. The rhythms of its programming—daytime, newstime, prime time, night time—serve as an implicit clock. Its inhabitants are as familiar to us as our neighbors and friends.

The TV set has become the primary source of news and entertainment for most Americans and a major force in the acculturation of children. Television has transformed the country's political processes. It is a fundamental component of the corporate marketing structure that underlies our consumer economy. Television, in short, pervades and alters the contemporary American environment.

Yet television also remains alien. It comes from *somewhere else.* It does not respond to us. Its images flicker before us like dreams.

Nor do we seem able to see television very clearly as an institution. To describe it as a "medium" is too colorless, too coldly technological. Television is not simply a medium of transmission, it is an active, pervasive force. It is, I believe, a *mediator* as well as a medium —a mediator between our individual lives and the larger life of the nation and the world; between fantasy and fact; between old values and new ideas; between our desire to seek escape and our need to confront reality.

Given the undeniable importance of television, the paucity of serious critical attention paid to it is striking. Television has been regularly attacked for being excessively violent, vulgar, or trivial. But only rarely has it received the kind of careful analysis and informed response that exist in abundance for literature, film, drama, and other performing arts.

There are good reasons for this, of course. Most obvious is the overall quality of television programming, which is generally regarded as being unworthy of serious critical interest. It is surely true that most of what appears on television is mediocre or worse. But the same is true of every medium, every art form.

It may be that television is actually being judged by a set of standards higher than those applied to other media. Neil Postman has noted that when a medium "saturates the culture in a cumulative way, like television, people have their expectations exaggerated to such an extent they tend to apply unrealistic criteria." Because television is always available to us at the turn of a switch, we tend to sample more of it and to expect that it will satisfy us. As a result, Postman suggests, "people think that television should have a substantially higher percentage of what they construe as quality shows than any other medium. It is a demand which no medium could meet."

The quality of television programming also is limited to some extent by the technical characteristics of the medium. The small size and low resolution of the TV screen precludes visual complexity, while television's low fidelity sound discourages the use of music and limits the impact of sound generally. These limitations mean that television is poorly suited to the presentation of dramatic spectacle (a fact which film makers have recognized and exploited). On the other hand, television's capacity for instantaneous transmission make it an ideal vehicle for sports, news, and live events. But the aesthetic of real-time happenings is not one easily recognized by traditional criticism.

Another limitation of the medium derives from the setting in which it is viewed. Our relationship to television is more like our relationship to the daily newspaper than to a film or play, which are experienced outside our normal routine. We seek out films and plays, and they begin and end in darkness and silence. But the TV set is turned on casually, and television programs are surrounded by commercials and other programs. We rarely give television our full attention. The inevitable commercial interruptions further discourage prolonged absorption.

The result is that it is easy to watch television but difficult to talk about it intelligently. Although we learn at an early age to become critical readers, we learn at an even earlier age to become uncritical viewers. Seldom if ever do we subject what we see on television to critical scrutiny.

An even more significant barrier to serious criticism is the nature of the institutions that control television. It was decided more than fifty years ago that although the airwaves belonged to the public, television in this country would be allowed to develop as a privately controlled, adertiser-supported private enterprise. Because of the way the medium evolved, American television came to be dominated by the three national commercial networks. Together, they account for approximately ninety percent of all television viewing time.

It is no secret that the networks are profitmaking institutions. Their business consists of attracting viewers and delivering them to advertisers, who represent the industry's only source of revenue. In this system, the measure of a program's success is not its quality nor whether it provides information or enlightenment—or even good entertainment. What matters is the size of the audience it attracts. As a result, the programming available in this country has been largely determined by the competition among the three networks for a dominant share of the available viewing audience. These constraints leave little room for innovation or excellence.

The place where innovation and excellence should most often be found is on public television. Because it is not subject to commercial pressures, public television is free to provide programs of the highest quality. And because it does not need to compete for ratings, it is able to provide programs of the highest quality.

Unfortunately, public television has not been able to capitalize on these advantages. Noncommercial television in this country came about as an afterthought to commercial television, and it has suffered from the lack of a clear mandate and wide popular support. Even today, it remains handicapped by undesirable channel allocations, inadequate and uncertain financing, political vulnerability, and a persistent confusion over its proper role. Until these problems are solved, public television will not provide a full-fledged alternative to the commercial networks.

Despite all these limitations and constraints, the fact remains that television is too important to ignore. The critic John Leonard has claimed that "television is now our only way of talking to each other about who we think we are." What he means, I think, is that television has not only become our primary channel for information and entertainment, but also the principal source of the imaginative forms through which we perceive ourselves and the world.

In the final analysis, American television is worth studying because it is a vivid and authentic expression of American culture. The medium's preoccupation with materialism and physical appearances, its irreverent, sometimes vulgar humor, its fascination with violence, even its sentimental optimism that goodness will eventually prevail—all these values are ingrained in the American character. Turning on the TV is like tuning in to the collective consciousness of the country. Whatever is important to the society—sexual standards, race relations, the conduct of government, crime and justice—finds expression somewhere on television.

I have come to the conclusion that the main reason we refuse to take television seriously is because it is so important to us. It is noteworthy that film studies did not begin to be respectable until television arrived to replace the movies as the country's dominant mass medium. In fact, there is an almost direct parallel between the decline in movie attendance after World War II and the rise of film studies. In this light, it is intriguing that television studies seem to be gaining acceptance just at the time when a whole range of new technologies—including cable, satellites, and the video-disc—are beginning to challenge the dominance of the networks.

Television as we know it is not about to disappear, of course, any more than the movies disappeared when television arrived. But it will change. In fact, it may be that just as television freed the film to grow in new directions, so the new media may liberate television from the constraints imposed on it by its own enormous success. At some future date, we may look back to the three decades from 1950 through 1980 as the Age of Broadcast Television.

In attempting to explain our difficulties in understanding American literature, D. H. Lawrence wrote that "it is hard to hear a new voice, as hard as it is to listen to an unknown language. We just don't listen." Our task as television critics is simply to learn to listen and to watch, consciously and carefully; to find the words to describe accurately what we have seen; and to think about the significance of what we have seen; and then, only then, to pass judgment. This book is intended to provide an introduction to the language and literature of television.

Part 1.
Overviews

The essays in this section take a broad look at television as a whole. The authors attempt to identify television's distinctive characteristics, define the roles it plays in our lives, or describe its effects.

The first essay was published in 1936 at the very dawn of the age of television. Psychologist Rudolph Arnheim examines what the new medium of television has in common with earlier media and distinguishes the ways in which it differs from them. He concludes with the prophetic warning that, although television can enrich us, it also has the potential "to put our minds to sleep"—a theme which has recurred in much subsequent criticism. Indeed, Douglass Cater's essay, written several decades later, picks up this theme as he considers why television has failed so far to live up to its initial promise.

The final two essays in this section focus on the impact of television. Michael Novak speculates about how the structure and pace of television may be shaping our perceptions. George Comstock summarizes what existing scientific research can tell us about the effects of television on us.

A Forecast
of Television

Rudolph Arnheim

Man's range of interest goes beyond the reach of his senses. Of the technical inventions that serve to diminish this disproportion, television is the latest and perhaps the most important. The new gadget seems magical and mysterious. It arouses curiosity: How does it work? What does it do to us? To be sure, when the television sets will have appeared on the birthday tables and under the Christmas trees, curiosity will abate. Mystery asks for explanation only as long as it is new. Let us take advantage of the propitious moment.

First of all, what is the fundamental problem involved in television? Eyes and ears have quite different tasks and, correspondingly, are made differently. The eye gives information about shape, color, surface qualities, and motion of objects in three-dimensional space by registering the reactions of these objects to light. The ear reveals little about the objects as such; it only reports on some of their activities, which happen to produce sound waves. On the whole, the eye takes little interest in the nature, place, and condition of the light

*This article was written and first published in 1935.

sources that make the light rays fall upon the retina. The ear is interested in the source of the sound; it wants the sound waves, on their way to the eardrum, to be as little modified as possible in order to keep the message from the source unaltered. Sound is produced by an object but tells us little about that object's shape, whereas the eye, in order to fulfill its task, must reckon with the fact that a suitable likeness of a three-dimensional object must be at least two-dimensional. The projection of a three-dimensional body upon a two-dimensional plane will give a one-sided but often informative picture. No satisfactory information would be obtained after the even more radical reduction of a body to a one-dimensional object—whether the reduction be spatial, that is, like a line on paper, or temporal, that is, a sequence of changes taking place in one point.

Any sense organ can register only one stimulus at a time so that the eye in order to produce a two-dimensional recording has to consist of numerous receptors that operate one next to the other. The mosaic that results from this collaboration of the receptors depicts three-dimensional space and volume as best it can. The time dimension, which is available in addition, uses the change of stimulation in each receptor to record motion and action.

A different situation is found in hearing. The sounds that exist in auditory space at any one time are not recorded separately but add up to one, more or less complex vibration, which can be received by a single membrane, such as the eardrum. This unitary vibration may be produced by the simple sound of a tuning fork or the complex noises of a crowd of excited people or a symphony orchestra. To some extent the ear succeeds in teasing the complex vibration apart, but it offers scant information about the locations of the different sound sources. The ear, like the eye, operates with a battery of receptors, and they, too, are arranged in a two-dimensional surface. The receptors of the cochlea are parallel fibers, as different in length and tension as the strings of a harp, and apparently for a similar purpose. The "strings" of the cochlea seem to be activated by resonance when vibrations of corresponding frequencies impinge upon them. This means that the ear uses its receptor field to distinguish between pitches, whereas the eye uses its to distinguish between spatial locations.

Whatever our hearing tells us about space and the directions from which sounds reach us is not strictly indispensable. Radio and phonograph often eliminate the resonance that gives information about space, and never tell about the direction but only about the distance of the sound source from the microphone. Auditory space, as transmitted by these mechanical devices, knows neither right nor left, neither above nor below. It only distinguishes between near and far, and yet we receive a rather complete or at least satisfactory impression. Whatever spatial qualities *are* transmitted, are derived from modifications sustained by the sound as it moves through space: distant sound is blurred, it is relatively weaker, and so forth.

If we do without directional hearing, the ear needs only three kinds of data, namely, the amplitude of the vibration, which produces loudness, the speed of the vibration, which produces pitch, and the shape of the vibration, which produces timbre (the difference between a flute, a bell, a soprano, a dog's bark). Since all the sounds that occur at a given moment fuse into one complex vibration, only one receptor is needed for the physical recording and transportation of sound. The eye, on the other hand, has to deal with millions of point-sized stimuli, which constitute the visual field. Therefore, in order to see space, volume, and shape, we require a battery of innumerable eyes—all of which are served by one common lens in the human receptor organ whereas insects have individual lenses for every eye. The sensitive surface formed by these eyes reproduces a projection of three-dimensional space.

These are the conditions that determine our modern ways of sending pictures, music, and speech through space. When light and sound do the transmitting themselves, the result is not very accurate even though the distance may be relatively small and our eyes and ears reinforced by mechanical receptor devices. Colors fade, shapes become fuzzy, sounds are blurred as the vibrations that carry them travel through space. In vision, the size of the retinal image depends on the visual angle, which may make objects shrink beyond recognition even at moderate distances. Therefore, definite progress was made as soon as it became possible to translate properties of sound and light messages into properties of electrical waves, for these waves travel through open space or wire without undergoing relevant changes; they adapt themselves to the curvature of the earth, and their speed is so nearly infinite that emission and reception become practically simultaneous. Space and time are annihilated.

It still strikes us as uncanny that pictures can be sent by telephone, and that we can see by radio. This is so because the electric transmission of sound was invented first. There is nothing inherently more or less mysterious in the one than in the other. The electrical waves will transmit the equivalents of amplitude, frequency, and shape of vibration, that is, all the essential properties of the phenomena in question. The particular problem of television is, of course, that pictures are two-dimensional. If analyzed, they decompose into a large number of brightness and color values, only one of which can be transmitted by one transmitter at a given moment. If we consider that the retina of the eye employs something like one hundred and fifty million receptors to produce an image, it seems that millions of telephones or radio stations should be needed to send just one picture. Fortunately, our eyes retain a given impression for a definite, though small span of time so that if all the stimuli that make up the picture are shown within a fraction of a second they will seem to appear all at once. Short though these time intervals need to be, they are long enough for electricity to send the point-sized stimuli one after the other over one and the same transmitter. The problem has been solved, in other words, by translating spatial relations (within the picture) into temporal ones, that is, by transforming a two-dimensional phenomenon into a one-dimensional one.

Speed of transmission is necessary also because visual objects change and move. The motion picture has taught us that a minimum of sixteen to twenty-four images per second is needed to produce smooth motion. Therefore the cathode ray must scan any one image fast enough to deal with a sufficient number of them every second. The scanning device must take care of the first, the second, and the fourth dimensions practically all at once.

Television enormously increases the capacity of radio for documentary information. The auditory world, available to the listener, is poor in documentary qualities. Hearing excels in transmitting speech and music, that is, products of the spirit; it renders little of physical reality. Without the services of a commentator or reporter, the event that radio purports to send over the air waves remains fragmentary to the point of being incomprehensible. Sometimes the rhythmical noise of marching feet, the scraps of band msic and voices may add up to the picture of a large crowd moving through the streets of a city. But the concreteness of such an experience is more to the credit of the listener's imagination than to what comes actually through the loudspeaker. The ear is a tool of reasoning; it is best qualified to receive material that has been given shape by man already—whereas seeing is direct experience, the gathering of sensory raw material.

Through television radio becomes a documentary medium. Only when it ministers also to the eye, radio fulfills its task—not its only task and perhaps not its most important—of making us witness immediately what is going on in the wide world around us. We see the citizens of a neighboring town assembled in the market square, the Prime Minister of a foreign country making a speech, two boxers fighting for the world championship in an arena across the ocean, the British dance bands performing, an Italian coloratura singer, a German professor, the smoldering remains of a wrecked railway train, the masked street crowds at the carnival, the snow-capped mountains of the Alps as they appear through clouds from an airplane, tropical fish through the windows of a submarine, the machines of a car factory, an explorer's ship battling the polar ice. We see the sun shining on Mount Vesuvius and, a second later, the neon lights that illuminate Broadway at the same time. The detour via the describing word becomes unnecessary, the barrier of foreign languages loses importance. The wide world itself enters our room.

Television is a relative of motorcar and airplane: it is a means of cultural transportation. To be sure, it is a mere instrument of transmission, which does not offer new means for the artistic interpretation of reality—as radio and film did. But like the transportation machines, which were a gift of the last century, television changes our attitude to reality: it makes us know the world better and in particular gives us a feeling for the multiplicity of what happens simultaneously in different places. For the first time in the history of man's striving for understanding, simultaneity can be experienced as such, not merely as translated into a succession in time. Our slow bodies and nearsighted eyes no longer hamper us. We come to recognize the place where we are located as one among many: we become more modest, less egocentric.

The technical gadget of the television set, however, does not cause these beneficial changes by itself. It offers possibilities, which the public must seize. Although the new victory over time and space represents an impressive enrichment of the perceptual world, it also favors the cult of sensory stimulation, which is characteristic of the cultural attitude of our time. Proud of our inventions—photography, the phonograph, film, radio—we praise the educational virtues of direct experience. We believe in traveling, and use pictures and movies in the schools. But as we render man's image of his world immensely more complete and accurate than it was in the past, we also restrict the realm of the spoken and the written word and thereby the realm of thinking. The more perfect our means of direct experience, the more easily we are caught by the dangerous illusion that perceiving is tantamount to knowing and understanding.

Television is a new, hard test of our wisdom. If we succeed in mastering the new medium it will enrich us. But it can also put our mind to sleep. We must not forget that in the past the inability to transport immediate experience and to convey it to others made the use of language necessary and thus compelled the human mind to develop concepts. For in order to describe things one must draw the general from the specific; one must select, compare, think. When communication can be achieved by pointing with the finger, however, the mouth grows silent, the writing hand stops, and the mind shrinks.

A good documentary or educational film is not raw experience. The material has passed the mill of reason, it has been sifted and interpreted. The direct transmissions of television will not offer much opportunity for such shaping of the stuff. Even so, people who know how to observe and to draw conclusions from what they see will profit greatly. Others will be taken in by the picture on the screen and confused by the variety of visible things. After a while they may even cease to feel confused: proud of their right to see everything and weaned from the desire to understand and to digest, they may feel great satisfaction—like those hardy British spinsters who after a trip around the world contentedly arrive in the train station of their home town in the same state of mind in which they left.

The senses are useful when their contribution is not over-estimated. In the culture we happen to live in, they teach us relatively little. The world of our century is a poor actor: it does show its variegated outside, but its true nature is not immediately apparent either to the eyes or to the ears. The newsreels tell us little, not only because the material is often badly chosen or because we do not know how to observe. They fail because the characteristics of the present world situation, or of a political event, or of a form of government are not as clearly expressed in their perceivable manifestations as a man's personality may be expressed in his face. Symptoms do not reveal much unless there is a physician to interpret them. In order to understand our present time, one must talk to the people, to the industrialists, or read the memoirs of the diplomats. If television is to make us understand the world rather than merely showing it to us, it will, at least, have to add the voice of the commentator to the pictures and the music and the noises—for words can speak of the general when we see the specific, and discuss the causes when we are faced with the effects.

How about the asocial traits, which television inherits from radio? Granted that when large masses of people see the same programs a certain unification of outlook will result. Also the exchange of programs can make for rapprochement among nations. When official pronouncements, parliamentary sessions, ceremonies, or court trials are transmitted, the citizen may feel more intimately concerned with the ways of his country. The complicated system of indirect government by which the central forces of public life reach the individual only through innumerable intermediaries is supplemented by the "wireless participation" of everybody in the affairs of state.

But doing things at the same time and doing them together is not quite the same. Radio and television do give a cozy family touch to public life, but they also keep the individual citizen from meeting his fellows. No longer does one need to be in company in order to celebrate or to mourn, to learn, to enjoy, to hail or to protest. It is true that our concert halls and theaters do not create much group feeling either. Strangers sit in rows, everyone watches and listens by himself, and the presence of the others is disturbing rather than helpful. But whenever the audience makes itself part of the event by laughing, shouting, answering, cheering, and booing, whenever the distinction between active and passive participants breaks down, something happens to the actor, the speaker, the teacher, or the preacher, as well as to the audience, the constituency, the pupils, and the congregation that cannot be replaced by electronics.

Television will make up for actual physical presence even more completely than does radio. All the more isolated will be the individual in his retreat, and the balance of trade will be correspondingly precarious: an enormous influx of riches, consumption without services in return. The pathetic hermit, squatting in his room, hundreds of miles away from the scene that he experiences as his present life, the "viewer" who cannot even laugh or applaud without feeling ridiculous, is the final product of a century-long development, which has led from the campfire, the market place, and the arena to the lonesome consumer of spectacles today.

Television and Thinking People

Douglass Cater

In January, 1949, only 2.3 percent of American homes had the box with the cathode-ray tube. Five years later, more than half of our homes had been penetrated by television. Today, 97 percent have one or more sets—a distribution roughly matching that of indoor plumbing. With American TV approaching its quarter-century anniversary as a household phenomenon, one might think we would have devoted serious attention by now to the effects of this medium on our culture, our society, our lives. Certainly we might expect at this point to be trying to articulate the consequences of the even more enveloping telecommunications environment which lies ahead. Yet, as the prescient Mr. Marconi predicted a long time ago, telecommunications has quickly become part of the "almost unnoticed working equipment of civilization."

Why unnoticed? What has prevented thinking people from applying their critical faculties to this medium, which reaches greater masses than all the other mass media combined (nearly twice as many sets in U.S. homes as the total daily circulation of newspapers)? Why haven't more of our talented scholars been attracted to the study of this new environment? Why do the media themselves devote so little attention to serious television analysis and criticism? Why have our foundations provided only very limited resources for the study of communications, which is as fundamental to society as education, health, or our physical environment?

I would suggest three speculative reasons for these failures. In the first place, scientific evidence suggests that thinking people—at least those over the age of twenty-five—are left-brained in development. They rely predominantly on the left hemisphere, which controls sequential, analytical tasks based on the use of propositional thought. TV, we are informed, appeals mainly to the right hemisphere of the brain, which controls appositional thought.

Scientists and theologians alike have pondered how the two halves of the brain relate—whether they ignore, inhibit, cooperate, compete, or simply take turns at the control center. But whole cultures seem to show preference for one or the other mode of thought, and thinking people of the Western world have up until now plighted their troth with propositional thought. But after five centuries of slowly acquired sophistication in distinguishing the truth from the trickery transmitted by Mr. Gutenberg's invention, we now find ourselves having to master the non-linear logic created by a steady bombardment of sights and sounds on our senses. The thinking person is apt to be somewhat bewildered by the telly and to regard it in the same way a back-sliding prohibitionist regards hard liquor—as something to be indulged in with a sense of guilt. The "educated viewer," according to Robert T. Bower's analysis of viewing habits, has learned to live with ambivalence: Although he may be scornful of commercial TV fare, "he watches the set (by his own admission) as much as others during the evening and weekend hours . . . even when he had a clear choice between an information program and some standard entertainment fare, he was just as apt as others to choose the latter."[1]

The peculiar structure of the American television industry is a second reason why the thinking person refuses to think seriously about the medium. The broadcast industry is based on a marketplace unlike any other in our private enterprise economy. It offers its product "free" to the consumer and depends on advertising to supply, by latest count, gross annual revenues of $4.5 billion. As a result, commercial TV's prime allegiance is to the merchant, not the viewer. To attract the advertising dollar, the programmer seeks to capture the dominant share of the viewers and to hold them unblinking for the longest period of time. Everything else is subordinated to this dogged pursuit of mankind in the mass. A program attracting many millions is deemed a failure and discarded if it happens to be scheduled opposite a program attracting even more millions.

Within this iron regime of dollars and ratings, a few ghettos of do-goodism exist. Network news and documentaries as well as occasional dramas of exceptional quality reveal an upward striving in television (dismissed by some cynics as tithing to the Federal regulators). But these programs fare poorly in the competition for television's most precious commodity—time. A former network news chief has remarked, "They don't mind how much money and talent we devote to producing documentaries so long as we don't ask for prime time evening hours to show them." Even the daylight hours have to be tightly rationed when the marathon melodramas of Washington start competing with the soap operas of Hollywood.

Thinking people do not know how to cope with a system whose economic laws, they are led to believe, are immutable. Any suggestions they may have for TV's betterment are characterized as naive, elitist, and offensive to the First Amendment. The proper posture is to sit back and be thankful when broadcast officialdom chooses to violate its own laws and reveal fleetingly what a fantastic instrument of communication television can be.

A third reason why thinking people have difficulty coming to grips with television is that we have yet to develop satisfactory measures with which to gauge this environmental phenomenon. Consider, as an example, the Surgeon General's inquiry into televised violence and its effect on the behavior of children. Conducted over three years at a cost of $1.8 million, and based on twenty-three separate laboratory and field studies, this was the most far-reaching probe to date into the social consequences of television. In its final report the Surgeon General's Committee could acknowledge only "preliminary and tentative" evidence of a causal relationship between TV violence and aggression in children.

For an industry dedicated to the proposition that thirty-second commercials can change a viewer's buying behavior, it would be folly to ignore this warning about the not-so-subliminal effects of its program content. But these studies, mostly gauging immediate response to brief TV exposure, could not adequately measure the impact of the total phenomenon—the experience of the child who spends up to six hours a day, year in and year out, before the set. This is what makes television different from reading books or going to the movies.

How to measure the long-term, less flamboyant effects of the environment created by television? In 1938, E. B. White witnessed a TV demonstration and wrote, "A door closing, heard over the air, a face contorted, seen in a panel of light, these will emerge as the real and the true. And when we bang the door of our own cell or look into another's face, the impression will be of mere artifice." Now, a third of a century later, comes Tony Schwartz to carry the speculation further.[2] Mr. Schwartz' insights have peculiar power because he was the creator of the ill-famed political commercial in 1964 showing a child innocently picking daisy petals as a countdown for a hydrogen blast. Though there was no mention of the presidential candidate against whom the message was aimed, the effect of the commercial was so unnerving that it was withdrawn by its sponsors after a single showing. Schwartz appears to know whereof he theorizes.

Gutenberg man, he writes, lived by a communication system requiring the laborious coding of thought into words and then the equally laborious decoding by the receiver—akin to the loading, shipping and unloading of a railway freight car. Electronic man dispenses with this, communicating experience without the need of symbolic transformations. What the viewer's brain gets is a mosaic of myriad dots of light and vibrations of sound which are stored and recalled at high speed. Amid this electronic bombardment, Schwartz speculates, a barrier has been crossed akin to the supersonic sound barrier, or, in his image, the 90-mile-an-hour barrier when a motorcycle racer must turn *into* rather than *out with* a skid: ". . . in communicating at electronic speed we no longer direct information into an audience but try to evoke stored information out of them in a patterned way."

The function of the electronic communicator, according to Schwartz, "is to achieve a state of resonance with the person receiving visual and auditory stimuli." The Gutenberg communicator—for the past five hundred years patiently transmitting experience line by line, usually left to right, down the printed page—is no longer relevant. TV man has become conditioned to a total communication environment, to constant stimuli which he shares with everyone else in society and to which he is conditioned to respond instantly. Schwartz believes that the totality and instantaneousness of television, more than its particular program content, contributes to violence in society.

His premises lead him to the shattering conlusion that "truth is a print ethic, not a standard for ethical behavior in electronic communication." We must now be concerned not with Gutenberg-based concepts of truth but with the "effects" of electronic communication: "A whole new set of questions must be asked, and a whole new theory of communications must be formulated."

Without going all the way with Schwartz, we clearly need to examine TV's effects more diligently. What, for example, is television doing to the institutions and forms and rituals of our democracy? In 1968, sitting in Washington, I watched TV coverage of the disastrous Democratic Convention in Chicago. At one moment, all hell broke loose in the area where the Wisconsin delegation was seated. Immediately, the TV cameras zoomed in and reporters rushed there with walkie-talkies. In an instant, the whole viewing nation knew the cause of the trouble, while Speaker Carl Albert, presiding over the convention, didn't know. Yet Albert was the one who had to decide what to do about the problem. In microcosm, one witnessed how leadership can be hustled by such a formidable communications system.

Politicians are struggling to learn the grammar of TV communication and to master the body English so different from that of the stump speech. TV has markedly influenced the winnowing process by which some politicians are sorted out as prospects for higher office and others are not. TV has contributed to abbreviation of the political dialogue and even changed the ground rules by which candidates map their campaign itineraries.

TV has nurtured widespread illusions about recreating a Greek marketplace of direct democracy. When citizens can see and hear what they believe to be the actuality, why should they rely on intermediating institutions to make the decisions for them? When political leaders can reach directly to their constituents without the help of a political party, why should they not opt for "the people's" mandate rather than "the party's"? Recent Presidents and Presidential candidates have been notably affected by this line of reasoning. It exposes an ancient vulnerability of our republic in which so much political lip service is paid to the notion that public opinion should rule everything.

How can democracy be strengthened within the environment of television? Why, in an age of abundant communication, has there been a continuing decline in voter participation? Michael Robinson, a political scientist, cites surveys which indicate that heavy TV viewers are more apt than light viewers to be turned off by politics.[3] He speculates that the more dependent an individual becomes on TV as his principal source of information, the more likely he is to feel that he cannot understand or affect the political process. TV, unlike newspapers, reaches many who are not motivated to seek information about public affairs and these "inadvertent" audiences, in Robinson's view, are frequently confused and alienated by what they see. Such a proposition runs directly counter to the usual reformist instinct to prescribe more programming to overcome voter apathy. Professor Robinson's speculations need to be probed more deeply.

What will be the future? George Orwell had a vision of a time—less than a decade away—when the communciations environment would be employed for the enslavement rather than the enlightenment of mankind. Orwell called his system "Big Brother." For the present anyway, we can conceive of a less ominous communications future with MOTHER, which is the acronym for "Multiple Output Telecommunication Home End Resources."

What will be the technical characteristics of MOTHER? First, she will offer infinitely more channels—via microwave, satellite, cable, laser beam—than the present broadcast spectrum provides. There will also be greater capacity crammed within each channel—more information "bits" per gigahertz—so that one can simultaneously watch a program and receive a newspaper print-out on the same channel.

A life-sized MOTHER, giving the illusion of three dimensions, will be able to narrowcast to neighborhoods or other focused constituencies. She will be "interactive," permitting us to talk back to our television set by means of a digital device on the console. Recording and replay equipment, already being marketed, will liberate us from the tyranny of the broadcast schedule, and computer hookup and stop-frame control will bring the Library of Congress and other Gutenberg treasuries into our living room.

Finally, via the satellite, MOTHER will offer world-wide programming in what the communications experts artfully call "real time" (even if real time means that Mohammed Ali must fight at 4:00 a.m. in Zaire in order to suit the prime time of New Yorkers). Although MOTHER will be able to beam broadcasts from the People's Republic of China directly to a household in the U.S. and vice versa, she may face political barriers.

Until recently, prophets foresaw that the cable and other technological advances would transform television from a wholesale to a retail enterprise, directly offering the consumer a genuine diversity of choice. The "television of abundance" would bring not just greater variety of programs but also new concepts of programming—continuing education, health delivery, community services. Television would become a participatory instrument of communication rather than a one-way flow.

Today, these visions are not so bright. Some critics now glumly predict that the new technology will suffer the fate of the supersonic transport. Others expect the technology to be developed, but it will serve strictly commercial rather than social purposes. Computer may be talking to computer by cable and satellite, but householders will still be watching "I Love Lucy" on their TV sets.

My own expectation is that the next decade or two will radically alter America's communications. The important issue is whether it will be for better or for worse. If it is to be "for better," we must give more critical attention to TV than we have given in the past. Too much critical time has been wasted worrying about the worst of television. More attention should be paid to the best, not simply laudatory attention but a systematic examination of style and technique and message. Criticism should also extend its reach beyond the intellectual elite into elementary and secondary schools, where children can be stimulated to think about the medium which so dominates their waking hours. We must endeavor to raise the viewers' capacity to distinguish truth from sophistry, or at least their awareness, in Schwartz's vocabulary, of the "resonance" being evoked from them.

There needs to be more widespread analysis and debate of the potential for new media and for new forms within the media. Could an electronic box office for pay programming repeal the iron laws governing "free" commerical television? How do we move beyond the limits of present broadcasting toward broader social purposes for television? In an era when life-long learning has become essential to prevent human obsolescence, television surely has a role to play. And television might regularly deliver some types of health service now that the doctor is seldom making house-calls. Health and education are gargantuan national enterprises costing upwards of $200 billion annually. Yet only paltry sums are being invested for research and demonstration to develop TV's capacity to enrich and extend them.

Finally, we must move beyond our preoccupation with the production and transmission processes in media communication. An equally important question is what gets through? The editors of *Scientific American* report that man's visual system has more than a million channels, capable of transmitting instantly 10^7 bits of information to the brain. Yet the brain has the capacity for receiving only twenty-seven bits of information per second. These are the raw statistics of communication within the human anatomy. They lead Sir John Eccles, the Nobel Prize-winning physiologist, to believe that the most important frontier of brain research involves the study of inhibition—our capacity to censor stimuli in order to prevent overload. Sir John makes the comparison: "It's like sculpture. What you cut away from the block of stone produces the statue."

Our journalists, both on TV and in print, pledge fealty to the proposition that society thrives by the communication of great gobs of unvarnished truth. Our law courts make us swear to tell "the truth, the whole truth, and nothing but the truth." Yet we only dimly understand how, in an all-enveloping information environment, man chisels his little statues of perceived reality. As we approach a time when communication threatens to fission like the atom, we need to delve more deeply into these mysteries.

Looking far ahead, Robert Jastrow, Director of the Goddard Institute of Space Studies, foresees a fifth communications revolution more radical even than the previous four revolutions of speech, writing, printing, and radio. "In the long term, the new satellites will provide a nervous system for mankind, knitting the members of our species into a global society," Jastrow predicts and compares this to that change in the history of life several billion years ago when multicellular animals evolved out of more primitive organisms.

Before such an awesome prospect, thinking people may feel overwhelmed. Or else we can screw up our courage, ask the fundamental questions, and make the critical choices to shape our destiny.

Footnotes

1.   Robert T. Bower, *Television and the Public* (Holt, Rinehart and Winston, Inc., 1973).

2.   See his recent book, *The Responsive Chord* (Anchor/Doubleday, 1973).

3.   See his essay, page 97.

Television Shapes
the Soul

Michael Novak

For twenty-five years we have been immersed in a medium
never before experienced on this earth. We can be forgiven if we do
not yet understand all the ways in which this medium has altered us,
particularly our inner selves: the perceiving, mythic, symbolic—and
the judging, critical—parts of ourselves.

Media, like instruments, work "from the outside in." If you
practice the craft of writing sedulously, you begin to think and perceive differently. If you run for twenty minutes a day, your psyche is
subtly transformed. If you work in an executive office, you begin to
think like an executive. And if you watch six hours of television, on
the average, every day . . . ?[1]

Innocent of psychological testing and sociological survey, I
would like to present a humanist's analysis of what television seems
to be doing to me, to my students, to my children, and, in general, to
those I see around me (including those I see on television, in movies,
in magazines, etc.). My method is beloved of philosophers, theologians, cultural critics: try to *perceive,* make *distinctions, coax into*

the light elusive movements of consciousness. It goes without saying that others will have to verify the following observations; they are necessarily in the hypothetical mode, even if some of the hypotheses have a cogency that almost bites.

Two clusters of points may be made. The first, rather metaphysical, concerns the way television affects our way of perceiving and approaching reality. The second cluster concerns the way television inflicts a class bias on the world of our perceptions—the bias of a relatively small and special social class.[2]

Television and Reality

Television is a molder of the soul's geography. It builds up incrementally a psychic structure of expectations. It does so in much the same way that school lessons slowly, over the years, tutor the unformed mind and teach it "how to think." Television *might* tutor the mind, soul, and heart in other ways than the ways it does at present. But, to be concrete, we ought to keep in view the average night of programming on the major networks over the last decade or so—not so much the news or documentaries, not so much the discussion on public television or on Sundays, not so much the talk shows late at night, but rather the variety shows, comedies, and adventure shows that are the staples of prime-time viewing. From time to time we may allow our remarks to wander farther afield. But it is important to concentrate on the universe of prime-time major network programming; that is where the primary impact of television falls.

It is possible to isolate five or six ways in which television seems to affect those who watch it. Television series represent genres of artistic performance. They structure a viewer's way of perceiving, of making connections, and of following a story line. Try, for example, to bring to consciousness the difference between the experience of watching television and the experience of learning through reading, argument, the advice of elders, lectures in school, or other forms of structuring perception. The conventions of the various sorts of television series re-create different sorts of "worlds." These "worlds" raise questions—and, to some extent, illuminate certain features of experience that we notice in ourselves and around us as we watch.

(1) Suppose that you were a writer for a television show—an action-adventure, a situation comedy, even a variety show. You

would want to be very careful to avoid "dead" spots, "wooden" lines, "excess" verbiage. Every line has a function, even a double or triple function. Characters move on camera briskly, every line counts, the scene shifts rapidly. In comedy, every other line should be a laugh-getter. Brevity is the soul of hits.

Television is a teacher of expectations; it speeds up the rhythm of attention. Any act in competition with television must approach the same pace; otherwise it will seem "slow." Even at an intellectual conference or seminar we now demand a swift rhythm of progressive movement; a leisurely, circular pace of rumination is perceived as less than a "good show."

(2) But not only the pace is fast. Change of scene and change of perspective are also fast. In a recent episode of *Kojak,* action in three or four parts of the city was kept moving along in alternating sequences of a minute or less. A "principle of association" was followed; some image in the last frames of one scene suggested a link to the first frames of the new scene. But one scene cut away from another very quickly.

The progression of a television show depends upon multiple logics—two or three different threads are followed simultaneously. The viewer must figure out the connections between people, between chains of action, and between scenes. Many clues are *shown,* not *said.* The viewer must detect them.

The logic of such shows is not sequential in a single chain. One subject is raised, then cut, and another subject is picked up, then cut. Verbal links—"Meanwhile, on the other side of the city . . ."—are not supplied.

In teaching and in writing I notice that for students one may swiftly change the subject, shift the scene, drop a line of argument in order to pick it up later—and not lose the logic of development. Students understand such a performance readily. They have been prepared for it. The systems of teaching which I learned in my student days—careful and exact exegesis proceeding serially from point to point, the careful definition and elucidation of terms in an argument and the careful scrutiny of chains of inference, and the like—now meet a new form of resistance. There has always been resistance to mental discipline; one has only to read the notebooks of students from medieval universities to recognize this well-established tradition of resistance. But today the minds and affections of the brighter students are teeming with images, vicarious experiences, and indeed of actual travel and accomplishments. Their minds race ahead and around the flanks of lines of argument. "Dialectics" rather than "logic" or "exegesis" is the habit of mind they are most ready for. I say this neither in praise nor in blame; pedagogy must deal with this new datum, if it is new. What are its limits and its possibilities? What correctives are needed among students—and among teachers?

(3) The periodization of attention is also influenced by the format of television. For reasons of synchronized programming the ordinary television show is neatly divided into segments of approximately equal length, and each of these segments normally has its own dramatic rhythm so as to build to dramatic climax or sub-climax, with the appropriate degree of suspense or resolution. Just as over a period of time a professor develops an instinct for how much can be accomplished in a fifty-minute lecture, or a minister of religion develops a temporal pattern for his sermons, so also the timing of television shows tutors their audience to expect a certain rhythm of development. The competitive pressures of television, moreover, encourage producers to "pack" as much action, intensity, or (to speak generally) entertainment into each segment as possible. Hence, for example, the short, snappy gags of *Laugh-In* and the rapid-fire developments of police shows or westerns.

Character is as important to successful shows as action; audiences need to "identify" with the heroes of the show, whether dramatic or comic. Thus in some ways the leisure necessary to develop character may provide a counter-tendency to the need for melodramatic rapidity. Still, "fast-paced" and "laugh-packed" and other such descriptions express the sensibility that television both serves and reinforces.

(4) Television tutors the sensibilities of its audience in another way: it can handle only a limited range of human emotions, perplexities, motivations, and situations. The structure of competitive television seems to require this limitation; it springs from a practiced estimation of the capacity of the audience. Critics sometimes argue that American novelists have a long tradition of inadequacy with respect to the creation of strong, complicated women and, correspondingly, much too simple and superficial a grasp of the depths and complexitites of human love. It is, it is said, the more direct "masculine" emotions, as well as the relations of comradeship between men, that American artists celebrate best. If such critical judgments may be true of our greatest artists working in their chosen media, then, a fortiori, it is not putting down television to note that the range of human relations treated by artists on television is less

than complete. The constraints under which television artists work are acute: the time available to them, the segmentation of this time, and the competitive pressures they face for intense dramatic activity. To develop a fully complicated set of motivations, internal conflicts, and inner contradictions requires time and sensitivity to nuance. The present structure of television makes these requirements very difficult to meet.

This point acquires fuller significance if we note the extent to which Americans depend upon television for their public sense of how other human beings behave in diverse situations. The extent of this dependence should be investigated. In particular, we ought to examine the effects of the growing segregation of Americans by age. It does not happen frequently nowadays that children grow up in a household shared by three generations, in a neighborhood where activities involve members of all generations, or in a social framework where generation-mixing activites are fairly common. I have many times been told by students (from suburban environments, in particular) that they have hardly ever, or never, had a serious conversation with adults. The social world of their parents did not include children. They spent little time with relatives, and that time was largely formal and distant. The high schools were large, "consolidated," and relatively impersonal. Their significant human exchanges were mostly with their peers. Their images of what adults do and how adults think and act were mainly supplied by various media, notably television and the cinema. The issue such comments raise is significant. Where *could* most Americans go to find dramatic models of adult behavior? In the eyes of young people does the public weight of what is seen on television count for more than what they see in their private world as a model for "how things are done"? Indeed, do adults themselves gain a sense of what counts as acceptable adult behavior from the public media?

If it turns out to be true that television (along with other media like magazines and the cinema) now constitutes a major source of guidance for behavior, to be placed in balance with what one learns from one's parents, from the churches, from one's local communities, and the like, then the range of dramatic materials on television has very serious consequences for the American psyche. While human behavior is to a remarkable extent diverse and variable, it tends to be "formed" and given shape by the attraction or the power of available imaginative materials: stories, models, symbols, images-in-action. The storehouse of imaginative materials available to each person provides a sort of repertoire. The impact of new models can be a powerful one, leading to "conversions," "liberations," or "new directions." The reservoir of acquired models exerts a strong influence both upon perception and upon response to unfamiliar models. If family and community ties weaken and if psychic development becomes somewhat more nuclearized or even atomized, the influence of television and other distant sources may well become increasingly powerful, moving, as it were, into something like a vacuum. Between the individual and the national source of image-making there will be little or no local resistance. The middle ground of the psyche, until recently thick and rich and resistant, will have become attenuated.

The point is not that television has reached the limit of its capacities, nor is it to compare the possibilities of television unfavorably with those of other media. It is, rather, to draw attention to television as it has been used in recent years and to the structures of attention that, by its presentations, it helps to shape.

The competitive pressures of programming may have brought about these limits. But it is possible that the nature of the medium itself precludes entering certain sorts of depths. Television may be excellent in some dimensions and merely whet the appetite in others.

(5) Television also seems to conceive of itself as a national medium. It does not favor the varieties of accent, speech patterns, and other differences of the culture of the United States. It favors a language which might be called "televisionese"—a neutral accent, pronunciation, and diction perhaps most closely approximated in California.

Since television arises in the field of "news" and daily entertainment, television values highly a kind of topicality, instant reflection of trends, and an effort to be "with it" and even "swinging." It values the "front edge" of attention, and it dreads being outrun by events. Accordingly, its product is perishable. It functions, in a way, as a guide to the latest gadgets and to the wonders of new technologies, or, as a direct contrary, to a kind of nostalgia for simpler ways in simpler times. Fashions of dress, automobiles, and explicitness "date" a series of shows. (Even the techniques used in taping shows may date them.)

Thus television functions as an instrument of the national, mobile culture. It does not reinforce the concrete ways of life of individual neighborhoods, towns, or subcultures. It shows the way things are done (or fantasized as being done) in "the big world." It is an organ of Hollywood and New York, not of Macon, Peoria, Salinas, or Buffalo.

I once watched television in a large hut in Tuy Hoa, South Vietnam. A room full of Vietnamese, including children, watched Armed Forces Television, watched Batman, Matt Dillon, and other shows from a distant continent. Here was their glimpse of the world from which the Americans around them had come. I wanted to tell them that what they were watching on television represented *no place,* represented no neighborhoods from which the young Americans around them came. And I began to wonder, knowing that not even the makers of such shows lived in such worlds, whose real world does television represent?

There are traces of local authenticity and local variety on national television. *All in the Family* takes the cameras into a neighborhood in Queens. The accents, gestures, methods and perceptions of the leading actors in *Kojak* reflect in an interesting and accurate way the ethnic sensibilites of several neighborhoods in New York. The clipped speech of Jack Webb in *Dragnet* years ago was an earlier break from "televisionese." But, in general, television is an organ of nationalization, of homogenization—and, indeed, of a certain systematic inaccuracy about the actual, concrete texture of life in the United States.

This nationalizing effect also spills over into the news and the documentaries. The cultural factors which deeply affect the values and perceptions of various American communities are neglected; hence the treatment of problems affecting such communities is frequently oversimplified. This is especially true when matters of group conflict are involved. The tendency of newsmen is subtly to take sides and to regard some claims or behavior as due to "prejudice," others as rather more moral and commendable.

The mythic forms and story lines of the news and documentaries are not inconsonant with the mythic forms represented in the adventure stories and Westerns. "Good" and "evil" are rather clearly placed in conflict. "Hard-hitting" investigative reporting is mythically linked to classic American forms of moral heroism: the crime-buster, the incorruptible sheriff. The forces of law and progress ceaselessly cut into the jungle of corruption. There is continuity between the prime-time news and prime-time programming—much more continuity than is detected by the many cultivated Cyclopses who disdain "the wasteland" and praise the documentaries. The mythic structure of both is harmonious.

It should prove possible to mark out the habits of perception and mind encouraged by national television. If these categories are not decisive, better ones can surely be discerned. We might then design ways of instructing ourselves and our children in countervailing habits. It does not seem likely that the mind and heart tutored by many years of watching television (in doses of five or six hours a day) is in the same circumstance as the mind and heart never exposed to television. Education and criticism must, it seems, take this difference into account.

The Class Bias of Television

Television has had two striking effects. On the one hand, as Norman Podhoretz has remarked, it has not seemed to prevent people from reading; more books are being published and mass marketed than ever before in American history. It is possible that television stimulates many to go beyond what television itself can offer.

Secondly, television works, or appears to work, as a homogenizing medium. It presents a fairly non-representative, non-concrete, imagined world to a national audience. In many respects, it could be shown, the overall ideological tendency of television productions—from the news, through the talk shows, to the comedy hours, variety shows, and adventure, crime, and family shows—is that of a vague and misty liberalism: belief in the efficacy of an ultimate optimism, "talking through one's problems," a questioning of institutional authorities, a triumph of good over evil. Even a show like *All in the Family,* beneath its bluster and its violation of verbal taboos, illustrates the unfailing victory of liberal points of view: Archie Bunker always loses. A truly mean and aggressive reactionary point of view is virtually nonexistent. There is no equivalent on national television to *Human Events* and other right-wing publications, or to the network of right-wing radio shows around the nation. While many critics of right and left find prime-time television to be a "wasteland," few have accused it of being fascist, malicious, evil, or destructive of virtue, progress, and hope. Television's liberalism is calculated to please neither the new radicals nor the classic liberals of the left, nor the upbeat, salesmanlike exponents of the right. In harmony with the images of progress built into both liberalism and capitalism, television seems, however gently, to undercut traditional institutions and to promote a restless, questioning attitude. The main product—and attitude—it has to sell is the new.

This attachment to the new insures that television will be a vaguely leftist medium, no matter who its personnel might be. Insofar as it debunks traditions and institutions—and even the act of *representing* these in selective symbolic form is a kind of veiled threat to them—television serves the purposes of that larger movement within which left and right (in America, at least) are rather like the two legs of locomotion: the movement of modernization. It serves, in general, the two mammoth institutions of modern life: the state and the great corporations. It serves these institutions even when it exalts the individual at the expense of family, neighborhood, religious organizations, and cultural groups. These are the only intermediate institutions that stand between the isolated individual and the massive institutions.

Thus the homogenizing tendencies of television are ambivalent. Television can electrify and unite the whole nation, creating an instantaneous network in which millions are simultaneous recipients of the same powerful images. But to what purpose, for whose use, and to what effect? Is it an unqualified good that the national grid should become so pre-eminent, superior to any and all local checks and balances? The relative national power and influence of state governors seems to have been weakened, for example; a state's two senators, by comparison, occupy a national stage and can more easily become national figures.

But in at least five other ways national television projects a sense of reality that is not identical to the sense of reality actual individuals in their concrete environments share. Taken together, these five ways construct a national social reality that is not free of a certain class and even ethnic bias.

(1) The television set becomes a new instrument of reality—of "what's happening" in the larger, national world, of "where it's at." In some sense what isn't on television isn't quite real, is not part of the nationally shared world, will be nonexistent for millions of citizens. Three examples may suggest the power of this new sense of reality.

Experiments suggest (so I am told) that audiences confronted with simultaneous projection on a large movie screen and on a television set regularly and overwhelmingly end up preferring the image on the smaller set. The attraction of reality is somehow there.

On a political campagin, or at a sports event, individuals seem to seek to be on camera with celebrities, as if seeking to share in a precious and significant verification of their existence. A young boy in

Pittsburgh exults, "I'm real!" as he interposes himself between the grinding cameras and a presidential candidate in the crowd. Not to be on television is to lack weight in national consciousness. Audience "participation" (the ancient platonic word for being) fills a great psychic hunger: to be human in the world that really counts.

Finally, anyone who has participated in a large-scale event comes to recognize vividly how strait and narrow is the gate between what has actually happened and what gets on television. For the millions who see the television story, of course, the story is the reality. For those who lived through a strenuous sixteen-hour day on the campagin trail, for example, it is always something of a surprise to see what "made" the television screen—or, more accurately, what the television screen made real. That artificial reality turns out to have far more substance for the world at large than the lived sixteen hours. According to the ancient *maya,* the world of flesh and blood is an illusion. And so it is.

(2) Television is a new technology and depends upon sophisticated crafts. It is a world of high profit. Its inside world is populated by persons in a high income bracket. Moreover, television is a world that requires a great deal of travel, expense-account living, a virtual shuttle service between Los Angeles and New York, a taste for excellent service and high prestige. These economic factors seriously color television's image of the world.

The glitter of show business quickly spread to television. In the blossomy days when thinkers dreamed of an affluent society and praised the throwaway society, the shifting and glittering sets of television make-believe seemed like a metaphor for modern society. Actually, a visit to a television studio is extraordinarily disappointing, far more so, even, than a visit to an empty circus tent after the crowd has gone. Cheaply painted pastel panels, fingerprints sometimes visible upon them, are wheeled away and stacked. The cozy intimacy one shares from one's set at home is rendered false by the cavernous lots of the studio, the tangle of wires, the old clothing and cynical buzzing of the bored technicians, crews, and hangers-on. Dust and empty plastic coffee cups are visible in corners where chairs compete for space. There is a tawdriness behind the scenes.

In a word, the world of television is a radically duplicitous world. Its illusions pervade every aspect of the industry. The salaries paid to those who greet the public remove them from the public. The settings in which they work are those of show business. Slick illusion is the constant temptation and establishes the rules of the game.

Moreover, the selling of products requires images of upward mobility. The sets, designs, and fluid metaphors of the shows themselves must suggest a certain richness, smoothness, and adequacy. It is not only that writers and producers understand that what audiences desire is escape. (One can imagine a poor society in which television would focus on limited aspiration and the dramas of reality.) It is also the case, apparently, that an inner imperative drives writers, producers, and sponsors to project their *own* fantasies. Not all Americans, by far, pursue upward mobility as a way of life. A great many teach their children to have modest expectations and turn down opportunies for advancement and mobility that would take them away from their familiar worlds.

The myths of the upwardly mobile and the tastes of the very affluent govern the visual symbols, the flow, and the chatter of television.

(3) The class bias of television reality proceeds not only from the relative economic affluence of the industry and its personnel. It springs as well from the educational level. "Televisionese" sends a clear and distinct message to the people, a message of exclusion and superiority. (George Wallace sends the message *back*; he is not its originator, only its echo.) It is common for a great many of the personnel connected with television to imagine themselves as anti-establishment and also perhaps as iconoclastic. Surely they must know that to men who work in breweries or sheet metal plants, to women who clean tables in cafeterias or splice wires in electronic assembly plants, they must seem to be at the very height of the Establishment. Their criticisms of American society—reflected in *Laugh-In*, in the night-club entertainers, and even in the dialogue of virtually every crime or adventure show—are perceived to be something like the complaints of spoiled children. There seems to be a self-hatred in the medium, a certain shame about American society, of which Lawrence Welk's old-fashioned, honeyed complacency and the militant righteousness of Bob Hope, John Wayne, and *Up With America!* are the confirming opposites. To confuse the hucksterism of television with the real America is, of course, a grievous error.

Television is a parade of experts instructing the unenlightened about the weather, aspirins, toothpastes, the latest books or proposals for social reform, and the correct attitudes to have with respect to race, poverty, social conflict, and new moralities. Television is preeminently a world of intellectuals. Academic persons may be astonished to learn of it and serious writers and artists may hear the theme with withering scorn, but for most people in the United States television is the medium through which they meet an almost solid phalanx of college-educated persons, professionals, experts, thinkers, authorities, and "with it," "swinging" celebrities: i.e., people unlike themselves who are drawn from the top ten percent of the nation in terms of educational attainment.

It is fashionable for intellectuals to disdain the world of television (although some, when asked, are known to agree to appear on it without hesitation). Yet when they appear on television they do not seem to be notably superior to the announcers, interviewers, and performers who precede them on camera or share the camera with them. (Incidentally, although many sports journalists write or speak condescendingly of "the jocks," when athletes appear as television announcers—Joe Garagiola, Sandy Koufax, Frank Gifford, Alex Karras, and others—the athletes seem not one whit inferior in intelligence or in sensitivity to the journalists.) Television is the greatest instrument the educated class has ever had to parade its wares before the people. On television that class has no rival. Fewer than ten percent of the American population has completed four years of college. That ten percent totally dominates television.

It is important to understand that the disdain for "popular culture" often heard in intellectual circles is seriously misplaced. Television, at least, more nearly represents the world of the educated ten percent than it reflects the world of the other ninety percent. At most, one might say in defense, the world of television represents the educated class's fantasies about the fantasies of the population. To say that *kitsch* has always required technicians to create it is not a sufficient route of escape. Do really serious intellectuals (i.e., not those "mere" technicians) have better understandings of where the people truly are? What, then, are those better understandings?

The interviews recorded by Robert Coles, for example, tend to show that persons of the social class represented by Archie Bunker are at least as complicated, many-sided, aware of moral ambiguities, troubled and sensitive, as the intellectuals who appear on television, in novels, or in the cinema. Artists who might use the materials of ordinary life for their creations are systematically separated from ordinary people by the economic conditions of creativity in the United States.

(4) The writers, producers, actors, and journalists of television are separated from most of the American population not only by economic standing, and not only by education, but also by the cul-

ture in which their actual lives are lived out. By "culture" I mean those implicit, lived criteria that suggest to each of us what is real, relevant, signifianct, meaningful in the buzzing confusion of our experience: how we select out and give shape to our world. The culture of prime-time television is, it appears, a serious dissolvant of the cultures of other Americans. The culture of television celebrates to an extraordinary degree two mythic strains in the American character: the lawless and the irreverent. On the first count, stories of cowboys, gangsters, and spies still preoccupy the American imagination. On the second, the myth of "enlightenment" from local standards and prejudices still dominates our images of self-liberation and sophistication. No doubt the stonghold of a kind of priggish righteousness in several layers of American history leads those who rebel to find their rebellion all too easy. It is as though the educated admonish one another that they "can't go home again" and that the culture against which they rebel is solid and unyielding.

But what if it isn't? What if the perception of culture on the part of millions is, rather, that chaos and the jungle are constantly encroaching and that the rule of good order is threatened in a dozen transactions every day—by products that don't work, by experts and officials who take advantage of lay ignorance, by muggings and robberies, by jobs and pensions that disappear, by schools that do not work in concert with the moral vision of the home?

Television keeps pressing on the barriers of cultural resistance to obscenities, to some forms of sexual behavior, and to various social understandings concerning work and neighborhood and family relationships. A reporter from the *New York Times* reports with scarcely veiled satisfaction that *Deep Throat* is being shown in a former church in a Pennsylvania mining town, as though this were a measure of spreading enlightenment. It might be. But what if our understanding of how cultural, social, and moral strands are actually interwoven in the consciousness of peoples is inadequate? What if the collapse of moral inhibition in one area, for a significant number of persons, encourages a collapse at other places? What if moral values cannot be too quickly changed without great destructiveness? The celebration of "new moralities" may not lead to the kind of "humanization" cultural optimists anticipate.

Television, and the mass media generally, have vested interests in new moralities. The excitement of transgressing inhibitions is gripping entertainment. There are, however, few vested interests wishing to strengthen the inhibitions which make such transgressions good entertainment. Television is only twenty-five years old. We have very little experience or understanding proportionate to the enormous moral stakes involved. It is folly to believe that *laissez-faire* works better in moral matters than in economic matters or that enormous decisions in these matters are not already being made in the absence of democratic consent. When one kind of show goes on the air others are excluded during that time. The present system is effectively a form of social control.

I do not advocate any particular solution to this far-ranging moral dilemma; I do not know what to recommend. But the issue is a novel one for a free society, and we do not even have a well-thought-out body of options from which to choose. In that vacuum a rather-too-narrow social class is making the decisions. The pressures of the free market (so they say) now guide them. Is that so? Should it be so?

(5) Because of the structure and history of the social class that produces prime-time television, group conflict in the United States is also portrayed in a simplistic and biased way. The real diversity of American cultures and regions is shrouded in public ignorance. Occasional disruptions, like the rebellion of West Virginia miners against certain textbooks and the rebellion of parents in South Boston against what they perceived as downward mobility for their children and themselves, are as quickly as possible brushed from consciousness. America is pictured as though it were divided between one vast homogeneous "middle America," to be enlightened, and the enlighteners. In fact, there are several "middle Americas."

There is more than one important Protestant culture in our midst. The Puritan inheritance is commonly exaggerated and the evangelical, fundamentalist inheritance is vastly underestimated (and under-studied). Hubert Humphrey is from a cultural stream different from that of George Wallace or of John Lindsay. There are also several quite significant cultural streams among Catholics; the Irish of the Middle West (Eugene McCarthy, Michael Harrington) often have a quite different cultural tradition from the Irish of Philadelphia, Boston, or New York. Construction workers on Long Island are not offended by "pornography" in the same way as druggists in small midwestern towns; look inside their cabs and helmets, listen to their conversations, if you seek evidence. There is also more than one cultural stream among American Jews; the influence of the Jews of New York has probably misled us in our understanding of the Jewish experience in America.

It seems, moreover, that the social class guiding the destiny of television idealizes certain ethnic groups—the legitimate minorities—even while this class offers in its practices no greater evidence of genuine egalitarianism than other social classes. At the same time this class seems extremely slow to comprehend the experiences of other American cultures. One of the great traumas of human history was the massive migration to America during the last 100 years. It ought to be one of the great themes of high culture, and popular culture as well. Our dramatists neglect it.

Group conflict has, moreover, been the rule in every aspect of American life, from labor to corporate offices to neighborhoods to inter-ethnic marriages. Here, too, the drama is perhaps too real and vivid to be touched: *these* are inhibitions the liberal culture of television truly respects. Three years ago one could write that white ethnics, like some others, virtually never saw themselves on television; suddenly we have had *Banacek, Colombo, Petrocelli, Kojak, Kolchack, Rhoda, Sanford,* and *Chico.* Artists are still exploring the edges of how much reality can be given voice and how to voice it. These are difficult, even explosive matters. Integrity and care are required.

It must seem odd to writers and producers to be accused of having a "liberal" bias when they are so aware of the limitations they daily face and the grueling battles they daily undergo. But why do they have these battles except that they have a point of view and a moral passion? We are lucky that the social class responsible for the creative side of television is not a reactionary and frankly illiberal class. Still, that it is a special class is itself a problem for all of us, including those involved in it.

Footnotes

1. There is no discernible variation between the hours spent watching television by the college-educated, or by professors and journalists, and the public as a whole.

2. The second theme is explored in more detail in my essay, "The People and the News," appearing in *Moments of Truth?* (The fifth Alfred I. duPont-Columbia University Survey of Broadcast Journalism), Marvin Barrett, ed. New York: Thomas Y. Crowell Company, 1975.

Television and Human Behavior

George Comstock

Television has introduced a fifth and artificial season to the four natural ones around which people have always organized their lives. This new influence, like the natural seasons, has a specific place in the calendar. Each fall and winter, new programs are introduced, accompanied by increased viewing and attention. It even has its own holiday, Super Bowl Sunday. It differs from the natural seasons by remaining with us in some guise throughout the year. By 1976, almost every American home had television, and that fall the average television household had a set on almost seven hours a day. It is difficult to conceive that in December of 1945, Gallup was asking the country:

"Do you know what television is?"
"Have you ever seen a television set in operation?"

Now, 25 years after television began to become common in the American home, the resulting scientific literature consists of about 2500 items—experiments, surveys, case studies, content analyses, and various interpretive reviews and commentaries. What does it tell us?

The study of the role of the mass media in American life has been filled with controversy, principally over the capability of social and behavioral science to say anything with much authority about such a complex issue. The controversy has been particularly noisome because there are few persons who do not think of themselves as experts in regard to the mass media. As a citizen wrote the National Institute of Mental Health after the Surgeon General's study of television violence, "You should have asked me. You could have saved the money."

The themes are as old as the mass media and tools of investigation, as this account about the effects of a different medium illustrates:

ELLINGTON REFUTES CRY THAT
SWING STARTED SEX CRIMES

In refutation of the hue and cry against swing music by Arthur Cremin, of the New York Schools for Music, in which the instructor attributed the recent wave of sex crimes to the current "hot" jazz vogue, Duke Ellington, prominent composer-pianist-bandsman, denounced Cremin's psychological experiments as being totally unfair and completely lacking in authoritative material.

Cremin, in his recent attack, said he would prove through tests he conducted that swing music produced debased emotions in human beings. He is reported to have placed a young man and woman in a room alone, first playing a series of symphonic recordings followed by a set of swing recordings. According to the teacher, the young couple remained formal throughout the first renditions, but as the music turned to jazz, they became familiar and more personal towards one another.

"If this experiment is earnestly offered as proof for the ill effects derived from swing music," said Duke Ellington, in discussing the matter before the Musician's Circle of New York, "then the facts must be totally discounted as not being a true psychology test, for there was no 'proper constant'—a prerequisite of an accurate experiment of this nature."

Ellington, who studied psychology during his collegiate courses at Howard University, further commented . . . "Music invigorates emotions to certain degrees, but on the other hand, so do baseball and football games. If music can be proved a neurotic influence, then I'm certain you will find Stravinsky's 'Le Sacre Du Printemps' a great deal more exciting, emotionally, than a slow 'ride' arrangement of 'Body and Soul' or even a fast rendition of 'Tiger Rag.' " (*down beat,* December 1937)*

An aside by Thomas Pynchon in "Gravity's Rainbow" is relevant here:

Proverbs for Paranoids, 3: If they can get you asking the wrong questions, they don't have to worry about answers.

This is the key to making good use of evidence from social and behavioral science on the role of television in our lives. Ask science a question its methods can answer. For example, science cannot tell us conclusively whether television violence contributes to serious crime because its methods are too imperfect. It can empirically test hypotheses whose confirmation or disconfirmation alters the probability that such a proposition is true and verify the consistency of observed fact with such a proposition. Conclusions of a grander sort depend on judgments about the acceptability of various assumptions and the risk of error that is tolerable. Consequently, the argument that there is no conclusive scientific evidence on this and other broad causal relationships is not impressive. The wrong question is being asked.

From the beginning, television has been principally entertainment. Only a small proportion of total broadcast time has been devoted to news and public affairs, although the coverage of certain specific events—election campaigns, assassinations, congressional investigations, and space flights—has absorbed the nation's attention. The shape of that entertainment has been remarkably constant despite oscillations in violence, the decline of westerns, the fall and rise of game shows, and the rise and fall from popularity of featured performers. Fiction in some guise has been the principal component.

---

*Reprinted by permission of *down beat* magazine.

In the daytime, it appears as soap operas and situation comedies. In prime time, it has appeared as general drama, feature films, situation comedy, westerns, and mystery, suspense, and detective-and-police tales. Action and adventure have always been central in evening entertainment. Variety has been peripheral because of its dependence on extraordinary personalities, a sparse commodity. In the mid-1970s, situation comedy became increasingly common, partly as the result of the search by the networks for programming in which the infliction of injurious or lethal violence is unlikely. Sports draw huge audiences, but account for a relatively small portion of total viewing time.

The dominant figure in television drama has been the youthful adult white male. For 25 years, he has occupied a large majority of major roles. Women have far less often been seen in central roles. The elderly, children, and blacks and other minorities have been seen relatively infrequently, although appearances of blacks increased sharply in the late 1960s as the result of network policy.

Occupationally, television drama is a world of law enforcement or crime, professionals, males, and persons with atypical or no visible means of support. The departure from reality into the fantasy of violence, upper status, and freedom from economic restraint is marked.

The quantity of violent programs in a season has oscillated over the years. The oscillations apparently are caused by the rush of the industry toward a violent genre as soon as ratings demonstrate its popularity, followed by a retreat as the newly formed mob of violent programs dilute the audience for violence and ratings for many fall below acceptability. Interpersonal physical and verbal abuse, however, has been demonstrated to be unrelated either to the size of audience for the episodes of network series or to the liking for episodes expressed by viewers.

Violence is often the means to an end in television drama. The use of illegal or socially disapproved means to achieve socially approved ends is a staple. Otherwise, television appears to be noncontroversial in its treatment of topics, with some tendency to favor the interests of advertisers. For example, in the portrayal of behavior related to the environment, the totality of messages has been in accord with public dispositions regarding pollution, nature, and conservation, evasive where there is high controversy (as in the case of population control), and in accord with the interests of advertisers favoring private over public transportation.

The quantity of violence in television prime-time drama and on

Saturday mornings, like the number of programs of a violent type, has oscillated over the years. The principal result so far of efforts to reduce violence has been a decline in killing. Downward trends in other measures have generally been followed by upward shifts. Increased pressures—from the government and the public, but particularly from advertisers—conceivably may foretell a different story. One of the most striking aspects of television violence so far has been the high degree to which characters fall victim to crime or violence, for a rate of victimization far in excess of that risked by the average viewer. Women have seldom been seen as professionals. Typically, they have been sex objects and providers of affection and support to the achieving male.

Male dominance has also been typical in commercials. Women have usually been portrayed in a few limited roles, principally leisure activities. When the sexes are fairly evenly divided in the audience, male appearances predominate. When women are almost certain to be the major purchasers of a product (as they are particularly of products advertised in the daytime)—and even in the commercials they are usually shown as its users—males are nevertheless most often seen as informed experts about the product's value and use.

The segment of the broadcast schedule the networks devote to news has regularly been the focus of debate. The principal issue has been bias, either in the reporting of controversial events such as the Vietnam war and the subsequent invasion of Cambodia, or in election campaign coverage. It is, of course, impossible to reach conclusions about coverage that has not been studied, or about future coverage. The question is made particularly difficult by two factors: the criteria for judging bias is itself often a matter of debate, and news is inevitably the creature of events which may favor one side or another. Many critics of national television have been able to offer arguments that merit attention. However, the many analyses of news content do *not* provide much support for the contention of bias, either in regard to major stories or election campaigns. Nor do the various strong criticisms of network coverage during the Nixon years by officials associated with that Administration appear to have affected coverage, except perhaps to introduce a very slightly greater degree of caution in the handling of stories.

Public television—as those who advocate it in the interests of diversity would expect—differs sharply. The principal difference is the presentation of a greater proportion of children's, news, and public affairs programming. However, a major trend discernible over the past decade has been toward a greater emphasis on entertainment, although entertainment different in character from that on commercial television.

One thoroughly studied topic is the public's viewing behavior. Over the past 15 years, the amount each television household uses its set has steadily increased. Use of television has always been greater in the United States among those of lower socioeconomic status. However, when the increasing consumption by those of lower socioeconomic status began to level off—as would be expected because of the ceiling imposed on total possible viewing time by other activities —the viewing by those of higher socioeconomic status began to climb more sharply. By the mid-1970s, viewing was greater by those of higher socioeconomic status than it had been a decade before by those of lower status. This appears to represent a final step in the pervasive adoption of television by our society in which those at first most resistant—possibly because of greater affinity for "print" and "book" culture—began to approach the amount of viewing of those who turned to television more readily.

However, the convergence in amount of viewing by those of lower and higher socioeconomic status conceivably may not end in the greater homogeneity of media experience that these trends imply. The new technologies—such as cable television and in-home playback—require greater income for access, and thus may lead to those of higher socioeconomic status fashioning a television environment of their own.

Average amount of viewing changes throughout the life cycle. Viewing increases from childhood through elementary school, decreases through the high school and college years, then increases again to a level that persists throughout adult life until a further increase in the later years. Those over 65 view more than adults in general. Viewing tends to vary inversely with other demands. Thus, it is decreased by the social and educational demands of adolescence, and by the demands on younger adults of child-rearing, social life, and career development, and increased by the reduced occupational demands of retirement. Certain segments of the audience definitely are heavier-than-average viewers. Among these are women, blacks, the elderly, and children.

Viewing over a typical day arches up sharply, like the back of a beast ready to pounce. The pattern for the fall of 1976 is typical, although average hours of weekly viewing are less in summer and greater in winter. In the morning hours, only about 9 percent of

Americans of all ages were watching television. By early evening the figure was 30 percent. Later, the figure approached 45 percent, before declining to about 17 percent around midnight. The peak is an audience of more than 95 million.

It would be a mistake to think that the arch is identical for all segments of the audience. The viewing cycle differs over the day and week by age and sex. Younger adult women (18-49 years of age) reach an early peak in mid-afternoon, decline, then rise to a much higher prime-time peak between 8:00 and 10:00 pm. Adult men view little during the day and begin their rise in early evening to their sole, prime-time peak. Older women and men (50-plus) behave similarly, except that the peaks occur sooner, viewing by both men and women is heavier, and viewing by men is proportionately greater. During the weekend, viewing by men and women, both older and younger, is similar.

The cycle for children and teenagers is very different. Young children (2-5 years of age) reach an early peak in mid-morning, decline until mid-afternoon, then rise to a new, markedly higher peak at about 5:00 pm, followed by a slight decline (presumably because of some meals without television), then rise to a final similar peak about 8:00 pm. Older children (6-11 years of age) reach a slight, presumably preschool, peak at 8:00 am, then decline until mid-afternoon when the rising curve resembles that for young children with two notable exceptions: the final evening peak is much higher, and viewing into the later evening is heavier. Teenagers behave similarly to adult males with viewing slight until early evening when the rise to a prime-time peak begins. Viewing by teenage girls is typically heavier than by boys except for a sharp 5:30-7:30 pm dip—an unexplained phenomenon alternatively attributable to kitchen chores, some other activity, a distaste for news, or some combination of these factors.

The data make clear the large place of television viewing in the lives of the young. At their first daily peak in the morning in the fall of 1976, less than a third of all young children were in the audience; during two evening peaks, the figure was about 45 percent. At their first evening peak, about 40 percent of all older children were in the audience, and at the second, the figure was about 55 percent. By 10:00 pm, only about 12 percent of younger children remained in the audience, but the figure for older children was almost twice that. Teenagers are generally not heavy viewers, but in their prime-time peak about 40 percent were in the audience. Slightly more than half of all children under 12 were in the audience between 8:00 and 9:00 pm weekdays. The figure declined to 30 percent for 9:00-10:00 pm and to 13 percent during the half-hour before 11:00 pm. The huge size of the prime-time audience means that children make up a modest proportion, but their rate of viewing means that in absolute numbers the evening audience of younger children is very large—in the fall of 1976, about 18 million at any given moment in the 8:00-9:00 pm period. On Saturday mornings, when children dominate the much smaller audience, the number of younger children viewing during the peak between 9:00 and 11:00 am was only slightly greater—about 19 million.

These varied viewing patterns reflect the effects of available time, alternative demands and opportunities, and the appeal of programming at the various hours. From the perspective of the television industry, which seeks to maximize its audience, these data pose the question of how the height of these curves can be increased. In their various applications in programming decisions, they lead to such industry concepts as "audience flow" (the shifts of viewers away from and toward the medium and from channel to channel during the broadcast day), "lead-in" (usually applied to a program but more properly thought of as the demographic composition of the audience at a given time that may affect the size and character of the audience for subsequent programming), and "least objectionable programming" (that content which will attract the maximum audience as the result of the phenomenon that many choose to view before deciding what to view). From the perspective of the social or behavioral scientist, these data represent the fit of the medium to the varied lives of these disparate segments of the audience. From the perspective of the public-interest advocate concerned about the effects of television, they are the facts of who is viewing what, and therefore the metric of possible impact.

Another measure of the public's response to television is its beliefs about the medium and its evaluation of the medium's performance. There are several main threads. Between 1960 and 1970, the public became somewhat disenchanted with television, although its evaluation of the medium remained on the whole highly favorable. Compared to the other mass media—magazines, newspapers, and radio—television has risen in esteem. It has dramatically replaced the newspaper as the medium first in public favor. The most criticized aspects of television are commercials. A majority believe that there are too many, but an identical majority believe the presence of commercials is a fair price to pay for television. Other aspects drawing considerable criticism, particularly in regard to children, are sex-related and other content judged inappropriate for the young, and violence. Despite the generally favorable evaluation given television compared to other media, it is also more often cited as the medium that is getting worse. It is not waggish to suggest that this is not an anomaly but a reflection of greater sensitivity to the medium that has become predominant among the mass media.

When the public focuses on news, television increasingly has received acclaim. In 1960, television was slightly overshadowed by newspapers in being judged by the public as the principal source of news, the provider of the most complete coverage, and the most credible source. By 1970, television had become the unambiguous leader on all these counts. Despite this generally favorable evaluation, about a fourth of the public believes television news is biased. However, complaints come about equally from conservatives and liberals. This means that to the degree that people believe the news to be biased, it is equally so to partisans, not that there is unanimous perception of nonbias.

The widely declared esteem for television news is qualified by certain facts. The term "television news" to which the public responds in most studies encompasses both network national news and local news. A large proportion of the adult public—in one national sample more than half over a two-week period—do not watch network national news. Reading of newspapers appears to be more frequent. The viewing of local news, ignored implicitly or explicitly in many studies, is greater. The esteem for television decreases and that for newspapers increases when the subject is local and not national news. The implication is that to some degree the public's expression of reliance on "television news" represents a response to the medium as symbol or eternal presence at the hearth rather than a measure of its actual importance as a regular news source.

Like television viewing, favorability toward the medium—in beliefs and in the evaluation of its performance—is inversely related to socioeconomic status, as measured by income or education. Favorability also is greater among blacks and older adults. However, when the viewing choices of those higher and lower in socioeconomic status are compared, differences are minor, and even total amount of viewing by the mid-1970s had become more similar. The implication is that television so well performs its function as an entertainer that it largely overcomes scruples based on attitudes.

There are a variety of ways in which television affects the experiences of its audience beyond hours spent viewing. These concomitants of television include the behavior before the set during viewing, the effects on allocation of leisure time, the influence on other activities, the dynamics of program choice, the impact on other media, and the various uses and gratifications of the medium.

Television certainly brought something new to the household by dimming the lights and turning faces toward the screen. Behavior before the set is unique to television because, despite the similarities to the movies, the home is not a theater. The viewing of television is typically discontinuous and accompanied by some other activity. Eating very often accompanies viewing. People leave and enter the room, sew, converse, play games, read, give full attention to something else, turn back to the screen. Any given time estimate of viewing represents continuing attention and withdrawal. This oscillating inattention is not unrelated to content; people give least constant attention to commercials and news, and the most to movies and other drama.

The impact of television on the expenditure of leisure time has been sizable. Television has markedly increased the total amount of time spent with the mass media. Television viewing as a primary activity, excluding very disrupted viewing while doing something else, consumes more of the leisure time of Americans than any other activity. Among almost 40 kinds of primary activities—exclusive categories into which the 24 hours of the day can be divided—television viewing falls behind only sleep and time spent at work. Despite the variations in total viewing attributable to sex, age, ethnicity, and socioeconomic status, it is a rare set of circumstances where television viewing is not the predominant leisure activity.

Television's absorption of leisure naturally occurs at the expense of other activities. One of television's most marked effects appears to have been to reduce time spent sleeping. It also appears to have reduced time spent in social gatherings away from home, in radio listening, in reading books, in miscellaneous leisure, in conversation, in travel related to leisure, in movie-going, in religious activities, and in household tasks. Television appears in some instances to have increased public participation by drawing attention to events that might otherwise be overlooked. Thus, it may boost a previously not-so-popular sport or cultural activity. However, in the case of minor league baseball in the United States, it appears to have severely reduced attendance by bringing major league baseball into the home.

The conflict of taste among family members that is implied by the decision to view one program rather than another is sharply attenuated by the growing number of multiset homes and by the degree to which only one or a few family members are viewing at a particular time of day. By the mid-1970s, more than half of households of three or more persons had more than one set. During the day, an adult female is typically alone to choose programs, or else she is there with her child or children. Disagreement increases with the group's heterogeneity, and is resolved by a democratic majority, or by normative social standing and authority. Children and parents will view separately when there is disagreement in a multiset household. When there is only one set or children and parents are committed to viewing together, children's tastes rule about as often as do the tastes of parents. When parents agree, they typically prevail over children. When a child and either parent agree, they typically prevail over the other parent. When husbands and wives disagree, which is about half the time, husbands more often prevail. When children disagree, the older is likely to prevail. Parents report considerable lack of mutual agreement, but children report little conflict, which suggests that children do not believe the existing lack of agreement as a very serious matter.

The greater amount of time spent with television increases the incursion of common experience bearing on an extraordinary range of topics, from political and social crises to relations between the sexes. This increase, of course, is attributable to the attention given television and involves some decrease in the time given to other media. The basic rule is that a new mass medium will displace older media when it performs their functions either with greater convenence, reduced financial expenditure, or in a more satisfying way. However, a mass medium may also alter the character and the functions served by other media as these older media attempt to compete. The popularity of a new medium implies a redistribution of media use because consumer expenditures for media are roughly a constant proportion of income, so that expenditures for a new medium imply a reduction in expenditures for old. Television has reshaped the other media, and it is likely that the television we know will itself be reshaped by new technology offering different opportunities and options in regard to information, news, and entertainment.

Any medium and any content may serve for a given individual almost any purpose and may provide almost any conceivable gratification. For a few, a crime caper movie may serve as a lesson about the unlawful acquisition of wealth; for the majority, it will serve simply as entertainment. Television news may be viewed by many for information and some will use such information as the weather report to plan the following day's activities, while for others it will serve simply as diversion, like the presentations preceding or following. However, every medium and every type of content has its normative or central character. In American society, the central use and gratification of television is entertainment. Entertainment is not only predominant in content, but the seeking of entertainment is the predominant rationale offered by the public for viewing television. Television also appears to be largely viewed for itself, rather than for the specific programs; the decision to view is typically more influential than the decision what to view at any particular part of the day.

A major focus has been television's role in the lives of the young. Children as a group are heavy viewers, with viewing increasing through elementary school. Viewing decreases during the high school and college years, but adolescents nevertheless view substantial amounts of television. The major concern has been over possible negative effects. In this respect, television has inherited the villainous posture attributed by critics to whatever mode of storytelling at the time—comic book, movie, radio drama, or ancient tale-spinning and epic poetry—seemed to attract the young. Nevertheless, there are certain traits peculiar to television which justify concern—it occupies extraordinary amounts of time, it is omnipresent, access is difficult to regulate, and most of its programming is designed for adults with no regard for the responses of children.

What research depicts is quite complex, not without apparent inconsistencies, and leaves many questions unanswered. Regular viewing begins long before the first grade, and preferences and tastes begin almost as soon as viewing. Sex differences in taste and preference appear early and continue. Age differences are noticeable, and with them come differences between blacks and whites. There are marked individual differences in amount of viewing and in tastes and preferences. The most plausible way to examine television is as a factor whose place and influence varies with the characteristics and particular age or developmental stage of the young person.

Four topics in particular have drawn attention—television advertising, political socialization, antisocial effects, and "prosocial" effects.

Research on the influence of commercials during growing up is just beginning. Attention to commercials appears to decrease with age, which means exposure is inversely related to the knowledge and experience necessary for critically evaluating them. Very young children do not comprehend the self-interested persuasive nature of commercials. With such understanding comes skepticism and distrust. Even among adolescents, who display the most distrust, there is some attention to and acquisition of information from commercials. Commercials appear to inspire appeals to parents to purchase products. One study found that by the end of the five weeks of the campaign, Christmas toy advertising overcame the defenses of early resisters and those who previously did not prefer television-advertised items began to choose them. The major questions, such as influences on health-related practices, such as dietary preferences, and on basic values, such as materialism or acquisitiveness, remain to be addressed.

Television is *probably* an important factor in the image and expectations young persons hold in regard to politics and government. This is probably so despite the modest degree of attention young persons give to news and public affairs programming. The very nature of public events makes the mass media a major source of information. Children and adolescents frequently cite television as their main source of public-affairs knowledge. Television appears to be more important than teachers or parents for information on continuing events, such as the Vietnam war. However, parents appear to have a strong influence on the direction of opinion. There are many questions not yet studied. To some degree, the wrong question may have been asked in studies which dismissed television as unimportant because it did not change attitudes. The wrong question may also be asked when the focus is solely on news and public-affairs programming, because political socialization involves many issues, such as what constitutes power, the appropriate means for problem solving, and the character of law enforcement, on which there is a large quantity of relevant portrayals in television entertainment. The varied studies so far suggest that television's influence is usually indirect, principally by providing information whose evaluation and eventual influence depends heavily on interpersonal relationships, but nevertheless important because information is a major ingredient in political socialization.

The most studied topic has been the influence of television on antisocial behavior. Television viewing itself appears to be unrelated to either aggression or antisocial behavior. The viewing of television violence appears to increase the likelihood of subsequent aggressiveness. This conclusion derives from the pattern of results of dozens of laboratory experiments, field experiments, and surveys. It also hides many complexities. The relationship of television violence to aggression and antisocial behavior is a topic that reveals the strengths and weaknesses of social and behavioral science, and illustrates many of the problems in drawing generalizations applicable to future events from the limited circumstances of specific studies.

The evidence is that television may increase aggression by teaching viewers previously unfamiliar hostile acts, by generally encouraging in various ways the use of aggression, and by triggering aggressive behavior both imitative and different in kind from what has been viewed. Effects are never certain because real-life aggression is strongly influenced by situational factors, and this strong role for situational factors means that the absence of an immediate effect does not rule out a delayed impact when the behavior in question may be more propitious. The likelihood of subsequent aggressiveness is increased by portrayals in which the aggressor is justified in his act, is rewarded, escapes punishment, or is engaged in the intent to inflict harm. Such likelihood is also increased by portrayals which are realistic and by similarities between cues in the portrayal and in the environment.

Television violence under certain circumstances is capable of reducing subsequent aggressiveness, but the cause appears to be inhibition following upon anxiety over aggression rather than catharsis. The quantity of studies with consistent results provides considerable confidence about the relationship between television violence and subsequent aggression, but the studies do not provide direct evidence on whether television contributes widely or generally to serious antisocial behavior.

In recent years, increasing attention has been given to television's contribution to socially desirable, or "prosocial," behavior. The few studies done to date indicate that television portrayals can increase the likelihood of certain kinds of behavior other than aggression, although there are many differences between raising the likelihood of negatively sanctioned behavior, such as aggression, and doing so for positively sanctioned behavior.

Learning appears to underlie all other influences. Children and adolescents learn from television in a variety of ways. Both knowledge and behavior are subject to influence by television. Television probably should be considered a major agent of socialization, although its influence is often indirect and contingent on interpersonal relations and other factors.

Four other segments of the audience—women, blacks, the poor, and the elderly—are also of high interest. Each has an atypical relationship to television. They are all, as groups, heavy viewers. They are usually portrayed on the screen either in trite fashion, in lesser roles, or relatively infrequently. Increasingly, they have become the subject of concern over whether they are served well by the mass media. Women and the elderly are heavy viewers because they are less frequently in the labor force, and instead remain at home, where television is adjacent. The social roles assigned women apparently fate them to be heavy viewers, for both younger and older women view more on the average than their male peers. Blacks are extraordinarily favorably disposed toward television. The reasons are highly speculative, but one possibility is a fortuitous conjunction of the histories of the medium and the group. The poor typically rely heavily on television among the media, probably because of a lack of the education that would orient them more toward print media. Blacks, the poor, and the elderly are all more likely to look upon television as a source of knowledge and information. The larger effects of television on these portions of the audience are unknown, but there are intriguing bits of data and much speculation.

There are two bodies of findings which can best be examined together in order to interpret the evidence most easily, because in both cases there are calculated attempts to persuade—these are the data on television and politics, and on television and advertising. When they are examined together, political and campaign news coverage, political advertising, and product advertising, display certain similarities and differences.

In both areas, there are instances in which paid-for campaigns appear to have had a significant impact. However, the very many factors which influence decisions make the clear-cut demonstration of effects on behavior uncommon. In politics, television appears to affect knowledge and information and to define the context in which voting decisions are made. Along with the other mass media, it helps to establish the agenda of personalities and issues to which the public responds. Television has an important role because it is the ultimate mass medium in focusing the nation's attention on the same topics, persons, and messages. During elections, it is now a principal means of increasing the salience of politics, stimulating the expression of partisanship, and orienting the public toward the eventual act of voting. However, television's influence on the outcome of elections is limited by voters' party allegiances prior to a specific campaign and

their tendency typically to reach a decision by the time of the nominating conventions, the carrying by television of roughly balanced
news coverage and political advertising for the various candidates
(this becomes to some degree self-canceling with respect to the
emphasis given one side or another), and the preoccupation of television news with events and personalities amenable to visual coverage
rather than issues.

The trend toward reduced party allegiance over the past 15 years
and the presence of unusual numbers of undecided or wavering
voters (such as in the 1976 presidential election), increase the opportunity for television to have an effect. The evidence from the many
studies of the 1960 Nixon-Kennedy debates does not lead to any
conclusion about their effect on the outcome, although it appears
that individual voters were affected in various ways in their beliefs
and perceptions. Evidence from 1976 suggests that in this close election, where voter indecision was high and the Ford-Carter debates
were an electoral media event, television played a particularly significant role in facilitating the reaching of a decision by individual
voters about which of the major candidates to vote for.

Television has probably altered the way political campaigns are
fought, and thereby reshaped politics, but this is precisely the important kind of "effect" that is not readily measurable by social and
behavioral science. Politics and advertising most overlap in the case
of political advertising, which despite certain sharp differences shares
many similarities with product advertising. Advertising obviously can
affect knowledge, information, attitudes, and behavior, but the various conditions on which such effects are contingent are numerous
and complex.

There is a very large scientific literature on the effects on subsequent behavior of exposure to a television portrayal. This literature
derives from a number of disparate theories of human behavior, and
although much of it deals with effects on aggressive or antisocial
behavior, the implications apply to a far wider, highly varied range of
behavior. Among the concepts or conditions on which a behavioral
effect appears to be contingent are the state of physiological arousal,
the perceived consequences of the behavior in question, the perceived reality or "authenticity" of the television portrayal, the alternatives for behaving in the situation at hand, the salience of the
behavior in question at the particular time and in the particular circumstances, and the opportunity to perform it.

It is likely that social and behavioral science will assume an increasing role in television policy-making. Its impact is likely to be particularly great in the regulation of television advertising, where new issues have emerged in regard to effects on children, and in the highly varied self-regulatory actions undertaken by the television industry in response to pressure from the government and public. However, it also has a role in the evaluation of the effectiveness of policies adopted primarily on legal, economic, or ideological grounds. There is a lengthy agenda of topics which future research should address, many with significance for future policy. Progress in the practical application of research to the problems of mass communications depends on the solution of three problems. (1) The difficulty of generalizing from research to real life can be alleviated (a) by the use of multiple methods of investigation, dissimilar in their deficiencies, to focus on the same question, and (b) by the further development of theory, which implies the wide use—despite the objections raised against its artificiality in the case of television—of the laboratory-type experiment. (2) The polyglot and fragmented nature of the scientific study of television can be partially overcome (a) by the use of focused, coordinated research programs directed by persons expert and sophisticated in communications studies in which research is organized around a theme or topic, with particular attention to encouraging cooperation among investigators, insuring coverage of important issues, and the avoiding of redundancy, with a publications program to bring about speedy, effective dissemination of results to social and behavioral scientists, the television industry, and the public, and (b) by the inauguration of a specialized information service specifically designed to address the needs of the field. (3) The usefulness of social and behavioral science in policymaking of all kinds, in the government, in the industry, and on the part of citizen and advocacy groups, can be increased (a) by altering the intellectual milieu in which social and behavioral scientists function to give them greater knowledge of the way broadcasting operates so that they can devise research that is more pertinent, and (b) by altering the organizational milieu in which policymakers function to give them greater and more effective access to social and behavioral science's expertise.

Part 2.
Critical Approaches

The essays in this section are concerned with specific critical approaches for examining and evaluating the content of television. Starting from the premise that television serves the same function for society that dreams do for individuals, Peter Wood demonstrates how psychoanalytic theory can be applied to the interpretation of television drama as dreams. David Thorburn focuses on television melodrama and argues that characteristics usually considered limitations may actually be strengths.

Arthur Asa Berger then explains how the concepts and insights of semiotics can be applied to television criticism, while Herb Zettl offers an approach to television aesthetics based on the audio and visual resources of television and the ways in which they are used. Finally, David Littlejohn surveys the field of television criticism as it has been practiced in this country over the past several decades.

Television as Dream

Peter H. Wood

There are dreams as distinct as actual experiences, so distinct that for some time after waking we do not realize that they were dreams at all; others, which are ineffably faint, shadowy and blurred; in one and the same dream, even, there may be some parts of extraordinary vividness alternating with others so indistinct as to be almost wholly elusive. Again, dreams may be quite consistent or at any rate coherent, or even witty or fantastically beautiful; others again are confused, apparently imbecile, absurd or often absolutely mad. There are dreams which leave us quite cold, others in which every affect makes itself felt—pain to the point of tears, terror so intense as to wake us, amazement, delight, and so on. Most dreams are forgotten soon after waking; or they persist throughout the day, the recollection becoming fainter and more imperfect as the day goes on; others remain so vivid (as, for example, the dreams of childhood) that thirty years later we remember them as clearly as though they were part of a recent experience. Dreams, like people, may make their appearances once and never come back; or the same person may dream the same thing repeatedly, either in the same form or with slight alterations. In short, these scraps of mental activity at night-time have at command an immense repertory, can in fact create everything that by day the mind is capable of—only, it is never the same.[1]

—Sigmund Freud

Not long ago the austere American diplomat and scholar, George F. Kennan, commiserated with a group of Oxford and Cambridge graduates that they lived in a world changing too fast for its own good. It is "a world," Kennan moralized, "given increasingly to the primitive delights of visual communication."

Ever since monks stopped illuminating their manuscripts and turned to the dull efficiencies of the printing press, academics and other bibliophiles have taken a condescending stance toward any non-linear forms of information exchange. Particularly offensive to shareholders in the print economy is television, that newest process of illumination which changes light into an electrical image and back to light again. There is something threatening, confusing, paralyzing about its "primitive delights"; it is a bad dream, and they wish it would go away.

But George Kennan and all the king's men could never devise an adequate "containment theory" for American television. The cornucopia-shaped tube is in 98 percent of American dwellings, and, for at least a quarter of every day, it is scanning electrons toward us at a rate of over 30,000 lines per second. It has become a real and permanent fixture in our homes and in our heads. TV is no dream. Or is it?

If television is not the meaningless nightmare deplored by numerous elders, could it in fact be something of the inverse: a significant flow of collective dream materials which we have not yet begun to interpret adequately? Most of us can recall incidents where television contributed to our own dreams. (After all, TV frequently serves to put us to sleep these days—both figuratively and literally.) And the recent Surgeon General's report on TV violence even hinted at simple substitution, reporting that those who watch more TV dream less. But if we can accept the idea that TV *affects* the dream-life of individuals, can we entertain the thought that TV may also *constitute*—in some unrecognized way—part of the collective dream-life of society as a whole? Is there room, in other words, for *the interpretation of television as dream*?

A few people are beginning to think so. A recent issue of the California bulletin, *Dreams and Inner Spaces*, for example, dealt with the parallels between dreams and TV. Among those who have already considered this concept, the most notable is anthropologist Ted Carpenter. Carpenter has co-edited *Explorations in Communication* with Marshall McLuhan, and written a book called *They Became What They Beheld* (not about television!) with photographer Ken Hyman. The fall 1972 issue of *Television Quarterly* carried a piece by communications professor John Carden entitled, "Reality and Television: An Interview with Dr. Edmund Carpenter," in which Carpenter suggests that the viewer of media events "participates solely as dreamer." He observes that, "Television is the real psychic leap of our time. . . .Its content is the stuff of dreams and its form is pure dream."

If there are grounds for such an approach, as I myself am increasingly convinced, then it bears directly on the concept which we accept as "TV criticism" (or, more significantly, "TV analysis"). Therefore, one point should be stressed at the outset: raising the prospect of analyzing "TV as dream" does not in any way negate traditional approaches to television. If valid, it would necessarily reinforce existing modes of media criticism. It would neither supplant them nor be irrelevant to them; it would simply offer an additional related perspective.

Where does TV criticism stand now? To some it seems suitably rich and diversified; to others it appears depressingly homogenized and inconsequential. But value judgments aside, almost *all* current criticism falls into one or both of the following modes: art commentary, or industry commentary. Stated another way, TV criticism, as it presently exists, derives from two sources: traditional artistic and literary criticism on the one hand, and the modern newspaper-magazine genre which might be called "Hollywood commentary" on the other.

The artistic or cultural approach, though by no means highbrow, involves a slight distancing from the material. It addresses matters drawn from traditional art forms, particularly drama, such as the subtlety of the story line and the skill of the actors. Unfortunately, as Marvin Barrett of the Columbia School of Journalism points out, most network shows measured on these scales "don't even register in the aesthetic area." The TV critic applying traditional dramatic and cultural standards confronts, in Barrett's phrase, "continuous mediocrity." But if the Marvin Barretts dread and deprecate such mediocrity, the Rona Barretts extol and expand it. The mode of industry criticism which has grown up around film, TV's celluloid godparent, shapes a vast range of television commentary. It encompasses both pure network handouts and hard-nosed exposés. But whether adulatory or critical, intimate or detached, this mode depends upon at least an appearance of investigative reporting and it overflows with personal and production details. "Which people?" "What expenses?" "Why—when—how?" It is the "low-down" by and for the would-be insider.

As much as anything else, it is these two roots, epitomized by drama criticism and Hollywood coverage, which have given TV analysis its current shape. From the former, it derives a strongly judgmental and crudely critical tone. Appraisers of prime-time television make heavy use of such words as "good" and "bad," "should" and "shouldn't," far beyond their limited role as consumer counsellors. From the latter, TV analysis derives a directness, a narrowness, a literal-mindedness. There is a willingness to deal with separate segments of shows or personalities in isolation; there is a tendency to accept, and even stress, surface appearances. While other ways to categorize TV criticism are obviously available, anyone doubting the existence of these two roots can examine them, thoroughly entwined, in a publication such as *TV Guide*.

Commenting along these lines in the interview mentioned above, Ted Carpenter stated:

> I'm convinced that we judge television as if it were a modified form of print—and, of course, find it wanting. What we overlook is the reality it reveals. Unlike print, television doesn't transmit bits of information. Instead it *transports* the viewer. . . .*All television becomes dream.* This is the inner trip, the search for meaning beyond the world of daily appearance.

The question being posed below is whether art analysis and industry analysis of TV could not be complemented by a new and separate form of "dream analysis," a form which might take us, in Carpenter's words, "beyond the world of daily appearance."

Before addressing this serious question directly, consider it in a playfully inverted form: what could current television analysts tell you about the workings of your individual subconscious? Suppose for a moment the TV critics' tendencies to stress surface content and to emphasize value judgments were applied to the interpretation of your own dreams. The results, of course, would be ludicrous. To learn that a given dream was a "tedious rerun," containing "entirely too much sex, though humorous in places," would provide limited enlightenment at best. For in dream interpretation, the "originality" of the plot and dialogue, the "level" of acting, the "uniqueness" of the characters, the "realism" of the setting, and the "logic" of the ending all become matters of little or no relevance. In short, the questions which are currently deemed most appropriate, useful, and legitimate in TV analysis are the very ones which seem most inappropriate, useless, and illegitimate in dream analysis.

But if dream interpretation can have anything to offer television, basic similarities between TV and dream must first be established. Therefore, begin by considering a list of half a dozen general congruities:

1. *Both TV and dreams have a highly visual quality.* The word "tele-vision" and the much older medieval phrase "dream vision" underscore this point. "In dreams we go through many experiences," Freud wrote in his *General Introduction to Psychoanalysis.* "For the most part our experiences take the form of visual images; there may be feeling as well, thoughts, too, mixed up with them, and the other senses may be drawn in; but for the most part dreams consist of visual images."

2. *Both TV and dreams are highly symbolic.* As Michael Arlen noted in an excellent *New Yorker* column (April 7, 1975), TV "transforms experience into symbols" in accordance with an incessant and deeply felt human need. Dreams do the same. "Symbolism," Freud stated, "is perhaps the most remarkable part of our theory of dreams."

3. *Both TV and dreams involve a high degree of wish-fulfillment.* The enemies and the exponents of television, for different reasons, have acknowledged the degree to which the medium provides an escape and a release into a world of fantasy—fantasy which often

gains its power as a heightened and intensified version of reality. "That dreams are brought about by a wish and that the content of the dream expresses this wish," Freud wrote, "is one main characteristic of dreams." He continued, "the dream does not merely give expression to a thought, but represents this wish as fulfilled, in the form of an hallucinatory experience." It is "almost like being there" in each instance, living through some form of an experience which is greatly desired or—equally important and not entirely opposite— which is greatly feared. Thus real and implied violence has a heightened place in both the prime-time dreaming of individuals and the prime-time television of our culture. Chase scenes and sexual hints are as commonplace in one as in the other.

4. *Both TV and dreams appear to contain much that is disjointed and trivial.* But the contents of dreams, and perhaps someday of television, can be shown to be consistent and coherent. We have all heard TV content dismissed vehemently as being beneath serious concern, much as Freud once heard verbal slips and then dreams dismissed. "A certain element of exaggeration in a criticism may arouse our suspicions," he wrote, intrigued as always by the implications of resistance. "The arguments brought against the dream as an object of scientific research are clearly extreme. We have met with the objection of triviality already in 'errors,' and have told ourselves that great things may be revealed by small indications." It will take time and patience to determine which—if any—great things stand to be revealed by the trivia of prime-time television.

5. *Both TV and dreams have an enormous and powerful content, most of which is readily and thoroughly forgotten.* Freud wrote that, "Most dreams cannot be remembered at all and are forgotten except for some tiny fragments." It is relatively easy, and apparently necessary, for individual dreamers to avoid or forget much of the content of most of their dreams. They are able, at least with effort and practice, to awaken from dreams they cannot handle. However, they are also able to return to and recall dreams with which they are ready to deal. Avoiding conscious recollection of a dream does not erase its content; the themes continue to recur and impinge. All this is quite similar with television, where avoidance mechanisms (beyond direct forgetfulness) function at a variety of levels from living room channel switching to FCC censorship. (It may not be surprising that Timothy Leary and others who began experimenting with non-sleep dreaming through drugs adopted a terminology drawn from television: "turn on," "tune in," "turn off.") Is it conceivable

that television, like dreams, could be repetitive, boring, and mundane on the surface precisely because its latent content is so relevant, powerful, and pervasive?

6. *Finally, both TV and dreams make consistent use—overt and disguised—of materials drawn from recent experience.* Freud stated in the *General Introduction* that, "we want to know further from what cause and to what end we repeat in dreams this which is known to us and has recently happened to us." We wish to know much the same thing about television. Like dream, television's brief and non-linear visual images invoke—and also evoke—a great wealth of familiar and often current material stored in the viewer's mind.

If, for the sake of experimentation or argument, one goes along with all or most of these rough generalizations, an interesting and somewhat heretical critical perspective begins to open up. But to explore it depends upon the tentative acceptance, or at least upon the consideration, of two further and somewhat novel assumptions. The first has to do with whether television is—as we often more than half seriously say it is—a "mindless" phenomenon.

When Freud began his consideration of dreams in the 1890s, others had been involved in related speculations for several decades. But their conclusions (not unlike those of the first generation of TV critics) tended to stress the ways in which dream failed to measure up to reality. Freud wrote that, "they are content with the bare enumeration of the divergences of the dream-life from waking thought with a view to depreciating the dreams: they emphasize the lack of connection in the associations, the suspended exercise of the critical faculty, the elimination of all knowledge, and other indications of diminished functioning." The mind, they concluded, was at rest, too relaxed to "make sense"; dreams were therefore to be understood in somatic or bodily terms. It was Freud's insight to turn this assumption upside down: "let us accept as the basis of the whole of our further enquiry the following hypothesis—that dreams are not a somatic, but a mental phenomenon." He went on to ask, "but what is our justification in making this assumption? We have none, but on the other hand there is nothing to prevent us."

Where lack of sense, lack of importance or meaning, had been assumed, Freud postulated the opposite. What happens if we make the same assumption about TV, using the same justification at first —that is, "there is nothing to prevent us"? In so doing, we set aside, for the moment, somatic interpretations of television (TV as SOMA?)

which stress the physical origins and characteristics of each show, series, or network, much less of the medium as a whole. We assume that beyond inadvertency ("Some guy just came up with that line," or "The tight budget meant they just happened to cut the scene here"), and beyond specificity ("Peter Falk always acts that way," or "All Norman Lear shows are like that"), there also exists some larger consciousness to which television can be linked.

But what is this collective consciousness which at some level can be said to create and consume the images of television? Here we must add a second hypothesis. Just as our dreams, contrary to traditional logic, have been proven to be the product of our individual subconscious, so perhaps TV may eventually be understood as a form of dream-equivalent within the "collective subconscious." I do not employ this last phrase in any strict parallel to Jung's similar term, although it is suggestive that TV is built around archetypes, many of them similar to the primordial images which Jung believed to be stored in the "collective unconscious" of the entire species. Instead I refer, for the moment, to the entity of our own American society, virtually all of whose homes are reached by television. It is the hypothesis that, within this entity, whatever can be said validly on one level about the separate consciousness of distinctive and discernible audiences, producers, etc., something else can be said on another level about the consciousness of the entire entity as a whole. At that level such little-understood social phenomena as feedback and simultaneity and information-storage do away with the separateness of image-viewer and image-maker in a single collective consciousness, sharing simultaneously in powerful ephemeral images. To quote Ted Carpenter again:

> We live inside our media. *We* are their content. Television images come at us so fast, in such profusion, that they engulf us, tattoo us. We're immersed. It's like skin diving. We're surrounded, and whatever surrounds, involves. Television doesn't just wash over us and then "go out of mind." It goes *into* mind, deep into mind. The subconscious is a world in which we store everything, not something, and television extends the subconscious.

It is paradoxical, but also logical, that by definition this media consciousness (in which we are all infinitely small participating parts) is not aware of the workings of its collective subconscious on the surface, but only at some lower level. That is to say, if we know about it, we don't know we know, and I would argue that, to a re-markable degree, this applies just as much to the so-called "creators" as to the so-called "viewers." As Freud wrote about the creators of individual dreams, "I assure you that it is not only quite possible, but highly probable, that the dreamer really does know the meaning of his dream; *only he does not know that he knows, and therefore thinks that he does not*" (italics in original).

By implication then, and in contrast to most of what we have heard, learned, or experienced, it may be that *we ourselves are in some way responsible for television; we create it. More than any previous medium including drama and film, TV is a vivid projection of our collective subconscious.* Obviously, in practical, individual terms, we are not "responsible" for TV in whole or in part. We lack the technical understanding, the financial capacities, and per-haps even the will and insight to "create" television programs. And yet, all logic and commentary notwithstanding, we can be discovered to shape television more than it shapes us. This is true not merely in the material sense that audiences build ratings which sell products which buy programs, but also in a larger and less conscious way. Much as individuals purposefully and unconsciously create their own dream world and then react to it, I speculate that a TV society pur-posefully and unconsciously creates its own video world and then reacts to it.

Susan Sontag, who has speculated about the relations of dream and film, suggests in *Against Interpretation* that in one sense Freud was *too* successful in his efforts to get below the surface of things, since the influence of psychoanalysis on artistic criticism has grown overly great. But she offers a clear summary of this powerful mode: "All observable phenomena are bracketed, in Freud's phrase, as *manifest content*. This manifest content must be probed and pushed aside to find the true meaning—the *latent content*—beneath." This approach can be adapted to studying television, especially in the con-text of what Freud called "dream-work."

Since dreams involve repressed thoughts or wishes that cannot be handled fully or directly by the conscious individual, these hidden or latent thoughts are translated through dreaming into a series of sensory and visual images. Freud defined this transformation of a wish into a dream as "dream-work," and he referred to the opposite process of unravelling the dream-work as "interpretation." "Let me remind you," he stated with emphasis, "that *the process by which the latent dream is transformed into the manifest dream is called THE DREAM-WORK;* while the reverse process, which seeks to progress from the manifest to the latent thoughts, is our work of interpretation; the work of interpretation therefore aims at demolishing the dream-work." It was as though a powerful message was translated into an acceptable code for presentation, so that the presentation itself could then be decoded in order to discover the original message.

According to Freud, the original coding process, the dream-work, proceeds through several different means. The first and most self-explanatory means is *condensation*, the process of compressing, combining, fragmenting, or omitting elements of the latent thoughts as they become content in the manifest dream. The second means is *displacement*, whereby "a latent element may be *replaced*, not by a part of itself, but by something more remote, something of the nature of an allusion," or "the *accent* may be transferred from an important element to another which is unimportant, so that the center of the dream is shifted as it were, giving the dream a foreign appearance." A third means, sometimes labelled *inversion*, involves both the "regressive translation of thoughts into images" and also the fact that these visual images themselves are often "inverted," containing multiple, contradictory or opposite meanings. An ambiguity, an ambivalence, is set up, the consideration of which can be an important aspect of interpretation. A fourth element of dream-work, implicit in each of the preceding three, might be called *dramatization*, for the transformation of latent thoughts into manifest dreams involves continuous and inclusive working of material into some dramatic form, whether vivid or sketchy, polished or loose, elaborate or mundane.

What is striking about these central aspects of dream-work is that they all apply with uncanny directness to television. If we can accept the earlier hypotheses (and, admittedly, they are difficult to concede at first, whether taken literally or metaphorically) that media society as a whole has a consciousness somewhat like that of an individual, and that one way this collective consciousness deals with latent thoughts is by transforming them into the manifest content of television, then each separate process of dream-work can be seen to have its equivalent in what we might choose to call "TV-work."

Each of these correlations can be illustrated briefly. It goes without saying, first of all, that *TV-work involves dramatization*.

What applies to "Kojak" or "The Waltons," to Norman Lear and Associates or Mary Tyler Moore Productions, also applies to the creations of "CBS News" and "ABC Sports"; all prime-time television partakes heavily of drama. But it is less the drama of a playwright, with continuity which allows development, than the drama of a dream, with immediacy which provides belief. "Television," Carpenter states, "seems complete in itself. Each television experience seems distinct, self-sufficient, utterly true as itself, judged and motivated and understood in terms of itself alone. Concepts such as causation and purpose appear irrelevant."

Secondly, *TV-work involves condensation*—drastic, continuous and creative condensation. To take simply one example, Rhoda Morganstern of "Rhoda" is introduced as a "window decorator." This single tag, while entirely plausible and mundane in itself, is rich in associative meanings along several dimensions (just as Art Carney on "The Honeymooners" used to work in the sewers). Rhoda is pretty enough to be a window decoration herself, but she is also competent enough to decorate windows. That is, she has a useful money-earning job outside the home, yet the job is strikingly similar in content to traditional unpaid work within the home. In fact, "window decorating" connotes on one level all that is regarded as superficial, transparent and peripheral about women's traditional roles. However, on another level, it connotes central aspects of female sexuality presented as decorous virginity. And so on.

Also, *TV-work involves displacement* (and it is interesting to assume in this regard, as one does with dreams, that the more jumbled or obscure a presentation seems to be, the more displacement there has been in the process of TV-work). As a simple example, consider an element of a recent "Mary Tyler Moore Show" episode in which Mary finds herself serving dinner to Lou, her manly but insecure middle-aged "boss." (In condensed TV, as in condensed dream, one often "finds oneself" doing something with limited lead-in or prior explanation.) Much of "MTM" deals with displaced sexual wishes—the show is introduced by a song about "making it"—though this scene is more apparent than most. Among the things Mary wants to have at this Friday night rendezvous is a bottle of champagne, and the visual imagery and verbal dialogue of the scene, heavy with double meanings, focuses around how to open the bottle satisfactorily. Lou, uncertain but pretending to know how to do it, receives friendly encouragement and guidance from the more experienced and competent Mary. When he finally holds the large bottle erect in front of him and uncorks it, the prized white liquid comes bubbling out, giving Mary pleasure and transforming Lou's anxiety to satisfaction. The entire sequence, lasting only a few seconds, can be interpreted as wish fulfillment for both sexes around the prevalent concern of male impotence, all displaced in an acceptable but unmistakable way to a champagne bottle and the popping of its cork.

Lastly, *TV-work involves inversion*—the inversion of latent thoughts into meaningful and often ambiguous verbal and visual symbols, and also, to quote Freud, the "inversion of situations or of relations existing between two persons, as though the scene were laid in a 'topsy-turvy' world." "All In The Family" illustrates this point on a regular basis. Archie's steady flow of seemingly random but obviously meaningful verbal slips (such as "the infernal revenue system") are set against a series of larger situational inversions, each of which is absurd, but not *"merely"* absurd. The argumentative Bunkers function through an unending series of oppositions: male-female, young-old, white-black, liberal-conservative, us-them. . . . Yet it is significant that the presentation of contradicting arguments invariably becomes contradictory in its own right. No one ever argues a consistent "line," despite the perpetual tone of certainty. Hence, the important factor for analysis, most commentators notwithstanding, is not who comes out on which side so much as the presentation of a confusing issue. Since so much of prime-time TV deals with this kind of back-and-forth inversion, it is worth quoting Freud once again on opposites:

> One of our most surprising discoveries is the manner in which opposites in the latent dream are dealt with by the dream-work. We know already that points of agreement in the latent material are replaced by condensation in the manifest dream. Now contraries are treated in just the same way as similarities, with a marked preference for expression by means of the same manifest element. An element in the manifest dream which admits of an opposite may stand simply for itself, or for its opposite, or for both together; only the sense can decide which translation is to be chosen.

In this context, the entire question of how any given show "turns out in the end" takes on a new significance, or rather insignificance.

In the final analysis, the test of such speculations and hypotheses will be pragmatic. Their validity and usefulness must be demonstrated repeatedly over time. No one successful exercise will confirm their rightness, but then again, no single unconvincing effort will prove their wrongness. As with any propositions, we eventually accept or discard them at our own peril.

With this in mind, it seems only fair and logical to conclude with several brief attempts at specific TV analysis of the sort hinted at in the generalizations above. Let me discuss two separate shows aired during 1975, an episode of the short-lived series, "Kung Fu," and a one-hour incident from the venerable "Gunsmoke." Both are Westerns, but they are entirely different in their outward or manifest style and, I shall argue, in their primary latent content.

Take the episode of "Kung Fu" entitled *The Predators*. The story-line, or manifest content, is as follows. The Asian-American hero, Caine, stands falsely accused of killing a sheriff. Having escaped his sentence to hang, he comes across an Apache, Hoskay, whose brother has been killed by white scalp-hunters. After risking his life to protect the Indian from these bounty hunters, Caine follows them and is provoked into a conflict with the renegade Navajo, Mutala, who does much of their dirty work. In their fight Caine neutralizes his opponent and looks beyond him to the white leader, Rafe, whom he suddenly body-checks over the edge of a cliff, following after him in a dramatic free fall to the river below ("Rafe tumbling, Caine in control," according to the script). There the Apache, Hoskay, attacks Rafe in revenge. The Indian is wounded, and Caine is obliged to lead these two enemies from the canyon together. He finally succeeds, negotiating a settlement between Apaches and scalpers. In the process, he also wins an acknowledgement of his identity and wisdom from Rafe.

This story is paralleled by a sequence of flashbacks to China as young Caine watches the progress of his fellow disciple Teh Soong from youthful zealotry to the beginnings of mature self-awareness. The entire episode is built around little more than a series of unlikely fights and confrontations, the sort of dramatization from which most dreams and television are made. But more interesting is the condensation of several separate social themes from the past several years into a single plausible narrative.

The topical anxieties which provide the story's latent content are generational and racial conflict in the United States and the war in southeast Asia. Each of these themes is partially hidden by displacement. For example, the Indians in fact represent Black Americans. Hunted by rednecks (working for the man who actually killed the lawman), the Apache seeks revenge on them for killing his brother, but he hates all whites because of "all his fallen brothers." In contrast to this militant, Mutala (Mulatto?) the Navajo wears a Civil War army cap and literally fights the White Man's battle for him in the most unseemly way. He has fully accepted his role, and while it fills him with hate, this hatred is directed toward those (Caine and the Apaches) who are both more liberated and liberating.

If racial antagonisms are displaced to the West, some of those between generations are displaced to the Far East. Through the device of flashbacks to Asia, we see Teh Soong, slightly older than Caine, experience the classic student evolution of the sixties. He begins by dropping out of school. (Master Kan: "You will not be dissuaded . . . ?") His purpose is to fight injustice. (The people are living like "slaves" while the mandarins continue to "demand tribute.") While his elders seemingly do nothing, he expects to do everything. ("I will take up the cause of the people . . . I will lead them . . . speak for them . . . fight for them.") When bloodied in the movement ("beset by soldiers"), he returns to Kan's paternal care, though as young Caine observes to the Master, "Teh Soong accepts your kindness, and, at the same time, defies you." Recovered, he tries to lead the people against "the soldiers and the mandarins," only to turn from the cause and put on "the rags of a beggar," admitting openly that he had been more concerned with his own glory than with the burdens of the people.

Both of Caine's brother figures, Hoskay and Teh Soong (Ho and Tse Tung?), represent generalized aspects of anti-colonial struggle. But much of the show's dialogue concerning Vietnam is remarkably explicit. Standard words and phrases, even whole exchanges, from the war debate recur in only slightly disguised form. At the outset Rafe (Fear, but also Fa——er?) tells Caine, "Chinee, you're a caution," but proceeds to disregard him as a representative both of draftable American youth ("My father was born here") and the powerful Chinese presence. Master Kan explains of Teh Soong's radical acts, "He led a revolt in a village to the north. (sadly) Now the village has been destroyed." Note the ambiguity of the phrase "*to* the North" and also the similarity in tone and words with a well-meaning and patronizing American father (officer, editor, etc.) explaining why a village has been destroyed in order to be saved.

In the midst of these fragments from the Vietnam debate, it is worth recalling an important observation about dream dialogue. Freud claimed that *"the dream-work cannot create conversation in dreams;* save in a few exceptional cases, *it is imitated from, and made up of, things heard or even said by the dreamer himself* on the previous day, which have entered into the latent thoughts as the material or incitement of his dream" (emphasis added). Thus we hear Rafe's gun-carrying supporters say, as was often said of Uncle Sam, "I ain't seen no one lick Rafe yet." Caught in the Canyon (LBJ's tunnel?) with Caine, Rafe asks him tauntingly whether he thinks he knows the way to get out. It is a familiar American question and tone from the late sixties and early seventies and Caine's reply ("There is no choice. The way in is the way out.") paraphrases the simple and bitter response emblematic of the anti-war argument: "You can leave the way you came—in boats." But the way out is made hard when it becomes entangled in questions of "honor," whether real or pretended. "You have no honor?" Caine asks Rafe, inverting the question which older Americans had so steadily asked their young.

Equally resonant is the final dialogue between Teh Soong, returning to his studies from the resistance, and Master Kan, accepting him back, as Young Caine, who admires them both, looks on. One could hardly dream up a more succinct dramatization of the draft-resister dilemma that preoccupied Americans of the mid-seventies and that symbolized the interface between issues of generational and military conflict:

MK: Will you abide with us?

TS.   You will allow me?

MK: Our hearts are open.

TS: I beg your forgiveness, Master . . . And yours, Student Caine.

MK: You have my love.

YC: Mine as well.

TS: . . . Forgiveness?

MK: If you will find that, it must come from the one who has condemned you, Teh Soong. I would hope he would be generous. Surely there has been enough destruction.

But the latent content of a TV show is not always so heavily social; it can deal with far more personal material. This was driven home to me recently when I settled down to test out some of these ideas again at random. An episode of that most long-lived series, "Gunsmoke," had just gotten underway. A common farmer near Dodge City, legal guardian for a kindly but slow-witted younger man, is in love with a golden-haired and golden-hearted woman "working" above the Longbranch Saloon. His past is as shady as hers and as difficult to bury, when he is spotted by an old partner-in-crime who feels betrayed in a long-forgotten but unsolved bank robbery in a distant state. The farmer survives a duel with his one-time companion (the cause of which is kept from Marshal Dillon) and cements his relation to the saloon girl, only to be killed in the end by the youth for whom he holds responsibility. This devoted and dull-witted sidekick has also fallen in love with the saloon girl in his own child-like way, inspired by her beauty and her affectionate, mothering manner towards him. Needing money to "marry" her, he turns in his reformed-robber protector to Sheriff Dillon for the posted reward, not sensing the consequences for the couple he loves and depends on. Finally, overwhelmed by what he has done, the youth pulls a gun on the sheriff but shoots his unarmed benefactor instead.

In terms of "art" and "industry" criticism, I wanted an ingenious but rather far-fetched and implausible plot, conveyed better than adequately by the usual cast and aided by three talented outsiders in the feature roles. The slightly crude theme is handled creditably; overt violence, though stereotyped, is minimal; and the ending, however implausible, is suitably tragic. But what did I watch in terms of dream interpretation? The latent meaning behind the manifest content seems to be quite different and considerably more plausible. The entire hour is not only understandable, but in fact *best understood* as a direct and detailed treatment of the Oedipus Complex. It transposes to the archetypal American setting of Dodge City the universal drive summarized in the song, "I Want a Girl Just Like the Girl that Married Dear Old Dad."

Though condensation and inversion are evident, displacement is the primary element of the TV-work in this instance. In order to see the latent material clearly, it is necessary to understand that the traditional oedipal triangle has been skewed slightly—disguised—so that no one is in quite their proper role. "Father" is not the real father, only a guardian of the youth and a suitor of the saloon girl. "Mother" is not the real mother, only a kindly woman-of-the-evening who is eager to settle down. "The son" is not a real son, only a man whose slight retardedness gives him all the innocence of a child and forces him to act out, or dramatize, what others might only think.

In this context, consider three of the program's central scenes. The first scene, though ostensibly concerned with an innocent knife-game on the saloon steps, deals directly with the Son's awakening sexuality. Doc and Festus (delivering a box tied up in pink to Miss Kitty) pass the young man playing mumblety-peg, sticking his knife into the front steps of the Longbranch. He is trying to master a new feat called "over the cowshed," in which he throws his knife up in front of himself. Doc warns him not to throw it into the Longbranch and then proceeds through the (emblematic) swinging doors into the saloon-whorehouse. There he and Festus have a brief but meaningful exchange (while eyeing several prostitutes) about Doc's comparative experience and proficiency at "mumblety-peg," and the double meaning is not to Doc as a surgeon. Meanwhile, the Son tries the hard trick and pulls it off, but gets in trouble when his knife sticks close to the boots of some older men. They humiliate and taunt the young innocent by taking away his knife and passing it under and around their horses, leaving him crying in the dust until he summons his "parents" from the saloon. The scene ends when the Mother picks up the knife and restores it to the Son, while looking lovingly at the Father.

In a second central scene, the Father must undertake "man's business," which he cannot explain to his dependent, and he leaves the Son with the Mother inside the Longbranch. Her mind is elsewhere, on the man's impending (gun)fight with the old (out)law partner, but she indulges the youth's fantasies, having sworn to look after him if the male guardian is killed. When she says she would like to live in his house, he hears it innocently as an expression of sexual rather than maternal love. The forbidden oedipal wish has been stated and its fulfillment seemingly promised.

Later he is outraged when he is "treated like a kid" and denied money by his guardian and rival. His futile attempt to rob the funds he needs to be his own man and "wed" the saloon girl-Mother, brings Marshall Dillon to the house. Having innocently but ingeniously exposed his Father for robbery and won the Mother for companionship, he finally kills the person who has been the focus of his childlike anger and frustration. The forgiving Father dies lying on top of him, trying to take the smoking gun from his hand. Implausible scenes such as these, repeated endlessly each night in the privacy of our homes, may, when we get the hang of it, make more sense in psychological terms than in traditional dramatic terms.

Having suggested that the latent wishes of a generalized consciousness by means of so-called "TV-work" which bears a close resemblance to dream-work, one final question must be raised regarding any possible usefulness of this approach. Dream analysis, after all, began as, and has remained, a part of a broader process of therapy for individuals. But could the interpretation of TV as dream ever have any collective therapeutic value? The answer depends in part upon a much more thorough definition of the collective subconscious and the hows and whys of TV-work—the process of disguising societal needs and wishes in acceptable video form. The relation of each individual to this hypothetical collective consciousness will also demand further thought and speculation, as will the question, so familiar to dream analysts, of whether "working through" a fantasy periodically by some kind of mental process makes one (or in this case *all*) more aware of, and receptive toward, the underlying problem or more resigned to its continuing existence in a suppressed and unacknowledged form.

Walter Benjamin (1892-1940), the sensitive literary interpreter and cultural critic of the Frankfort School, once stated that, "During long periods of history, the mode of human sense perception changes with humanity's entire mode of existence." Benjamin, whose essays are published under the revealing title *Illuminations*, continued, "The manner in which human sense perception is organized, the medium in which it is accomplished, is determined not only by nature but by historical circumstances as well." Historical circumstances have put us in the middle of a new media world. However primitive the "delights of visual communication" may still seem to most people, it is now possible to speculate that television may someday present new and necessary "illumination" as our modes of collective perception are reorganized. After all, the video medium is young, and we have scarcely begun to understand it.

Footnote

1.   This quotation is from *A General Introduction to Psychoanalysis* (1924), p. 95 of the Pocket Book edition. Other quotations from Freud in the paper are all drawn from this same paperback edition of the *General Introduction*.

Television Melodrama

David Thorburn

I remember with what a smile of saying something daring
and inacceptable John Erskine told an undergraduate class
that some day we would understand that plot and melodrama were good things for a novel to have and that
Bleak House was a very good novel indeed.
　　　　　　　　　　　　　　—Lionel Trilling,
　　　　　　　　　　　　　　A Gathering of Fugitives

Although much of what I say will touch significantly on the
medium as a whole, I want to focus here on a single broad category
of television programming—what *TV Guide* and the newspaper listings, with greater insight than they realize, designate as "melodrama."
I believe that at its increasingly frequent best, this fundamental television genre so richly exploits the conventions of its medium as to be
clearly distinguishable from its ancestors in the theater, in the novel,

and in films. And I also believe, though this more extravagant corollary judgment can only be implied in my present argument, that television melodrama has been our culture's most characteristic aesthetic form, and one of its most complex and serious forms as well, for at least the past decade and probably longer.

Melo is the Greek word for music. The term *melodrama* is said to have originated as a neutral designation for a spoken dramatic text with a musical accompaniment or background, an offshoot or spin-off of opera. The term came into widespread use in England during the nineteenth century, when it was appropriated by theatrical entrepreneurs as a legal device to circumvent statutes that restricted the performances of legitimate drama to certain theaters. In current popular and (much) learned usage, *melodrama* is a resolutely pejorative term, also originating early in the last century, denoting a sentimental, artificially plotted drama that sacrifices characterization to extravagant incident, makes sensational appeals to the emotions of its audience, and ends on a happy or at least a morally reassuring note.

Neither the older, neutral nor the current, disparaging definitions are remotely adequate, however. The best recent writings on melodrama, drawing sustenance from a larger body of work concerned with popular culture in general, have begun to articulate a far more complex definition, one that plausibly refuses to restrict melodrama to the theater, and vigorously challenges long-cherished distinctions between high and low culture—even going so far as to question some of our primary assumptions about the nature and possibilities of art itself. In this emerging conception, melodrama must be understood to include not only popular trash composed by hack novelists and film-makers—Conrad's forgotten rival Stanley Weyman, for example, Jacqueline Susann; the director Richard Fleischer—but also such complex, though still widely accessible, art-works as the novels of Samuel Richardson and Dickens, or the films of Hitchcock and Kurosawa. What is crucial to this new definition, though, is not the actual attributes of melodrama itself, which remain essentially unchanged; nor the extension of melodrama's claims to prose fiction and film, which many readers and viewers have long accepted in any case. What is crucial is the way in which the old dispraised attributes of melodrama are understood, the contexts to which they are returned, the respectful scrutiny they are assumed to deserve.[1]

What does it signify, for example, to acknowledge that the structure of melodrama enacts a fantasy of reassurance, and that the happy or moralistic endings so characteristic of the form are reductive and arbitrary—a denial of our "real" world where events refuse to be coherent and where (as Nabokov austerely says) harm is the norm? The desperate or cunning or spirited strategems by which this escape from reality is accomplished must still retain a fundamental interest. They must still instruct us, with whatever obliqueness, concerning the nature of that reality from which escape or respite has been sought. Consider the episode of the Cave of Montesinos in *Don Quixote*, in which the hero, no mean melodramatist himself, descends into a cavern to dream or conjure a pure vision of love and chivalry and returns with a tale in which a knight's heart is cut from his breast and salted to keep it fresh for his lady. This is an emblem, a crystallizing enactment, of the process whereby our freest, most necessary fantasies are anchored in the harsh, prosaic actualities of life. And Sancho's suspicious but also respectful and deeply attentive interrogation of Quixote's dream instructs us as to how we might profitably interrogate melodrama.

Again, consider the reassurance-structure of melodrama in relation to two other defining features of the form: its persistent and much-condemned habit of moral simplification and its lust for topicality, its hunger to engage or represent behavior and moral attitudes that belong to its particular day and time, especially behavior shocking or threatening to prevailing moral codes. When critics or viewers describe how television panders to its audience, these qualities of simplification and topicality are frequently cited in evidence. The audience wants to be titillated but also wants to be confirmed in its moral sloth, the argument goes, and so the melodramatist sells stories in which crime and criminals are absorbed into paradigms of moral conflict, into allegories of good and evil, in which the good almost always win. The trouble with such a view is not in what it describes, which is often accurate enough, but in its rush to judgment. Perhaps, as Roland Barthes proposes in his stunning essay on wrestling, we ought to learn to see such texts from the standpoint of the audience, whose pleasures in witnessing these spectacles of excess and grandiloquence may be deeper than we know, and whose intimate familiarity with such texts may lead them to perceive as complex aesthetic conventions what the traditional high culture sees only as simple stereotypes.[2]

Suppose that the reassuring conclusions and the moral allegorizing of melodrama are regarded in this way, as *conventions*, as "rules" of the genre in the same way that the iambic pentameter and the rimed couplet at the end of a sonnet are "rules" for that form. From this angle, these recurring features of melodrama can be perceived as the *enabling conditions* for an encounter with forbidden or deeply disturbing materials: not an escape into blindness or easy reassurance, but an instrument for seeing. And from this angle, melodrama becomes a peculiarly significant public forum, complicated and immensely enriched because its discourse is aesthetic and broadly popular: a forum or arena in which traditional ways of feeling and thinking are brought into continuous, strained relation with powerful intuitions of change and contingency.

This is the spirit in which I turn to television melodrama. In this category I include most made-for-television movies, the soap operas, and all the lawyers, cowboys, cops and docs, the fugitives and adventurers, the fraternal and filial comrades who have filled the prime hours of so many American nights for the last thirty years.[3] I have no wish to deny that these entertainments are market commodities first and last, imprisoned by rigid timetables and stereotyped formulas, compelled endlessly to imagine and reimagine as story and as performance the conventional wisdom, the lies and fantasies, and the muddled ambivalent values of our bourgeois industrial culture. These qualities are, in fact, the primary source of their interest for me, and of the complicated pleasures they uniquely offer.

Confined (but also nourished) by its own foreshortened history and by formal and thematic conventions whose origins are not so much aesthetic as economic, television melodrama is a derivative art, just now emerging from its infancy. It is effective more often in parts of stories than in their wholes, and in thrall to censoring pressures that limit its range. But like all true art, television melodrama is cunning, having discovered (or, more often, stumbled upon) strategies for using the constraints within which it must live.

Its essential artistic resource is the actor's performance, and one explanation—there are many others—for the disesteem in which television melodrama is held is that we have yet to articulate an adequate aesthetics for the art of performance. Far more decisively than the movie-actor, the television-actor creates and controls the meaning of what we see on the screen. In order to understand television drama, and in order to find authentic standards for judging it as art, we must learn to recognize and to value the discipline, energy, and intelligence that must be expended by the actor who succeeds in creating what we too casually call a *truthful* or *believable* performance. What happens when an actor's performance arouses our latent faculties of imaginative sympathy and moral judgment, when he causes us to acknowledge that what he is doing is true to the tangled potency of real experience, not simply impressive or clever, but *true*—what happens then is art.

It is important to be clear about what acting, especially television-acting, is or can be: nothing less than a reverent attentiveness to the pain and beauty in the lives of others, an attentiveness made accessible to us in a wonderfully instructive process wherein the performer's own impulses to self-assertion realize themselves only by surrendering or yielding to the claims of the character he wishes to portray. Richard Poirier, our best theorist of performance, puts the case as follows: "performance . . . is an action which must go through passages that both impede the action and give it form, much as a sculptor not only is impelled to shape his material but is in turn shaped by it, his impulse to mastery always chastened, sometimes made tender and possibly witty by the recalcitrance of what he is working on."[4]

Television has always challenged the actor. The medium's reduced visual scale grants him a primacy unavailable in the theater or in the movies, where an amplitude of things and spaces offers competition for the eye's attention. Its elaborate, enforced obedience to various formulas for plot and characterization virtually require him to recover from within himself and from his broadly stereotyped assignment nuances of gesture, inflection, and movement that will at least hint at individual or idiosyncratic qualities. And despite our failure clearly to acknowledge this, the history of television as a dramatic medium is, at the very least, a history of exceptional artistic accomplishment by actors. The performances in television melodrama today are much richer than in the past, though there were many remarkable performances even in the early days. The greater freedom afforded to writers and actors is part of the reason for this, but (as I will try to indicate shortly) the far more decisive reason is the extraordinary sophistication the genre has achieved.

Lacking access to even the most elementary scholarly resources —bibliographies, systematic collections of films or tapes, even moderately reliable histories of the art—I can only appeal to our (hopefully) common memory of the highly professional and serious acting regularly displayed in series such as "Naked City," "Twilight Zone," "Route 66," "Gunsmoke," "The Defenders," "Cade's County," "Stoney Burke," "East Side, West Side," "The Name of the Game," and others whose titles could be supplied by anyone who has watched American television over the past twenty or twenty-five years. Often the least promising dramatic formulas were transformed by vivid and highly intelligent performances. I remember with particular pleasure and respect, for example, Steve McQueen's arresting portrayal of the callow bounty hunter Josh Randall in the western series, "Wanted: Dead or Alive"—the jittery lean grace of his physical movements, the balked, dangerous tenderness registered by his voice and eyes in his encounters with women; the mingling of deference and menace that always enlivened his dealings with older men, outlaws and sheriffs mainly, between whom this memorable boy-hero seemed fixed or caught, but willingly so. McQueen's subsequent apotheosis in the movies was obviously deserved, but I have often felt his performances on the large screen were less tensely intelligent, more self-indulgent than his brilliant early work in television.

If we could free ourselves from our ingrained expectations concerning dramatic form and from our reluctance to acknowledge that art is always a commodity of some kind, constrained by the technology necessary to its production and by the needs of the audience for which it is intended, then we might begin to see how ingeniously television melodrama contrives to nourish its basic resource—the actor—even as it surrenders to those economic pressures that seem most imprisoning.

Consider, for example, the ubiquitous commercials. They are so widely deplored that even those who think themselves friendly to the medium cannot restrain their outrage over such unambiguous evidence of the huckster's contempt for art's claim to continuity. Thus, a writer in the official journal of the National Academy of Television Arts and Sciences, meditating sadly on "the total absence" of serious television drama, refers in passing to "the horrors of continuous, brutal interruption."[5]

That commercials have shaped television melodrama decisively is obvious, of course. But, as with most of the limitations to which the genre is subjected, these enforced pauses are merely formal conventions. They are no more intrinsically hostile to art than the unities observed by the French neoclassical theater or the serial installments in which so many Victorian novels had to be written. Their essential effect has been the refinement of a segmented dramatic structure peculiarly suited to a formula-story whose ending is predictable—the doctor will save the patient, the cop will catch the criminal—and whose capacity to surprise or otherwise engage its audience must therefore depend largely on the localized vividness and potency of the smaller units or episodes that comprise the whole.

Television melodrama achieves this episodic or segmented vividness in several ways, but its most dependable and recurring strategy is to require its actors to display themselves intensely and energetically from the very beginning. In its most characteristic and most interesting form, television melodrama will contrive its separate units such that they will have substantial independent weight and interest, usually enacting in miniature the larger patterns and emotional rhythms of the whole drama. Thus, each segment will show us a character, or several characters, confronting some difficulty or other; the character's behavior and (especially) his emotional responses will intensify, then achieve some sort of climactic or resolving pitch at the commercial break; and this pattern will be repeated incrementally in subsequent segments.

To describe this characteristic structure is to clarify what those who complain of the genre's improbability never acknowledge: that television melodrama is in some respects an *operatic* rather than a conventionally dramatic form—a fact openly indicated by the term *soap opera*. No one goes to Italian opera expecting a realistic plot, and since applause for the important arias is an inflexible convention, no one expects such works to proceed without interruption. The pleasures of this kind of opera are largely (though not exclusively) the pleasures of the brilliant individual performance, and good operas in this tradition are those in which the composer has contrived roles which test as fully as possible the vocal capacities of the performers.

Similarly, good television melodramas are those in which an intricately formulaic plot conspires perfectly with the commercial interruptions to encourage a rich articulation of the separate parts of the work, and thus to call forth from the realistic actor the full energies of his performer's gifts. What is implausible in such works is the continual necessity for emotional display by the characters. In real life we are rarely called upon to feel so intensely, and never in such neatly escalating sequences. But the emotions dramatized by these improbable plots are not in themselves unreal, or at least they need not be—and television melodrama often becomes more truthful as it becomes more implausible.

As an example of this recurring paradox—it will be entirely
familiar to any serious reader of Dickens—consider the following
generically typical episode from the weekly series, "Medical Center."
An active middle-aged man falls victim to an aneurysm judged
certain to kill him within a few years. This affliction being strategic-
ally located for dramatic use, the operation that could save his life
may also leave him impotent—a fate nasty enough for anyone, but
psychologically debilitating for this unlucky fellow who has divorced
his first wife and married a much younger woman. The early scenes
establish his fear of aging and his intensely physical relationship
with his young wife with fine lucid economy. Now the plot elaborates further complications and develops new, related centers of
interest. His doctor—the series regular who is (sometimes) an arresting derivation of his television ancestors, Doctors Kildare and Ben
Casey—is discovered to be a close, longtime friend whose involvement in the case is deeply personal. Confident of his surgeon's
skills and much younger than his patient, the doctor is angrily
unsympathetic to the older man's reluctance to save his life at the
expense of his sexuality. Next, the rejected wife, brilliantly played
by Barbara Rush, is introduced. She works—by a marvelous arbitrary coincidence—in the very hospital in which her ex-husband
is being treated. There follows a complex scene in the hospital
room in which the former wife acts out her tangled, deep feelings
toward the man who has rejected her and toward the woman who
has replaced her. In their tensely guarded repartee, the husband
and ex-wife are shown to be bound to one another in a vulnerable
knowingness made in decades of uneasy intimacy that no divorce
can erase and that the new girl-wife must observe as an outsider.
Later scenes require emotional confrontations—some of them equally
subtle—between the doctor and each wife, between doctor and
patient, between old wife and new.

These nearly mathematic symmetries conspire with still further
plot complications to create a story that is implausible in the extreme. Though aneurysms are dangerous, they rarely threaten impotence. Though impotence is a real problem, few men are free to
choose a short happy life of potency, and fewer still are surrounded
in such crises by characters whose relations to them so fully articulate such a wide spectrum of human needs and attitudes. The test
of such an arbitrary contrivance is not the plausibility of the whole
but the accuracy and truthfulness of its parts, the extent to which
its various strategies of artificial heightening permit an open en-

actment of feelings and desires that are only latent or diffused in the muddled incoherence of the real world. And although my argument does not depend on the success or failure of one or of one dozen specific melodramas—the genre's manifest complexity and its enormous popularity being sufficient to justify intensive and respectful study—I should say that the program just described was for me a serious aesthetic experience. I was caught by the persuasiveness of the actors' performances, and my sympathies were tested by the meanings those fine performances released. The credibility of the young wife's reluctant, pained acknowledgement that a life without sex *would* be a crippled life; the authenticity of the husband's partly childish, partly admirable reverence for his carnal aliveness; and, especially, the complex genuineness of his ambivalent continuing bonds with his first wife—all this was there on the screen. Far from falsifying life, it quickened one's awareness of the burdens and costs of human relationships.

That the plots of nearly all current television melodramas tend, as in this episode of "Medical Center," to be more artificially contrived than those of earlier years seems to me a measure not of the genre's unoriginality but of its maturity, its increasingly bold and self-conscious capacity to *use* formal requirements which it cannot in any case evade, and to exploit (rather than be exploited by) various formulas for characterization. Nearly all the better series melodramas of recent years, in fact, have resorted quite openly to what might be called a *multiplicity principle*: a principle of plotting or organization whereby a particular drama will draw not once or twice but many times upon the immense store of stories and situations created by the genre's brief but crowded history. The multiplicity principle allows not less but more reality to enter the genre. Where the old formulas had been developed exhaustively and singly through the whole of a story—that is how they became stereotypes—they are now treated elliptically in a plot that deploys many of them simultaneously. The familiar character-types and situations thus become more suggestive and less imprisoning. There is no pretense that a given character has been wholly "explained" by the plot, and the formula has the liberating effect of creating a premise or base on which the actor is free to build. By minimizing the need for long establishing or expository sequences, the multiplicity principle allows the story to leave aside the question of *how* these emotional entanglements were arrived at and to concentrate its energies on their credible and powerful present enactment.

These and other strategems—which result in richer, more plausible characterizations and also permit elegant variations of tone —are possible because television melodrama can rely confidently on one resource that is always essential to the vitality of any art-form: an audience impressive not simply in its numbers but also in its genuine sophistication, its deep familiarity with the history and conventions of the genre. For so literate an audience, the smallest departure from conventional expectations can become meaningful, and this creates endless chances for surprise and nuanced variation, even for thematic subtlety.

In his instructive book on American films of the '40s and '50s, Michael Wood speaks nostalgically of his membership in "the universal movie audience" of that time. This audience of tens of millions was able to see the movies as a coherent world, "a country of familiar faces, . . . a system of assumptions and beliefs and preoccupations, a fund of often interchangeable plots, characters, patches of dialog, and sets." By relying on the audience's familiarity with other movies, Wood says, the films of that era constituted "a living tradition of the kind that literary critics always used to be mourning for."[6]

This description fits contemporary television even more closely than it does those earlier movies, since most members of the TV audience have lived through the whole history of the medium. They know its habits, its formulas, its stars, and its recurring character actors with a confident, easy intimacy that may well be unique in the history of popular art. Moreover, television's capacity to make its history and evolution continuously available (even to younger members in its universal audience) is surely without precedent, for the system of reruns has now reached the point of transforming television into a continuous, living museum which displays for daily or weekly consumption texts from every stage of the medium's past.

Outsiders from the high culture who visit TV melodrama occasionally in order to issue their tedious reports about our cultural malaise are simply not seeing what the TV audience sees. They are especially blind to the complex allusiveness with which television melodrama uses its actors. For example, in a recent episode of the elegant "Columbo" series, Peter Falk's adventures occurred onboard a luxury liner and brought him into partnership with the captain of the ship, played by Patrick Macnee, the smooth British actor who starred in the popular spy series, "The Avengers." The scenes between Falk and Macnee were continuously enlivened not simply by the different acting styles of the two performers but also by the attitudes toward heroism, moral authority, and aesthetic taste represented in the kinds of programs with which each star has been associated. The uneasy, comic partnership between these characters —Falk's grungy, American-ethnic slyness contrasting with, and finally mocking, Macnee's British public school elegance and fastidiousness—was further complicated by the presence in the show of the guest villain, played by yet another star of a successful TV series of a few years ago—Robert Vaughn of "The Man From U.N.C.L.E." Vaughn's character had something of the sartorial, upper-class *elan* of Macnee's ship's master but, drawing on qualities established in his earlier TV role, was tougher, wholly American, more calculating, and ruthless. Macnee, of course, proved no match for Vaughn's unmannerly cunning, but Falk-Columbo succeeded in exposing him in a climax that expressed not only the show's usual fantasy of working-class intelligence overcoming aristocratic guile, but also the victory of American versions of popular entertainment over their British counterparts.

The aesthetic and human claims of most television melodrama would surely be much weakened, if not completely obliterated, in any other medium, and I have come to believe that the species of melodrama to be found on television today is a unique dramatic form, offering an especially persuasive resolution of the contradiction or tension that has been inherent in melodrama since the time of Euripides. As Peter Brooks reminds us in his provocative essay on the centrality of the melodramatic mode in romantic and modern culture, stage melodrama represents "a popular form of the tragic, exploiting similar emotions within the context of the ordinary." Melodrama is a "popular" form, we may say, both because it is favored by audiences and because it insists (or tries to insist) on the dignity and importance of the ordinary, usually bourgeois world of the theater-goer himself. The difficulty with this enterprise, of course, is the same for Arthur Miller in our own day as it was for Thomas Middleton in Jacobean London: displacing the action and characters from a mythic or heroically stylized world to an ordinary world—from Thebes to Brooklyn—involves a commitment to a kind of realism that is innately resistant to exactly those intense passionate enactments that the melodramatist wishes to invoke. Melodrama is thus always in conflict with itself, gesturing simultaneously toward ordinary reality *and* toward a moral and emotional heightening that is rarely encountered in the "real" world.

Although it can never be made to disappear, this conflict is minimized, or is capable of being minimized, by television—and in a way that is simply impossible in the live theater and that is nearly always less effective on the enlarged movie-screen. The melodramatic mode is peculiarly congenial to television, its inherent contradictions are less glaring and damaging there, because the medium is uniquely hospitable to the spatial confinements of the theater and to the profound realistic intimacy of the film.

Few would dispute the cinema's advantages over the theater as a realistic medium. As every serious film theorist begins by reminding us, the camera's ability to record the dense multiplicity of the external world and to reveal character in all its outer nuance and idiosyncrasy grants a visually authenticating power to the medium that has no equivalent in the theater. Though the stage owns advantages peculiar to its character as a live medium, it is clearly an artform more stylized, less visually realistic than the film, and it tests its performers in a somewhat different way. Perhaps the crucial difference is also the most obvious one: the distance between the audience and the actor in even the most intimate theatrical environment requires facial and vocal gestures as well as bodily movements "broader" and more excessive than those demanded by the camera, which can achieve a lover's closeness to the performer.

The cinema's photographic realism is not, of course, an unmixed blessing. But it is incalculably valuable to melodrama because, by encouraging understatement from its actors, it can help to ratify extravagant or intense emotions that would seem far less credible in the theater. And although television is the dwarf child of the film, constrained and scaled down in a great many ways, its very smallness can become an advantage to the melodramatic imagination. This is so because if the cinema's particularizing immediacy is friendly to melodrama, certain other characteristics of the medium are hostile to it. The extended duration of most film, the camera's freedom of movement, the more-than-life-sized dimensions of the cinematic image—all these create what has been called the film's mythopoeic tendency, its inevitable effect of magnification. Since the natural domain of melodrama is indoors, in those ordinary and enclosed spaces wherein most of us act out our deepest needs and feelings—bedrooms, offices, courtrooms, hospitals—the reduced visual field of television is, or can be, far more nourishing than the larger, naturally expansive movie-screen. And for the kind of psychologically nuanced performance elicited by good melodrama, the smaller television screen would seem even more appropriate: perfectly adapted, in fact, to record those intimately minute physical and vocal gestures on which the art of the realistic actor depends, yet happily free of the cinema's malicious (if often innocent) power to transform merely robust nostrils into Brobdingnagian caverns, minor facial irregularities into craterous deformities.

Television's matchless respect for the idiosyncratic expressiveness of the ordinary human face and its unique hospitality to the confining spaces of our ordinary world are virtues exploited repeatedly in all the better melodramas. But perhaps they are given special decisiveness in "Kojak," a classy police series whose gifted leading player had been previously consigned almost entirely to gangster parts, primarily (one supposes) because of the cinema's blindness to the uncosmetic beauty of his large bald head and generously irregular face. In its first two years particularly, before Savalas' character stiffened into the macho stereotype currently staring out upon us from magazine advertisements for razor blades and men's toiletries, "Kojak" was a genuine work of art, intricately designed to exploit its star's distinctively urban flamboyance, his gift for registering a long, modulated range of sarcastic vocal inflections and facial maneuvers, his talent for persuasive ranting. The show earned its general excellence not only because of Savalas' energetic performance, but also because its writers contrived supporting roles that complemented the central character with rare, individuating clarity, because the boldly artificial plotting in most episodes pressed toward the revelation of character rather than shoot-em-up action, and because, finally, the whole enterprise was forced into artfulness by the economic and technological environment that determined its life.

This last is at once the most decisive and most instructive fact about "Kojak," as it is about television melodrama generally. Because "Kojak" is filmed in Hollywood on a restricted budget, the show must invoke New York elliptically, in ingenious process shots and in stock footage taken from the full-length (and much less impressive) television-movie that served as a pilot for the series. The writers for the program are thus driven to devise stories that will allow the principal characters to appear in confined locations that can be created on or near studio sound-stages—offices, interrogation rooms, dingy bars, city apartments, nondescript alleys, highway underpasses, all the neutral and enclosed spaces common to urban life generally. As a result, "Kojak" often succeeds in projecting a sense of the city that is more compelling and intelligent than that which is offered in many films and television movies filmed on location: its menacing closeness, its capacity to harbor and even to generate certain kinds of crime, its watchful, unsettling accuracy as a custodian of the lists and records and documents that open a track to the very center of our lives. "Kojak's" clear superiority to another, ostensibly more original and exotic police series, "Hawaii Five-O," is good partial evidence for the liberating virtues of such confinement. This latter series is filmed on location at enormous expense and is often much concerned to give a flavor of Honolulu particularly. Yet it yields too easily to an obsession with scenic vistas and furious action sequences which threaten to transform the program into a mere travelogue and which always seem unnaturally confined by the reduced scale of the television screen.

That the characters in "Kojak" frequently press beyond the usual stereotypes is also partly a result of the show's inability to indulge in all the outdoor muscle-flexing, chasing, and shooting made possible by location filming. Savalas' Kojak especially is a richly individuated creation, his policeman's cunning a natural expression of his lifelong, intimate involvement in the very ecology of the city. A flamboyant, aggressive man, Kojak is continually engaged in a kind of joyful contest for recognition and even for mastery with the environment that surrounds him. The studio sets on which most of the action occurs, and the many close-up shots in each episode, reinforce and nurture these traits perfectly, for they help Savalas to work with real subtlety—to project not simply his character's impulse to define himself against the city's enclosures but also a wary, half-loving respect for such imprisonments, a sense indeed that they are the very instrument of his self-realization.

Kojak's expensive silk-lined suits and hats and the prancing vitality of his physical movements are merely the outer expressions of what is shown repeatedly to be an enterprise of personal fulfillment that depends mostly on force of intellect. His intelligence is not bookish—the son of a Greek immigrant, he never attended college—but it is genuine and powerfully self-defining because he must depend on his knowledge of the city in order to prevent a crime or catch a criminal. Proud of his superior mental quickness and urban knowingness, Kojak frequently behaves with the egotistical flair of a bold, demanding scholar, reveling in his ability to instruct subordinates in how many clues they have overlooked and even (in one episode) performing with histrionic brilliance as a teacher before a class of students at the police academy. Objecting to this series because it ratifies the stereotype of the super-cop is as silly as objecting to Sherlock Holmes on similar grounds. Like Holmes in many ways, Kojak is a man who realizes deeply private needs and inclinations in the doing of his work. Not law-and-order simplicities, but intelligence and self-realization are what "Kojak" celebrates. The genius of the series is to have conceived a character whose portrayal calls forth from Savalas exactly what his appearance and talents most suit him to do.

The distinction of "Kojak" in its first two seasons seems to me reasonably representative of the achievements of television melodrama in recent years. During the past season, I have seen dozens of programs—episodes of "Harry-O," "Police Story," "Baretta," "Medical Center," the now-defunct "Medical Story," several made-for-TV movies, and portions at least of the new mini-series melodramas being developed by ABC—whose claims to attention were fully as strong as "Kojak's." Their partial but genuine excellence constitutes an especially salutary reminder of the fact that art always thrives on restraints and prohibitions, indeed that it requires them if it is to survive at all. Like the Renaissance sonnet or Racine's theater, television melodrama is always most successful when it most fully embraces that which confines it, when *all* the limitations imposed upon it—including such requirements as the 60 or 90-minute time slot, the commercial interruptions, the small dimensions of the screen, even the consequences of low-budget filming—become instruments of use, conventions whose combined workings create unpretentious and spirited dramatic entertainments, works of popular art that are engrossing, serious, and imaginative.

That such honorific adjectives are rarely applied to television melodrama, that we have effectively refused even to consider the genre in aesthetic terms is a cultural fact and, ultimately, a political fact almost as interesting as the art-works we have been ignoring. Perhaps because television melodrama is an authentically popular art—unlike rubber hamburgers, encounter-group theater or electric-kool-aid journalism—our understanding of it has been conditioned (if not thwarted entirely) by the enormous authority American high culture grants to avant-garde conceptions of the artist as an adversary figure in mortal conflict with his society. Our attitude toward the medium has been conditioned also by even more deeply ingrained assumptions about the separate high dignity of aesthetic experience—an activity we are schooled to imagine as uncontaminated by the marketplace, usually at enmity with the everyday world, and dignified by the very rituals of payment and dress and travel and isolation variously required for its enjoyment. It is hard, in an atmosphere which accords art a special if not an openly subversive status, to think of television as an aesthetic medium, for scarcely another institution in American life is at once so familiarly *un*special and so profoundly a creature of the economic and technological genius of advanced industrial capitalism.

Almost everything that is said or written about television, and especially about television drama, is tainted by such prejudices; more often it is in utter servitude to them. And although television itself would no doubt benefit significantly if its nature were perceived and described more objectively, it is the larger culture— whose signature is daily and hourly to be found there—that would benefit far more.

In the introduction to *The Idea of a Theater*, Francis Fergusson reminds us that genuinely popular dramatic art is always powerfully conservative in certain ways, offering stories that insist on "their continuity with the common sense of the community." Hamlet could enjoin the players to hold a mirror up to nature, "to show . . . the very age and body of the time his form and pressure" because, Fergusson tells us, "the Elizabethan theater was itself a mirror which had been formed at the center of the culture of its time, and at the center of the life and awareness of the community." That we have no television Shakespeare is obvious enough, I guess. But we do already have our Thomas Kyds and our Chapmans. A Marlowe, even a Ben Jonson, is not inconceivable. It is time we noticed them.[7]

Footnotes

1. The bibliography of serious recent work on melodrama is not overly intimidating, but some exciting and important work has been done. I list here only pieces that have directly influenced my present argument, and I refer the reader to their notes and bibliographies for a fuller survey of the scholarship. Earl F. Bargainnier summarizes recent definitions of melodrama and offers a short history of the genre as practiced by dramatists of the eighteenth and nineteenth centuries in "Melodrama as Formula," *Journal of Popular Culture*, 9 (Winter, 1975). John G. Cawelti's indispensable *Adventure, Mystery, and Romance* (Chicago, 1976) focuses closely and originally on melodrama at several points. Peter Brooks' "The Melodramatic Imagination," in *Romanticism: Vistas, Instances, Continuities*, ed. David Thorburn and Geoffrey Hartman (Cornell, 1973), boldy argues that melodrama is a primary literary and visionary mode in romantic and modern culture. Much recent Dickens criticism is helpful on melodrama, but see especially Robert Garis, *The Dickens Theatre* (Oxford, 1965), and essays by Barbara Hardy, George H. Ford, and W. J. Harvey in the Dickens volume of the twentieth-century views series, ed. Martin Price (Prentice-Hall, 1967). Melodrama's complex, even symbiotic linkages with the economic and social institutions of capitalist democracy are a continuing (if implicit) theme of Ian Watt's classic *The Rise of the Novel* (University of California Press, 1957), and of Leo Braudy's remarkable essay on Richardson, "Penetration and Impenetrability in Clarissa," in *New Approaches to Eighteenth-Century Literature*, ed. Phillip Harth (Columbia University Press, 1974).

2. Roland Barthes, "The World of Wrestling," in *Mythologies*, trans. Annette Lavers (Hill and Wang, 1972). I am grateful to Jo Anne Lee of the University of California, Santa Barbara, for making me see the connection between Barthes' notions and television drama.

3. I will not discuss soap opera directly, partly because its serial nature differentiates it in certain respects from the prime-time shows, and also because this interesting subgenre of TV

melodrama has received some preliminary attention from others. See, for instance, Frederick L. Kaplan, "Intimacy and Conformity in American Soap Opera," *Journal of Popular Culture*, 9 (Winter, 1975); Renata Adler, "Afternoon Television: Unhappiness Enough and Time," *The New Yorker*, 47 (February 12, 1972); Marjorie Perloff, "Soap Bubbles," *The New Republic* (May 10, 1975); and the useful chapter on the soaps in Horace Newcomb's pioneering (if tentative) *TV, The Most Popular Art* (Anchor, 1974). Newcomb's book also contains sections on the prime-time shows I am calling melodramas. For an intelligent fan's impressions of soap opera, see Dan Wakefield's *All Her Children* (Doubleday, 1976).

4.   Richard Poirier, *The Performing Self* (Oxford, 1971), p. xiv. I am deeply indebted to this crucial book, and to Poirier's later elaborations on his theory of performance in two pieces on ballet and another on Bette Midler (*The New Republic*, Janaury 5, 1974; March 15, 1975; August 2 & 9, 1975).

5.   John Houseman, "TV Drama in the U.S.A.," *Television Quarterly*, 10 (Summer, 1973), p. 12.

6.   Michael Wood, *America in the Movies* (Basic Books, 1975), pp. 10-11.

7.   Though they are not to be held accountable for the uses to which I have put their advice, the following friends have read earlier versions of this essay and have saved me from many errors: Sheridan Blau, Leo Braudy, John Cawelti, Peter Clecak, Howard Felperin, Richard Slotkin, Alan Stephens, and Eugene Waith.

Semiotics and TV

Arthur Asa Berger

In his *Course in General Linguistics,* first published in 1916, Saussure postulated the existence of a general science of signs, or Semiology, of which linguistics would form only one part. Semiology therefore aims to take any system of signs, whatever their substance and limits; images, gestures, musical sounds, objects, and the complex associations of all these, which form the content of ritual, convention or public entertainment: these constitute, if not languages, at least systems of signification. There is no doubt that the development of mass-communications confers particular relevance today upon the vast field of signifying media . . .

—Roland Barthes
Elements of Sociology

I'm not sure whether semiology (sometimes also called *semiotics*) is a subject, a movement, a philosophy, or a cult-like religion. I do know that there is a large and rapidly expanding literature on the subject and that many of the writings by semiologists are difficult and highly technical. My mission, then, is challenging, for not only am I to explain the fundamental notions of semiology, I am also to apply them to television and television productions. It is a large undertaking for a short essay, but I think it can be done. However, the price I must pay involves a certain amount of simplification and narrowness of focus. I hope that between this essay and the annotated bibliography, those interested in the subject will probe more deeply at their own convenience.

A Brief History of the Subject

Although an interest in signs and the way they communicate has had a long history (medieval philosophers, John Locke, etc.), modern semiological analysis can be said to have begun with two men—a Swiss linguist, Ferdinand de Saussure (1857-1913), and the American philosopher Charles Saunders Peirce (1839-1914). Saussure's book, *Course in General Linguistics*, published posthumously in 1916, suggested the possibility of semiological analysis. It dealt with many of the concepts which can be applied to signs and which are explicated in this essay. Two of Saussure's concepts were of crucial importance for the development of semiology: (1) his division of the sign into two components, the *signifier,* or "sound-image," and the *signified,* or "concept"; and (2) his suggestion that the relationship between signifiers and signified is arbitrary. Peirce, on the other hand, focused on three aspects of signs—their *iconic, indexical,* and *symbolic* dimensions—as illustrated below in Figure 1.

Dimension:	Iconic	Indexical	Symbolic
Signified by:	Resemblance	Causal connections	Conventions
Examples:	Pictures and statues	Smoke/fire Symptom/disease	Words, numbers, flags
Process of Perception:	Can be seen	Can be figured out	Must be learned

Fig. 1. Peirce's Three Dimensions of Signs

From these two points of departure a movement was born and semiological analysis has spread all over the globe. Important work was done in Prague and in Russia early in the twentieth century, and semiology is now well-established in France and Italy (where Roland Barthes, Umberto Eco, and many others have done inventive theoretical as well as applied work). There are also outposts of progress in England and the United States.

Semiology has been applied, with interesting results, to film, theatre, medicine, architecture, zoology, and a host of other areas that involve or are concerned with communication and the transfer of information. In fact, some semiologists, perhaps carried away with things, suggest that *everything* can be analyzed semiologically and see semiology as the queen of the interpretive sciences, the key that unlocks the meaning of all things great and small. Whether this is the case is questionable, but without doubt semiology has been used by all kinds of people in a variety of interesting ways. It has only recently been taken seriously in America, however, and it is still not widely used or taught here.

There are several reasons for the slow acceptance of semiology in this country. First, we Americans tend to be pragmatic and down-to-earth; abstruse, theoretical and formalistic methodologies are not congenial to us. Also, there is a kind of international cultural lag that exists, and it takes some time for movements that are important in the European intellectual scene to become accepted, let alone popular, in the United States. Thus, although important work was done here by Charles Saunders Peirce early in the century, we had to wait for semiological analysis to evolve and mature in Europe before it began to catch our attention here. (As a matter of fact, now that Americans are getting around to semiology, it may be passé in Europe. But that's beside the point.)

The Problem of Meaning

The essential breakthrough of semiology is to take linguistics as a model and apply linguistic concepts to other phenomena of communication—films, television programs, fashion, foods, almost anything that involves the transfer of information. In the analysis of these phenomena, which are called *texts* by semiologists, the basic concern is to determine *how meaning is generated and conveyed*. Let me quote Jonathan Culler's *Structuralist Poetics: Structuralism,*

Linguistics and The Study of Literature (1976, p. 4):

> The notion that linguistics might be useful in studying
> other cultural phenomena is based on two fundamental
> insights: first, that social and cultural phenomena are not
> simply material objects or events but ... objects and
> events with meaning, and hence signs; and second, that
> they do not have essences but are defined by a network
> of relations ...

Signs and *relations*—these are two of the key notions of semiological analysis. In semiological analysis we make an arbitrary and
temporary separation of content and form and focus our attention
on the system of signs that makes up a text. Thus, a meal (to stray
from television for a moment) is not seen as steak, salad, baked
potato, and apple pie but rather as a sign system conveying meanings
related to matters such as status, taste, sophistication, nationality,
and so on. Similarly, in television, a text like "Star Trek" can be
thought of as a system of signs. The meaning in the television series
stems from the signs and from the system that ties the signs together. This system is generally not obvious and must be elicited
from the text.

Perhaps it is best now to quote from Saussure, who wrote in his
Course in General Linguistics (1916, p. 16):

> ... Language is a system of signs that express ideas and is
> therefore comparable to a system of writing, the alphabet
> of deaf-mutes, symbolic rites, polite formulas, military sig-
> nals, etc. But it is the most important of all these systems.
>
> *A science that studies the life of signs within society* is
> conceivable; it would be a part of social psychology and
> consequently of general psychology; I shall call it *semi-
> ology* (from Greek *semeion,* "sign"). Semiology would
> show what constitutes signs, what laws govern them. Since
> the science does not yet exist, no one can say what it
> would be; but it has a right to existence, a place staked out
> in advance.

This is the charter statement of semiology, a statement which opens
the study of media to us; for not only can we study symbolic rites
and military signals, we can also study television commercials,

soap operas, situation comedies, and almost anything else as "sign systems."

Saussure offered another crucial insight that is relevant here: the suggestion that concepts have meaning because of relations and that the basic relationship of concepts is oppositional. Thus, "rich" means nothing unless there is "poor," nor "happy" unless there is "sad." As he put it, "concepts are purely differential and defined not by their positive content but, negatively, by their relations with the other terms of the system" (p. 117). The "most precise characteristic" of a concept within some kind of a system "is in being what the others are not" (p. 117). We can see this readily enough in language, but it also holds for texts. Nothing has meaning in itself!

So where are we now? I have suggested that semiological analysis is concerned with meaning in texts and that meaning stems from relationships—in particular, the relationship among signs. But what, exactly, is a sign?

Signs

A sign, Saussure tells us, is a combination of a concept and a sound-image, a combination which cannot be separated (see Figure 2). But because these terms are not quite satisfactory for Saussure, he modifies them slightly:

> I propose to retain the word "sign" *[signe]* to designate the whole, and to replace "concept" and "sound-image" respectively by *signified [signifié]* and *signifier [signifiant]*; the last two terms have the advantage of indicating the opposition that separates them from each other and from the whole of which they are parts. (p. 67)

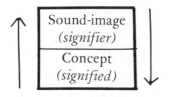

Fig. 2. Saussure's Diagram of a Sign

The relationship between the signifier and signified—and this is crucial—is arbitrary, unmotivated, unnatural. There is no logical connection between a word and a concept or a signifier and signified, a point which makes for finding meaning in texts interesting and problematical.

Saussure offers a diagram comparing the *sign* and the *symbol* "tree" as an example (see Figure 3).

Fig. 3. Saussure's Diagram of the Sign and Symbol "Tree"

The difference between the sign and the symbol in this diagram, Saussure suggests, is that *a symbol has a signifier that is never wholly arbitrary.* He writes:

> One characteristic of the symbol is that it is never wholly arbitrary; it is not empty, for there is a rudiment of a natural bond between the signifier and signified. The symbol of justice, a pair of scales, could not be replaced by just another symbol, such as a chariot. (p. 68)

How do signifiers generate meaning? And how is it that we know these meanings? If the relationship between a signifier and signified is arbitrary, the meanings these signifiers hold must be learned somehow. This implies that there are certain structured associations, or *codes,* which we pick up in order to interpret signs. (I will deal with this subject in more detail shortly.)

Let's look at "Star Trek" in terms of its signifiers and what is signified. Anyone who has seen the series (and I use it because it is continually being rerun) knows that it is a space adventure. We know this because we are "told" so at the beginning of each episode, when the Starship Enterprise is sent on a mission in outer space—to explore new worlds and seek out new civilizations, to "boldly go where no man has gone before." In addition, we are provided with a number of other signifiers throughout the program: rocket ships, futuristic uniforms, ray guns, advanced computer technology, extraterrestrials with strange powers, and feats of magic/science, among other things.

It is precisely the fact that the program is so rich in signifiers that the legions of "Trekkies" are able to (and inspired to) hold conventions, wear costumes, sell "phasers," and so on. For when one has assumed some of the signifiers, one can claim to have "appropriated" the signified. This, I might point out, is the basis of many television commercials. Consumers purchase the "right" products with the assumption (or hope) that these products will signify a certain social class, status, or life-style.

All of this is based on associations we learn and then carry around with us. And anyone who communicates uses these associations between signifiers and signified. Since in real life the relationships are arbitrary and change rapidly, one must be on his or her toes all the time. Signifiers can become dated and change their significance all too quickly. In a sense, then, we are all practicing semiologists who pay a great deal of attention to signs—to signifiers and signifieds—although we have probably never heard of the terms.

Language and Speaking

Earlier I suggested that texts (such as films, television programs, commercials, etc.) are like languages and that the rules of linguistics can be applied to them. Language enables us to communicate information, feelings, ideas, and the like by establishing systems and rules that people learn. And just as there is a grammar for writing and speaking, there is also a grammar for different media.

Saussure made a distinction between *language (langue)* and *speaking (parole)* that is useful here: Language is a social institution made up of systematized rules and conventions that enable us to speak and, more broadly, to communicate with one another. Each person speaks in his or her own individual manner, but this speaking is based on the language and the rules that everyone learns. In addition, people are "speaking" all the time, even when they aren't saying anything with their mouths. Our hairstyles, eyeglasses, clothes, facial expressions, posture, gestures, and many other things about us are continually communicating (that is, signifying) for those who are sensitive to such things and who are mindful of signs and signifiers.

Similarly, a television program such as "Star Trek" can be looked upon as a "language" which is intelligible to its audience because the audience knows the signs and what they signify. They also know the conventions of the genre, what is acceptable and unacceptable. In other words, they know the codes!

Let me offer a brief summary here:

1. Our concern is how *meaning* is created and conveyed in texts.

2. Our focus is upon the *signs* we find in these texts. We understand that signs are combinations of *signifiers* and *signifieds*.

3. Since nothing has meaning in itself, the *relationships* that exist among signs are crucial. It is the way that words are combined which determines what they mean. *Language* is a social institution that tells us how words are to be used; *speaking* is an individual act based on language.

4. *Texts* can be looked upon as being similar to speech and implying grammars or languages that make these texts meaningful. There are codes and conventions which make the signs in a narrative understandable and which also shape the actions of the narrative.

The Synchronic and the Diachronic

As Saussure uses the terms, *synchronic* means analytical and *diachronic* means historical. A synchronic study of a text looks at the relationships that exist among its components; a diachronic study looks at the way the narrative evolves. Another way of putting this is that a synchronic analysis of a text looks for the pattern of paired oppositions buried in the text (the *paradigmatic* structure), whereas a diachronic analysis focuses upon the chain of events (the *syntagmatic* structure) that forms the narrative. Figure 4 shows these relationships more clearly.

Synchronic Analysis	Diachronic Analysis
Simultaneity	Succession
Static	Evolutionary
Relations in a system	Relations in time
Paradigmatic	Syntagmatic

Fig. 4. Synchronous versus Diachronic Analysis

Syntagmatic Analysis

A syntagm is a chain; a syntagmatic analysis of a text looks at the text as a sequence of events that form some kind of a narrative. The Russian folklorist Vladimir Propp devised such analysis in his pioneering book, *Morphology of the Folktale* (1973), first written in 1928. Morphology means the study of forms—that is, the component parts of something and their relationship to each other and the whole. Propp did his work on a group of fairy tales and describes his method as follows:

> We are undertaking a comparison of the themes of these tales. For the sake of comparison we shall separate the component parts of fairy tales by special methods; and then, we shall make a comparison of the tales according to their components. The result will be a morphology (i.e., a description of the tale according to its component parts and the relationship of these components to each other and to the whole). (p. 19)

The essential narrative unit that Propp used in his analysis was what he called a *function.* As he writes:

> *Function is understood as an act of a character, defined from the point of view of its significance for the course of the action.*

The observations cited may be briefly formulated in the following manner:

1. Functions of characters serve as stable, constant elements in a tale, independent of how and by whom they are fulfilled. They constitute the fundamental components of a tale.

2. The number of functions known to the fairy tale is limited. . . .

3. The sequence of functions is always identical. . . .

4. All fairy tales are of one type in regard to their structure. (pp. 21-23)

Whether or not Propp was correct in all his assertions is not of great importance to us here. His concept of functions has significance for us because it can be applied to all kinds of texts (films, television programs, comics, other kinds of narratives) with interesting results.

Propp gives a summary of the essence of each function, an abbreviated definition of it in one word, and a conventional sign for it. Some functions are rather complicated and have numerous subcategories, all of which fulfill the same task. I will quote Propp's first function so you can see what a simple one is like and how he elaborates it (1973, p. 26):

I. ONE OF THE MEMBERS OF A FAMILY ABSENTS HIMSELF FROM HOME. (Definition: *absentation.* Designation: β.)

    1. *The person absenting himself can be a member of the older generation* (β_1). Parents leave for work (113). "The prince had to go on a distant journey, leaving his wife to the care of strangers" (265). "Once, he (a merchant) went away to foreign lands" (197). Usual forms of absentation: going to work, to the forest, to trade, to war, "on business."

    2. *An intensified form of absentation is represented by the death of parents* (β_2).

    3. *Sometimes members of the younger generation absent themselves* (β_3). They go visiting (101), fishing (108), for a walk (137), out to gather berries (244).*

This is one of Propp's briefer functions; some, like number eight (about a villain doing harm or injury to a member of a family), have 19 subcategories.

Even though we do not possess all the subcategories of each function it is still possible to use Propp's 31 functions to make syn-

---

*The numbers in parentheses refer to specific fairy tales that Propp studied.

tagmatic analyses of selected texts, and I am providing a chart with these functions and a brief description of each. What will become obvious to you, as you use these functions, is the degree to which many contemporary stories contain many of Propp's functions. His definition of the hero as (1973, p. 50):

> . . . that character who either directly suffers from the action of the villain . . . or who agrees to liquidate the misfortune or lack of another person. . . .

is also worth considering. Heroes also, he tells us, are supplied with magical agents or helpers that they make use of, from time to time.

The chart that follows (which is a simplification and slight modification of Propp's list) gives each function and briefly describes it.

	Propp's Functions	
α	*Initial situation*	Members of family or hero introduced
β	*Absentation*	One of the members of a family absents himself from home
γ	*Interdiction*	An interdiction is addressed to the hero
δ	*Violation*	An interdiction is violated
ϵ	*Reconnaissance*	The villain makes an attempt at reconnaissance
ζ	*Delivery*	The villain receives information about his victim
η	*Trickery*	The villain attempts to deceive his victim
θ	*Complicity*	The victim submits to deception, unwittingly helps his enemy
A	*Villainy*	The villain causes harm or injury to a member of a family
a	*Lack*	One member of a family lacks something or wants something
B	*Mediation*	Misfortune is made known, hero is dispatched
C	*Counteraction*	Seekers agree to decide on counteraction
$\uparrow$	*Departure*	The hero leaves home
D	*1st function of donor*	Hero is tested, receives magical agent or helper
E	*Hero's reaction*	Hero reacts to actions of the future donor
F	*Receipt of magic agent*	Hero acquires the use of a magical agent
G	*Spatial transference*	Hero led to object of search
H	*Struggle*	Hero and villain join in direct combat
J	*Branding*	Hero is branded
I	*Victory*	Villain is defeated
K	*Liquidation*	Initial misfortune or lack is liquidated
$\downarrow$	*Return*	The hero returns
Pr	*Pursuit*	A chase: the hero is pursued

(cont.)

O	*Unrecognized arrival*	The hero, unrecognized, arrives home or in another country
L	*Unfounded claims*	A false hero presents unfounded claims
M	*Difficult task*	A difficult task is proposed to the hero
N	*Solution*	The task is resolved
Q	*Recognition*	The hero is recognized
Ex	*Exposure*	The false hero or villain is exposed
T	*Transfiguration*	The hero is given a new appearance
U	*Punishment*	The villain is punished
W	*Wedding*	The hero is married and ascends the throne

There are seven dramatis personae in Propp's scheme and they are listed below and described:

1.	*Villain*	Fights with hero
2.	*Donor*	Provides hero with magical agent
3.	*Helper*	Aids hero in solving difficult tasks, etc.
4.	*Princess and her father*	Sought-for person Assigns difficult tasks
5.	*Dispatcher*	Sends hero on his mission
6.	*Hero*	Searches for something or fights with villain
7.	*False Hero*	Claims to be hero but is unmasked

I will now apply Propp's functions to an episode of the television series "The Prisoner" in order to show how Propp's analytical design can uncover the morphology of a narrative text. "The Prisoner," a remarkable "existential" series broadcast a number of years ago, is regarded by many people as a television classic. It is about a spy who resigns from some mysterious organization, returns to his London apartment where he is gassed, and then wakes up in a strange, resort-like prison, The Village, where everyone is called by a number. In the seventeen episodes of the series, the hero, "the prisoner," is locked into battles with various adversaries. At the end, the prisoner escapes from The Village, which he destroys, and returns to his apartment.

The following is a synopsis of the first episode, titled "Arrival":

The program opens with the hero, unnamed, in an office with some officials. He is resigning; he pounds the table, leaves, and returns to his apartment. As he begins packing, he is gassed and passes out. He awakes in "The Village," a resort-like prison (and a totalitarian society) in which everyone has numbers instead of names.

The prisoner is told that he is Number Six and is pitted against Number Two, who wishes to find out why Six resigned. Six tries to escape by running along the seashore but is "captured" by a huge and terrifying rubber sphere, Rover, which is kept beneath the sea and is controlled by Number Two.

Six is then sent to The Village hospital, where he shares a room with an old friend, also a spy. While Six is taken out of the room for an "examination" by a doctor, there is a commotion in the hospital. Six rushes back to his room and is told that his friend has committed suicide.

After Six is released from the hospital he notices a woman acting strangely at his friend's burial procession. Six talks with the woman, who tells him that she was the friend's lover and that they were planning to escape from the island. She has a watch with a special device that will enable Six to evade Rover and steal a helicopter.

Six takes the watch and "escapes" via the helicopter, but shortly after he has left the island he discovers that the helicopter is rigged and controlled by Number Two. The episode ends with the helicopter returning to The Village and with the prisoner's supposedly dead friend telling Two that Six is an unusual person who will need special treatment.

Although "The Prisoner" is not a fairy tale, it contains, like many contemporary narrative texts, the elements of the classic fairy tale. The following chart (see Figure 5) lists a sampling of the Proppian functions that could be applied to events in the "Arrival" episode of "The Prisoner." (This analysis could have been extended by citing some of the subcategories Propp uses in *Morphology of the Folk Tale,* but I merely want to suggest the possibilities of this kind of analysis.

There are several important things we learn from a syntagmatic analysis, such as that designed by Propp. First, narratives, regardless of kind or genre, are composed of certain functions (or elements) which are essential for the creation of a story. Propp's analytical functions lead us, then, to an understanding of the nature of formulas. Second, the order in which events take place in a narrative is of great importance. There is a logic to narrative texts, and the arrangement of elements in a story greatly affects our perception of what anything "means."

Propp's Functions	Events in "Arrival"
Initial situation.	Six shown resigning.
Interdiction violated.	(Implicit) Spies can't resign.
Villain causes injury.	Six abducted to The Village.
Receipt of a magical agent.	Woman gives Six watch with device.
False hero exposed.	Friend shown with Two.

Fig. 5. Proppian Functions in "Arrival" Episode of *The Prisoner*

Paradigmatic Analysis

The paradigmatic analysis of a text involves searching for a hidden pattern of oppositions which generate meaning. As Alan Dundes writes in his introduction to Propp's *Morphology of the Folk Tale,* the paradigmatic form of structural analysis

> seeks to describe the pattern (usually based upon an *a priori* binary principle of opposition) which allegedly underlies the folkloristic text. This pattern is not the same as the sequential structure at all. Rather, the elements are taken out of the "given" order and are regrouped in one or more analytic schema. (p. *xi*)

There is a reason why we search for binary or polar oppositions. It is because meaning is based upon establishing relationships, and the most important relationship in the production of meaning in language is that of opposition.

We return here to Saussure's notion that ". . . in language there are only differences." Or, as Jonathan Culler writes in *Structural Poetics* (1976): "Structuralists have generally followed Jakobsen and taken the binary opposition as a fundamental operation of the human mind basic to the production of meaning." (p. 15).

Thus, in all texts (whether narrative or not) there must be some kind of a systematic and interrelated set of oppositions that can be elicited. Most people are not conscious of these polar oppositions— and sometimes they are implied and not given. But without these differences there can be no meaning.

Some critics argue that the oppositions and other structures which semiologists "elicit" from texts are not really there. They assert that semiologists do not *discover* systems of relationships but, instead, *invent* them. This controversy is sometimes known as the "hocus-pocus" versus the "God's truth" argument.

I personally believe that the bipolar oppositions which semi-oticians find in texts are actually there. Not only that, I believe that they *have* to be there. Finding meaning without discerning polar oppositions is like trying to listen to the sound of one hand clapping.

Since I've used "The Prisoner" already, let me offer a brief para-digmatic analysis of the "Arrival" episode in order to show the ideational structure upon which the narrative is hung. The most important opposition found in this episode is between freedom and control; I therefore use these two concepts at the head of my list in Figure 6:

Freedom	*Control*
Number Six	Number Two
The individual	The organization
Willpower	Force
Escape	Entrapment
Trust	Deception

Fig. 6. **Polar Oppositions in "Arrival" Episode of** *The Prisoner*

Claude Lévi-Strauss, the distinguished French anthropologist, suggests that the syntagmatic analysis of a text reveals its manifest meaning (what happens) whereas a paradigmatic analysis reveals latent meaning (what the text is about). Lévi-Strauss's interest is the way narratives are organized or structured and how their organiza-tion generates meaning. He has done a great deal of work (much of it highly controversial) on myths, kinships systems, and related mat-ters. There are, he believes, fundamental or minimal units of myths, what he calls *mythemes,* which combine in certain ways to give messages. These mythemes can be expressed in short sentences which express an important relationship. For example, in the Oedipus myth, Lévi-Strauss offers such mythemes as "Oedipus kills his father

Laius" or "Oedipus marries his mother" or "Oedipus immolates the Sphinx."

These mythemes and their rules of combination (what Lévi-Strauss calls *bundles* of relations) are the stuff out of which myths are made. And what is most significant about myths, in the opinion of Lévi-Strauss, is the stories they tell, not their style. Myths are important not only because they function as charters for the groups that tell and believe in the stories, but also because they are the keys to the ways in which the human mind works.

Thus, it is the structured relationships among the characters and what these relationships ultimately mean that should be the object of one's attention, not the way a story is told. Myths, Lévi-Strauss believes, give coded messages from cultures to individuals, and the task of the analyst is to discover these masked or hidden messages by "cracking the code," so to speak. In the final analysis, this involves eliciting the paradigmatic structure of a text.

In making a paradigmatic analysis of a text, one must be careful to avoid two common errors. First, make certain you elicit true oppositions (as opposed to negations). I would suggest, for example, that "poor" is the opposite of "rich" and should be used instead of such negations as "unrich" or "nonrich." And second, be sure that your oppositions are tied to characters and events in the text.

Metaphor and Metonymy

Metaphor and *metonymy* are two important ways of transmitting meaning. In metaphor, a relationship between two things is suggested through the use of *analogy*. Thus, we might say "My love is a red rose." One of the most common metaphoric forms is the *simile*, in which "like" or "as" is used to state the comparison ("he's as sharp as a razor"; "she sings like an angel").

In metonymy, a relationship is suggested through *association*. As James Monaco writes in *How to Read a Film* (1977):

A metonymy is a figure of speech in which an associated detail or notion is used to invoke an idea or represent an object. Etymologically, the word means "substitute naming" (from the Greek *meta*, involving transfer, and *onoma*, name). Thus, in literature we can speak of the king (and the idea of kingship) as "the crown." (p. 135)

A common form of metonymy is the *synecdoche,* in which a part stands for the whole or vice versa.

A good example of metaphor in film is the famous scene in Chaplin's *The Gold Rush* in which he cooks his boots and eats the shoelaces the way one would eat spaghetti. A good example of filmic metonymy would be the monstrous weather balloon Rover in "The Prisoner" The balloon is associated, of course, with the oppressive regime that runs The Village. The following chart (see Figure 7) compares and contrasts metaphor and metonymy and should help clarify the two concepts.

Metaphor	Metonymy
Resemblance based on *analogy.*	Resemblance based on *association.*
Meta: transfer, beyond. *Phor:* to bear.	*Meta:* transfer. *Onoma:* name.
Chaplin eats shoelaces like spaghetti.	Rover kills one of the villagers on command of Number Two.
Simile: Important subcategory in which comparison is stated using "like" or "as."	Synecdoche: Important subcategory in which part stands for the whole or the whole for a part.
No man is an island . . .	Red suggests passion.
Costume of Spider-Man.	Uncle Sam "stands for" America.
Long, thin objects can be seen as penises.	The bowler suggests an Englishman; the cowboy hat is associated with the American West.

Fig. 7. Metaphor and Metonymy Contrasted

Generally speaking, we find metaphor and metonymy all mixed together. Indeed, sometimes a given object might have both metaphoric and metonymic significance. The distinction is important, because it enables us to see more clearly how objects and images (as well as language) will generate meaning. In the case of metonymy, it also enables us to see that people's minds carry around *codes,* highly complex patterns of associations, which enable them to interpret metonymic communications correctly. Just as you can't tell the players without a program, you can't understand the meaning of most social interaction without knowing the code.

Codes

Codes, as I have suggested, are highly complex patterns of associations which we all learn within the society and culture. These codes, or "secret structures" in our minds, affect the way we interpret the signs and symbols found in the media. They therefore affect the way we live as well. From this perspective, cultures are codification systems which play an important (though often unperceived) role in our lives. To be socialized means, in essence, to be taught a number of codes, most of which are quite specific to a person's social class, geographical location, ethnic group, etc.

We all recognize that in order to be able to drive on the highways a code is needed. This code is a collection of rules which tell us what to do in most conceivable situations. In like manner, with television, we are all taught what certain media signs "mean." Quite obviously, the codes and understandings that we accept about life we also carry over to media productions—thus, the creation, as we now put it, of a "mass-mediated culture"; and, thus, the considerable potential for misunderstandings to arise between those who create television programs and those who view them.

In his essay, "Toward a Semiotic Inquiry into the Television Message" (1972), Umberto Eco, the distinguished Italian semiologist, suggests that "aberrant decoding ... is the rule in the mass media" (p. 106). This is because people bring different codes to a given message and thus interpret the message in different ways. As Eco puts it:

> Codes and subcodes are applied to the message in the light of a general framework of cultural references which constitutes the receiver's patrimony of knowledge: his ideological, ethical, religious standpoints, his psychological attitudes, his tastes, his value systems, etc. (p. 115)

Eco offers two examples of how these aberrant decodings might take place: (1) foreigners in strange cultures who do not know the codes, and (2) people who interpret messages in terms of their own codes rather than according to the codes in which the messages were originally cast. Eco believes that such aberrant decodings were the exception, not the rule, before the development of the mass media. Now, he argues, aberrant decodings have become the norm because of the wide gap that exists between those who create and generate the material carried by the media and those who receive this material.

In other words, the transmitters of messages, because of their social class, educational level, political ideologies, world view, ethos, etc., do not share the same codes as their audiences, who differ from the message transmitters in some or even most of the above respects and who interpret the messages they receive from their own perspectives. To see how this might be possible, let me mention the work of the British sociolinguist Basil Bernstein. His research leads him to conclude that British children learn either of two linguistic codes, what he calls the *elaborated* and the *restrictive* codes, and that these codes play a major role in the future development and adult lives of the children.

The chart below (see Figure 8) shows the difference between these two codes.

Elaborated Code	*Restricted Code*
Middle classes.	Working classes.
Grammatically complex.	Grammatically simple.
Varied vocabulary.	Uniform vocabulary.
Complex sentence structure.	Short, repetitious sentences.
Careful use of adjectives and adverbs.	Little use of adjectives and adverbs.
High-level conceptualization.	Low-level conceptualization.
Logical.	Emotional.
Use of qualifications.	Little use of qualifications.
Users aware of code.	Users unaware of code.

Fig. 8. The Two Linguistic Codes of British Children

According to Bernstein, the elaborated and restrictive codes become the matrix through which thought is filtered, leading to very different value systems, belief systems, attitudes about the world, and so on. It has been said that the Americans and British are two nations separated by a common language. The different classes in Britain, with their different codes, seem to be separated in the same way.

Bernstein's work enables us to see how language shapes us. His research was also meant to demonstrate the enormous problems we face in trying to resocialize the hard-core poor and other disadvantaged elements in society. Moving from language to the media, where there are aesthetic codes and iconic codes separating people, we must consider the fact remarkable that the media can communicate with any degree of effectiveness.

Semitoics of the Television Medium

Each medium, because of its nature, imposes certain limitations on whichever popular art form, or genres, it carries. Because of the small screen and the nature of the television image, for instance, it is difficult to present effective epic scenes on television. Television is a "close-up" medium which is better at revealing character than capturing action.

In applying semiology to television, then, we should be concerned with aspects of the medium that *function* as "signs" (as distinguished from the aspects that *carry* signs). What is most interesting about television, from this point of view, are the kinds of shots and the camera and editing techniques employed in the medium (see the list in Figure 9).

Signifier	Definition	Signified (Meaning)
Close-up.	Face only.	Intimacy.
Medium shot.	Most of body.	Personal relationship.
Full shot.	Full body of person.	Social relationship.
Long shot.	Setting and characters.	Context, scope, public distance.
Pan down.	Camera looks down.	Power, authority.
Pan up.	Camera looks up.	Smallness, weakness.
Zoom in.	Camera moves in.	Observation, focus.
Fade.	Blank screen gets image.	Beginning.
Dissolve.	Screen goes blank.	Ending.
Cut.	Switch from one image to another.	Simultaneity, excitement.
Wipe.	Image wiped off screen.	Imposed conclusion.

Fig. 9. The Grammar of the Television Medium

There are other matters that might be considered here as well, such as the lighting techniques and the uses of color, sound effects, and music. All of these are signifiers which we learn and which help us interpret what we see and hear on television. Television is a highly complex medium which uses verbal language, visual images, and sound to generate impressions and ideas in people. It is the task of the television semiotician to determine, first, how this is possible and, second, how this is accomplished.

Some Criticisms of Semiological Analysis

You will notice that very little has been said, to this point, about aesthetic judgments. This points to one of the major criticisms of semiological analysis, namely that in its concern for the relationship of elements and the production of meaning in a text, semiology ignores the quality of the work itself. That is, semiology is not really concerned with art but rather with meaning and modes of cognition (the codes needed to understand a text). It is, the critics say, as if one judged a meal by the quality of the ingredients, without much concern for how the food was cooked and how it tastes.

Another complaint about semiological analysis, especially of television and televised texts, is that the semiologist lacks a strong theoretical foundation that would facilitate work in these areas. Most of the work done in semiology in recent years has concerned iteself with film, not television. Without a strong and well-articulated body of theoretical criticism, work in the applied semiological analysis of television texts must remain tentative.

Nevertheless, a great deal is possible; and if the analyst can avoid extremism in discovering and interpreting the signifying systems in our texts, semiology will produce critical readings of considerable value and utility. We have enough theory to get started, and a future body of applied semiological analyses will lead to further advances in critical theory.

In the material that follows, I suggest some activities that should be undertaken in making a semiological analysis of a television text. I have concentrated on the narrative in this article, but much of what I've discussed is applicable as well to all kinds of television programs.

A. *Isolate and analyze the important signs in your text.*

    1. What are the important signifiers and what do they signify?

    2. What is the system that gives these signs meaning?

3. What codes can be found?
4. What ideological and sociological matters are involved here?

B. *What is the paradigmatic structure of the text?*
1. What is the central opposition in the text?
2. What paired-opposites fit under the various categories?
3. Do these oppositions have any psychological or social import?

C. *What is the syntagmatic structure of the text?*
1. What functions from Propp can be applied to the text?
2. How does the sequential arrangement of elements affect meaning?
3. Are there formulaic aspects which have shaped the text?

D. *How does the medium of television affect the text?*
1. What kinds of camera and editing techniques are used?
2. How are lighting, color, music, and sound used to give meaning to signs?

E. *What contributions have theorists made that can be applied?*
1. What have semiological theorists written that can be adapted to television?
2. What have media theorists written that can be applied to semiological analysis?

I hope that what I have written will give a sense of the semi-ological approach and enable my readers to apply this fascinating—and powerful—analytical tool. Once you begin seeing everything as signs, you'll know you have contracted the semiological disease. Be warned that there is no known remedy!

An Annotated Bibliography

Barthes, Roland. *Mythologies.* Hill and Wang, 1972. A collection of short essays on everyday life topics, such as wrestling, soap powders, margarine, steak and chips, etc. and a long essay on semiological aspects of myth. A fascinating book and one of the most interesting examples of applied semiological analysis.

Barthes, Roland. *Writing Degree Zero and Elements of Semiology.* Beacon Press, 1970. In the latter book Barthes deals with the basic concepts used in semiological analysis. He makes reference to some of the work he's done on food, fashion, furniture and automobiles.

Coward, Rosalind, and John Ellis. *Language and Materialism: Developments in Semiology and the Theory of the Subject.* Routledge & Kegan Paul, 1977. An important theoretical work which deals with semiological thought and its relation to Marxism, the work of the French post-Freudian Lacan and other topics.

Culler, Jonathan. *Structuralist Poetics: Structuralism, Linguistics and the study of Literature.* Cornell University Press, 1976. An excellent discussion of the basic principles of semiological analysis and application to literature. His book, *Ferdinand de Saussure,* in the Penguin Modern Masters series is also highly recommended.

Eco, Umberto. "Toward a Semiotic Inquiry into the Television Message," in *Working Papers in Cultural Studies,* No. 3, Autumn 1972. A provocative analysis of mass-media content and communication.

Fiske, John, and John Harley. *Reading Television.* Methuen & Company, 1978. This is one of the most useful applications of semiological theory to television to be found. The authors devote a good deal of attention to codes and to specific texts.

Guiraud, Pierre. *Semiology.* Routledge and Kegan Paul, 1975. A very brief but interesting explication of semiological principles, originally published in the French "Que sais-je?" series. Focus is on functions of media, signification and codes.

Leach, Edmunch. *Claude Lévi-Strauss.* Viking Press, 1970. One of the more successful attempts to make Lévi-Strauss understandable to the general reader. Has some biographical material as well as chapters on myth, kinship and symbolism.

Lévi-Strauss, Claude. *Structural Anthropology.* Doubleday Anchor Books, 1967. A collection of essays on language, kinship, social organization, magic, religion and art by the distinguished French anthropologist. An original mind and a great literary stylist.

Monaco, James. *How to Read a Film.* Oxford University Press, 1977. An inventive and fascinating analysis of the film medium.

Propp, V. *Morphology of the Folktale.* University of Texas Press, 1973. A classic "formalist" analysis of fairy tales which has implications for the analysis of all kinds of other mass-mediated culture.

De Saussure, Ferdinon. *Course in General Linguistics.* McGraw-Hill, 1966. One of the central documents in semiological analysis and the source of many of the concepts used in the field.

Scholes, Robert. *Structuralism in Literature.* Yale University Press, 1974. An introduction to structuralist thinkers with a focus on the analysis of literary texts but with obvious implications for other kinds of texts. The ideas of thinkers such as Jakobson, Lévi-Strauss, Jolles, Souriau, Propp and Barthes are dealt with.

Sebeok, Thomas A. ed. *A Perfusion of Signs* and *Sight, Sound and Sense.* Indiana University Press, 1977 and 1978. Two important collections of applied semiological theory. Topics dealt with include: clowns, medicine, faces, religion, nonsense, architecture, music, culture, etc.

Wright, Will. *Sixguns and Society: A Structural Study of the Western.* University of California Press, 1975. An ingenious application of the ideas of Lévi-Strauss, Propp, and others to the Western genre.

Television Aesthetics

Herbert Zettl

If asked to comment on the aesthetics of television, some of us would probably describe the "quality" programming—the televised symphony concerts, ballets, some of the BBC imports, etc. If pressed a little harder, we might acknowledge some of the better-known video artists who have managed to find sanctuary and limited exposure within the protective walls of respectable museums. Most likely, we would mention only in passing, if at all, the medium itself and *its* aesthetic characteristics—the various field forces of light, time, motion, and sound that operate within the small area of the television screen.

This should not be surprising. Firmly rooted in the tradition of literary analysis, we feel more comfortable in discussing the aesthetic merits of content and style than in analyzing the characteristics and potentials of the medium through which such content is communicated. In the aesthetics of literature, the transmission medium—the book—has precious little influence on the message, the literary content, and the structure of the work.[1] The German proverb, *Papier ist geduldig,* "paper is tolerant," aptly describes the relatively neutral position of the transmission medium in the literary communication process.

Not so in television—the television medium is anything but tolerant. Rather, it has precise and decisive aesthetic requirements that can make or break a message, regardless of the significance and integrity of the initial intent of the "communicators." Indeed, the whole television apparatus—people and machines—exerts such a strong influence on what is being communicated that we must examine the medium itself on at least an equal basis with its content.

What are the aesthetic requirements of television? And, more importantly, what are the aesthetic potentials of the medium? How, if at all, do they correlate with the experiential phenomena of our *Zeitgeist,* such as our preoccupation with the fleeting moment, our often painful awareness of the multi-layeredness and complexity of experience, and our social need for a multiplicity of perspectives on events? How, if at all, can an awareness of the aesthetic variables of television, and a knowledge of their communication codes, help us in generating more effective television communication?

In our search for the fundamental aesthetic elements of television, we might be guided by the efforts of Wassily Kandinsky and his colleagues at the *Bauhaus,* who overturned the traditional approach to the aesthetics of painting.[2] While the traditionalists were still examining the finished product, the painting, by such established criteria as subject matter, composition, unity, variety, technical treatment, and symbolic meaning of codes and subcodes, Kandinsky insisted on isolating and examining the basic elements—the points, lines, and planes—by which paintings are created.[3] In addition, instead of working deductively, from a finished product to its components, Kadinsky proceeded inductively, from a description of the fundamental image elements to their various combinations and structures.

In the same way, if we free ourselves from trying to make sense of the *content* presented on television, we can begin to look at the television screen and listen to the sound so as to isolate and identify the fundamental perceptual—that is, aesthetic—elements of the medium: (1) *light and color;* (2) *two-dimensional space* (the area and the field forces within the screen); (3) *three-dimensional space* (the depth and volume of the screen image); (4) *time and motion;* and (5) *sound.*[4] While admitting to the variability and contextual interdependability of these elements, we will, in this essay, touch only upon the variables that are especially pertinent to the aesthetics of television.

Field Analysis: Light and Color

The television image is composed of electrical energy, a rapidly scanning electron beam or series of beams which we perceive as variations in light and color (or shades of gray). The *materia* of television are not illuminated objects and people, but constantly changing patterns of light and color whose very existence depends upon the fluctuating energy of the electron beam. Thus, the television image is a product of external light—the light reflected into the lens of the television camera—and internal light, the electron beam that activates the many thousands of phosphorus dots or rectangles that make up the screen "mosaic." For optimal communication, the medium requires a careful interplay of external and internal light.

Although our basic lighting objectives in television may be to reveal the three-dimensionality and the general texture of an object, or to establish a certian mood, we must also contend with the electronic requirements and limitations of the television camera. While we may prefer extremely high-contrast chiaroscuro lighting, for example, with deep shadows and brilliant highlights for dramatic effect, we have to yield to the television camera's need for a more subtle contrast ratio by rendering the shadows somewhat translucent. Thus, shadow control, rather than illumination, is one of the key considerations in structuring the first aesthetic field of the television medium.

On the other hand, the "internal lighting" potential of television provides us, more so than in any other medium, with a variety of aesthetic opportunities. Whereas changes in external lighting may affect our perception of the appearance of an event and our orientation as to space, time, and mood, internal lighting can reveal and change the inner structure of an event. Let us assume for a moment that we want to intensify an especially energetic portion of an exuberant dance. With external lighting, we could bathe the whole scene in red or another high-energy color, or we might have the dancers move into bright pools of light, or we could render them as silhouettes against a brightly illuminated background. But with a simple manipulation of the internal lighting (beam) controls of the television camera, we can create extremely high contrasts in the scene, or we can colorize dancers and background in such a way that the highly saturated color fields pulsate against one another, or we can have the entire image vibrate in response to the energy and rhythm of the dance.

To cite another example, we are all familiar with the almost comic displays of contortions or the brutally detailed closeups by which death is usually treated in films and television shows. Even the most skillful external mood lighting can only begin to suggest the tragic implications that are intended for the death scene. With internal lighting, however, we may be able to portray the ultimate structure change, the event of a death, with both tragic impact and dignity.

Picture the closeup of a soldier's face. Mortally wounded, his expression is one of disbelief. He slowly lowers his head so that it comes to rest on the bottom edge of the screen. And then we begin to debeam the image, to reduce the energy of the life-giving electron beam. The contrast increases, the dark areas of the picture become voids, the light areas begin to glow. We have the feeling that the soldier is making one last effort to gather and contain life's energy. But the image begins to disintegrate. The life force, which had previously been formalized in timebound human actions, transforms back into the original cosmic energy. What we witness is total structural change —a metamorphosis.

Color can also be manipulated both externally and internally. We can use colors on the set and in costumes, but we can also induce a color scheme electronically in a scene which has been originally videotaped in black and white. Through internal lighting controls, for example, we can change the color scheme of a scene from low-energy to high-energy. In this way, we might intensify the mounting inner stress of a person by matting in highly saturated backgrounds or by electronically "burning up" a normally tinted scene through intense reds and yellows. We could also decelerate a scene by changing it from high-energy colors to more tranquil, pastel-colored hues.

Figures 1-3B

Fig. 2

Fig. 3

Fig. 1

Fig. 3B

Fig. 3A

119

Field Analysis: Two-Dimensional Space

One of the most obvious characteristics of the television screen is that it is relatively small. And yet, the restricted area of this two-dimensional field has several significant aesthetic implications.[5] While the large area of the cinemascope screen thrives on spectacular vistas without sacrificing scenic detail, the small television screen demands closeup views. Consequently, the deductive approach of the cinema, by which we move from the overall view to event detail, is much less effective on the television screen. Television works most effectively if it presents inductive visual sequences, in which we move from closeup to closeup, forcing the viewers to perceive the overall vista through psycholgoical closure rather than from the screen image.

In film, the closeup is an emphatic statement, whether it is used in the "simulated binocular" fashion, to give us a detailed view of a scene, object, or person, or in the more interpretive sense of "combining gaze with motive."[6] In short, in film, the closeup is a special occasion. For television, on the other hand, the closeup is a common occurrence. The extreme closeup, which on the large cinema screen still manages to maintain a figure-ground relationship, becomes on television a new perceptual phenomenon. With figure and ground becoming ambiguous, we tend to confuse the image on the screen with the screen itself. The distinction between symbol (the screen image) and referent (the actual person photographed) has become temporarily suspended. The extreme closeup has become an event which, as Christian Metz would say, has its own image as referent.[7]

When watching an extreme closeup of a person on television, we may very well be seduced into accepting the resulting image as the primary event rather than its representation. Perhaps it is the frequent and consistent use of very tight closeups that makes soap opera characters appear so real to so many television viewers. On the small television screen, the spectacle of things is de-emphasized, but human actions gain special prominence. The closeup shot not only brings the event closer to us, but sometimes even seduces us as spectators to move closer to the event. While we tend to look *at* the spectacle on the movie screen, with television we are permitted a look *into* the event. Our viewing of landscape has changed into a perception of inscape.[8]

Such a personalization of events puts a premium on the use of the human image. Like the theatre, television relies heavily on human events—what people think, feel, and do. Perhaps this is one of the reasons why abstract television—the use of nonrepresentational moving images—cannot be successfully sustained, even if done with skill and artistic integrity.[9] This does not mean that television cannot show abstract images. But they seem to work best when integrated into some human activity, or if they have as their origin human form and energy, such as the electronically manipulated image of an athlete's or dancer's leap.

Even pantomime, seemingly well-suited for the small screen, in fact runs counter to the iconic image requirement of television. When the highly abstract event of pantomime appears on the small television screen, we are apparently unwilling or unable to flesh out the minimal visual clues of mime in order to imagine more of an event than what we see. We tend to perceive the abstract motions of mime merely as jerky movements rather than as symbolic acts. Similarly, the pantomimist's makeup is seen as a painted face rather than as the universal mask of humanity.

On the other hand, we as viewers are quite willing to extend an event that plays in the small actual space of the television screen, the *on-screen space,* into the *off-screen space* surrounding the television set.[10] In fact, the off-screen space is always an important consideration for the television production designer when he or she is structuring the two-dimensional and three-dimensional aesthetic fields of the on-screen space. Designers must make the off-screen space believable by translating certain on-screen design elements into *vectors* that suggest an off-screen continuation of the on-screen space, or that provide a plausible contiguity and/or continuity between different on-screen shots.

A vector indicates a certain directional force, either by implication, as, for example, objects that are arranged in a certain way, or by an explicit pointing or movement of something in a specific direction. We can distinguish among three major types of design vectors: (1) *graphic vectors,* (2) *index vectors,* and (3) *motion vectors.* Graphic vectors are created by stationary elements that are arranged in such a way as to lead our eyes along. A line, a row of bottles, or even a row of letters in a screen title, can act as a graphic vector. An arrow, a person pointing or looking in a particular direction, a pointed gun are all examples of index vectors, while a moving car, a dancer moving from screen-right to screen-left, or a person running might serve as a motion vector.[11]

Since vectors represent dynamic screen forces, they are well-suited to the moving image of television. Indeed, we can combine various types of vectors into vector fields and use them not only in the analysis, but also in the building of screen space within a single shot, from shot to shot, or even from screen to screen in multi-screen presentations. Next to music, the proper structuring of vectors is one of the most important aesthetic factors in helping the television designer to apply closure to a related sequence of shots.

Here is a simple example of vector continuity over a sequence of shots. We have a closeup of a speaker and subsequent closeups of members of the audience. Figure 4 shows the speaker with a high-magnitude screen-right index vector. Figure 5 shows the audience members with index vectors that also point to screen right. The shots obviously would not cut together, since, in a sequence of such shots, the speaker and the audience would be looking away rather than toward each other. In other words, the index vectors are continuing, rather than converging (see Figure 6).

Fig. 4   SPEAKER

Fig. 5   AUDIENCE

Television viewers might accept such a vector discrepancy if the sequence of closeups has been preceded by an overview of the whole scene. But in any inductive shooting, in which the overall view is built through a sequence of closeups, such mistakes in vector design would disorient the viewers. The solution, as television directors have learned, is to prepare a simple vector diagram (Figure 7) and follow it during the actual shooting. The viewers are then assured of proper vector convergence (Figure 8).

Fig. 6   CONTINUING VECTORS

Fig. 7   CONVERGING VECTORS

Fig. 8   VECTOR DIAGRAM FOR PROPER VECTOR CONVERGENCE

One experimental method for expanding television on-screen space, without sacrificing the concentrated space-time field of the relatively small television screen, is to use several screens, either side by side or in some other configuration (see Figure 9). Television multi-screens represent a simple, yet organic, extension of the television mosaic. However, vector control becomes even more of a necessity with such an extension, especially if the individual space-time units of the individual screens are to be perceived as a structural entity.

For example, if we want to perceive a continuous landscape on three side-by-side screens, we need to ensure a continuity of the graphic vectors (see Figure 10). Discontinuous vectors will not only interrupt the horizonline of the landscape, but also destroy the three-screen structural unity (see Figure 11). On the other hand, the continuity and careful structuring of vectors can help to direct the viewer's eyes to a particular screen within the multi-screen setup. As we can see in Figure 12, two high-magnitude vectors inevitably lead our eyes to the lower-magnitude target, the right screen.[12]

Fig. 9   MULTI-SCREEN CONFIGURATIONS

Fig. 10   GRAPHIC VECTORS CONTINUED

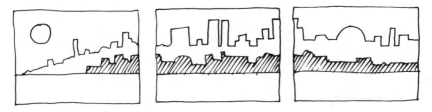

Fig. 11   GRAPHIC VECTORS DISCONTINUED

Fig. 12   COMBINED INDEX VECTORS TO RIGHT-SCREEN TARGET

Field Analysis: Three-Dimensional Space

The illusory third dimension, depth, proves to be the most flexible space dimension for the television screen. While screen height (the y-axis in a normal coordinating system) and width (the x-axis) have definite actual limits, screen depth (the z-axis) can extend all the way to the horizon. Technically, the camera can "see" much more readily into the distance than sideways. The camera need not move at all to cover an articulated z-axis and little, if at all, for object motion toward and away from the camera.

Thus, when structuring the three-dimensional field, the television technician is particularly concerned with the articulation of the z-axis. What the technician does, in effect, is to try to place objects and people at varying distances from the camera so that the viewer will be able to distinguish various depth planes, or grounds—most basically, a foreground, a middleground, and a background—on the two-dimensional screen.

Because of the importance of z-axis articulation, the depth characteristics of various camera lenses or, in the case of television, zoom-lens positions become especially important. With the wide-angle lens, for example, the television camera can increase the illusion of depth—or, to use the new terminology, the camera increases the length of the z-axis. People seem to stand farther apart than they really are, rooms look larger, hallways longer, buildings higher. In addition, with the use of a wide-angle lens the motion along the z-axis—toward and away from the camera—seems faster than it really is. Finally, and most importantly, the wide-angle lens can intensify the dramatic quality of a shot. As simple a gesture as extending one's hand toward the camera can become a menacing act when shot with a wide-angle lens.

The narrow-angle, or telephoto, lens also has a more far-reaching aesthetic impact than simply reducing the illusion of z-axis space by crowding objects closer together than they really are. For example, a director can prolong for a television audience the brief yet intense agony of two lovers trying to meet by having the actors run toward each other through the dense z-axis space created by the telephoto lens. Like slow motion, the telephoto lens seems to increase atmospheric density. (To the contrary, the wide-angle lens seems to create not only more space but, like accelerated motion, a thinner atmosphere.)

Like z-axis staging, which means the articulation of the space from foreground to background, z-axis blocking, the movement of objects and performers toward or away from the camera, is one of the peculiar consequences of the small screen that has been turned into an aesthetic asset.

In television, for example, the psychological depth of the story is intensified by having the actors move along the z-axis—toward and away from the camera—thereby emphasizing the screen depth. A scene which would look and feel quite ordinary when played sideways takes on significance and heightened conflict when confined to z-axis space.

On the other hand, lateral motion, the movement from side to side, looks nondramatic and flat on the small television screen. It is not by accident, then, that situation comedies are blocked with a predominance of sideways motion. The "flat" movement, coupled with high-key, flat lighting, helps to render the action light, external, and appropriately situational.

Field Analysis: Time-and-Motion

Obviously, the concepts of time and motion have a significant bearing on any analysis of a medium that deals basically with the moving image. We get an inkling of the importance of time in television when we read about the thousands of dollars an advertiser must pay for each second of commercial airtime, or when on special occasions we see the magic word "live" superimposed over the televised event. Then, when another superimposed title informs us later that the "live" telecast is actually a playback of an event recorded earlier, we feel strangely let down. Some of the original excitement and energy seem to have gone out of the process. What happened? Why do we feel obliged to inform the public of this type of aesthetic manipulation? Why don't we advertise the time-space manipulation, if not violations, that occur inevitably during postproduction editing?

In our attempt to answer these questions and to discuss the peculiar temporal aspects of television, we will place the medium in the context of some of the prevailing experiential phenomena of our time: the instantaneousness of the moment, the complexity of experience, and the multiplicity of viewpoint.

Instantaneousness of the moment. In our efficiency-oriented society, time has become a commodity. We bargain about the cost of time, and the networks ask for, and receive, thousands of dollars for each second of advertising airtime. They have rate cards that show the current cost of time and warn the prospective customer that "time is not sold in bulk."

Far removed from the concepts of time which in the past signaled us to rest, seek shelter, hunt, or prepare for the eternal afterlife, we now see time as an existential phenomenon. We place a premium on the now. We tend to measure the worth of work more by how fast than by how well we can do things. As a "now generation," we seek instant information to make instant decisions about events that are about to happen the very next instant. Instant pudding and hot news are just two manifestations of our "now society."

Television represents the ultimate instrument with which to express this reverence for the now. With television we can intensify and distribute an event all over the world while the event is still in the process of becoming. Live television puts a premium on the non-causal development of the moment: We do not know what will happen next and cannot, therefore, predict causal relationships with any degree of accuracy. Since the present has, in the words of Saint Augustine, "no space,"[13] it is much more apt to reflect the quality of an event than its linear progression.

Qualitative criteria, such as the perceived intensity of a televised event and the degree of our involvement in it, seem much more appropriate for the analysis of live television—the present—than the usual quantitative criteria, such as how long the event lasted. I remember getting up very early to watch the first U.S. manned space shot. Although the live telecast lasted for several hours, I had no feeling of the passage of time. All I remember experiencing was a moment of extreme intensity. As Stephen C. Pepper points out, "In an actual event the present is the whole texture which directly contributes to the quality of the event."[14]

A similar thing happens when we watch a live sports telecast. While structured by the rules of the game, the event nevertheless moves from moment to moment in unpredictable ways. There is no set plot structure that builds systematically from crisis to crisis. Sports have no such deterministic designs. It is the quality of the moment that counts and that television transmits not only with a minimum of energy loss, but with a clarification and an intensification of that quality. When done with skill, the live transmission of an event can change us readily from viewers to percipients, or even to participants.

Of course, not every event gains from being transmitted live. A basically historical event, such as a prescripted drama in which every external and internal development is carefully predetermined, gains little from being produced live. On the contrary, the control afforded by videotape and postproduction is a welcome factor in the deliberate building of the drama of such a screen event. The "golden era" television plays of the 1950s, which had to be done live by necessity, often provided more excitement for the production crews and actors than for the home audience.

Why, we may ask, should television creators not try to establish a format for television drama that capitalizes on the medium's live quality? Before we try our hand in suggesting a new dramaturgy for television, it might be useful to analyze even further the peculiar aliveness of the television image. A brief comparison with the film image will aid in this analysis:

Film is by nature a historical medium. It photographs and records parts of an event or several events for later manipulation. Structurally, film is visualized calculus. It shows change as a series of small, discontinuous, static increments. The fluid movement of the event is rather crudely chopped up into a series of still images, each of which shows a frozen segment of the motion. The Greek philosopher Zeno of Elea would have been delighted with film, since it offers convincing proof of his theory that motion is nothing but an illusion.[15] Film moves only in our imagination.

Film's structural dependence on sequence may well explain the medium's consistent and successful use of stories that have strong sequential developments; that is, plots in which a cause-effect development is clearly delineated. The filmic montage in which certain images are sequentially presented in order to create a *tertium quid*, a meaning that was only partially or not at all contained in any one of the juxtaposed shots, is the ultimate statement in filmic language.[16]

Because film deals essentially with a series of static images of past action, it affords the filmmaker a high degree of control over the filmic event. The filmmaker can put the beginning of the original event at the end of his new, filmic event, ignore some sections that seem redundant, put in other segments from another event, etc. Thus, film is basically *medium dependent*.

In contrast to the basic unit of film, the static frame, the television image is continuously moving. The scanning beam is constantly trying to complete an always incomplete image. Although we speak and work with television "frames," designating the time the screen has been scanned twice with interlaced fields, the television image, nevertheless, remains in motion. Contrary to the film image, which we can hold, look at, enlarge and treat like any other photographic snapshot, the basic television unit is ephemeral, forever fleeting. Like the Bergsonian *durée,* the basic television image knows no past.[17] It is in a continual process of becoming, regardless of whether the screen image has at its electronic base the television camera, the videotape, or any other electronic storage device.

It should be pointed out again that we are concerned here with the *basic* structural conditions of the television and film units, not with the way they can be treated in the actual production process. With modern computer-assisted editing equipment, for example, we can edit videotape frame by frame very much in the manner we can manipulate film in postproduction. However, such production similarities do not invalidate the fundamental structural differences between the two media. On the contrary, they can help us discover aesthetic potentials that have largely been ignored for the two media, or they can help to explain production techniques that have consistently, though mysteriously, proved effective for one or the other medium.

Now we have a basis from which to develop a television dramaturgy. The television image lives off the now. It is in a continual state of becoming. It is a process image. It has the capacity to treat the present not as an *ex post facto* reconstruction, but as it occurs. It can detect, clarify, and intensify the energy and quality of the moment.

Already we can see that the traditional construction of plot that leads from exposition to point of attack to rising action to climax to falling action and resolution is somewhat incongruent with the basic structure of the television image. Rather than trying to construct conflict through a sequential delineation of cause-effect action, television encourages us to become introspective, to look at our private actions, conflicts, tensions, rather than those of society at large. Somehow, Gotthold Lessing, John Galsworthy, and Lajos Egri seem to have anticipated television when they advocated that dramatic conflict should spring from character, not plot, and that "constant change is the very essence of existence."[18]

On a small scale, such a dramaturgy is established during a television interview. The television director who has enough courage and sensitivity to capitalize on closeups of the interview guests can utilize the aesthetic potentials of the medium to penetrate and communicate the moment as it occurs. Politicians have experienced both victory and defeat because of this aesthetic potential.

On a larger scale, in the realm of television drama, we still need to develop the proper dramaturgical format. Rehearsals frequently generate more excitement on the screen and transmit more energy than the final videotaping of the television play. Like sports, the rehearsal reflects a creative development, rather than a progression of precisely determined actions, and it leaves room for the now to be witnessed in its process of becoming.

The "happenings" of the 1960s were an attempt to work with the instantaneousness of the moment, the now. But the stage was the wrong medium for such events. It was not "a new form of theatre," as Michael Kirby claims, but rather events that, as Susan Sontag quite rightly observes, "state their freedom from time in their deliberate impermanence."[19] The proper medium for happenings is obviously television. Perhaps we can even say that live television *is* a happening.

The people who videotape with their small television camera-recorder units everything from the local school board meeting to a friend brushing his teeth, are also somehow closer to the essential quality of the medium and its aesthetic potential than those who spend millions on filming historical extravaganzas for television. Although videotaped, such unspectacular efforts nevertheless reflect life in a state of becoming, and when done with seriousness, integrity, and love, they manage quite frequently to elevate the ordinary moment to a significant statement about human dignity and joy.

The live telecasting of news is perhaps the format most congruent to the aesthetic requirements and potentials of television. It focuses on moments that are considered significant in human affairs and distributes these clarified and intensified moments with almost the speed of light to a potentially unlimited world audience. This potential of television to reflect instantly the developments of humankind has, unfortunately, been reduced to the static image of some authority figure reading newspaper stories, or, all too frequently, bedtime stories, to us. But with the availability of educated, sensitive reporters, highly portable cameras and microphones, and versatile transmission equipment, such as satellites and fiber-optic cables, the continual transmission of live events should become the norm rather than the exception.

The awesome potential of television to transmit the same information to a practically unlimited number of people has yet to receive proper attention. What are the sociological and psychological ramifications when we all receive the same audio-visual stimuli at the very same time? To what extent does receiving the same information at precisely the same moment through exactly the same channel—the television set—connect all of us? What experiences, if any, are generated by this common occurrence? What, if we persuade the entire audience to do the same thing, as we do so often and consistently in advertising? At what point might we change from the loose aggregate of individuals engaged in the same communication experience to a crowd whose members willingly yield their individual judgment to a collective mind?[20]

Complexity of experience. Each moment that we experience, even the simplest one, is conditioned by our conscious and unconscious awareness of past and future events. There is no way of isolating moments of our experience and making them fit a simplified experiential pattern. Even if we consciously try to reduce the complexity of our experience by setting some of the more aggravating problems aside, we soon discover that we have simply rearranged the pattern, assigned different priorities to our awareness, but not solved any of the problems. Thus, many of us find ourselves experiencing *Angst,* a free-floating anxiety, even when we have nothing to worry about.

The ordinary program fare on television does little to help us cope with the experiential complexities of the now. One-dimensional people who deal with one-dimensional problems do not provide appropriate models for our daily experiences. Neither do straightforward plots that move from predictable cause to predictable effect. How can we take as positive models characters who are only a few steps away from the black-hat-for-the-bad-guy and white-hat-for-the-good-guy variety? Why shouldn't we be upset with a police force that cannot locate a stolen bicycle, when, on the television screen, the police are consistently able to solve even the most complicated crimes in one hour, minus commercial time?

This is not to say that television should not produce such program fare. Escape is a very important function of television programming. But there should also be some shows that reflect, at least to some extent, the complexities of our daily experiences and that guide us in dealing with these difficulties in a positive way.

Some of the soap operas are notable exceptions to the standard television fare. At least the "soaps" occasionally admit that good does not always triumph over evil, or honesty over corruption, and that we all carry at least two Faustian souls in our breast.[21] Soap operas deal with such complexities by concentrating on character development. Because the same characters appear almost every day, there is ample time to reveal the multi-layeredness of their psychological makeup and crisis-ridden lives.

Multiplicity of viewpoint. Television, by its very nature, needs to be selective. An inductive presentation of events presupposes selective points of view. But this selection process is not in the hands of the perceivers, the viewing audience. Rather, it is done by a more or less sensitive television director or editor. We should not be too surprised, then, that television news stories and especially documentaries are accused of being slanted, skewed, even untrue, especially by the people who have actually been involved in the news events.

Television, with its basically one-way transmission and inductive presentation methods, is highly susceptible to autocratic persuasion. This communication tendency is in direct opposition to the democratic principle of not only having the privilege of, but the right to, various points of view. In the most obvious cases, editorials and political announcements, we require by law the opportunity for a different point of view.[22] But there are no such provisions for perceptual distortions: the way the shots are framed, the sequence of events, or the details selected for display.

Of course, various points of view might be presented sequentially, in the manner of "Rashomon." Television news could give the audience first one point of view of an event, then another, then a third, and so forth. But how often have we experienced such a multiple presentation of a single event? Occasionally, we hear political commentary presented sequentially by two people holding opposite views, or the various points of view are expressed by participants of a panel discussion. But most of the time, news is presented from a single perspective. Only "Sesame Street" seems to have the insight and wit to present single concepts from various points of view.

Again, multi-screen presentations, in which various aspects or points of view of an event are displayed simultaneously for the percipient, might be an appropriate communication method. Like the television director, who usually enjoys a multiple image display in the control room, the viewers too could be presented with a multiplicity of views of a single event or of several events of equal influence.

During a televised interview, for example, the television director is constantly pressed to make a choice between action and reaction shots. A two-shot, even if properly framed, usually produces too small an image or, rather, too low-energy an image, to communicate the various psychological subtleties of the people involved. But if closeups of the people were displayed on separate screens, we as viewers would not only enjoy a higher-information image; we would also have the choice of whether to watch the action or reaction.

Television also permits several points of view or events to be shown simultaneously on a single screen. A closeup of someone sleeping, with dream images superimposed over the face, or a super-imposition or a key of a closeup and longshot of a dancer, are examples of single-screen multiple viewpoints. Some sophisticated production equipment also allows for dividing the television screen into a number of areas that display a variety of scenes simultaneously. Such single-screen complexification is perfectly acceptable and appropriate for events that are to be impressionistically perceived, such as dance, rock music, or the various events going on during a track meet. But the viewer runs into difficulty if television attempts to communicate cognitive information in this way. There is just too much going on all at once for the viewer to make any complex judgments.

Multiple screen presentations seem to prevent such perceptual and cognitive difficulties, at least to some extent.[23] However, much more thinking and experimentation need to be done with this communication technique before we can predict, at least to some degree, the relative effectiveness of multi-screens in the presentation of multiple points of view.

Field Analysis: Sound

When thinking about television, we have the tendency to ignore sound, or, at best, to consider it subordinate to the pictures. The term "tele-vision," or "far-seeing," does little to remind us that sound is, in fact, an integral part of television communication. Sound ranks often as the primary factor in the cognitive as well as affective communication processes of television, even if its production usually takes second place to the video portion of television programming.

We all know how difficult it is to follow a story when there is trouble with the sound portion of a telecast. Pictures alone are rarely sufficient to supply us with specific information or to carry forward even a simple story. On the other hand, we can walk away from the television set from time to time and lose relatively little of what is going on, provided that we can hear the audio portion of the program.

It is hard to imagine silent television, the way we once had silent film.[24] Because film had developed a rather sophisticated visual language before the advent of sound, some film theorists felt that sound was, and ought to be, secondary to the visual imagery. Siegfried Kracauer, for example, believed that the film medium "calls for verbal statements which grow out of the flow of pictorial communications instead of determining their course," and that "many film makers have accordingly de-emphasized speech."[25] Even in some recent films, there is evidence that Kracauer's statements are taken to heart. When shown on television, such films sound strangely spotty and incomplete, especially when their narrative continuity is based on large-screen, high-definition vistas rather than on what people do and say. On television, verbal statements are symbiotically interconnected with the visual images; one lives off the other.

But what exactly makes sound so important on television? What functions are fulfilled by television sound? Sound gives the television viewer specific information, helps to make us feel in a certain way, predicts events about to happen, underlines events that are happening, makes an event more complex, supplies aesthetic energy, aids the viewer in connecting off-screen with on-screen space, and contributes a great deal toward making the viewer perceive inductively sequenced events as an organic whole.

On television, as in real life, we get a great amount of information from what people say. It would be extremely difficult, if not impossible, to produce a newscast that consisted only of visual images. The more we move from percept to concept, the more generalized the meaning of a word, the more we have to rely on the semantic and syntactic precision of speech for effective communication.

The prevailing and rather widespread aversion on the part of television producers and critics against "talking heads"—closeups of people who talk—is based on the erroneous assumption that television is principally a visual medium. There is nothing wrong with a talking head so long as it talks well and so long as the talk adheres to some of the peculiar aesthetic requirements of the medium. For instance, a closeup of a person talking requires an audio "closeup" as well. The voice quality, projection, and volume must all match the intimacy of the visual image. Shouting or unnatural voice projection are out of place for visual closeups.

Sound perspective, in which closeups are matched with close sounds and long shots with more distant sounds, is one of the key aesthetic requirements in television production. This is why sometimes even superb theatrical performances appear peculiarly artificial when seen on television. While the actor's movements are generally scaled down to fit the closeup requirements of the television camera, the voice projection is rarely made to follow suit. It is hard for the viewer who sits only a few feet away from the set to grant credibility to someone who is so insensitive as to shout. Many media advisors try to train public figures to speak low-key and with little projection, even when addressing a large crowd in a public place. They figure that more people will eventually witness the event on television than in the public place and that, therefore, it is better to adjust to the requirements of the television medium than to those of the live communication process.[26]

One of the forms of information exchange peculiar to television is the performer who speaks directly to the viewers. The personalization, if not incarnation, characteristics of television make it quite appropriate for someone on the television screen to talk to us as though we were partners in an intimate dialogue. We patiently listen to the screen image telling us what's new, what to buy, whom to vote for. We feel nothing special to have even presidents singling us out to confide their problems, aspirations, hopes. Such a method identifies the viewer, eliminates his or her anonymity, and transforms him or her from spectator to active participant in the communication process. In film, in which we are usually anonymous spectators, this method is not as successful. When the screen hero suddenly turns on us, we feel discovered, caught in the act. Besides, we do not want to see the much-admired screen hero step down and become one of us, our psychological equal.[27]

In addition to what people say on television, there are many literal sounds (for which the knowledge of the sound source by the viewer is important) and nonliteral sounds (for which we don't have to identify the originating source) that provide us with specific information not contained in the visual shorthand of television.

For example, we can easily locate an office in the downtown area by accompanying the closeup of a cluttered desk with typical literal downtown city sounds, such as traffic, police sirens, and overhead jet planes. By replacing these sounds with sounds of birds singing, the rustle of leaves, the murmurs of a brook, the identical shot of the cluttered desk now places the office in the country. The chirping of crickets puts the screen event convincingly into the evening or night, even if the lighting engineer might have had some problems with getting the scene dark enough because of the minimum light requirements of the television camera. Or we can use literal and nonliteral sounds to signal future events. The very distant sound of sirens, horns, and bells of fire engines and emergency vehicles gives an early cue to the viewer as to the upcoming tragedy while the visual scene still shows the senior citizen in a dilapidated sitting room, trying to light the candles on the birthday cake.

Reaction shots gain some of their significance and especially semantic definition through "off-screen" sound. If we see a closeup of a man smiling and hear at the same time the literal sounds of a terrible automobile accident, we will certainly attribute different character traits to him than if the identical closeup were accompanied by the nonliteral sounds of romantic music.

Such psychological closure is also achieved by supplementing the visual closeup with the off-screen environment through sound only. On television, we don't need to precede or follow the tight medium shot of two happy people sitting at a restaurant table with various environmental shots of the entire restaurant. The typical sounds of a restaurant mixed with some soft music gives us sufficient information to expand the on-screen scene into the off-screen space and to perceive the prevailing mood of the scene.

Music and sound effects are simple devices to sharpen a visual statement, render a scene appropriately complex, and provide, or add to, the impact or aesthetic energy of a scene. We not only accept, but seem to expect, the sports car which careens with squealing tires through the hairpin turns of a narrow mountain road to be followed closely by a large orchestra, producing high-pitched, dissonant music and pounding rhythms. Indeed, I witnessed a small boy singing some sort of musical scales while his friends, engaged in a mock battle, produced the typical loudspeaker-induced sounds of gunshots. It took me a few minutes to realize that the boy who sang had not lost his senses, but was simply providing the traditional aesthetic energy for the scene. His actions were not much different from the flute players of classical Greece, who provided similar aesthetic energy for the performances of great tragedies.

When dealing with television sound, great care must be taken not to have the audio become independent from the video, either structurally or as to intensity. Sometimes, when transmitting symphony concerts, public television stations have used their FM transmitters to simulcast the audio portion of the concert. As well-intentioned as such a service may be, it is rarely successful from an aesthetic point of view. Most often, the high-definition and high-quality sound that comes out of the speakers of the average home stereo system overpowers the low-definition video so much that audio and video seem woefully out of balance. The sensitive viewer, who expects a reasonable balance of aesthetic energy between pictures and sound, will first lower the volume, and then perhaps even go back to the low-definition speaker on the television set to achieve the proper audio-visual relationship.

Finally, sound provides the rubber band that helps to keep the various inductively shot details bound together. Given a tightly structured sound track, such as a fugue by Johann Sebastian Bach, we try to make the visual sequences adhere to it, regardless of whether they fit or not. As in real life, in television it is the rhythmic structure that generates the movement and the pulse of existence, that defines time and space, that makes us feel in depth, and that makes us perceive an event as a clarified and intensified aesthetic experience.

Footnotes

1. Rene Wellek and Austin Warren, *Theory of Literature* (New York: Harcourt, Brace, and Co., 1949), p. 142.

2. For more information on the Bauhaus approach, see Hans M. Wingler, *The Bauhaus* (Cambridge, Mass.: M.I.T. Press, 1969); László Moholy-Nagy, *Vision in Motion* (Chicago: Paul Theobald and Co., 1947); Johannes Itten, *Design and Form,* trans. John Maass (New York: Reinhold Publishing Co., 1964).

3. Wassily Kandinsky, *Point to Line to Plane,* trans. Howard Dearstyne and Hilla Rebay (New York: Solomon Guggenheim Foundation, 1947).

4. Herbert Zettl, *Sight Sound Motion: Applied Media Aesthetics* (Belmont, Calif.: Wadsworth Publishing Co., Inc., 1973).

5. Horace Newcomb, "Toward a Television Aesthetic," in Horace Newcomb, ed., *Television: The Critical View,* 2nd ed. (New York: Oxford University Press, 1979), p. 422.

6. John L. Fell, *Film and the Narrative Tradition* (Norman, Okla., 1974), pp. 224-5; Richard M. Blumenberg, *Critical Focus: An Introduction to Film* (Belmont, Calif.: Wadsworth Publishing Co., 1975), pp. 31-2.

7. Christian Metz, *Film Language: A Semiotics of the Cinema,* trans. Michael Taylor (New York: Oxford University Press, 1974), p. 106. For a more extensive treatment of the television closeup, see Philip S. Kipper, "The Meaning of the Closeup Shot in Television Drama" (Unpublished M.A. Thesis, San Francisco State University, 1978).

8. "Inscape" has been used in a similar way by George W. Linden, *Reflections on the Screen* (Belmont, Calif.: Wadsworth Publishing Co., 1970).

9. See some of the video-synthesized works by Nam June Paik, Bill Etra, Stephen Beck. Jonathan Price, in his book, *Video Visions: A Medium Discovers Itself* (New York: New American Library, 1977), p. 106, calls these images "uptight, metallic, unnatural." See also Ira Schneider and Beryl Korot, eds., *Video Art: An Anthology* (New York: Harcourt, Brace, Jovanovich, 1976).

10. Noël Burch devotes a whole chapter to these two kinds of space. See his *Theory of Film Practice,* trans. Helen R. Lane (New York: Praeger Publishers, 1973), pp. 17-31.

11. Zettl, *Sight Sound Motion,* pp. 140-5.

12. There are significant aesthetic differences between the single screen and multi-screen vector fields. See Herbert Zettl, "Toward a Multi-Screen Aesthetic: Some Structural Considerations," *Journal of Broadcasting,* Winter 1977, pp. 5-19.

13. Edward B. Pusey, trans., *The Confessions of Saint Augustine* (New York: Collier Books, 1961), p. 196.

14. Stephen C. Pepper, *World Hypotheses* (Berkeley: University of California Press, 1970), p. 242. See also Robert M. Pirsig, *Zen and the Art of Motorcycle Maintenance* (New York: Bantam Books, 1974), p. 241.

15. V. C. Chappell, "Time and Zeno's Arrow," *Journal of Philosophy,* 59 (1962), pp. 765-84; Adolf Grünbaum, "Modern Science and the Refutation of the Paradoxes of Zeno," *Scientific Monthly* 81 (1955).

16. Sergei Eisenstein, *Film Form and Film Sense,* ed. and trans. Jack Leyda (New York: World Publishing Company, 1957).

17. See Herbert Zettl, *Sight Sound Motion,* pp. 249-67; Henri Bergson, *Creative Evolution,* trans. Arthur Mitchell (New York: Modern Library Edition, Holt, Rinehart and Winston, Inc., 1944), pp. 335-6.

18. Lajos Egris, *The Art of Dramatic Writing* (New York: Simon and Schuster, 1960), p. 50.

19. Michael Kirby, *Happenings* (New York: E. P. Dutton and Co., 1966), p. 11; Susan Sontag, *Against Interpretation* (New York: Delta Books, Dell Publishing Co., 1966), p. 266.

20. For a definition of mass audience, see Charles R. Wright, *Mass Communication: A Sociological Perspective,* 2nd ed. (New York: Random House, 1975). For the psychological behavior of a crowd, see the classic work by Gustave LeBon, *The Crowd* (London: Ernest Benn, Ltd., 1930), pp. 25-6. See also Roger Brown, *Social Psychology* (New York: Free Press, 1965).

21. Herbert Zettl, "The Rare Case of Television Aesthetics," *Journal of the University Film Association 30*(2) (Spring 1978): 7-8.

22. For an explanation of the Fairness Doctrine and the Equal Time Section 315 of the Communications Act, see Sydney W. Head, *Broadcasting in America,* 2nd ed. (Boston: Houghton Mifflin Co., 1972), pp. 436-44.

23. Herbert Zettl, "Toward a Multi-Screen Television Aesthetic."

24. See Rudolf Arnheim, *Film as Art* (Berkeley: University of California Press, 1957); Theodor Adorno, *Eingriffe: Neun Kritische Modelle* (Frankfurt a. Main: Suhrkamp Verlag, 1963), p. 74.

25. Siegfried Kracauer, *Theory of Film* (New York: Oxford University Press, 1960), p. 106.

26. Tony Schwartz, *The Responsive Chord* (Garden City, N.Y.: Anchor Books, 1974).

27. Zettl, *Sight Sound Motion,* p. 335.

Thoughts on
Television Criticism

David Littlejohn

Television desperately needs criticism. Whether it gets the
kind of criticism it needs is something else again. The great
majority of the bashes aimed against it are superficial,
aimless, uninformed, distinguished by fury rather than
fact.

> —Hubbell Robinson, Jr.
> (former CBS Vice-President)
> "The Hatchet Men"
> *Saturday Review*
> (March 14, 1959)

. . . far too many TV critics in 1974 are continuing the
mindless—and anti-journalistic—practice of grinding out
fan-rot nonsense culled directly from network press
releases, or writing up fluffy and soporific phone interviews with fifth-billed stars of "Movie of the Week," or

spending hours in the unwarranted creation of "mailbox
columns" filled with phony queries.

—Gary Deeb
(former television critic for
the *Chicago Tribune*)
"TV Critics—The Hack Pack"
Variety (January 9, 1974)

Television criticism in this country has been regarded with scorn
almost from the start. Its practitioners have been called incompetent,
superficial, and corrupt not only by media professionals (who might
be expected to take offense), but by television critics themselves. In
a 1959 survey commissioned by the Fund for the Republic, Patrick
McGrady, Jr. wrote: "Television criticism is, by and large, the fitful
labor of tired writers of monumental good will, a degree of talent
and jaded perspective. As such, its effect is . . . generally inconsistent,
capricious and of questionable value to anyone." He characterized
Jack Gould, TV editor at *The New York Times* until 1971—and the
most prolific, most powerful regular television writer this country
has ever known—as "the poorest of the major critics . . . gratingly
insensitive and illogical . . . objectionable, whimsical and, perhaps,
dangerous." A fellow reviewer (Richard Burgheim of *Time*) once
called Gould "a menace as a reporter," a man in need of "vocational
guidance."

Have our television critics been as bad as these citations assert?
Does any one among them, during the years between 1949 and 1974,
stand out as distinctive and worth rereading—and if so, for what
reasons? What qualities, forms, and standards are common to television criticism? Are there special problems or limitations built into
the job which distinguish it from other forms of reviewing? Are there
untried or under-used approaches to criticism which might be considered by the observers of American television's second quarter-century? These are some of the questions I would like to raise, and begin
to answer.

Let me describe, first of all, how this project began and developed. It grew out of three presumptions:

(1) Television criticism in this country is, in general,
of a very low order—considerably below the standards set

by the better American criticism of film, drama, art, music and literature. Moreover, this criticism is unworthy of the immense influence (and occasional high achievements) of the medium.

(2) There may be a number of ways to stimulate a television criticism that is better written, better informed, more penetrating, more responsive to both the nature of the medium and the surrounding social context, and, finally, more useful to both the industry and the viewers.

(3) Any discussion of future models for American television criticism will be more rational and realistic if it is based on a judicious summary of the work done in this field over TV's first 25 years.

I began by collecting references to all the reviews and articles concerning television that had appeared between 1949 and 1974 in 30 national general-interest magazines and in hundreds of other American and British periodicals of more specialized interest, as well as several masters' theses and doctoral dissertations. I read most of the critical pieces during this period from *Commentary*, *The Nation*, *The New Republic*, *The New Yorker*, *The New York Times Magazine*, and *The Reporter*, and a sampling from *The Atlantic Monthly*, *Newsweek*, *Saturday Review*, and *Time*—a total of about 800 reviews. I also discovered at least 200 *books* about television (including collected reviews by critics like Michael Arlen, John Crosby, Gilbert Seldes, and Robert Lewis Shayon) and read many of them. Finally, I reviewed essays and criticism of television by literary critics and cultural historians (Boorstin, Hentoff, Hoggart, Podhoretz, Trilling, Vidal), film and drama critics (Alpert, Hewes, Kael, Kanfer, MacDonald, Schickel, Tynan), and even music critics like Irving Kolodin and Winthrop Sargeant, who review televised operas and concerts.

Of course, the great bulk of television reviewing appears in daily newspapers across the country. This presents a formidable problem of access and research, but I was fortunate enough to acquire, as a start, the complete sets of newspaper columns and articles by two veteran practitioners, Jack Gould of *The New York Times* (over 5,000 separate articles, dating from the late 1930s to 1971) and Dwight Newton of *The San Francisco Examiner* (1949 to the present). To complete my overview of newspaper criticism, I also read the television reviews of two other senior newspaper critics—Lawrence Laurent of *The Washington Post* and Cecil Smith of *The Los Angeles Times*.

Besides this review of major critical writings on American television, I devised two comparative surveys which should help to reveal the general critical standards (and deficiencies) of writing about television. In the first survey, I wrote in mid-1975 to the television writers of 25 of the country's leading daily newspapers and the two major wire services, enclosing a chronological list of some 200 television "events" since 1948 which they, or their predecessors, had probably written about: the first shows of significant or popular series, various "specials," one-time dramas or documentaries, important live-event coverage, and major controversies. Unfortunately, few of these TV writers had kept copies or clippings of their reviews over the years—or perhaps they lacked the time to ferret them out for an unknown researcher. In any case, I managed to obtain at least a respectable sampling of additional articles by TV critics in Chicago, Denver, Garden City (N.J.), Indianapolis, Milwaukee, New York, St. Louis, San Diego, and the UPI.

My second survey was designed to judge television criticism by the standards applied to other fields. Television has often presented adaptations of works originally written for other media (Shakespeare, opera, feature films, etc.) and the work of writers and directors who have performed in other fields (Chayevsky, Frankenheimer, Lumet, Penn). Together, these provide the student of television criticism with a good opportunity to compare *its* standards with those applied to the same work or creator in other fields. How did the television critics' reviews of the original "Days of Wine and Roses" or "Marty" compare with film critics' reviews of the subsequent movie versions? Is an opera—the U.S. premiere of a Bernstein or Menotti work, for example—reviewed more generously or less knowledgably when presented on TV than when presented on the stage? Are Frederick Wiseman's documentaries judged differently on the box than in the cinema?

The Job of the TV Critic

Television (as its reviewers have often pointed out) is "everything." It includes not only almost all the other arts (drama, film, music, dance, visual design of many sorts), but also various forms of journalism. In this latter role, it is expected to cover local, national, and international politics; wars and disasters, presidential speeches, inaugurations, and national funerals; and almost anything else that passes as a news event. It also presents popular sports, classes (at many levels and in many subjects), intellectual (and non-intellectual) discussion, quiz shows, game shows, and other diversions; and innumerable advertisements. It is a complex, profitable, and much-regulated industry. It is an even more complex technology.

The TV columnist, reporter, reviewer, or critic would ideally be able to write intelligently about all of these things. Of those I have read so far, a handful have risen respectably well to the challenge: John Crosby (*The New York Herald-Tribune*), Marvin Kitman (*Newsday*), and John Leonard (*Life*, then *Newsweek*)—all three humorists at least as much as critics; in recent years, Ron Powers of *The Chicago Sun-Times*, Norman Mark of *The Chicago Daily News*, and Dwight Newton of *The San Francisco Examiner* (at least on Sundays) along with three or four other daily reviewers; Neil Compton of *Commentary*, Robert Lewis Shayon of *Saturday Review*, and —the reigning master of this unrespected craft—Michael Arlen of *The New Yorker*.

One problem is that most "television critics" in this country are obliged to spend a great deal of their time writing things other than criticism. They write news of the networks and gossip and features about television personalities. They write of legal and economic matters, audience surveys, pressure groups, sponsors, and ratings. Many of them are also responsible for assembling program logs and doing other journalistic chores far removed from what is generally thought of as criticism. In fact, much of the low repute of television writing in American newspapers is based on the assumption that the writer's work is often not criticism at all, but oblique publicizing— a mere assembling and editing of producers' press releases.

Even the relatively independent television writers, whose work is more highly esteemed than that of most daily reviewers, do a great deal of writing that is not focused on a specific program or series. Television, by its very nature, cries out for critical analysis as a social institution, no less than advertising, public schools, comic books, or the two-party system. Television is, in the language of the 1974 Aspen conference, a very potent "social and cultural force."

Over a few months in 1971, Robert Lewis Shayon of the *Sat-*

urday Review (now professor at the Annenberg School of Communications in Philadelphia) dedicated articles to the Fairness Doctrine, the effects of TV violence on children, racism on Alabama ETV, closed-circuit TV, license-renewal challenges, minority programming, advertising on children's television, and other issues more appropriately called media news than television criticism. The most thoughtful people in this country who have written about television with any regularity have addressed themselves to such subjects frequently and provocatively, just as Pauline Kael has speculated on the effects of movie violence and Eric Bentley has discussed the social-realistic pretensions of Broadway plays.

Beyond this onerous obligation to write about "everything," there are a few other considerations that make television criticism—especially daily television criticism—very nearly unique:

(1) Reviewers in most fields are expected to serve not only as aesthetic judges but also as reporters and, to some degree, as historians. But the peculiarities of television make these latter roles especially important for its critics. Students of criticism belittle the "trade-reporter's role" which most newspaper TV editors are obliged to fulfill. But given the defensive arrogance of the television industry, and the thick wadding of public relations and special-interest pressures in which the industry often wraps its activities, some American TV writers (Jack Gould, Norman Mark, Robert Lewis Shayon, Dwight Newton, and the *Variety* staff come to mind) have done a very good job of reporting indeed, and it is useful to us all that they have done it.

But good reviewing is also a form of reporting—perhaps that before anything else. In the case of television (like film, dance, and art), reviewing is the attempt to recreate in words a primarily nonverbal experience. Regarded absolutely, this is an impossible task, but the challenge should appeal to good writers. Instead of rising to it, however, too many television critics of the past generation have settled either for plus-or-minus adjectives pasted onto opaque plot summaries, or for verbal screens and polemic smoke that camouflage altogether the televised event.

In the years before regular network previewing, a standard lament of daily television reviewers was that they were always obliged to print their reviews after a program had been broadcast and, hence, could be of little real service to the viewer. Apart from the fact that most concert reviewers are in exactly the same position, I think this complaint makes sense only if one regards criticism as nothing more than consumer reporting.

After-the-fact reviews of unique performances (and most American television programs, remember, are still units in a series) can serve a valuable *educational* function. If you have already witnessed an event, a subsequent reading of a good critic's analysis is likely to enlarge and illuminate your own remembered experience, to recall aspects of it out of decaying or unconscious memory, to reveal possibilities of coherence, purpose, meaning, and beauty that can then become your *own* convictions. I came across one recreation of an Ed Murrow "Small World" program by John Lardner (*The New Yorker*, April 18, 1959) which was so convincing that I honestly thought I had seen it.

The evocative, exact descriptive critique can give readers who have not seen a program a keen sense of what took place—the journalistic function. Such reviews can also serve future students of American television, who will have to depend considerably on TV reporters and critics to discover what actually went out over the air during TV's first 25 years—the historical function.

It is probably just as well that most critics don't think of themselves as indispensible historians, but they are—or at least, like other journalists, they are the daily chroniclers on whose reports historians will depend. My own "collected sets" of Jack Gould, Dwight Newton, Cecil Smith, and Lawrence Laurent—plus the bound volumes of *TV Guide* from 1953 on—aren't the easiest things in the world to read through. But in the shocking absence of any consultable archive of *actual* past television programs, they compose an indispensable resource and tell a story quite different in its emphasis, thoroughness, standards, and details from works like Erik Barnouw's *History of American Broadcasting*.

(2) The sheer quantity of available American television forces a very demanding job of discrimination on the reviewer. Although previews and videotape recording devices now make it possible for the critic to view two or more programs broadcast at the same time, he still must choose *what* to criticize out of mountains of material. (TV producers and their publicists, of course, are always ready and willing to help the reviewers make their choices.)

(3) The series or serial structure of most American television, the daily repetition of news and talk shows, and the use of reruns and old movies present a frustrating challenge rarely dealt with satisfactorily by most television writers. While most TV viewers perceive television as an event of daily/weekly recurrence, the

critics, in general, discuss television programs as discrete, one-time-only happenings: the first show of a new series, the "special," the unique drama, documentary, or televised real-world event.

(4) Along the same lines, few television critics "use" television in the same way their readers do. The TV critic is on the look-out for novelty, quality, controversy, the new and different (as, to a degree, is the Broadway playgoer or the art gallery habitue). The average lay television viewer, on the other hand, opts for relaxing diversion, familiar faces, a reassuring sameness—the very things the networks know so well how to provide, but which can drive the intelligent critic up the wall, or back to books.

The critic-reader relation in limited circulation, "quality" magazines (*Commentary, The New Republic, The New Yorker*) may be different from this, but I wonder. Few critics seem able to accept, or deal with, the relatively uncritical casualness with which even their discriminating readers make use of TV. (An exception may be the occasional use of the "domestic drama" type of review. In this format, the reviewer tells us about his spouse, his children, his household routine—all as facetious pretext for commenting on the programs they watched last night. This intimate, chatty format has never been utilized, to my knowledge, by critics in any other field.)

(5) There are worlds of difference between the working conditions of the TV editor of a large daily newspaper, the television critic of a weekly or monthly magazine (who may be asked to contribute to only occasional issues), and the intellectual who offers his thoughts on television in a single essay or book. The daily TV critic (whose work is typically subject to the greatest amount of outside abuse) works under an extraordinary set of pressures his more leisured counterparts know nothing of: daily deadlines, 600-word limits, the obligation to fit a paper's existing style, Newspaper Guild regulations, publishers' hiring habits, and the pressing expectations of hundreds of thousands of local readers to be informed regularly on new shows, new seasons, new stars, and current issues.

The television critic of a newspaper, or even a lower-circulation magazine, also finds himself subject to the "outside" pressures of passionate reader mail, an avalanche of press releases, special previews and junkets, the demands of station-owning publishers and irate congressmen and community leaders, and the countless daily personal phone calls and visits from TV performers and executives. All of this occurs on a scale undreamed of by the TV critics' freer, perhaps more fortunate colleagues responsible for classical music, live drama, books, or art. Only popular music and the movies—two other tightly centralized, billion-dollar industries—visit similar pressures on their regular critics. No one can write about television for very long without becoming cognizant of and influenced by questions of "power."

The Power of the TV Critic

The television critics of America—whether alone, together, or through the agency of others—*do* have a certain degree of power over programming. This is one reason why it would be to our advantage to have good television critics. TV programmers and producers *have* sometimes changed their ways in response to published criticism, although never to the degree they have reacted to ratings. People hostile to critics—usually performers who are criticized—enjoy pointing out how frequently the public disagrees with them. Most television reviewers I have read disliked Milton Berle from the start, when he was attracting three-quarters of the viewing audience. On the other hand, they devoted a great deal of favorable attention to documentaries and cultural programs that drew what were for television relatively small audiences.

In television, as in other fields, a single critic can rarely "make or break" a show or a performer. However, a particularly strong writer, backed by some display of public opinion (or an obvious consensus of critical opinion), *can* affect the shape of television programming in the long run. Individual instances of "critical power" are difficult to isolate, since so many other factors enter into programming decisions. A few cases do come to mind; but in most of them there has been a *third* party involved between critic and network—a third party who was both more sensitive to reasoned, nonmonetary argument than most television executives, and more directly influential than the television critic.

For example, certain television writers argued for years that a well-supported, noncommercial American network was the only way out of the eternal cycle of lowest common denominator programming on the three advertiser-dominated chains. But it was only by means of the more powerful agencies of the Ford Foundation, the Carnegie Commission on Educational Television, and, ultimately, the U. S. Congress that the critics can be said to have "brought about" the Public Broadcasting System. Similarly, the Massachusetts-based pressure group called Action for Children's Television, which has played a crucial intermediary role in reforming children's programming *may* have been partly stimulated into existence by years of columns on the subject by critics like Robert Lewis Shayon. NBC has doubtlessly been cheered by 20 years of almost automatic praise from most reviewers for the offerings of its occasional "Hallmark Hall of Fame." But my suspicion is that this praise was even more important to J. C. Hall, the president of the program's sponsoring company, who wanted support and acknowledgement for what he regarded as his own important (and costly) contributions to American culture.

The favorable notice usually given in newspaper columns to news-documentaries, from "Victory at Sea" to the latest "CBS Reports," and to the more popularly oriented educational or NET/PBS fare (from "Shakespeare on TV" to "Upstairs/Downstairs") have no doubt attracted great numbers of viewers to these programs who would never otherwise have watched them. A consensus, or "ganging-up" of TV writers has also been given credit for the repeated showings of certain TV dramas; or for the extended lifetimes of certain popular but insufficiently profitable series ("Father Knows Best," "Mr. Peepers," "I Remember Mama," "The Voice of Firestone"); or for keeping others alive by promoting syndicated, non-network sales ("Lassie," "Star Trek," "The Lawrence Welk Show"). Often, the critics won these battles by marshalling letter-writing campaigns from their readers. But such successes (for what they're worth) have never been more than temporary, and they have been greatly outnumbered by the failures, particularly in recent years. In the earlier years of television, local station managers (who perhaps felt more uncertain than they do today of "what the viewer wants") seemed to respond more acutely to criticism in their local press.

Good Critics in Bad Times

Television criticism needs well-informed, independent men and women of taste, men and women who are also good writers possessed of a broad background of cultural reference and some sense of social responsibility. Within very broad ranges, I do think one can make certain value distinctions in TV criticism: between the Uninformed and the Well-Informed; the Well-Written and the Ill-Written; the Coherent and the Incoherent. (One might also risk the Useful and the Less Useful, the Original and the Unoriginal, the Fair and the Unfair—but then we would have to ask: useful to whom? original to whom? fair to whom?)

Even my minimal list is of dubious value. I can imagine (if not lay my hands on) a piece of criticism that was ill-informed, ill-written, and incoherent, and yet still valuable and useful; because, let us say:

— it was lit up here and there by flashes of real insight or provocative thought, like a bad opera with one or two great arias.

— its clumsiness and incoherence were the authentic marks of a real and rugged effort to come to terms with difficult material, as opposed to the slickly packaged wit of many pros.

— its misinformation was simply the mark of a beginner who may be looking freshly and newly, as opposed to the tediously encyclopedic knowingness of the jaded professional.

This leaves one with almost no standards of better or worse criticism, and (abstractly, theoretically) I almost believe there are none. Plus-or-minus judgment is certainly no test. Wise men disagree radically about almost every event in the world of art and entertainment.

You can get literary-elitist, or academic-philosophical (or whatever other model you happen to admire), and position television critics accordingly on your ladder of excellence. The usual way to do this is to name a critic from some other field who has obtained satisfactory credentials—James Agee or Andre Bazin or Penelope Houston or Pauline Kael, Vasari or Winckelmann or Ruskin or Clement Greenberg, Dr. Johnson or Ste. Beuve or the Schlegels or Alfred Kazin—and then measure television critics against your choice. Do that, however, and I don't think you'll come up with anyone who appears to "measure up"—who writes as well, thinks as deeply, brings to bear such a broad ground of cultural reference and specific knowledge and insight, whose writing is likely to prove as enduring—with the possible exception of Michael Arlen.

American television—so far—has simply not been able to attract that kind of critic. The reasons usually given for this failure are the low status of the TV writer in any newspaper hierarchy; the claim that only a third-rate mind could willingly devote so many hours a week, year after year, to such a third-rate medium; the obligation to involve oneself so stickily with the shoddy thinking and vulgar values of network executives, TV actors, and agency men; and the refusal of broadly educated people to give to television the time they believe it is essential to give to other things—books, films, theater, music, conversation, and the world outdoors.

The three best-known and most influential sources of "journalistic," or regular, criticism of the arts and culture of the United States are *The New York Times*, *The New Republic*, and *The New Yorker*. It is for these three periodicals that a majority of the most-cited theatre, film, book, art, and music critics in this country have written. Each of these periodicals has also given considerable attention, if not always regular coverage, to the accomplishments and events of television.

For over 30 years, Jack Gould—directing, at his most influential, a staff of eight—reported for the *Times* on the intricate maneuvers and manipulations of the growing world of broadcasting. Employing the dogged, multi-column detail one expected of the *Times*, Gould was clearly more at home investigating and reporting, rather than reviewing. He lived in the *Times'* own special world of politics, money, and power, giving readers blow-by-blow, word-for-word accounts of the transfer of Channel 13 or of FCC hearings. He hectored and lectured the networks in thickset, avuncular prose, playing monitory moralist to the Sixth Avenue moguls. He was politically liberal and culturally conservative, forever counseling reason and the Middle Way.

When Gould retired, his reporting role was taken over by Les Brown of *Variety*. Brown is perhaps the one person in the country best-equipped to do the job properly, but he has none of Gould's "Golden Age" staff and is left to cover the gigantic TV newsbeat almost single-handedly. John J. O'Connor's appointment to fill the other half of Gould's role, as TV *critic*, marked a distinct improvement in this function. O'Connor writes better, thinks more interestingly, and seems less committed to television-as-it-is. On the whole, however, he seems hesitant to judge and fits in perhaps too easily with the *Times'* unexciting gallery of careful, relatively un-adventurous critics past and present, all of whom have been read by producers with an attention beyond their due.

Eight different men have written about television at one time or another for *The New Republic*: Saul Carson, John Cogley, John Gregory Dunne, David Ebbitt, Paul Goodman, Walter Goodman, Roger Rosenblatt, and Reed Whittemore. Each had something sound and distinctive to offer, along the magazine's liberal-critical line. The best writer among them was probably Reed Whittemore ("Sedulus"), but already his collected columns seem as dated (and sometimes as clever) as John Crosby's of the '50s. There is about them something of the tone of the elder pedagogue trying to relax, without total success. Reading his columns alongside Stanley Kauffmann's film reviews (where they were usually run) is an embarrassing reminder of the different levels of criticism the two fields have attracted.

Before Michael Arlen, *The New Yorker* offered Philip Hamburger, a predictable middlebrow entertainer; John (son of Ring) Lardner, who often said useful things well; and, in two reviews each, Renata Adler (on game shows and the Children's Television Workshop) and Jonathan Miller, who wrote one supremely witty "anti-television" essay so deftly, almost madly turned that one excuses it for saying so little. I apologize for quoting at such length, but Miller is irreducible as well as unique:

> Television is a vast, phosphorescent Mississippi of the senses, on the banks of which one can soon lose one's judgment and eventually lose one's mind. The medium itself is depressing. The shuddering fluorescent jelly of which it's made seems to corrode the eye of the spectator and soften his brain. In television, the bodies and faces, the dances and games are suspended in a coldly glowing magma that must surely be repulsive to the touch: at once palpable and intangible—quite uncanny. It is like ectoplasm, in fact, which makes the term "medium" doubly appropriate. Television is a low-grade domestic seance in endless session, and the set goes to it with a vengeance, mouthing its gobbet of luminous cheesecloth until the tube burns out . . . Telly is a mean, fidgeting irritant, far smaller than one's own field of vision, flickering away in the corner of the eye like a dull, damaged butterfly. It would be mad, and certainly unfair, to expect consistent marvels from such a mingy little electronic membrane as

this. Not to mention all the other drawbacks of the instrument—the frame rolls, the flickers, the snowstorms, the ghosts, the warps, the jumps, the judders, the chronic vibrato. Not to mention the commercials which inhabit the crevices of the programs like vile, raucous parasites, jumping out all over the living room, nipping, tweaking, and chattering unforgivably about joints, armpits, skin wrinkles, bowels, and blocked-up nasal passages. And not, furthermore, to mention the way in which Telly slithers into the home and stays in one corner of the room like a horrible electronic gossip. In the suggestive gloaming of the darkened parlor, Telly is just one of a number of bits of furniture vaguely discerned in the general moonglow.

The Exception: Michael Arlen

I'm pleased that a man like Michael Arlen (who took over at *The New Yorker* late in 1966, three years after Miller gave up) has chosen to write essays on American culture as reflected on the cathode-ray tube. I'd be happy if a few more writers of such breadth and verve and originality gave it a try. (Few "higher thinkers" or good writers seem able to endure regular reporting on television for more than a few years. On retiring from the job, John Crosby said, "I can't sit and stare at that box for another ten years. I'd go crazy.") Arlen has been able to crack open new ways of thinking about television, as James Baldwin was able to do with our thinking about American racism in the 1950s, by writing freshly and honestly about subjects with which everyone is familiar.

Beginning on October 1, 1966, Arlen wrote 36 biweekly essays for *The New Yorker*, later collected in *Living-Room War*. He stopped in September 1968, to write three distinguished books on other subjects: *Exiles*, *An American Verdict*, and *A Voyage to Ararat*. Arlen returned to the subject of television in *The New Yorker* at the end of 1974.

The variety of his writing projects over such a relatively short time suggests that Arlen, like other intelligent TV critics (Mannes, Leonard, Crosby, Goodman) is really a *writer* first, dedicated to the examination of self and society through the instrument of a highly personal style. The seriousness of his dedication to the phenomenon of television—while he is working on it—is beyond question: no critic in TV's short history comes close to the intensity of his scrutiny, the depth of his insight, or the marvels of his style. But for almost all fine minds who have tried to deal with American TV on a regular, critical basis, the subject seems to wear thin, or to exhaust the critic's patience, after a few months or years.

Arlen's superiority results, I think, from four things: his understanding of television, his "higher-critical" approach, his liberated responses, and his fine style:

(1) His radical understanding of how American television works has equaled or exceeded that of the most experienced TV reporters. He is fully aware of its financial power structure, its manipulation of politics, its cultural timidity, its over-readiness (before Watergate) to serve as a propaganda arm to the government. He observes, times, counts, telephones, and researches like the responsible journalist he wishes TV newsmen would try harder to be. But he also responds, emotionally and aesthetically, to TV *as TV*—not as a text with background illustrations.

> They spent most of the time, really, on what Reagan said and what people were saying about Reagan—speeches and interviews, dull stuff. They did it filmically, though, cutting and panning, but cutting and panning in terms of the material, not in terms of what some art director thought was sexy, and the result was that it wasn't dull at all.

He can even explain convincingly why "Batman" is better television than "Captain Kangaroo."

(2) From the start, Arlen had no particular interest in merely reviewing "TV-as-programs." ("What is one going to say about 'Petticoat Junction' anyway—beyond making a few arch, superior little cultural leaps in the air, and then jumping on its stomach?") His real concern was rather for TV "as something we are doing to ourselves." Generically speaking, this represents a quantum leap toward a kind of "meta-criticism" of the Mailer/Kael variety, a leap that a few architecture-environment critics are taking as well.

> A great many people obviously want the companionship of other voices as they pass through the day, with a sort of undemanding background picture thrown in to certify that the voices really exist as people . . .

> On the surface, television now gives us isolated facts. Some
> fun. Even, now and then, a tiny morsel of the world. But
> what it mostly gives us is some *other* world, the world we
> dream we live in. It tells us nothing, almost *nothing* about
> how life is and how we are . . .

This "higher criticism" reached a peak of indispensable insight into
"television's reality" in a long 1968 essay ("Television and the Press
in Vietnam," *Living-Room War*) that is the wisest thing I have
ever read on television news.

(3) Arlen is blessed by a cynical liberation from kneejerk
critical responses—especially to the kind of "liberal" pretentiousness
that the networks (including the noncommercial network) purvey
in their pompous self-defenses and proudly emit over the air in their
"serious" programming. An obvious 1950s-style message play or an
irresponsible piece of liberal propaganda in the guise of a documentary elicit from Arlen far more venomous contempt than does mere
mediocrity.

(4) Arlen's is a fluid, manic, mercurial style, sometimes brash
and colloquial ("Come off it, NBC!"). He has a helpless tendency to
wit of a wild and airy kind that *can* run to drunken excess: there are
novelistic fantasias and Tom Wolfeish montages that lose me altogether. Sentences dash and comma on, with breathless self-qualifying
doublebacks (ho!) and repeats—piling up, shifting tone, accreting
serio-comically along. There's a dilly in the great Vietnam piece
that sparks and leaps on for 190 words. This critic is not writing
for Everyman.

Rarely is Arlen's language mere style or self-expression, however. The anti-network ironies can have a savage directness. His near-
surrealistic, semi-colloquial style seems to me akin to TV itself,
which Arlen likes best when it is being its free, visual self, not some
strained imitation of literature. *My* kind of English cannot do justice
to most television; Michael Arlen's can. This is vanguard criticism;
an intensely alert and mobile mind, armed with appropriate rhythms
and diction, taking the phenomenon of American TV with total
seriousness.

The eight essays of his I have read since his 1974 return are
for the most part serious, well-reasoned critiques. Most valuable are
several radical assessments of the format and judgments of TV network news, which Arlen finds depressingly unchanged over the
eight-year gap in his TV writing—no more responsible as journalism,

no more representative of reality now than then, no better a contribution to reasoned political judgment.

But something vital is missing from these later essays: the wit, the freedom, the freakiness have virtually disappeared. There are a few flings at the "Old Arlen," and one attempt to find new meanings in the communications explosion. But much of the 1974-75 writing reminds one of the older defenders of fairness, reason, and responsibility-to-viewers—a worthy enough standard, but one Arlen far outreached in 1966-68. He praises "The Adams Chronicles" as a worthy venture in Bicentennial nationalism, and argues for more foreign correspondents in TV news. He honors Frederick Wiseman in the kind of inflated, predictable tones the younger Arlen would, I think, have surely and cynically mocked: "It's a fascinating film —in some ways frightening, and also humorous, and dealing, albeit indirectly, with questions as deep as the modern soul." "The modern *soul*," Michael? "Albeit"? "Thus, today, in the new year of 1975, we are ensnared as never before in the overseas world, and involved at least as much as ever before with our fellow man . . ." Shayon? Gould? Your local congressman?

The Average TV Critic

Michael Arlen was, though—and he may be again—our best. But to ask for a battalion of Arlens would be silly. For one thing, you can't cook up critics to taste: They come when they're needed, where they're needed, and serve the audiences who need them. For another, the sort of television critics *most* people need—the men and women who would serve television and its viewers reasonably well— are non-intellectuals: decent writers with open minds, active consciences, a broad range of tastes, and an accessibility to at least some of what Pauline Kael happily calls "trash." They are people who *like* to watch television, as do most of their readers. And they aren't writing for *The New Republic* or *The New Yorker*, for *Commentary* or *Atlantic*.

I started my long trek through the newspaper columns dismayed by the trivia, bothered by the gossip, the journalese, the easy put-downs and puffs, the predictable "standards." But the more I read, the more I found myself realizing that this writing was more *like* television-as-it-is: it wasn't fighting it. Perhaps these *were* the right people to be writing about most television, both when it was good and when it was bad. They struck me as journalists closer to sports writers than to drama critics—but doesn't that make some kind of sense? Gossip about stars *belongs* to the world of television, as do slick eight-inch columns, written under pistol-to-the-head deadlines. There's a correspondence, an aptness between form of object and form of critique that is missing in most magazine reviewers. As one of Britain's keenest TV reviewers (Clive James of *The Observer*) recently wrote, "Criticism which does not reflect the medium's ephemerality and multiplicity (which are aspects of each other) is lying."

One doesn't want to push this idea too far. Dull, trivial subjects need not call forth only dull, trivial criticism. There have been good critics in bad times, like George Bernard Shaw and James Agee, who were able to spin straw into gold. Still, it is a lazy professional writer who cannot find *some* subject in television—be it a program, a person, or an issue—worthy of his serious attention once a day.

What troubles me most in the daily reviewers I have sampled is not so much their opinions or ideas as the quality of their prose. Too often, their prose seems to be mindlessly spun out of Winchellese jargon and fruity old metaphors and cliches. People who write so gracelessly and carelessly cannot, I believe, think very well. Perhaps they are (as other newsmen have claimed) mainly incompetent ex-reporters who couldn't handle more substantial assignments. In any case, I was dismayed to find that the men who run many of America's large daily newspapers allow such poor and apparently unedited prose to get through.

Attempts at a style loftier than this norm usually fell into one of three categories:

(1) Self-preening gags (See how clever I am?) and obvious phrase-making wit.

(2) Routine, ritual praise of Programs of Pretension. A collection of the American reviews of Shakespeare on TV, from Charlton Heston in *Julius Caesar* to Richard Chamberlain in *Hamlet*, would be an embarrassing display of ignorant awe.

(3) Pompous sermonizing over responsibility and taste, as if in imitation of Jack Gould at his most preach-

erly. In papers more provincial than the *Times*, this often takes the form of a smug, lowbrow conservatism, forever carping over necklines, long hair, or Suggestive Situations. There is a certain amount of timid crowd-pleasing in this category of reviewing. Many writers for the daily press seem hesitant to commit themselves on "breakthrough" series like "Laugh-in," "All In The Family," or "Mary Hartman, Mary Hartman" until they have read the ratings. Similarly, reviews of some particularly sentimental dramas appear to be contrived with a finger on the public pulse. In general, however, I think that America's television reviewers share, rather than lead or shape, America's tastes, and that their frequent professions of disgust or of unashamed tears are probably sincere. They *did* hate the Beatles, and David Brinkley, and PBL; they *do* love the Waltons.

Millions of Americans dote on their "own" daily TV reviewers, for all their dismal prose and timid taste, as they never could with critics of a wiser, keener stamp. The public see their tastes reflected in print, and they respond with comfort and fellow-feeling. Reviewers write to them personally, cosily, in chatty, daily letters about programs and stars—and they write back, tens of thousands of them, every week. Let it be.

I said earlier that the Useful/Useless, Original/Unoriginal, Fair/Unfair distinctions were dubious ones, dependent on the person using the criticism (what's useful/original/fair to *me* may not be to you). But let me venture one personal, non-absolute criticism of the critics. There is one category of TV criticism—and it fills the books and magazines—that I *do* regard as virtually useless and tediously unoriginal. Moreover, it is generally unfair, since it is unrepresentative or undescriptive of the object. This category is what I would call "anti-television" cant—the stringing together of more or less witty insults, usually in the form of metaphors for refuse ("garbage," "trash," "scum," "wasteland"), accompanied by standard, meaningless adjectives ("utter," "unmitigated," "absolute," "total," etc.). This, I think, gets nobody anywhere.

Such criticism is nondescriptive—it doesn't tell the reader anything about what was seen. It is, obviously, non-analytic. It is culturally condescending, an *expression* rather than a statement of disgust—and, even then, it is often only stock-response disgust, not disgust of the real and passionate sort. At best, it can only amuse by its surface of spleen (a trivial goal) and form a loose, snobbish bond between the critic and other unthinkingly anti-television types among his or her readers.

Standards for Good Television Criticism

The full potential of television communication is unlikely ever to be realized, or even explored, unless independent and imaginative thinkers take the time and effort to consider critically what television has done and, even more important, what it *might* have done. It would be helpful to us all if so influential, so culture-determining a thing as television were to be looked at closely and thought about carefully by a lot of intelligent people. The fact that most television programming to date may seem vapid and uninteresting (or worse) may be an excuse for ignoring it. But it is not, I think, a wholly adequate one. Television is now at least as essential a force as formal education in shaping this country's culture, and it is a considerably more essential force than the art one finds in galleries and museums—two subjects good critics are all too happy to keep writing about. Television is too important to be left to its market researchers and "creative" insiders—or to second-rate reviewers. After 25 years, American intellectuals wake up to discover that the world around them has been radically re-ordered by this vulgar, lowbrow toy. Disgusted by what they see, they rail as eloquently and futilely at television as earlier generations of thinkers railed at radios and cars. It will no longer do.

What should a *good* television critic do? The TV columns of the daily press have traditionally played several roles. They have served as consumer directories ("What to Watch Tonight"); as oblique letters of advice to producers and performers; as platforms for witty verbal display; and as genial conduits and translators of reader opinion. These roles can be serviceable and entertaining. But there are worthier uses, I think, to which television criticism can be put. Without either declining into routine, anti-television cant, or wafting into graceless, academic prose, the good television critic can serve several useful functions—quite apart from any considerations of his power to alter programming or change industry policy.

1. *The good television critic can point out lies, errors, and*

serious distortions when he discovers them in news and documentary programs. Most documentaries in the past 25 years have been reviewed by simply retailing to the reader the information presented by the producer, with no critical consideration of possible bias or inaccuracy. Such reviews could as easily be the networks' own press releases, and sometimes they are.

John J. O'Connor has remarked that network documentaries have become so predictable he no longer bothers to review them. Other TV critics ignore them because most of their readers do, or review them uncritically because they haven't the special competence to do anything more. But even "small" national evening ratings may represent millions of viewers, for whom TV news-documentaries—suavely packaged, predictably structured, and persuasive—may be the most vivid presentation of an issue that they will ever receive.

If the presentation is false, then surely someone (other than wounded special-interest groups) should be around to say so. And, "special competence," as any good reporter knows, can be developed in a very short time by diligent research into libraries, files, and public records, as well as by asking intelligent questions of people who know the answers. Norman Mark of *The Chicago Daily News* has done an exemplary job of testing the claims of documentaries by these means.

2. The good critic can survey trends and types of programming over one or more so-called "seasons." This would provide him with the opportunity not only to analyze the content of different programs and to make comparative evaluations, but also to suggest relationships between these changing forms and the world outside the box. It has become almost obligatory for a TV reviewer to count up and bewail the imitative excesses of this or that popular type of program at the beginning and end of each season (family situation comedies, variety shows, westerns, giveaway shows, detective shows, police shows, etc.). But one can do more than this. In the 1960s, Marya Mannes of *The Reporter* wrote two extended analyses of commercials and two others of daytime soap operas. They represent her wisest and most thoughtful work as a television critic.

Of all the critics I have read, however, only Neil Compton (*Commentary*, 1964-70) attempted serious critical surveys of genres, types, and categories of programs on any regular basis. He took popular culture with the proper degree of seriousness and understood the realities of TV production and TV viewing. He always watched a great deal of television carefully before he wrote, and then he produced cogent critical essays in which he surveyed individual program-types over a season: Vietnam documentaries, pop music shows, children's daytime cartoons. He was never taken in by "prestige" programming, which is generally more pretention than substance.

On the whole, I found Compton to be a civilized critical chronicler, responsible but never pontifical, who remained readable without ever depending on the thin surface-sparkle of "wit":

> Perhaps it is naive to expect a medium which offers a service as domestic as a picture window and as continuous as running water to duplicate the conventional forms of theater and cinema, which are based on an audience which chooses freely among alternatives and commits time, energy, and money to the act of participation. The vast, unbuttoned universality of the television audience and the ritualistic repetitiveness of the weekly schedule mean that empathy is achieved, if at all, only after a half-dozen or more installments of a series have established a cadre of habitual viewers. Why should any dramatist choose to write to such a medium so long as theater and movies are open to him? Almost without exception, the best television dramas have been adaptations of works originally conceived for other media: the tendency of popular TV programs generally to be "spin-offs" of movies, comic books, novels, or musical comedies is more than a matter of mere witless imitation. (*Commentary*, April 1966)

3. *The good critic should also, from time to time, venture radical considerations of the very nature and creative possibilities of the medium.* How, for example, might the size of the television screen, the quality of its image, and the domestic locus of viewing affect the *kind* of comic or serious drama written for television, or the methods of directing and acting it? Producers, I am sure, ask such questions. But critics have usually dealt with them only in infrequent asides tucked into the format of a standard program review.

4. *Rather than simply attending to and then evaluating what appears on the television set, the good critic might on occasion inquire into the phenomenon and the social effects of those television programs which have now become either national rituals, or materials*

that we have come to ingest as naturally and unconsciously as the air through which they are transmitted. Some examples might be the annual Academy Awards and similar galas; the Miss America (etc.) competitions; the quadrennial national nominating conventions of the Democratic and Republican parties; the long moonshot watches; the three nightly half-hour network news presentations, with their studio "anchormen" and stand-up correspondents "on location"; the TV family that acts out comic situations in three eight-minute scenes between commercials; the humorless, ill-drawn adventures of cartoon heroes on Saturday mornings; or (reaching back into history) such things as the charity telethons of the early 1950s.

Some of these forms have already been studied for their own sake—especially network news. John Lardner once speculated at length on the "adult western" of 1957, and Horace Newcomb has written a sound and provocative book (*TV: The Most Popular Art*) on the mythical imagery of various popular TV genres. The 1958-59 quiz show scandal provoked a small library of inquiries into national values, and a few critics have puzzled over the "misery show" marvel, or the fact and effects of "commercial interruptions."

In 1963, Paul Goodman wrote a series of eleven essays on TV for *The New Republic* and, in the process, proved himself to be one of the few authentically radical thinkers to have addressed themselves to the medium. Some of the issues he raised were shocking in their simplicity, but they had rarely been raised before. A sample:

> On election night . . . there is a most impressive coverage of the returns in the race between the two matched pacers, and TV takes pride in this democratic service, though it defeats me exactly how democracy is served by it, since before TV people always managed to find out anyway who was elected President.

Normally, the harried daily reviewer cannot be expected to do any more than accept such phenomena as "givens" and compare one with another. Which network covered the convention best? Which station has the most appealing anchorman? Was this year's Emmy Show worse than the last? Perhaps I am the only person in the country who still regards the fact of an unstructured, two-hour long "talk show," nationally telecast every night, as an event utterly without reasonable explanation. Twenty years after Jack Paar first walked into *Tonight*, it still strikes me as an event worthy of radical investigation. What is—and *why* is—a Talk Show?

Most daily TV reviewers can protest that their readers and their editors have been conditioned to expect more simple, easily digestible fare than what I am proposing. But the Sunday editions of *The Los Angeles Times* and *The Washington Post* (to say nothing of the quality press of London and continental Europe) have demonstrated that editors and readers can accustom themselves to serious critical essays, at least once a week.

5. *The good critic should certainly investigate the commonplace notion that many people now depend on television for their conception of (or accept television in lieu of) the real world.* What exactly does this mean? What are the implications of this claim? Television shares certain basic qualities with cinema—both are made up of "motion pictures," usually photographed images of real things, displayed on a two-dimensional, rectangular screen. As a medium, then, and also in its individual programs, television invites the kind of theoretical speculation into its nature that has attended the study of film by such critics as Arnheim, Bazin, Kracauer, and Metz. Our manner of perceiving television lies open to both philosophical enquiry and physiological experimentation. Like cinema, it has evolved certain stock forms and fostered certain stereotypes and myths. Hence, like cinema, it affords rich material for criticism along generic and mythic lines.

Insofar as television shares other characteristics with still photography and journalism (the representation of real events), it also invites other forms of theoretical and critical investigation. One might examine, for instance, the relationship between the reality supposedly captured and transmitted by television (the battle of Con Thien, the life of the Loud family) and the translation of that reality into television's images and sounds. A serious critic might further examine the differences between our *experience* of such actual events, and our experience of television's versions of them.

6. *What appears on American television is at once the product of and (in a fuzzy way) a reflection of American society: "a window on the world," in the words of Sonny and Cher. A social critic possessed of sufficient temerity and self-assurance might well make use of the medium of television criticism to discuss both that window and that world.* Some critics have done this in limited ways, but usually by means of critical comment on disagreeable peculiar-

ities they find in television itself. (Commercials and giveaways, for instance, are frequently seen as a "reflection" of American greed.)

But the brave television critic can go even farther than this. He can (as the greatest critics have always done) analyze the *subject presented* as well as the means of presentation. There is no reason —other than fear of one's publisher, or one's own lack of competence—*not* to write of the state of American politics (or music, or foreign policy, or health care) in the context of an essay on TV's coverage of an election campaign (or "NBC Opera," or "CBS Evening News," or an "ABC Closeup" on doctors). With the bravery of hindsight, I was appalled to find how few daily TV critics in 1954 felt free or willing or able to say anything about the Army-McCarthy hearings other than the hours they were visible on TV. In recent years, the television critic who has taken greatest advantage of this opportunity—to write about "everything" in the process of writing about television—is Michael Arlen, whose *New Yorker* essays on "The Living Room War" began with, but then reached far beyond, a discussion of the television reporting on the Vietnam War.

7. *Every good critic is potentially a teacher.* I take it as axiomatic that the good critic of a particular field (perhaps not on first hiring, but certainly after a few dozen critical assignments) (a) knows more about the field than most of his readers; (b) attends more closely than they to particular events and therefore is, in Henry James' phrase, "one of those people on whom nothing is lost"; (c) is better able than they to articulate his response. As a result of these three superiorities, the good critic can (a) teach his readers more about the field—its methods of production, institutional structures, external and internal pressures and limitations; (b) train them to be better receivers of the art, to be more sensitive, more critical, more alert, and more attentive to all the possible sources of pleasure or information; and (c) enable them to give definable mental and verbal shape to (and, hence, retain as a permanent asset) this enhanced personal response.

Toward a New Criticism

Most books, and many articles, written so far on American television have been sociology, not criticism. A critic may, and perhaps should, be aware of the best social scientific research in his field. But it is not his role to practice it. To attempt to assess objectively what other people think about TV, or how much they need it, or how it affects them, has nothing to do with the art and practice of criticism, which depends for its basic data on the *individual* response (what Eric Sevareid condescendingly calls "the egocentric exercise of analyzing [one's] own reactions").

I think we are seeing the beginning of a new criticism, dependent on a new sensibility perhaps partly *formed* by television. It is based on a rich yet exact, a free yet knowing use of the English language. Its practitioners are able to modulate easily from the traditional to the vernacular, from the personal to the analytic. It is as intelligent as it is liberated. It is the language of (at their best) Norman Mailer, the editors of *Rolling Stone*, Pauline Kael—and Michael Arlen. It is a sort of late twentieth century, educated-American-demotic, unique (as far as I know) in the history of the language, although reminiscent of some of the juicier Victorians (Arnold, Carlyle, Dickens).

Along with this new use of language goes a happy, unfettered willingness to experience and deal with "popular" subjects. By this, I don't mean the earnest analyses of the Bowling Green Professor of Popular Culture, whose language, stance, background, and very life are usually alien to the popular subjects he tries to elevate and ennoble by his attention. I don't mean skittery verbal entertainers like Tom Wolfe, culturally slumming in an artificial prose, or a Marshall McLuhan; or most of the clumsy, inexpressive rock music reviewers, who haven't one-tenth the mind or style or lucidity or *reach* of the people I am describing.

The writers I'm referring to are very bright people, aware of and excited by contemporary culture, but in vital contact with past history as well. They can seem almost magically creative and free, and yet they are careful and correct in their use of the language. I suspect, in fact, that it's their very self-assurance and skill with the language that allows them their extraordinary insights into the things they discuss. This would also explain their excesses, their over-the-cliff fantasies (Mailer, Kael, *Rolling Stone*, and Arlen are all prone to these), the times when they get carried away by their own verbal and imaginative virtuosity. They also seem to share a near-manic taste for chaos and disorder, which may explain why they are able to tune in so clearly to the times of which they write:

It isn't, perhaps, that the world is deeper in chaos than it used to be, but that the element of chaos which has always been there in life, which really *is* life . . . is now coming more and more out from under wraps.

My own feelings—my own feelings (he mumbled) are that the divinity of man was a rather nice thing while it lasted but that we are now all so well along on the road to a life of metal and organization and technique and cultural technology and educational technology and sexual technology and all the rest of the morbid paraphernalia of modern life that it will take a few exertions of nothing much less than a kind of anarchism of the soul (well, there's a floaty expression for you) to even postpone the desert for a while.

The Flying Nun is interrupting Dean Rusk? Dean Rusk is interrupting *The Flying Nun*? This country seems to include both, in some mysterious, lunatic balance, and television includes both too . . .   (Michael Arlen, *Living-Room War*)

Put to the question, I would depend for the "future of television criticism" not on the egoistic pontificators; not on sociologists, futurologists, or cultural slummers; not on the "Isn't TV Awful?" wits, or the people who Don't Like Television Except When It's Very, Very Good; not even on traditional intellectuals like myself. I would depend, rather, on the good men and women who *like* TV and use it as most people do—but who, in addition, write clearly, have consciences, and are willing to live with the realities of the daily press. I would also depend on Front-Line writers and thinkers of the sort I have just tried to describe. They're rare, but there will be more. Television, I think, is helping to create them.

Part 3.
Drama

Television serves many functions, but none is more important to us than its role as storyteller. Without question, drama—fictional stories, both serious and comic, that are scripted and acted—represent the dominant form of television programming. The amount of drama to which we are exposed via television is unprecedented historically. It is often charged that television drama represents nothing more than pure escapism, but the authors of the essays in this section suggest that there is more to it than that.

Several essays focus on individual programs, such as "Dallas," "Maude," and the BBC's "An Englishman's Castle." Other essays attempt to explore the evolution and significance of entire genres—the soap opera, the media drama, the situation comedy. Also included are considerations of the curious phenomenon which has come to be known as docudrama and an analysis of the TV commercial as an art form.

Smooth Pebbles
at Southfork

Michael Arlen

It's easy to see why "Dallas" is one of the most popular shows in the country. It's juicily wicked, with plenty of Hollywood-style shimmer: all those designer dresses and helicopter-mounted hunting parties. Larry Hagman as bad J. R. Ewing is a most satisfying villain, especially in an era when heroes, anointed with the blessings of ambivalence, have all the good lines and evil is commonly represented by inarticulate psychopaths; Hagman's J.R. has a touch of Tennessee Williams' mean-weak young Southern gentlemen, a touch of old, snarly Dan Duryea, and a good deal of his own soft, spacy charm. Even the "Dallas" women hold their positions on the court better than most TV-pretty actresses, though the young ones all rather look alike; there's nothing really sexy ever going on, but there's a sort of subdued, genteel, panting quality in most of the episodes that keeps things interesting.

A lot of people seem to think of "Dallas" as soap opera—"prime-time soap opera" is what one of the news magazines called it a while ago—and one can hardly blame them. The hour-long scripts abound in infidelities and double-dealings of various kinds, and few of the principal characters appear to enjoy many moments of serenity—even a quiet evening at home now and then—free from the ravages of treachery and tantrum. Of course, "soap opera" has come to be one of those catch-all terms, applied to just about anything that seems to have a strong emotional or melodramatic tilt to it; I remember, for instance, President Nixon's "final days" and the BBC's version of "Anna Karenina" both being described as soap operas. But what is interesting, I think, about "Dallas" is the degree to which it *doesn't* resemble soap opera—at least, classic soap opera. In classic soap opera, after all, the fun is in the interaction of the characters, but what makes the whole thing work is the stability of the social framework: what used to be called the "manners" of society. In the early radio soaps, and in the famous television soaps of the nineteen-fifties and -sixties, these social conventions provided a framework not only for the story but also for the characters' emotions—an electrical field of force, as it were, that remained in place and that the characters bounced off (usually into one another) in a more or less continuing process. The key element was the *stability* of the framework—the established and agreed-upon nature of the rules. Thus, in classic soap opera, when a wife was unfaithful to her husband she knew (as did the audience) with reasonable exactitude how her husband and the community would respond to her infidelity. Frequently, the "manners" of the soap-opera story didn't correspond precisely to the "manners" of the audience, but that wasn't the point. The point was that for the story to make sense it needed limits; then the fun could begin, as the wife contrived to make a fool of her husband, or was tormented by guilt, and so forth. In this sense, all drama of manners —be it American soap opera, British drawing-room comedy, or Japanese *no* play—is a story of prisoners in a jail whose walls proclaim that certain things are *done* and certain things *not done.* Think of "As the World Turns." Think of the plays of Noël Coward. Think of "All in the Family." Ostensibly, this program enjoyed its tremendous success because of Norman Lear's masterly creation of the Archie Bunker family, because of the funny, pungent scripts, and because of the first-rate ensemble acting of the four principals. But surely the series worked as well as it did, and for as long as it did, because Lear had the good sense to preserve the social essence of Johnny Speight's "Till Death Us Do Part," the BBC series on which "All in the Family" was based, and which was intrinsically a comedy of manners: a drama of prisoners, first of the larger world of social conventions, then of the smaller world of family roles. At any given moment in "All in the Family," you knew exactly where Archie stood, where Edith stood, where Meathead stood, where Gloria stood. There were playful surprises but no real surprises: the framework was in place; the situation was stabilized.

"Dallas" seems to be different. Here it's not that the drama lacks "manners" but that the "manners" don't constitute a framework—not, at any rate, a framework of any stength and consistency. In "Dallas," when a wife cheats on her husband neither she nor her husband nor anyone else, including the audience, can be sure how the other parties will respond. For example, when Bobby (J.R.'s more or less good brother) suspects that his wife, Pam, is planning to have an affair with her boss during a forthcoming business trip to Paris, he neither confronts her with it nor believes her protestations of fidelity but on her departure takes up with an old girlfriend who happens along—and then doesn't sleep with her. What behavior pattern is this? Ambivalence? What code of manners is Bobby plugged into? Obviously, a code full of loopholes, but then most codes of manners contain a few loopholes. Essentially, one imagines, it is a code whose particulars seem to be in a state of flux or suspension—a code in which the rules have become destabilized and the players are making them up as they go along.

Sometimes, this improvisational quality adds a certain laid-back contemporaneity to the proceedings; at other times, though, it introduces an almost goofy absence of point of view into the otherwise taut structure. Sue Ellen and J.R., for example, clearly have one of the worst marriages in North America. He continually lies to her, betrays her, threatens her, and mostly has nothing to do with her; in turn, she lies to him, betrays him, is desperately trying to get a divorce, and is currently having him tailed by a private investigator. Hardly two lovebirds; moreover, the condition of their marriage is basically no secret to anyone else in the family. But when one evening, out of the blue, Sue Ellen, with apparent sweetness, gives a surprise anniversary party for her swinish mate (her secret motive is that she will use the party as evidence of wifely loyalty in the divorce proceedings), none of the other characters blink an eye or seem to think the little event at all strange or out of the ordinary. They stand around complaisantly, holding their cocktail glasses, like a Greek chorus that isn't "into" tipping off the audience about what's going on; like "townspeople" in a Western who have temporarily lost track of the moral drift of the situation. In fact, as an indication of the vagueness that shrouds the Ewings from time to time, J.R. not only doesn't find the party at all strange himself but rather imagines that it might be a jolly invitation from Sue Ellen (whose private investigator he has just laid a trap for) to a lovers' roll in the hay, which he later proposes—and only then discovers that the joke was on him: the party was a put-on.

The characters in "Dallas" are liberated from having to relate to a consistent perspective. They're also free to reinvent themselves. Consider the sudden and whimsical shift in the realtionship between Ray and Donna. Ray is the blond, good-looking manager of the Ewing ranch, Southfork, and Donna is the equally blond and good-looking young widow whom he has long had a crush on. In the beginning of their courtship, Ray appears very much the solid, soft-spoken Westerner: he don't say much but he's a good man. He's decent, strong, confident—a good match for Donna, who is described as "active in state politics." But no sooner does he get things going with Donna than he starts to turn into Hamlet. Donna has a party—not even a real party but just a little dinner, a cozy dinner with Ray and a couple of political friends, Texans, real nice folks, not exactly your Galbraith and Schlessinger crowd—and Ray gets all shy and dithery. He mutters that the only thing he knows about is ranch management, that he feels out of place, and so forth. If a Texas cowboy can pout, Ray comes close to pouting. In fact, he has stopped being a Texas cowboy—even a Texan; the framework has bent again, and that means that Donna is soon floating off into undiscovered or improvised territory. Since Ray won't marry her—being true to his new Hamlet role, and being apparently unaware of the thousands of cowboys who have had working wives, sometimes even educated working wives—a still more unlikely scene ensues when she goes to Ray's boss, old Jock Ewing, the family patriarch, and tries to persuade *him* to lean on Ray a little bit. Fortunately, Jock's role is still stabilized at this point, so he sends her packing.

Soap operas are almost never dreams. Daydreams, maybe: suppose the handsome doctor falls in love with the nurse; suppose the cute secretary steals the boss' affections. But most soap operas are too pragmatic to exist on a dream plane—are too full of the nuts and bolts of daily life. A good example of a classic, down-to-earth soap was the English "Upstairs, Downstairs"—that finely detailed rendering of the comings and goings of the Bellamy family and their servants in Edwardian England, which was such a hit with the American vid-lit audience when it was rebroadcast here by the Not Yet Ready for the

Public television system a few years back. I've even seen it suggested —I think by the Washington *Post*'s estimable Richard Cohen—that "Dallas" is a sort of homegrown, American version of "Upstairs, Downstairs." It's certainly true that "Dallas" is *ours,* and though a case might be made for the fact that "Upstairs, Downstairs" was also ours, the comparison is an interesting one. All the same, my guess is that a closer kin to "Upstairs, Downstairs" might be "All in the Family," for the two dramas share not only a rigid and coherent structure of manners but also a fondness for the grit and texture of social detail. When Lady Bellamy went on a trip, everything was done just right: the trunks, the packing, the right clothes for the voyage, the right clothes for the bottom of the trunk, the tissue paper for inside the sleeves. Similarly, when Edith Bunker gave a Tupperware party, not only did she have a complete set—and of the newest line—of Tupperware laid out on the table, but the Tupperware lady herself was on hand to make sure that Edith arranged things properly. But, unlike "Upstairs, Downstairs" and "All in the Family" and any number of recent television series that seem resolutely prosy, even journalistic, in their attention to detail, "Dallas" for the most part seems happily unfactual, undetailed, smooth—dreamlike. Some of the dream, of course, derives from the movie version of Edna Ferber's "Giant:" that huge Victorian house rising out of the flat Texas landscape in the middle of nowhere. The Ewings' ranch house is certainly cast in the same image, but, as the advertising people say, it is definitely downscale from "Giant." Large but not huge; white, serene, and grandly suburban, the Ewing domicile floats on a lake of pale-green lawn beneath a pale-blue sky—a dream not so much of oil or Texas or ranching as of American executive life. The Ewing driveway looks like one of those tasteful car commercials. Meals are genteely taken on the Ewing patio. Now and then, as if surprised by the camera, a Chicano servant is glimpsed in the background (somebody, presumably, has to pick up after the Ewings), but fleetingly, shyly, as if "they" weren't really there—or, at least, all took the bus back to town after work. It could be anywhere. Lake Forest: the Ewings of Lake Forest. It's hard to imagine that people watch "Dallas" because it's so American; there's no "downstairs" in evidence at Southfork, and the "upstairs" is alternately neurotic and criminal. Still, all the people in the audience who *aren't* corporate executives can probably get off on seeing what a mess those upscale Ewings are: all that boozing and sleeping around and driving full-size cars with rock-bottom E.P.A. ratings. Gold American Express cards sure don't buy a person happiness, do they?

"Dallas" isn't grainy, like real soap opera; it's smooth, like a river pebble, like a dream. Its characters don't so much lack manners as lack a stable relationship to manners. Young and old, new rich and old rich, good characters and bad characters share this stripped-down, improvisational sensibility. People make up "conventional" behavior on the spur of the moment. Consider, for example, the curious matter of the paternity complications that have recently surrounded Sue Ellen's baby. What's not especially curious is the paternity complications themselves, for we've been led to believe from the beginning that there was something fishy about the fathering of that child. In the first place, J.R. is as unspeakable a father as he is a husband; then, he and Sue Ellen rarely seem to be in a family-forming mood, what with his philandering and her long addiction to the bottle; then, too, there is Cliff, who is Sue Ellen's handsome and manly former lover, and who keeps popping up in the series like a jack-in-the-box. At any rate, for a variety of reasons a story to the effect that J.R. is not the real father appears in the newspaper. So far so good: a typically juicy "Dallas" imbroglio. But then Miss Ellie gets into the act. Miss Ellie, of course, is the beloved matriarch of the Ewings. Once upon a time, if memory serves, Barbara Bel Geddes, the daughter of the designer Norman Bel Geddes, was an ingenue on Broadway who enjoyed a somewhat risqué reputation in the *ancien régime* as a result of having to say the word "virgin" aloud in a comedy called "The Moon Is Blue;" now she plays Miss Ellie, a Texas lady of the old school. She has piles of money, sure. But values, too. Miss Ellie rules the roost; she sets the tone. She has *standards*. What, then, is her response to the paternity problem surrounding the birth of her grandchild? She gives a cocktail party. That's right: she, along with J.R., Sue Ellen, Bobby, Pam, etc., gives a cocktail party at Southfork, to which all Dallas society is invited. All Dallas society naturally shows up, and, as a result, another goofy scene takes place, in which the elegantly gowned and coiffed ladies of *tout* Dallas mill around the Ewing house with their prosperous husbands (making Sue Ellen so nervous that she has to sneak off to phone her current lover, Dusty) until the arrival, naturally, of the Ewing lawyer with the blood-test results, which are quickly announced to the assembled cocktailers, and which prove, to the surprise of everyone—not least Sue Ellen and J.R.—that J.R. is indeed the father of the child.

Miss Ellie, in this instance, was clearly destabilized, but what's interesting, it seems to me, is the degree to which "Dallas" has attuned itself to an intrinsically destabilized view of manners and social conventions and remained perfectly on target with its audience. And the Ewings of Southfork are not the only television pioneers in our new era of behavioral improvisation. Not only does Billy Ikehorn, the heroine of the mini-series "Scruples" (based with scholarly fidelity on Judith Krantz's novel of that name), travel light—another pebble-smooth, untextured creature of the late twentieth century, hurtling through time warps of social convention with no aerodynamic drag—but her behavior patterns seem to be imprinted on a constantly changing assortment of computer chips. To begin with, we are told that Billy is by birth "a Winthrop"—albeit a poor Winthrop. Aside from the fact that to be even a poor Winthrop in America is presumably to carry with one a greater imprint of social definition than, say, a Rockefeller does (at least, as Rockefellers have reportedly found out from time to time on marrying Winthrops), from a less genealogically fine-tuned point of view there are still some possibilities of good old-fashioned melodramatic conflict here; for instance, the girl of simple virtue rebelling against the upper-crust pretensions of her rich relatives. But no such luck. Billy is quite happy being a Winthrop —whatever being a Winthrop may mean. The only problem is being a poor Winthrop. Accordingly, she marries a tough old Jewish tycoon from Southern California and becomes rich, and when he dies she opens a fancy Beverly Hills super-boutique—called Scruples—and becomes even richer.

In other times, one imagines, a best-selling novelist might have focused on Billy's fairly remarkable journey from Winthrop Country to Mr. Ikehorn's bed and then to Scruples, but in our present era of social aerodynamics such journeys are apparently no problem—not really interesting. Too grainy, maybe; the content level may be too high. What we get, at any rate, is scenes of Billy's rich, good life, presented in the form of a continuing sequence of quasi television commercials, in which the stylishly dressed participants give every evidence of belonging to a recognizable social group and being connected to a comprehensible system of manners but in fact are floating free, not merely of background but of behavior; computer chips imprinted with different, and even contradictory, circuits of behavior get switched in and out as the occasion warrants.

At one point, for example, Billy, recently widowed and in the South of France, is invited to a dinner party by some swanky Hollywood people. Billy's arrival at the party is a car commercial; Billy herself is a clothes commercial; the setting for the party is a champagne commercial. Clearly, it is a fancy affair, with everyone very grownup and "social" and dressed to the nines, and with the fussy hostess worrying about the seating arrangements for dinner. Of course, Billy, being a Winthrop by birth, and educated at the proper schools, takes a back seat to nobody in matters of dinner-party etiquette—except here, when, before dinner, she meets a man she finds attractive and they both duck out to spend the evening by themselves. Neither Billy nor her escort seems to think it at all unusual that they should duck out of a seated dinner before dinner is even announced. Granted, there's a hallowed Hollywood tradition that enables high-spirited young lovers to vamoose from stuffy formal parties, but in this instance there's nothing high-spirited or rebellious about Billy's departure; the two would just rather be somewhere else —in a French-tourism commercial. Nor, apparently, does the once-fussy hostess think there's anything odd about the disappearance into the bushes, so to speak, of two of her more visible guests before her doubtless fabulous seated dinner begins; she's floating, too.

Like Miss Ellie and the "Dallas" gang, Billy Ikehorn and the hostess and the rest of the "Scruples" crowd drift in and out of various conceptions of proper behavior as if they were trying on clothes. Since the characters are destabilized, they can do anything; but since they answer neither to God nor to any framework of social conventions, it is hard to know whom or what they do answer to. "Themselves" is probably the missing word, but since these new selves appear to consist of such replaceable circuitry, it's hard to know what that means, either. In an earlier scene in "Scruples," when Billy is in California with her husband and he is barely alive after a stroke, she tires of hanging around the house and casually accepts an invitation from her sick husband's male nurse to an all-night party that he and some pals are giving—which she goes to, and where she is drugged and messed around with. I guess it's possible that the wife of a barely alive Southern California industrialist might accept from someone who was not only an employee but also a virtual stranger an invitation to an all-night party in another stranger's house; still, one imagines that there might be a certain eccentricity attached to the act. But where there's no framework, no code, there can't be eccentricity. Billy Ikehorn, as far as one can tell, is regarded by herself and all the other characters in "Scruples" as completely normal, well-behaved, even proper: once a Winthrop, as the saying goes, always a Winthrop. Similarly, the Ewings of Southfork, while periodically prone to helpless bouts of infidelity and private naughtiness, nonetheless seem to regard themselves, at least in social terms, as models of decorum and correctly observed convention. When nothing has a place of its own, everything, just possibly, may have a place *somewhere*. We're living in strange, smooth times, aren't we? Travelin' light, gathering no moss, making up new identities as we go along. Out in the audience, our citizens reconstitute themselves ever more rapidly according to fashion "looks" (proletarian, Russian, Chinese, Navajo, cowboy, preppy), and search for texture in the feel of denim, in imported whole-wheat bread, in the resonance of stereo tracks. Meanwhile, our new television favorites float free above their glossy plots: figures without background or definition, without entries in their passports. In other words, ourselves aerodynamically advanced, we cheer the streamlined, destabilized characters we so resemble. Who'd want it any other way?

Search for Tomorrow in Today's Soap Operas

Tania Modleski

In soap operas, the hermeneutic code predominates: "Will Bill find out that his wife's sister's baby is really his by artificial insemination? Will his wife submit to her sister's blackmail attempts, or will she finally let Bill know the truth? If he discovers the truth, will this lead to another nervous breakdown, causing him to go back to Springfield General where his ex-wife and his illegitimate daughter are both doctors and sworn enemies?" Tune in tomorrow, not in order to find out the answers, but to see what further complications will defer the resolutions and introduce new questions. Thus the narrative, by placing ever more complex obstacles between desire and its fulfillment, makes anticipation of an end an end in itself. Soap operas invest exquisite pleasure in the central condition of a woman's life: waiting—whether for her phone to ring, for the baby to take its nap, or for the family to be reunited shortly after the day's final soap opera has left *its* family still struggling against dissolution.

According to Roland Barthes, the hermeneutic code functions by making "expectation . . . the basic condition for truth: truth, these narratives tell us, is what is *at the end* of expectation. This design implies a return to order, for expectation is a disorder."[1] But, as several critics have observed, soap operas do not end. Consequently, truth for women is seen to lie not "at the end of expectation," but *in* expectation, not in the "return to order," but in (familial) disorder.

As one critic of soap opera remarks, "If . . . as Aristotle so reasonably claimed, drama is the imitation of a human action that has a beginning, a middle, and an end, soap opera belongs to a separate genus that is entirely composed of an indefinitely expandable middle."[2] The importance of this difference between classical drama and soaps cannot be stressed enough. It is not only that successful soap operas do not end, it is also that they cannot end. In *The Complete Soap Opera Book,* an interesting and lively work on the subject, the authors show how a radio serial forced off the air by television tried to wrap up its story.[3] It was an impossible task. Most of the storyline had to be discarded, and only one element could be followed through to its end—an important example of a situation in which what Barthes calls the "discourse's instinct for preservation"[4] has virtually triumphed over authorial control. Furthermore, it is not simply that the story's completion would have taken too long for the amount of time allotted by the producers. More importantly, I believe it would have been impossible to resolve the contradiction between the imperatives of melodrama—i.e., the good must be rewarded and the wicked punished—and the latent message of soaps—i.e., everyone cannot be happy at the same time, no matter how deserving they are. The claims of any two people, especially in love matters, are often simply mutually exclusive.

John Cawelti defines melodrama as having

> as its center the moral fantasy of showing forth the essential "rightness" of the world order. . . . Because of this, melodramas are usually rather complicated in plot and character; instead of identifying with a single protagonist through his line of action, the melodrama typically makes us intersect imaginatively with many lives. Subplots multiply, and the point of view continually shifts in order to involve us in a complex of destinies. Through this complex of characters and plots we see not so much the working of individual fates but the underlying moral process of the world.[5]

It is scarcely an accident that this essentially nineteenth-century form continues to appeal strongly to women, whereas the classic (male) narrative film is, as Laura Mulvey points out, structured "around a main controlling figure with whom the spectatator can identify."[6] Soaps continually insist on the insignificance of the individual life. A viewer might at one moment be asked to identify with a woman finally reunited with her lover, only to have that identification broken in a moment of intensity and attention focused on the sufferings of the woman's rival.

If, as Mulvey claims, the identification of the spectator with "a main male protagonist" results in the spectator's becoming "the representative of power,"[7] the multiple identification which occurs in soap opera results in the spectator's being divested of power. For the spectator is never permitted to identify with a character completing an entire action. Instead of giving us one "powerful ideal ego . . . who can make things happen and control events better than the subject/spectator can,"[8] soaps present us with numerous limited egos, each in conflict with one another and continually thwarted in its attempts to "control events" because of inadequate knowledge of other peoples' plans, motivations, and schemes. Sometimes, indeed, the spectator, frustrated by the sense of powerlessness induced by soaps, will, like an interfering mother, try to control events directly:

> Thousands and thousands of letters [from soap fans to actors] give advice, warn the heroine of impending doom, caution the innocent to beware of the nasties ("Can't you see that your brother-in-law is up to no good?"), inform one character of another's doings, or reprimand a character for unseemly behavior.[9]

Presumably this intervention is ineffectual, and feminine powerlessness is reinforced on yet another level.

The subject/spectator of soaps, it could be said, is constituted as a sort of ideal mother: a person who possesses greater wisdom than all her children, whose sympathy is large enough to encompass the conflicting claims of her family (she identifies with them all), and who has no demands or claims of her own (she identifies with no one character exclusively). The connection between melodrama and mothers is an old one. Harriet Beecher Stowe, of course, made it explicit in *Uncle Tom's Cabin,* believing that if her book could bring its female readers to see the world as one extended family, the world would be vastly improved. But in Stowe's novel, the frequent shifting of perspective identifies the reader with a variety of characters in order ultimately to ally her with the mother/author and with God who, in their higher wisdom and understanding, can make all the hurts of the world go away, thus insuring the "essential 'rightness' of the world order." Soap opera, however, denies the "mother" this extremely flattering illusion of her power. On the one hand, it plays upon the spectator's expectations of the melodramatic form, continually stimulating (by means of the hermeneutic code) the desire for a just conclusion to the story, and, on the other hand, it constantly presents the desire as unrealizable, by showing that conclusions only lead to further tension and suffering. Thus soaps convince women that their highest goal is to see their families united and happy, while consoling them for their inability to bring about familial harmony.

This is reinforced by the image of the good mother on soap operas. In contrast to the manipulating mother who tries to interfere with her children's lives, the good mother must sit helplessly by as her children's lives disintegrate; her advice, which she gives only when asked, is temporarily soothing, but usually ineffectual. Her primary function is to be sympathetic, to tolerate the foibles and errors of others.

It is important to recognize that soap operas serve to affirm the primacy of the family not by presenting an ideal family, but by portraying a family in constant turmoil and appealing to the spectator to be understanding and tolerant of the many evils which go on within that family. The spectator/mother, identifying with each character in turn, is made to see "the larger picture" and extend her sympathy to both the sinner and the victim. She is thus in a position to forgive most of the crimes against the family: to know all is to forgive all. As a rule, only those issues which can be tolerated and ultimately pardoned are introduced on soaps. The list includes careers for women, abortions, premarital and extramarital sex, alcoholism, divorce, mental and even physical cruelty. An issue like homosexuality which, perhaps, threatens to explode the family structure rather than temporarily disrupt it, is simply ignored. Soaps, contrary to many people's conception of them, are not conservative but liberal, and the mother is the liberal *par excellence.* By constantly presenting her with the many-sidedness of any question, by never reaching a permanent conclusion, soaps undermine her capacity to form unambiguous judgments.

These remarks must be qualified. If soaps refuse to allow us to condemn most characters and actions until all the evidence is in (and of course it never is), there is one character whom we are allowed to hate unreservedly: the villainess,[10] the negative image of the spectator's ideal self. Although much of the suffering on soap operas is presented as unavoidable, the surplus suffering is often the fault of the villainess who tries to "make things happen and control events better than the subject/spectator can." The villainess might very possibly be a mother, trying to manipulate her children's lives or ruin their marriages. Or perhaps she is avenging herself on her husband's family because it has never fully accepted her.

This character cannot be dismissed as easily as many critics seem to think.[11] The extreme delight viewers apparently take in despising the villainess[12] testifies to the enormous amount of energy involved in the spectator's repression and to her (albeit unconscious) resentment at being constituted as an egoless receptacle for the suffering of others. This aspect of melodrama can be traced back to the middle of the nineteenth century when *Lady Audley's Secret,* a drama about a governess turned bigamist and murderess, became one of the most popular stage melodramas of all time.[13] Discussing the novel upon which the stage drama was based, Elaine Showalter shows how the author, while paying lipservice to conventional notions about the feminine role, managed to appeal to "thwarted female energy:"

> The brilliance of *Lady Audley's Secret* is that Braddon makes her would-be murderess the fragile blond angel of domestic realism. . . . The dangerous woman is not the rebel or the blue-stocking, but the "pretty little girl" whose indoctrination in the female role has taught her secrecy and deceitfulness, almost as secondary sex characteristics.[14]

Thus the villainess is able to transform traditional feminine weaknesses into the sources of her strength.

Similarly, on soap operas, the villainess seizes those aspects of a woman's life which normally render her most helpless and tries to turn them into weapons for manipulating other characters. She is, for instance, especially good at manipulating pregnancy, unlike most women, who, as Mary Ellmann wittily points out, tend to feel manipulated by it:

At the same time, women cannot help observing that conception (their highest virtue, by all reports) simply happens or doesn't. It lacks the style of enterprise. It can be prevented by foresight and device (though success here, as abortion rates show, is exaggerated), but it is accomplished by luck (good or bad). Purpose often seems, if anything, a deterrent. A devious business benefitting by indirection, by pretending not to care, as though the self must trick the body. In the regrettable conception, the body instead tricks the self—much as it does in illness or death.[15]

In contrast to the numerous women on soap operas who are either trying unsuccessfully to become pregnant or have become pregnant as a consequence of a single unguarded moment in their lives, the villainess manages, for a time at least, to make pregnancy work for her. She gives it "the style of enterprise." If she decides she wants to marry a man, she will take advantage of him one night when he is feeling especially vulnerable and seduce him. And if she doesn't achieve the hoped-for pregnancy, undaunted, she simply lies about being pregnant. The villainess thus reverses male/female roles: anxiety about conception is transferred to the male. He is the one who had better watch his step and curb any promiscuous desires or he will find himself saddled with an unwanted child.

Moreover, the villainess, far from allowing her children to rule her life, often uses them in order to further her own selfish ambitions. One of her typical ploys is to threaten the father or the woman possessing custody of the child with the deprivation of that child. She is the opposite of the woman at home, who at first is forced to have her children constantly with her, and later is forced to let them go—for a time on a daily recurring basis and then permanently. The villainess enacts for the spectator a kind of reverse *fort-da* game,[16] in which the mother is the one who attempts to send the child away and bring it back at will, striving to overcome feminine passivity in the process of the child's appearance and loss. Into the bargain, she also tries to manipulate the man's disappearance and return by keeping the fate of his child always hanging in the balance. And again, male and female roles tend to get reversed: the male suffers the typically feminine anxiety over the threatened absence of his chidren.

The villainess thus continually works to make the most out of events which render other characters totally helpless. Literal paralysis turns out, for one villainess, to be an active blessing, since it prevents her husband from carrying out his plans to leave her; when she gets back the use of her legs, therefore, she doesn't tell anyone. And even death doesn't stop another villainess from wreaking havoc; she returns to haunt her husband and convince him to try to kill his new wife.

The popularity of the villainess would seem to be explained in part by the theory of repetition compulsion, which Freud saw as resulting from the individual's attempt to become an active manipulator of her/his own powerlessness.[17] The spectator, it might be thought, continually tunes in to soap operas to watch the villainess as she tries to gain control over her feminine passivity, thereby acting out the spectator's fantasies of power. Of course, most formula stories (like the Western) appeal to the spectator/reader's compulsion to repeat: the spectator constantly returns to the same story in order to identify with the main character and achieve, temporarily, the illusion of mastery denied him in real life. But soap operas refuse the spectator even this temporary illusion of mastery. The villainess' painstaking attempts to turn her powerlessness to her own advantage are always thwarted just when victory seems most assured, and she must begin her machinations all over again. Moreover, the spectator does not comfortably identify with the villainess. Since the spectator despises the villainess as the negative image of her ideal self, she not only watches the villainess act out her own hidden wishes, but simultaneously sides with the forces conspiring against fulfillment of those wishes. As a result of this "internal contestation," the spectator comes to enjoy repetition for its own sake and takes her adequate pleasure in the building up and tearing down of the plot. In this way, perhaps, soaps help reconcile her to the meaningless, repetitive nature of much of her life and work within the home.

Soap operas, then, while constituting the spectator as a "good mother," provide in the person of the villainess an outlet for feminine anger: in particular, as we have seen, the spectator has the satisfaction of seeing men suffer the same anxieties and guilt that women usually experience and seeing them receive similar kinds of punishment for their transgressions. But that anger is neutralized at every moment in that it is the special object of the spectator's hatred. The spectator, encouraged to sympathize with almost everyone, can vent her frustration on the one character who refuses to accept her own powerlessness, who is unashamedly self-seeking. Woman's anger is directed at woman's anger, and an eternal cycle is created.

And yet . . . if the villainess never succeeds, if, in accordance with the spectator's conflicting desires, she is doomed to eternal repetition, then she obviously never permanently fails either. When, as occasionally happens, a villainess reforms, a new one immediately supplants her. Generally, however, a popular villainess will remain true to her character for most or all of the soap opera's duration. And if the villainess constantly suffers because she is always foiled, we should remember that she suffers no more than the good characters, who don't even try to interfere with their fates. Again, this may be contrasted to the usual imperatives of melodrama, which demands an ending to justify the suffering of the good and punish the wicked. While soap operas thrive, they present a continual reminder that woman's anger is alive, if not exactly well.

We must therefore view with ambivalence the fact that soap operas never come to a full conclusion. One critic, Dennis Porter, who is interested in narrative structures and ideology, completely condemns soap operas for their failure to resolve all problems:

> Unlike all traditionally end-oriented fiction and drama, soap opera offers process without progression, not a climax and a resolution, but mini-climaxes and provisional denouements that must never be presented in such a way as to eclipse the suspense experienced for associated plot lines. Thus soap opera is the drama of perepetia without anagnorisis. It deals forever in reversals but never portrays the irreversible change which traditionally marks the passage out of ignorance into true knowledge. For actors and audiences alike, no action ever stands revealed in the terrible light of its consequences.[18]

These are strange words indeed, coming from one who purports to be analyzing the ideology of narrative form! They are a perfect illustration of how a high-art bias, an eagerness to demonstrate the utter worthlessness of "low" art, can lead us to make claims for high art which we would ordinarily be wary of professing. Terms like "progression," "climax," "resolution," "irreversible change," "true knowledge," and "consequences" are certainly tied to an ideology; they are "linked to classical metaphysics," as Barthes observes. "The hermeneutic narrative, in which truth predicates an incomplete subject, based on expectation and desire for its imminent closure, is . . . linked to the kerygmatic civilization of meaning and truth, appeal and fulfillment."[19] To criticize classical narrative because, for example, it is based on a suspect notion of progress and then criticize soap opera because it *isn't* will never get us anywhere—certainly not "out of ignorance into true knowledge." A different approach is needed.

This approach might also help us to formulate strategies for developing a feminist art. Claire Johnston has suggested that such a strategy should embrace "both the notion of films as a political tool and film as entertainment:"

> For too long these have been regarded as two opposing poles with little common ground. In order to counter our objectification in the cinema, our collective fantasies must be released: women's cinema must embody the working through of desire: such an objective demands the use of the entertainment film. Ideas derived from the entertainment film, then, should inform the political film, and political ideas should inform the entertainment cinema: a two-way process.[20]

Clearly, women find soap operas eminently entertaining, and an analysis of the pleasure that soaps afford can provide clues not only about how feminists can challenge this pleasure, but also how they can incorporate it. For, outrageous as this assertion may at first appear, I would suggest that soap operas are not altogether at odds with a possible feminist aesthetics.

"Deep in the very nature of soaps is the implied promise that they will last forever."[21] This being the case, a great deal of interest necessarily becomes focused upon those events which retard or impede the flow of the narrative. The importance of interruptions on soap operas cannot be overemphasized. A single five-minute sequence on a soap opera will contain numerous interruptions both from within and without the diegesis. To give an example from a recent soap opera: a woman tries to reach her lover by telephone one last time before she elopes with someone else. The call is intercepted by the man's current wife. Meanwhile, he prepares to leave the house to prevent the elopement, but his ex-wife chooses that moment to say she has something crucial to tell him about their son. Immediately there is a cut to another couple embroiled in an entirely different set of problems. The man speaks in an ominous tone: "Don't you think it's time you told me what's going on?" Cut to a commercial. When we return, the woman responds to the man's question in an evasive manner. And so it goes.

If, on the one hand, these constant interruptions and deflections provide consolation for the housewife's sense of missed opportunities, by illustrating for her the enormous difficulty of getting from desire to fulfillment, on the other hand, the notion of what Porter contemptuously calls "process without progression" is one endorsed by many innovative women artists. In praising Nathalie Sarraute, for example, Mary Ellmann observes that she is not

> interested in the explicit speed of which the novel is capable, only in the nuances which must tend to delay it. In her own discussions of the novel, Nathalie Sarraute is entirely antiprogressive. In criticizing ordinary dialogue, she dislikes its haste: there not being "time" for the person to consider a remark's ramifications, his having to speak and to listen frugally, his having to rush ahead toward his object—which is of course "to order his own conduct."[22]

Soap opera is similarly antiprogressive. Just as Sarraute's work is opposed to the traditional novel form, soap opera is opposed to the classic (male) film narrative, which, with maximum action and minimum, always pertinent dialogue, speeds its way to the restoration of order.

In soaps, the important thing is that there always be time for a person to consider a remark's ramifications, time for people to speak and listen lavishly. Actions and climaxes are only of secondary importance. I may be accused of wilfully misrepresenting soaps. Certainly they appear to contain a ludicrous number of climaxes and actions: people are always getting blackmailed, having major operations, dying, conducting extramarital affairs, being kidnapped, going mad, and losing their memories. The list goes on and on. But just as in real life (one constantly hears it said) it takes a wedding or a funeral to reunite scattered families, so soap opera catastrophes provide convenient occasions for people to come together, confront one another, and explore intense emotions. Thus in direct contrast to the male narrative film, in which the climax functions to resolve difficulties, the "mini-climaxes" of soap opera function to introduce difficulties and to complicate rather than simplify characters' lives.*

---

*In a provocative review of *Scenes from a Marriage*, Marshá Kinder points out the parallels between Bergman's work and soap operas. She speculates that the "open-ended, slow paced, multi-climaxed structure" of soap operas is "in tune with patterns of female sexuality" and

Furthermore, as with much women's narrative (such as the fiction of Ivy Compton-Burnett, who strongly influenced Sarraute), dialogue in soap operas is an enormously tricky business. Again, I must take issue with Porter, who says, "Language here is of a kind that takes itself for granted and assumes it is always possible to mean no more and no less than what one intends."[23] More accurately, in soaps the gap between what is intended and what is actually spoken is often very wide. Secrets better left buried may be blurted out in moments of intensity, or they are withheld just when a character most desires to tell all. This is very different from nighttime television programs and classic Hollywood films with their particularly naive belief in the beneficence of communication. The full revelation of a secret on these shows usually begins or proclaims the restoration of order. Marcus Welby can then get his patient to agree to treatment; Perry Mason can exonerate the innocent and punish the guilty. The necessity of confession, the means through which, according to Michel Foucault, we gladly submit to power,[24] is wholeheartedly endorsed. In soap operas, on the other hand, the effects of confession are often ambiguous, providing relief for some of the characters and dreadful complications for others. Moreover, it is remarkable how seldom in soaps a character can talk another into changing his/her ways. Ordinarily, it takes a major disaster to bring about self-awareness—whereas all Marcus Welby has to do is give his stop-feeling-sorry-for-yourself speech and the character undergoes a drastic personality change. Perhaps more than men, women in our society are aware of the pleasures of language—though less sanguine about its potential as an instrument of power.

---

thus perhaps lends itself more readily than other forms to the portrayal of feminine growth and developing self-awareness (*Film Quarterly* [Winter 1974-75], p. 51). It would be interesting to consider Kender's observation in the light of other works utilizing the soap opera format. Many segments of "Upstairs, Downstairs," for instance, were written by extremely creative and interesting women (Fay Weldon, for one). The only disagreement I have with Kinder is over her contention that "The primary distinction between *Scenes from a Marriage* and soap opera is the way it affects us emotionally. . . . Instead of leading us to forget about our own lives, and to get caught up vicariously in the intrigues of others, it throws us back on our own experience" (p. 53). But soap opera viewers constantly claim that their favorite shows lead them to reflect upon their own problems and relationships. Psychologists, recognizing the tendency of viewers to make comparisons between screen life and real life, have begun to use soap operas in therapy sessions (see Dan Wakefield, *All Her Children* [Garden City, New York: Doubleday & Company, 1976], pp. 140-43). We may not like what soap operas have to teach us about our lives, but that they *do* teach and encourage self-reflection appears indisputable.

An analysis of soap operas reveals that "narrative pleasure" can mean very different things to men and women. This is an important point. Too often feminist criticism implies that there is only one kind of pleasure to be derived from narrative and that it is essentially a masculine one. Hence, it is further implied, feminist artists must first of all challenge this pleasure and then out of nothing begin to construct a feminist aesthetics and a feminist form. This is a mistaken position, in my view, for it keeps us constantly in an adversary role, always on the defensive, always, as it were, complaining about the family but never leaving home. Feminist artists *don't* have to start from nothing; rather, they can look for ways to rechannel and make explicit the criticisms of masculine power and masculine pleasure implied in the narrative form of soap operas.

One further point: feminists must also seek ways, as Johnston puts it, of releasing "our collective fantasies." To the dismay of many feminist critics, the most powerful fantasy embodied in soap operas appears to be the fantasy of a fully self-sufficient family. Carol Lopate complains:

> Daytime television ... promises that the family can be everything, if only one is willing to stay inside it. For the woman confined to her house, daytime television fills out the empty spaces of the long day when she is home alone, channels her fantasies toward love and family dramas, and promises her that the life she is in can fulfill her needs. But it does not call to her attention her aloneness and isolation, and it does not suggest to her that it is precisely in her solitude that she has a possibility for gaining a self.[25]

This statement merits close consideration. It implies that the family in soap operas is a mirror-image of the viewer's own family. But for most viewers, this is definitely not the case. What the spectator is looking at and perhaps longing for is a kind of *extended* family, the direct opposite of her own isolated nuclear family. Most soap operas follow the lives of several generations of a large family, all living in the same town and all intimately involved in one another's lives. The fantasy here is truly a "collective fantasy"—a fantasy of community, but put in terms with which the viewer can be comfortable. Lopate is wrong, I believe, to end her peroration with a call for feminine solitude. For too long women have had too much solitude and, quite rightly, they resent it. In a thought-provoking essay on the family,

Barbara Easton persuasively argues the insufficiency of feminist attacks on the family:

> With the geographical mobility and breakdown of communities of the twentieth century, women's support networks outside the family have weakened, and they are likely to turn to their husbands for intimacy that earlier generations would have found elsewhere.[26]

If women are abandoned to solitude by feminists eager to undermine this last support network, they are apt to turn to the right. People like Anita Bryant and Mirabel Morgan, says Easton, "feed on fears of social isolation that have a basis in reality."[27] So do soap operas.

For it is crucial to recognize that soap opera allays *real* anxieties, satisfies *real* needs and desires, even while it may distort them.[28] The fantasy of community is not only a real desire (as opposed to the "false" ones mass culture is always accused of trumping up), it is a salutary one. As feminists, we have a responsibility to devise ways of meeting these needs that are more creative, honest, and interesting than the ones mass culture has come up with. Otherwise, the search for tomorrow threatens to go on, endlessly.

THE SOAP FORMULA

Currently, twelve soap operas are shown daily, each half an hour or an hour long. The first goes on the air at about 10:00 am, and they run almost continuously until approximately 3:30 pm. With the exception of "Ryan's Hope," which takes place in a big city, the soaps are set in small towns and involve two or three families intimately connected with one another. Families are often composed of several generations, and the proliferation of generations is accelerated by the propensity of soap characters to mature at an incredibly rapid rate; thus, the matriarch on "Days of Our Lives," who looks to be about 65, has managed over the years to become a great-great grandmother. Occasionally, one of the families will be fairly well-to-do, and another will be somewhat lower on the social scale though still, as a rule, identifiably middle-class. In any case, since there is so much intermingling and intermarrying, class distinctions quickly become hopelessly blurred. Children figure largely in many of the plots, but they don't appear on the screen all that often; nor do the very old. Blacks and other minorities are almost completely excluded.

Women as well as men frequently work outside the home, usually in professions such as law and medicine, and women are generally on a professional par with men. But most of *everyone's* time is spent experiencing and discussing personal and domestic crises. Kathryn Weibel (see note 11) lists "some of the most frequent themes:"

> the evil woman
> the great sacrifice
> the winning back of an estranged lover/spouse
> marrying her for her money, respectability, etc.
> the unwed mother
> deceptions about the paternity of children
> career vs. housewife
> the alcoholic woman (and occasionally man)
> (Weibel, p. 56)

(cont.)

Controversial social problems are introduced from time to time: rape was recently an issue on several soap operas and was, for the most part, handled in a sensitive manner. In spite of the fact that soaps contain more references to social problems than do most other forms of mass entertainment, critics tend to fault them heavily for their lack of social realism (on this point, see Edmondson and Rounds [note 3], pps. 228-247). As for the fans, most insist on soap opera's extreme lifelikeness and claim that the characters have to cope with problems very like their own.

Footnotes

1. Roland Barthes, *S/Z,* Richard Miller, trans. (New York: Hill and Wang, 1974), p. 76.

2. Dennis Porter, "Soap Time: Thoughts on a Commodity Art Form," *College English* (April 1977), p. 783.

3. Madeleine Edmondson and David Rounds, *From Mary Noble to Mary Hartman: The Complete Soap Opera Book* (New York: Stein and Day, 1976), pps. 104-110.

4. Barthes, p. 135.

5. John Cawelti, *Adventure, Mystery, and Romance* (Chicago: The University of Chicago Press, 1976), pps. 45-46.

6. Laura Mulvey, "Visual Pleasure and Narrative Cinema" in *Women and the Cinema.* Karyn Kay and Gerald Peary, eds. (New York: E. P. Dutton, 1977), p. 420.

7. Mulvey, p. 420.

8. Mulvey, p. 420.

9. Edmondson and Rounds, p. 193.

10. There are still villains in soap operas, but their numbers have declined considerably since radio days—to the point where they are no longer indispensable to the formula. "The Young and the Restless," for example, does without them.

11. See, for example, Kathryn Weibel, *Mirror Mirror: Images of Women Reflected in Popular Culture* (New York: Anchor Books, 1977), p. 62. According to Weibel, we quite simply "deplore" the victimizers and totally identify with the victims.

12. "A soap opera without a bitch is a soap opera that doesn't get watched. The more hateful the bitch the better. Erica of 'All My Children' is a classic. If you want to hear some hairy rap, just listen to a bunch of women discussing Erica.
    'Girl, that Erica needs her tail whipped.'
    'I wish she'd try to steal my man and plant some marijuana in my purse. I'd be mopping up the street with her new hairdo.'"
    Bebe Moore Campbell, "Hooked on Soaps." *Essence* (November 1978), p. 103.

13. "The author, Mary Elizabeth Braddon, belonged to the class of writers called by Charles Reade 'obstacles to domestic industry.'"
    Frank Rahill, *The World of Melodrama* (University Park: The Pennsylvania University Press, 1967), p. 204.

14. Elaine Showalter, *A Literature of Their Own* (Princeton, New Jersey: Princeton University Press, 1977), p. 165.

15. Mary Ellmann, *Thinking About Women* (New York: Harvest Books, 1968), p. 181.

16. The game, observed by Freud, in which the child plays "disappearnace and return" with a wooden reel tied to a string. "What he did was to hold the reel by the string and very skilfully throw it over the edge of his curtained cot, so that it disappeared into it, at the same time uttering his expressive

'o-o-o-o.' [Freud speculates that this represents the German word *'fort'* or 'gone.'] He then pulled the reel out of the cot again by the string and hailed its reappearing with a joyful *'da'* ['there'] ." According to Freud, "Throwing away the object so that it was 'gone' might satisfy an impulse of the child's, which was suppressed in his actual life, to revenge himself on his mother for going away from him. In that case it would have a defiant meaning: 'All right, then go away! I don't need you. I'm sending you away myself.'" Sigmund Freud, *Beyond the Pleasure Principle,* James Strachey, trans. (New York: W. W. Norton, 1961), pps. 10-11.

17.   Speaking of the child's *fort-da* game, Freud notes, "At the outset he was in a *passive* situation—he was overpowered by experience; but by repeating it, unpleasurable though it was, as a game, he took on an *active* part. These efforts might be put down to an instinct for mastery that was acting independently of whether the memory was in itself pleasurable or not." Freud, p. 10.

18.   Porter, pps. 783-784.

19.   Barthes, p. 76.

20.   Claire Johnston, "Women's Cinema as Counter-Cinema" in *Movies and Methods,* Bill Nichols, ed. (Berkeley: University of California Press, 1976), p. 217.

21.   Edmondson and Rounds, p. 112.

22.   Ellmann, pps. 222-223.

23.   Porter, p. 788.

24.   Michel Foucault, *La Volunté de Savoir* (Paris: Editions Gallinard, 1976), esp. pps. 78-84.

25.   Carol Lopate, "Daytime Television: You'll Never Want to Leave Home," *Radical America* (January-February 1977), p. 51.

26. Barbara Easton, "Feminism and the Contemporary Family," *Socialist Review* (May-June 1978), p. 30.

27. Easton, p. 34.

28. A point Hans Magnus Enzensberger makes about mass consumption in general. See *The Consciousness Industry* (New York: Continuum Books, 1974), p. 110.

Trials and Tribulations—
Thirty Years of Sitcom

Arthur Hough

Between 1948 and 1978, during the first three decades of American network television, some 400 situation comedies were produced and aired. These 400 series represented approximately 20,000 individual prime-time episodes, which amounts to nearly 700 half-hour television comedy episodes a year. In an attempt to chart the length and breadth and depth of this phenomenon, I entered hundreds of items of data from each of these sitcom series into a computer at San Francisco State University. Then, with thousands of statistics and frequencies spread out before me, I began looking for a way to discover the story of American television sitcom in terms of itself, leaving the more delicate linkage of sitcom trends with social trends to other students of the American scene. It was like trying to gauge the thickest ice on a vast expanse of frozen lake covered with statistical snow.

Finally, one evening, the snow blew away and revealed a single, beautifully clear spot. That spot was *1965*—just beyond the halfway point of the first 30 years of television situation comedy. The year 1965 was, apparently, both the pinnacle of public popularity for sitcoms and the transitional point between the old traditional domestic comedies and a half-dozen new television comedy genres. Situation comedies took 10 places in the top 20 Nielsen rankings of both the 1964-65 and 1965-66 seasons. Out of network television's total of 400 sitcom series between 1948 and 1978, 52 of the programs, or 13 percent, were on the air at some time during 1965. In fact, anyone watching television in 1965 was viewing a microcosm of two decades of situation comedy, with "Ozzie and Harriet"* and some form of "I Love Lucy" reaching all the way back to the early 1950s and "My Three Sons," "Bewitched," "The Beverly Hillbillies," and, of course, "Lucy" continuing uninterrupted into the 1970s.

In 1965, if you were a domestic comedy buff, you had your choice of sixteen nuclear-family shows, seven single-parent (all widowed) families, six sets of young marrieds, and three seasoned married couples. You could watch nine fantasy sitcoms all of which were concealing something dreadful, like an alien origin, a genie, a witch, a robot, an angel, a family of grotesques, or an English-speaking horse or car. The year 1965 was also the peak season for rustic comedies, for military farce, and for combinations of the two ("No Time for Sergeants," "Gomer Pyle," and "F Troop.").

And look who was working in television comedy that year: Eddie Albert, Lucille Ball, Joey Bishop, Shirley Booth, Ernest Borgnine, Walter Brennan, Edgar Buchanan, George Burns, Bing Crosby, Bill Dana, Buddy Ebson, John Forsythe, Tony Franciosa, Eva Gabor, Andy Griffith, Fred Gwynne, Glynis Johns, Jack Klugman, Fred MacMurray, Mary Tyler Moore, Agnes Moorehead, Jim Nabors, Mickey Rooney, the Smothers brothers, and Dick Van Dyke.

The turnover was just as dramatic. Twenty casts were fired in 1965 when their shows folded, and sixteen new casts were hired. It was the year of a great crossover—the linkage year between two distinct strains of American television comedy. One comedy period was dying but had not yet rolled over, and another more vigorous trend was just being born. Television situation comedy and the American television audience began to grow up in 1965.

In order to place 1965 in its proper context, we should look at the major trends in sitcom over the seventeen years which preceded it and the thirteen years which followed. But, first, let us clarify the meaning of "situation comedy."

There is no authoritative definition of situation comedy, so the most useful handle we can get on it is to examine the shows which

---

*The editor chooses to use the convention of enclosing show titles in quotation marks. I urge students and scholars not to follow this style. All television series titles represent complete works, and therefore should be in italics, quotation marks being reserved for individual episode titles.

1965: SITCOM'S BANNER YEAR

1953 54 55 56 57 58 59 60 61 62 63 64

19 66 67 68 69 70 71 72 73 74

Winter — Spring — Summer — Fall

1965

Ozzie & Harriet
Donna Reed
My Three Sons
Andy Griffith
Joey Bishop
Hazel
Mr. Ed
Dick Van Dyke
(Summers only)
McHale's Navy
Beverly Hillbillies
Lucy Show
Glynis
Patty Duke
Bill Dana
Petticoat Junction
My Favorite Martian
Farmer's Daughter
Bing Crosby
No Time for Sergeants
Wendy & Me
Tycoon
Bewitched
Addams Family
Valentine's Day
Broadside
Cara Williams
Munsters
Gilligan's Island
My Living Doll

F Troop
Please Don't Eat the Daisies

Lucy/Desi

Here's Lucy

Gidget

Green Acres

Camp Runamuck
Hank
Hogan's Heroes
Mr. Roberts

Smothers Brothers
Tammy
Get Smart

I Dream of Jeannie
John Forsythe
My Mother the Car

I Love Lucy

Ball

Less Than a Year:

Mickey
Many Happy Returns
Baileys of Balboa
Harris Against the World
Karen
Tom, Dick & Mary
Mona McCluskey
OK Crackerby

22 YEAR SPAN

have been *called* sitcoms and then create our definition from that. A sitcom is normally an open-ended series of thirty-minute self-contained television episodes which revolve around a single umbrella plot or situation and a regular cast of core characters. Sitcom is distinguished from other television drama in that its dominant themes and style are broadly played comedy; it generally involves stereotypical characters and ritualistic humor (repetition and "running gags"); and it frequently incorporates an irrational approach to reality, leaning strongly on blindness and concealment.

Sitcom also differs from other television drama in that it is usually staged in limited, shallow, unconnected sets with broad, flat lighting, suggesting that it is being played through a proscenium arch to a real audience. However, most sitcoms employ a laugh track even when played before a live audience.

The typical story formula for sitcom is "establishment, complication, confusion and resolution." Plots tend to be superficial and simplistic, and there is seldom any genuine villainy or dramatic depth. All shows have happy or at least upbeat endings.

Having said all that, I hasten to add that situation comedy does at one time or another escape every one of these characteristics. In the process of producing 20,000 sitcom episodes in thirty years, television producers and writers have reached out to every dramatic device known, and the results have occasionally transcended the genre. Pehaps the most tempting innovation in all situation comedy occurs when a plot walks precariously along the edge of serious drama, taking a *kamikaze* dive into tragedy and then pulling out at the last second to waggle its wings at the audience. "All in the Family" dared to do a rape scene as comedy; "Barney Miller," "M*A*S*H," and "Mary Tyler Moore" frequently subdued comic formulas to treat serious themes.

Development of the Domestic Sitcom

The 398 Sitcoms of 1948-1978

1948

Laytons
Laurel and Hardy

When *domestic* sitcoms are isolated from the nondomestic, slightly over half of all sitcoms since 1948, or 215 titles, fall into the domestic category. Among these domestic comedies, four major subgenres have evolved.

The domestic comedies began with *traditional families* (1948-55), continued with *nuclear families* (1955-65), adapted to the times with *eccentric families* (1965-70), and finally achieved a new category of *social* and *ethnic families* (1970-78).

The Traditional Family (1948-1955)

You probably don't remember the first domestic sitcom, "Mary, Kay and Johnny." It started in 1947 and had a healthy run of three years. It was a network jumper, starting on the Dumont network, then skipping over to NBC, then to CBS, and finally back again to NBC. It was so traditional that it wasn't even a dramatic invention. Instead, it concerned the family life of a real couple, Mary Kay Stearns and her husband Johnny (who wrote the scripts).

The Stearns were painfully typical. They began the show as newlyweds, and she was the flighty scatterbrained wife—a theme that was to become common in the early domestic comedies. They lived in an apartment (as did 67 other later sitcom couples), in a metropolitan setting (along with 211 other sitcom casts), and in New York City (where 93 other sitcoms have been set). In fact, Mary Kay, like Lucille Ball, actually became pregnant during the run of the show, and the baby was worked into the television script within a month after his birth.

So television sitcom began in the late 1940s with a single "authentic" family. Tradition and conservatism were strong elements in early sitcom. You couldn't get much more traditional than the Norwegian emigrant family of "I Remember Mama"—or more kosher than "The Goldbergs."

Life with Luigi
Heaven for Betsy
Adventures of Ozzie
and Harriet
Our Miss Brooks
Doc Corkle
Leave It to Larry
I Married Joan
Meet Millie
My Hero

1953

Private Secretary
Ethel and Albert
My Son Jeep
Life with Elizabeth
Bonino
My Favorite Husband
Ray Milland Show
Marge and Jeff
Jamie
Make Room for Daddy
Pride of the Family
Colonel Humphrey
Flack
Where's Raymond?
Topper
Take It from Me
Life with Father

1954

Duffy's Tavern
That's My Boy
World of Mister Sweeny
The Marriage
The Duke
Mayor of the Town
Joe Palooka Story
Mickey Rooney Show
It's a Great Life
Dear Phoebe
Willy
Father Knows Best
December Bride
Donald O'Connor
Texaco Show
Honestly Celeste
Halls of Ivy

1955

So This Is Hollywood

But there was also the middle-American influence of "The Aldrich Family" and "The Adventures of Ozzie and Harriet," as well as the bumbling husband themes of "The Stu Erwin Show" ("The Trouble with Father," 1950-55), "The Ruggles" (1949-52), and "The Life of Riley" (1949-58). The scatterbrained wife and the henpecked husband became the very heart of domestic comedy as Desi Arnaz and Lucille Ball joined the scene in their phenomenally popular and long-lived show. Sixteen of these earliest shows came directly from radio, where verbal nagging and screwball bumbling had been honed to a fine edge for years.

The computer research verified all of the above generalizations. The period from 1948 to 1955 presented the highest incidence of seasoned married couples, of scatterbrained wives (who were seldom given children to raise), of henpecked husbands, and of minor children. This period also represented the largest number of television shows originating from books and radio. Finally, this period gave us the highest number of middle-class situation comedies: 72 shows were about "I-Love-Lucy"-middle-class people. Only four shows depicted "Honeymooners"-lower-class level, and two shows dealt with the upper class (e.g., Ezio Pinza played an affluent, world-famous concert singer in "Bonino").

The Nuclear Family (1955-1965)

In the tight little sitcom family of the early 1960s, sons and daughters struggled to grow up and learn the rules of survival in a changing world. Mother and father pondered and explained while little Beaver Cleaver and his brother Wally compared notes on what the

Bob Cummings Show
Norby
Professional Father
The Soldiers
Those Whiting Girls
Great Gildersleeve
It's Always Jan
Joe and Mabel
Phil Silvers Show
Honeymooners
People's Choice

1956

Charlie Farrell Show
His Honor Homer Bell
Hey Jeannie
Stanley
Gale Storm Show
The Brothers
Adventures of Hiram
Holliday

1957

Blondie
Mr. Adams and Eve
Marge and Gower
Champion
A Date with the Angels
Tugboat Annie
Bachelor Father
Sally
Eve Arden Show
Dick and the Duchess
Real McCoys
Leave It to Beaver

1958

Love that Jill
How to Marry a
Millionnaire
This Is Alice
Donna Reed Show
Ed Wynn Show
Ann Sothern Show
George Burns Show

1959

Peck's Bad Girl
Too Young to Go Steady
Fibber McGee and
Molly
Love and Marriage

world was all about; "Dennis the Menace" tried to do his bit for those around him, but generally muffed it; and Dobie Gillis tried to reconcile his urges for women, money, and cars with the values of Maynard, his "beatnik" best friend. These were the "Donna Reed" years, in which one sitcom family after another struggled with the big domestic issues of the time, "measles, girl friends, school problems, and little white lies."

The early 1960s had the highest statistical incidence of family shows, relatives, household pets, and young marrieds, as well as a heavy complement of minor children and grandparents. But a new element was creeping in. The nuclear-family concept was softening as the single-parent family appeared in "Bachelor Father," "Andy Griffith," and "My Three Sons." Widowhood was the typical explanation for such a fracturing of the nuclear family; however, the first divorcee had also appeared—Vivian Vance in "The Lucy Show" (but only as a sidekick to widowed Lucy).

The family also began to need some outside augmentation, some surrogate parenting. During the early sixties, maids and housekeepers were in greater abundance than at any other time in sitcom history. "Hazel" became the family problem-solver; "The Farmer's Daughter" was a governess for a congressman's children; and the wealthy "OK Crackerby" hired a beautiful Harvard tutor to give "class" to his kids.

There were 22 maids, housekeepers, or household servants between 1960 and 1965, about twice as many as in any other five-year period. This seems particularly strange in a period when three out of four sitcoms depicted a middle-class setting. However, the upper-middle class also had its highest incidence in the early 1960s, as did shows with

Dennis O'Keefe Show
Hennessey
Many Loves of Dobie
Gillis
Betty Hutton Show
Dennis the Menace

1960

Happy
Lucy in Connecticut
Jim Backus Show
Tab Hunter Show
Pete and Gladys
Tom Ewell Show
My Three Sons
Andy Griffith Show
My Sister Eileen
Angel
Bringing up Buddy
Peter Loves Mary
Harrigan and Son
Guestward Ho

1961

Yes Yes Nanette
One Happy Family
Holiday Lodge
Car 54, Where Are You
Joey Bishop Show
Ichabod and Me
Hazel
Father of the Bride
Mr. Ed
Window on Main Street
Dick Van Dyke Show
Gertrude Berg Show
Bob Cummings Show
The Hathaways
Margie

1962

Room for One More
Oh Those Bells
Lucy Desi Comedy Hour
McHale's Navy
It's a Man's World
Don't Call Me Charlie
Fair Exchange
Ensign O'Toole
McKeever and the
Colonel

lower-upper class characters. It appears, then, that this period presented sitcom's most affluent families.

The Eccentric Family (1965-1975)

During the decade from 1965 to 1975, the nuclear family began to give way rather seriously to the problems of the single parent. In this period, 59 percent of TV families involved single parents; and although widowhood was still dominant, divorced parents had taken hold.

The first divorced mother appeared in "Accidental Family" in 1967, but this show also hedged its bets by including a family comprised of a divorced mother *and* a widowed father (Jerry Van Dyke). By the late 1970s, there were 23 divorced characters in television comedy, and widowhood had begun to disappear as an explanation for the single parent.

Single-parent situations were, of course, popular with television writers and producers because the situations permitted more complicated and adult plots. Mother was allowed a limited and conservative sex life while searching for a new mate, and the resultant insecurity on the part of the children raised the ante in issues of domestic anxiety.

Sitcom producers ran the gamut between handling the single-parent problem whimsically, by making the surrogate father an incarnate spirit as in "The Ghost and Mrs. Muir" (1968), and hitting the problem head on, as an adult partnership between parent and child. In "The Courtship of Eddie's Father" (1969), for example, Bill Bixby was allowed to bring beautiful women home to little Eddie every week, on approval, while the untouchable Japanese housekeeper, Mrs. Livingston, became the quiet surrogate mother.

In the middle 1960s, real eccentricity was added to the American TV family with the emergence of fantasy as a popular television form. In 1964 alone, three peculiar family parodies appeared: two monster families, "The Addams Family" and "The Munsters," and the witchwife of "Bewitched" (which ran on for eight more years). Then, in 1965, Jeannie the genie ("I Dream of Jeannie") was introduced.

In every one of these magical-fantasy domestic shows there were two constant comic elements: the production of visual absurdities through television's electronic magic, and the legitimization of lying, deception, secrecy, and concealment. Everybody was hiding something from someone, a centuries-old source of domestic comedy.

Fantasy was not the only technique exploited for increasingly complicated domestic plots. The rambling extended family of "The Beverly Hillbillies" captured the ratings for nine years through the 1960s (the show ranked nine times among the fifty top-rated television programs of all times). The success of "The Beverly Hillbillies" helped to launch the seven-year run of a Hooterville widow and her three beautiful daughters in "Petticoat Junction." In the late 1960s, it seemed that family *qua* family was not rich enough for the comic needs of sitcom audiences. Each family plot had to be sweetened with its own *schtick*.

The Social Family (1970-1978)

The metamorphosis of the family into a loose, open, liberal, contractual affair between a miscellaneous number of big and

Mona McCluskey
OK Crackerby
Camp Runamuck
Hank
Hogan's Heroes
Mr. Roberts
Smothers Brothers
Tammy
Get Smart
I Dream of Jeannie

1966

Double Life of Henry
Phyfe
My Name's McGooley,
What's Yours
Love on a Rooftop
Pruitts of South-
hampton
The Rounders
Tammy Grimes Show
That Girl
The Hero
Hey Landlord
It's About Time
Family Affair
Jean Arthur Show
The Monkees
Run Buddy Run
Occasional Wife
Pistols 'n Petticoats

1967

Mr. Terrific
Captain Nice
Rango
Good Morning, World
He and She
Second Hundred Years
Flying Nun
Mothers-in-Law
Accidental Family

1968

Here's Lucy
Julia
Ghost and Mrs. Muir
Mayberry RFD
Doris Day Show
Good Guys
Ugliest Girl in Town

little adults finally occurred in the late 1970s. The "Brady Bunch" tried to hold onto what chroniclers Brooks and Marsh called the "old-style fun-around-the-house situation comedies, full of well-scrubbed children, trivial adventures, relentlessly middle-class parents,"[1] and a housekeeper, family cat, and shaggy dog. But the Bradys were also an example of the "created" family—a widow, a widower, the three sons of one, and the three daughters of the other.

Each new television family during this period added social complexity to its home life. The widowed "Partridge Family" went into the music business; "Sanford and Son" succeeded by combining three subplots: ethnic humor, small-business struggles, and an anti-hero caught in a generation gap. "All in the Family" turned domestic life into a battleground for bigotry, and "Maude" covered all the hypocritical explosions that can occur in a liberal household that dealt weekly with divorce, alcoholism, adultery, single-parent sex, political manipulation, medical incompetence, and reverse racial snobbery. "Rhoda" featured the failure of a wife who became a successful woman; "Phyllis" was the model neurotic mother; George Jefferson the power-mad black *nouveau riche;* "One Day at a Time" the day-by-day education of a single mother by her daughters and a naughty janitor; "Three's Company" a barely platonic *menage a trois,* and "The Odd Couple" the "marriage" of two heterosexual men. The statistics of the period from 1975 to 1978 show an abnormally high incidence of seasoned marrieds without children and the highest number of contrived families, divorced parents, working wives, and grandparents and in-laws.

Domestic Sitcom Comes of Age (1970-1978)

1969

Queen and I
Bill Cosby Show
My World and Welcome
to It
Debbie Reynolds Show
Courtship of Eddie's
Father
Governor and JJ
Brady Bunch
Mr. Deeds Goes to Town
To Rome with Love

1970

Nanny and the Professor
Tim Conway Show
Magnificent Six and
a Half
Bugaloos
Here Come the Double
Deckers
Nancy
Arnie
Mary Tyler Moore
Make Room for Grand-
daddy
Barefoot in the Park
Odd Couple
Partridge Family

1971

New Andy Griffith
Show
All in the Family
From a Bird's Eye View
Doctor in the House
Trouble with Tracy
Shirley's World
Chicago Teddy Bears
Getting Together
Good Life
New Dick Van Dyke
Show
The Partners
Jimmy Stewart Show

1972

Me and the Chimp

There is nothing ambiguous about the changes that occurred in domestic sitcom during the 1970s. The new family shows were heavy with widowed or divorced parents; childless seasoned couples had returned to prominence; and the stage was set for the big social bombshell to burst. Network programming executives had been hanging onto archaic standards of censorship for twenty years; they thought they were really loosening up when they had such giant breakthroughs as allowing "three 'hells' and a 'damn' per show." Then came Norman Lear, an articulate, persuasive, and determined producer who managed to talk CBS into an American remake of a funny but caustic British show about a lower-middle-class bigot and his family.

Lear, either by design or accident, then executed a social pincers movement with his startling new series. The liberals liked Archie Bunker because he was clearly a fool and his bigotry was thwarted and condemned within the plot of each show. On the other hand, conservative viewers were delighted at last to see one of their own kind being "honestly" portrayed, and the good-natured laughter came easily when Archie was put down, out-argued, or shamed by his liberal son-in-law, his humanistic wife, and his young black intellectual neighbor, Lionel Jefferson.

"All in the Family" had something for everybody, and that meant big numbers in the ratings, which meant, in turn, network support and the inevitable "cloning" of the show into spin-offs. "Sanford and Son" (1972-77) gave us an irascible black in the next season, and "Maude" (1972-78) became the noisy, hypocritical, and affluent liberal mirror image

Don Rickles Show
Corner Bar
The Super
Maude
Paul Lynde Show
Temperatures Rising
Little People
Bob Newhart Show
Bridget Loves Bernie
Anna and the King
M*A*S*H
Sandy Duncan Show

1973

A Touch of Grace
Thicker Than Water
Love Thy Neighbor
Dusty's Trail
Ozzie's Girls
Diana
Lotsa Luck
Adam's Rib
Calucci's Department
Girl with Something
Extra
Here We Go Again
Needles and Pins
Bob+Carol+Ted+Alice
Roll Out

1974

Happy Days
Good Times
That's My Mama
Rhoda
Paper Moon
Chico and the Man
Texas Wheelers
Friends and Lovers

1975

Barney Miller
Hot L Baltimore
Karen
Sunshine
Bob Crane Show
We'll Get By
No, Honestly
Doc
Big Eddie
Fay
Montefuscos

of Archie. In 1974, "Chico and the Man" (1974-78) gave Mexican-Americans and Puerto Ricans an ethnically oriented show of their own. Then came the black bigot, as "The Jeffersons" (1974++) blasted off from the Bunker spaceship.

"All in the Family" had not just given us permission to look at bigotry; it had opened up dozens of other socially urgent but unmentionable issues that the networks had been sanitizing for over two decades. Families now could quarrel on sitcom; married and unmarried sex could be discussed. Homosexuality, impotence, alcoholism, religion, women's rights, communism, and even rape became comic topics of the day. Sitcom was finally catching up with the problems of its audience.

The Ethnic Family (1972-1978)

Of course, the infusion of social issues into sitcom plots was nearly a decade *behind* the real issues, but the walls of censorship had been breached. As Ted Westover wrote in *TV Guide*, "Norman Lear toiled mightily in the 1970s to drag television situation comedy kicking and screaming into the 1960s. That's as much progress as the developer of "All in the Family" and "Maude" and many other series could hope for in injecting some reality into sitcoms."

Part of this new reality was a procession of ethnic shows, mainly black, in which the old stereotypes gave way to more complicated characters. In fact, producers were now so nervous about the old stereotypes that they overcompensated, and we had a string of super-blacks—characters who were twice as smart, twice as quick, twice as "reality oriented" as their white co-stars. We had, for example, Harris on "Barney Miller," Benson on "Soap" and "Benson," Curtis Baker on "Carter Country," and young Gary Coleman on "Diff'rent Strokes."

A few black shows struggled for authenticity. "Sanford and Son" gave us an irascible black single father, prejudiced but canny and sly. "Julia" (1968-71) featured a black mother in an integrated middle-class plot. Norman Lear spun off Florida Evans, the black maid in "Maude," and put her into a genuine lower-middle-class family setting in "Good Times" (1974-79), and an attempt was made to portray a young hip black barber in Washington, D.C., in the family comedy "That's My Mama" (1974-75). No one was bold enough to have a black family adopt a white child, but three white families brought black children into their midsts, in "The Cop and the Kid" (1975-76), "Fish" (1977-78), and "Diff'rent Strokes" (1978++).

The 1970s came in with 25 sitcoms having high black involvement, whereas there had only been five such shows in the previous 20 years. Latino participation in sitcoms also gained steadily from two shows in the 1950s to four in the 1960s and ten in the 1970s, with such dramas as "Chico and the Man" (1974-78), the poor Puerto Rican "Popi" (1976), and the Mexican-American family comedy "Viva Valdez" (1976). All in all, the Latino shows have been less successful than the black sitcoms, and such other ethnic or religious family groups as Asians, Native Americans, Catholics, and Jews have been held to their usual low levels of participation.

Development of the Nondomestic Sitcoms—
The Early Years (1948-1955)

1978

Baby, I'm Back
Quark
Husbands, Wives and
Lovers
AES Hudson Street
Another Day
Ted Knight Show
Joe and Valerie
Roller Girls
Free Country
Taxi
Mork and Mindy
WKRP in Cincinnati
In the Beginning
Waverly Wonders
Who's Watching the Kids
Apple Pie
Diff'rent Strokes

**Military Sitcoms
1948-1978**

1955

The Soldiers
Phil Silvers Show

1959

Hennessey
(Dobie Gillis)

1962

McHale's Navy
Don't Call Me Charlie
(McKeever and the
Colonel)

1964

No Time for Sergeants
Broadside
Gomer Pyle, USMC

Like many of the earliest domestic comedies, the nondomestic situational series began mainly as backdrops for "show biz" acts of one sort or another. There were shows featuring a nightclub singer, a song publisher, a theatrical agent, and a vaudeville agent. "Heavens to Betsy" (1949) concerned two girls seeking a career in show biz; "That Wonderful Guy" (1949-50) dealt with the trials and tribulations of a would-be actor; "The Peter Lind Hayes Show" (1950-51) always featured a guest star who had happened by Peter and Mary's for dinner.

Fourteen early sitcoms featured show business themes, more than in any subsequent period; and 18 of these earliest shows were also "star vehicles"—situations built loosely around a well-known entertainer and usually carrying the name of the star in the title. The vacillation between star vehicle and situation comedy became apparent when the networks began to change the series titles back and forth between star and situation titles:

"The Peter Lind Hayes Show," also known as "The Peter and Mary Show"; "The Danny Thomas Show," also known as "Make Room for Daddy"; "The Ray Bolger Show," also known as "Where's Raymond?"; "The Mickey Rooney Show," also known as "Hey Mulligan."

Star vehicles have remained a constant in television and became particularly strong again in the early 1960s. In this later resurgence, however, a mere backdrop for performance was not deemed sufficient for a more sophisticated audience. Instead, the

1965

F Troop
(Mona McCluskey)
Hogan's Heroes
Mr. Roberts
(I Dream of Jeannie)

1972

M*A*S*H

1973

Roll Out

1976

CPO Sharkey

1977

Operation Petticoat

**Business Sitcoms
1960-1965**

1961

Holiday Lodge
Ichabod and Me
Bob Cummings Show

1962

Oh Those Bells
I'm Dickens; He's
Fenster

1963

Mack and Myre for Hire
Grindl
Petticoat Junction
New Phil Silvers Show

1964

Bing Crosby Show
The Tycoon
Valentine's Day
Many Happy Returns
Cara Williams Show

1965

OK Crackerby
Tammy

stars were generally required to perform as characters in fairly strong situational plots. Recall, for example, the "Joey Bishop," "Bob Cummings," "Loretta Young," "Patty Duke," "Bill Dana," "Phil Silvers," and "Bing Crosby" shows.

Military Sitcoms (1955-1970)

The late 1950s introduced a 15-year cycle of a lightly disguised, all-male vaudeville act called the *military sitcom.* It started with a short summer show in which Hal March played himself as an army private in "The Soldiers" (1955). Then came the "Phil Silvers Show" (1955-59), the prototype for all future military shows (until "M*A*S*H" broke the mold in 1972).

"Phil Silvers" offered a satire on military life in which the enlisted men continually made fools of pompous officers. "Hennessey" (1959-62) followed with the misadventures of a navy doctor, and then the dogface shows tumbled over one another, crowding the 1960s with "McHale's Navy" (1962-66), "Don't Call Me Charlie" (1962-63), "No Time for Sergeants" (1964-65), "Broadside" (1964-65), "Gomer Pyle, USMC" (1964-70), "F Troop" (1965-67), "Hogan's Heroes" (1965-71), and "Mr. Roberts" (1965-66). Notwithstanding their quality, the military sitcoms were the first purely television-created genre, since both the show biz and the domestic comedies had really originated in radio.

Business Sitcoms (1960-1965)

The *business sitcom* enjoyed its highest popularity in the early 1960s, at the same time as the military comedies. Sixteen series during this period involved plots that dealt with small, medium, and big businesses, including a newspaper, a publishing house, a charter airline, two hotels, an employment agency, a factory, the complaint desk of a department store, and the career of an electrical engineer (Bing Crosby, of all people). These business themes fell off from sixteen to five in the second half of the sixties.

Fantasy Sitcoms (1965-1970)

Evidence that television was beginning to develop its own unique style occurred in the 1960s, as more and more sitcoms, both domestic and nondomestic, began using dramatic and electronic gimmicks to spice up the show. A total of 46 sitcoms used those devices, and half of them were aired during the 1960s.

The most popular gimmick consisted of an actor turning to the camera and addressing the audience directly. This was the hallmark of George Burns, but it spread in the 1950s and emerged in the 1960s with the new twists of a talking infant ("Happy," 1960-61), a talking horse ("Mr. Ed," 1961-65), a talking car ("My Mother the Car," 1965-66) and the audience asides in Thurber's "My World and Welcome to It" (1969-72).

Electronic flashbacks became a principal gimmick in "The Dick Van Dyke Show" (1961-66) as Rob Petrie replayed his army life and the dilemmas of early marriage. The success of this gimmick led to the dream sequence technique of "The Bill Dana Show" (1963-65), the fantasy sequences of "My World and Welcome to It" (1969-72), and the surrealistic film techniques of "The Monkees" (1966-68), in which fast and slow motion, distorted focus, and comic film-insert techniques were borrowed from the Beatles' film *Help.*

But by far the most popular gimmickry

1975

Far Out Space Nuts
Lost Saucer

1976

Good Heavens
Holmes and Yo Yo

1977

Year at the Top

1978

Quark
Mork and Mindy

Rural Sitcoms
(Hillbilly, cowboy,
farm, and small town)
1948-1978)

1949

Lum and Abner

1951

Egg and I

1957

Real McCoys

1960

Andy Griffith
Guestward Ho

1961

Ichabod and Me

1962

Beverly Hillbillies

1963

Petticoat Junction

appeared in the fantasy and science fiction genres, delightfully introduced by the erudite alien in "My Favorite Martian" (1963-66), a visitor with the powers of invisibility, telepathy, remote control of objects, and retractable antennae.

The success of "My Favorite Martian," and of gimmickry generally, set off a barrage of electronic sleight-of-hand on the small screen. In the 30 years of network television, there have been 26 fantasy shows, and the biggest collection of them occurred in the late 1960s, when 16 magical plots appeared in one lump.

We had, for example, the famous witch-wife of "Bewitched" (1964-72), the creatures of "The Addams Family" (1964-66), the monsters of "The Munsters" (1964-66), the beautiful robot of "My Living Doll" (1964-65), an angel in the form of Tommy Smothers ("The Smothers Brothers Show," 1965-66), the genie of "I Dream of Jeannie" (1965-70), and the super power pills of "Mr. Terrific" (1967) and "Captain Nice" (1967), who drank a magic liquid. "The Flying Nun" (1967-70) merely flew, and the ghost in "The Ghost and Mrs. Muir" (1968-70) simply faded in and out.

There was a hidden bonus for sitcom writers in most of the fantasy shows. First, they could attract the audience with the weird, the magical, and the absurd, and then they could base the remaining plot on concealing the "magic" from a husband, the neighbors, nosy investigators, and society at large. Concealment and deception were thus made moral, appropriate, and even necessary to the survival of their characters.

New fantasy shows came along in the 1970s, but without much innovation. They merely continued the procession of talking

THEMES OF TELEVISION NETWORK SITUATION COMEDY FROM 1948 TO 1978

	1948-1955 84 shows	1955-1960 46 shows	1960-1965 74 shows	1965	1965-1970 57 shows	1970-1975 61 shows	1975-1978 75 shows
DOMESTIC COMEDY	NUCLEAR FAMILY / TRADITIONAL FAMILY				ECCENTRIC FAMILY	SOCIAL FAMILY	
	+Family		*Domestic				*Family
	*Seasoned married		*Family				+Seasoned married
	*Scatterbrain wife		*Relatives		*Single parent	*Single parent	*Grandparents
	*Bumbling husband		+Minor children				*In-laws
			+Grandparents				*Contrived family
			+Widow		*Widow		*Divorced
			*Young married				*Working wife
			*Domestic animals				
			*Maid/servant (first divorce)				
SITUATIONAL COMEDY	*STAR VEHICLE						*Occupations
	*Show biz		*MILITARY		*FANTASY	+Occupations	*Blacks
	*Radio origination		*Business		*RURAL		*Latins
			*Secretaries		*ADVENTURE		
					*Historical period	*Historical period	
			*Gimmick		*Gimmick		

+ = high incidence
* = highest incidence

1964

(No Time for Sergeants)
(Gomer Pyle, USMC)

1965

(F Troop)
Green Acres

1966

The Rounders
Pistols 'n Petticoats

1967

Rango

1968

Mayberry RFD

1971

New Andy Griffith
Show

1973

Dusty's Trail

1974

Texas Wheelers

1977

Kallikas

animals, disembodied voices, space travel, ESP, angels, devils, witches, and robots.

The Rural Sitcoms (1960-1970)

The rustic sitcoms are a strange genre. They are easy to spot when the setting is truly rural, as in Betty McDonald's run-down chicken farm in "The Egg and I" (1951-52), or a cowboy show like "The Rounders" (1966-67). But the rustic sitcom is not always found in a rural setting. The hillbilly who comes to the big city or joins the Army is still giving us that naive, down-home barnyard philosophy no matter where we transplant him.

The prototype for the hillbilly rustic sitcom was "The Real McCoys" (1957-63), a show that ABC put on the air only reluctantly. The plot involved a West Virginia mountain family who moved to the San Fernando Valley. It took off with national audiences and lasted six years. Suddenly there was enthusiasm for the rural show.

The successful "Andy Griffith Show" (1960-68) became the brood sow for three other shows. In 1964, Jim Nabors spun off to take the hillbilly theme into "Gomer Pyle, USMC" (1964-70). When Andy Griffith left the show, it was rekindled as "Mayberry RFD" (1968-71), and once again a spin-off resulted, "The Don Knotts Show" (1970-71), in which Knotts was a television host who produced a weekly show-within-a-show called "The Front Porch."

The second cluster of rustic shows was fathered by "The Beverly Hillbillies" (1962-71), a totally hillbilly show set down in Hollywood. The Clampetts spun off "Petticoat Junction" (1963-70), which returned to the small town setting of Hooterville, and then "Green Acres" (1969-71), in which a sophisticated city couple returned to live on a farm.

CBS was the host network for both of these royal families of rustic Americana, so when the network made a decision in 1971 to cut back on rural-oriented programming, five shows bit the barnyard dust in one year. Apparently, the genre is now making a strong return with shows like "Sheriff Lobo" and "The Dukes of Hazzard," which feature rustic humor combined with the backroad-redneck-auto-demolition comedy popularized by the movies.

Adventure Sitcoms (1965-1970)

Adventure sitcoms are rather a specialized genre, expensive to produce, requiring more movement, location filming and special effects. There have been a few successful adventure sitcoms, however, and twice as many of them aired in the late 1960s as in any other period. "Gidget" (1965-66) took her cameramen out into the sun and surf; "Get Smart" (1965-70) needed lots of special effects and movement to sustain its "secret agent" parody; "Run Buddy Run" (1966-67) was a Hitchcockian spoof on a man who knew too much and had to escape from determined gangsters; "Pistols 'n Petticoats" (1966-67) centered around a bumbling western sheriff; and "Rango" (1967) featured Tim Conway's short-lived characterization of an inept Texas Ranger. The last show of this high adventure period was "The Queen and I" (1969), the misadventures of the scheming purser of a bankrupt ocean liner.

Working Group Sitcoms (1970-1978)

Had you been following the upper-, middle-, and lower-class make-ups of situation comedy during its three decades, you would have found exactly what you expected, that 84 percent of all sitcoms have middle-class settings. Within the middle-class category itself, however, are two subclasses, the *upper-middle* class, consisting of substantial business people and professionals, and *lower-middle* class, made up of small-business people, clerical workers, other low-level white-collar workers, and a few skilled workmen. Until 1970, the more affluent and "respectable" upper-middle-class nondomestic and domestic comedies had led the lower-middle-class. But abruptly, in the 1970s, this ratio reversed itself, and television comedies began featuring the lower-middle class.

The ethnic sitcoms (with the conspicuous exception of "The Jeffersons") usually depicted lower-middle-class settings. But there was an even more significant increase in comedies which featured occupations and work settings. In the three decades of sitcom, occupations had figured prominently in over 1,600 core characters. But the incidence of "working" characters had increased in each ten-year period, with over 400 working people in the 1950s, over 500 in the 1960s, and 650 in the 1970s.

Although not of statistical significance, there was also a new quality to many of the work-oriented shows. The old cliche of the struggle between the boss and the employee began to be replaced in the 1970s with a happier scene, the "cooperative working group." "M*A*S*H" broke through the established format of military shows and depicted a military group in which the traditional hierarchy was mangled beyond recognition by a democratically biased and fearless medical staff. "Calucci's Department" (1973) was a short-lived but gentle comedy of a kind and confused office manager of a state unemployment office. "Barney Miller" (1975++) and "Alice" (1976++) were teamwork-oriented shows which drew the working group together into a loose extended family. To some extent, this phenomenon also appeared in the police station setting of "Carter Country" (1977-79) and in the commercial photography studio of "We've Got Each Other" (1977-78). And, finally, in 1978, two more employee-dominated cooperative work groups appeared in "Taxi" and "WKRP in Cincinnati."

Through all of this decade, one working group above all others caught the eye and the heart of the American viewer week after week: "Mary Tyler Moore" and her colleagues at a television station programming department were not only typical of the cooperative work-group style, but in fact the prototype of such shows and of the many other series featuring single working women. "MTM" lasted seven years, spawned five other series, and introduced one of the most believable, lucid, and lovable portrayals of the single woman in American society of the seventies. When there are a thousand sitcoms in television history, "The Mary Tyler Moore Show" will probably still be among the top ten in terms of historical and social significance.

What's Going to Be Funny in the Eighties?

Sitcoms in the last 30 years haven't stood still. They have evolved—from the single, quasi-vaudevillian plots and traditional families of the 1950s, through the upper-middle-class nuclear families, the eccentric and fantasy families, and the military and rural themes of the 1960s, and then into the social sitcom of the 1970s, with its single parents, working wives, controversial social issues, emancipated women, ethnic plots, sexual issues, and reaffirmation of the work ethic.

Situation comedy has reached a high level of complexity and a moderately respectable maturity in dealing with some of the daily problems of our age. Where will it go from here? Will it double back on itself, as it has recently ("Happy Days," "Laverne and Shirley"), in order to give us nostalgic views of the revolutionary 1960s? Will there be another spate of science fiction and fantasy, or perhaps a subgenre of communal families, unemployed but ecologically involved? Will we tire of seeing one middle-class comedy after another and start enjoying plots about billionaires and paupers?

The "best" of the current situation comedies have given us, I think, an important clue about what may be the next trend of the medium. The common elements among such groundbreakers of the 1970s as "All in the Family" (with all its spin-offs), "M*A*S*H," "Mary Tyler Moore" (and her progeny), ""One Day at a Time," and "Barney Miller" are increased social content and intensified dramatic style. Humorous as the television writers may make them, these plots reflect the more serious problems of daily life, and they cannot be portrayed without some serious dramatic style. The move toward the heavily dramatic comedy has, I believe, already begun. It is the toughest of all comedy to write and to perform, because it involves the sensitive process of increasing audience tension with serious dramatic elements, and then breaking that tension with comic relief.

And it is not merely a matter of developing more dramatic content in the scripts; the style of sitcom is changing across the board. Sets are becoming more three-dimensional, giving greater aesthetic depth. Dramatic lighting, more precise editing, and more subjective camera techniques are demanded by producers and directors.

Finally, we are seeing television develop a cadre of rich character types, reminiscent of the British film tradition. Increasingly, the humor of sitcom is coming out of the character of the actor, rather than from the impersonal punchlines of parody and burlesque. Unfortunately, the networks, in this regard, are often their own worst enemy. They will put a sitcom on the air which depends upon its own dramatic depth and character, and then they will yank it off the air in a few weeks before either the audience or the actors have discovered the fullest potential of the plot and characterization. Both actors and audience need a seasoning which they seldom are allowed to have.

The 1960s were clearly more exciting than the 1950s in American sitcom, and the 1970s were more exciting still. There is hope, then, that the 1980s will give us another, even deeper and more insightful perspective on the humor of our human *situation.*

Footnote

1.   Tim Brooks and Earle Marsh, *The Complete Directory to Prime Time Network TV Shows, 1946-Present.* New York: Ballantine Books, 1979.

Was Anyone Afraid
of Maude Finlay?

Philip Wander

Disparagement as a *thema* in humor is alive and well. The
media abound with apparently amusing putdowns, slurs,
digs, and barbs. So do faculty meetings, business lunches,
factory cafeterias, and cocktail parties. . . . In Hazlitt's
words, "we grow tired of everything but turning others
into ridicule and congratulating ourselves on their defects."
—Dolf Zillman and S. Holly Stocking[1]

"Maude" may have been the best argument against traditional
liberalism ever to appear in the media. Her heart bled on or near
Country Club Place. Her life alternated between personal fears about
her age, weight, and attractiveness and social crusades for mental
health centers, school benefits, and the like. Her politics were ultimately an affair of conscience, having more to do with the spirit of
the activity than with its practical outcome.

"Maude" was, beyond everything else, a show about personal
relationships, about a woman who was bigger, brighter, and more

articulate than her husband. It was about a marriage, and a way of life, built on conflict. Each episode was a sequence of brilliantly delivered insults, or "put-downs," between Maude and Walter, between Maude and Arthur, between Maude and Carol, between Maude and X.

Social satire in general, and the put-down humor of "Maude" in particular, reach back to a very ancient theatrical tradition. To some extent, this type of humor also merely reflects real-life behavior. Nevertheless, the pervasiveness of this sort of humor on prime-time television raises some serious questions. Without becoming melodramatic, I think it fair to say that the sheer quantity of verbal abuse in our lives exceeds anything experienced by earlier generations. By the time a contemporary child reaches the age of sixteen, for example, he or she will have viewed on television some 40,000 threats, over 80,000 instances of rejection or insult, and nearly 200,000 portrayals of yelling and screaming—and all of this in addition to the same sort of thing occurring at home, in school, and in other of the mass media.[2]

There is, no doubt, a broad range of social and psychological effects resulting from such conditioning. But my interest lies specifically in the cultural implications of the insult of put-down as a form of communication. Whatever its intent, an insult conveys not only what is thought to be funny—at least by the speaker—but also what sort of behavior or opinion or appearance *ought* to be put-down. Sarcasm, barbs, gibes, digs—all forms of personal invective—are based upon standards against which people (or things) are to be evaluated and compared.

This becomes particularly clear when some such standard for comparison is called into question by the society. Certain insults become, in themselves, socially unacceptable acts—thus, in the past generation in our society, put-downs based on racial classification became "racism" and those based on sexual differences became "sexism." When forms of invective remain unquestioned, however, the standards upon which they are built begin to appear "natural," the normal way to look at things. Moreover, while the insult recommends standards for comparison, it also recommends the act of insulting others as a way of relating.

This sort of verbal warfare, explored on television during the 1950s and 1960s by Milton Berle, Jackie Gleason, Mort Sahl, Don Adams, Johnny Carson, Don Rickles, Carol Burnett, and many others, was refined and promoted as an art form by the Normal Lear productions of the early 1970s ("All in the Family," "The Jeffersons," "Sanford and Son," along with "Maude"). The Lear productions were successful in amassing a larger audience for put-down comedy than ever before on television. Tens of millions of people, week after week, year after year, viewed and presumbaly learned from the verbal conflict of Norman Lear's series.

The Lear style is nicely illustrated in an episode of "Maude" in which she and Walter have been invited to a party. Walter has overslept an afternoon nap and is grumpy when Maude gently awakens him. He proceeds to complain about being unable to find his toothpaste and then his tweezers. Maude is radiant, preparing for the night out. Finally, as Walter continues to grumble, she asks him what is wrong. His answer: "Cliff Naler."

"Cliff Naler," Maude responds, "is a kind and gentle person. What do you have against him?"

"He has a thing for you, Maude. He's always watching your behind. You'd think he was trying to read a bumper sticker."

The argument moves from Walter's jealousy to the revelation that Cliff is having an affair at "the club" with another woman, Harriet Powers. From preening over the prospect of Cliff Naler's attention, Maude is thrown into depression and petulance upon learning that Cliff pursues "anything in skirts." Physical appearance and fears of aging become the themes of the episode.

Maude and Walter begin their wrangle by insulting one another. At one point, Maude suggests to Walter that he donate his brain to science. Then: "Instead of waiting until tomorrow, I think I'll remove it myself, Walter, with your tweezers." Walter complains to Maude about the suit he must wear to the party: "My suit is wrinkled in the front," he whines.

"Well," Maude answers, "You're wrinkled in the front and back yourself, Walter."

Walter objects to hair in the sink and asks Maude if she has been combing her hair over the drain. "Look at my hair," she tells Walter, as he leans over the sink, his bald pate shining in the light, "then look at yours; then ask whose hair is likely to clog up the sink."

Projecting her own fears of aging onto Walter, Maude continues to insult him for being wrinkled and bald. These taunts are responses to Walter's attacks on her for being selfish and unfair, for not getting his garments pressed while hers are always ready, and for brushing her hair over the rug. As Walter reduces Maude on one scale, housekeeping, she reduces him on another, physical attractiveness. The transaction is one of escalating symmetry.[3]

In a symmetrical relationship, each party strives to maintain an equal footing; thus, an insult is received as a call for a response in kind—an eye for an eye ethic in face-to-face communication. The alternative lies in effecting a complementary relationship in which the one of the couple accepts a subordinate or inferior role. But although the media ordinarily couple women like Maude with meek, assenting, henpecked, ineffectual males—thereby ridiculing both active females and passive males—Walter was always a clever, resourceful, and aggressive person in his own right. Their relationship always possessed a kind of roughshod equality: the right to be equally angry, to be equally insulting.

With their equality re-established, Walter and Maude move away from insulting one another's appearance to using the appearance of a friend as a means of attack. When Maude enthuses over Cliff, Walter calls him a "pygmy." When Walter pities Cliff's wife, Joanne, Maude calls her a "chinless, grey person." After the revelation of Cliff's affair with Harriet Powers, Maude mentions Harriet's body hair ("she spends most of her time at the electrolysist") and her "thick" ankles. ("Anyone with ankles like hair Harriet Powers needs all the help she can get.")

Just as the insult can be used for purposes of competition in face-to-face communication, so can it be used for purposes of community. In this variation, two people bond together by putting down a third party. Maude and Walter conclude that Cliff is a wretch, and Maude therefore joins with Walter in putting Cliff down. However, Maude can claim that "Cliff is attracted to ugly women" (Joanne and Harriet) only at the risk of looking at herself. She resolves this dilemma by down-scaling Cliff from "handsome" to a "pygmy greaseball."

Maude and Walter are now drawn closer together in part because each is enhanced at Cliff's expense: X is less than either of us; both of us are better than X. Maude also suddenly realizes that Cliff's attentions are so important to her, not because she is sexually attracted to him, but because she feels she is growing older and less desirable, and his attentions are flattering. "Attractive is the consolation prize," she sobs to Walter, who has tried to be consoling. "I don't want to be attractive. I want to be beautiful. Let's face it; this face," moans Maude, looking into a mirror, "is on the way out, and I'm not ready for it. I'll never be ready for it."

With "Maude," animus was raised to an art and fashioned into a game. The audience became judges in a contest of wit. Wit, however, was equated with clever disparagement. Verbal play (allusion, puns, clever turns of phrase) took on one form, the insult, and assumed one function, the put-down. The effect, moderated by the fact that "Maude," week after week, managed to puncture a great deal of pomposity and prejudice, was probably ambivalent for the viewing public.

On the one hand, "Maude" challenged societal standards for evaluating a person's worth. The series confronted prejudice to teach us that discrimination based on race, on sex, on age, or occupation is more than wrong; it is a sign of ignorance. The same social consciousness informed all Lear productions and made them unique in a world of Ricardos, Bradys, and Cunninghams.

Yet where verbal aggression is treated as a natural, even therapeutic mode of human interaction, it formally reflects the *status quo*. We shore up our egos, gain a sense of self-worth, by putting other people in their place. However clever or appropriate, insults require victims.

Furthermore, while fighting against prejudice, "Maude" never seemed to question a world of competitive individuals obsessed with the need to rank one another. Her one-woman campaigns were only against the standards by which people are ranked and the consistency with which these standards are applied. The program's themes of discrimination against women and minorities, while challenging the prerogatives of white, middle-class males, tended to make the assumption that the prerogatives of the white, male, middle-class are worth having. This is why "Maude," as a species of social criticism, belongs not in the romantic, but in the rhetorical tradition. "Maude" offered not a new vision, but conventional forms—the family, competition, middle-class society—reflected in a new light.

Footnotes

1. Dolf Zillmann and S. Holly Stocking, "Putdown Humor," *Journal of Communication,* 26 (Summer, 1976), 154.

2. The typical sixteen-year-old has watched 5,000 hours of TV. In 68½ hours, representing one episode of all fictional TV shows telecast in the fall of 1975, there were 430 instances of insults and rejection, 193 threats, and 1,006 examples of yelling and screaming. In all, there were 1,629 instances of verbal aggression and 991 instances of physical aggression (hitting, shoving, shooting, etc.). See Bradly S. Greenberg, Charles K. Atkin et al., *Project Castle: Children and Social Television Learning* (Washington, D.C.: U.S. Office of Child Development, 1977), p. 28.

3. See Paul Watzlawick, Janet H. Beavin, and Don D. Jackson, *Pragmatics of Human Communication* (New York: W. W. Norton & Company, Inc., 1967), pp. 107-118. See also Chapter 5, "Who's Afraid of Virginia Woolf?", pp. 149-186.

Media Medicine
and Morality

Robert S. Alley

A skeptic could reasonably argue that any questions one might pose concerning the social thrust and moral impact of television programming have already been answered by the very dominance of the profit motive in that industry. Certainly, producers must be economically successful in order to survive. However, those who populate the television industry, even the economic royalists, have other interests and goals in addition to the accumulation of wealth and power. A look at how this industry has treated the medical field reveals much about these additional interests and goals.

Historically, television has been cautious in its approach to medical science. Its first venture, called "Medic," was a well-received and highly realistic examination of surgery. The program sought to document medical case histories and used some actual hospital footage. This series began in 1954 and helped to launch the career of

Richard Boone who, after two years, moved to the lucrative and long-running "Have Gun, Will Travel." During its brief tenure, "Medic" was praised for its "seriousness and high-mindedness,"[1] even though Jack Gould of the *New York Times* felt it was sometimes marred by sensationalism. However, "Medic" came to an end at least partially because the portrayal of a Caesarean section was condemned before being shown by Father T. J. Flynn, director of radio and TV for the Roman Catholic Archdiocese of New York. This episode, entitled *The Glorious Red Gallagher*, was withdrawn by NBC after protest. General Electric and Procter and Gamble cancelled their sponsorship of the series, and the Los Angeles County Medical Association withdrew its endorsement. In May of 1956, the *Times* reported that NBC had decided to take "Medic" off the air.[2]

During the 1950s, medicine was a growth industry, a science, a pioneering profession seeking to provide better health and longer life—an extremely serious business. The adversary was disease and/or ignorance. Thus, "Medic" had attempted to convey information on such subjects as alcoholism, civil defense, and birth in a taut and intense manner, without humorous relief. Moreover, because the American public had been conditioned by a tense international political atmosphere, and was thinking cold war and brinksmanship, it was prepared to respond in dead earnest even to such trivial television fare as the one-dimensional dramas of the western genre: "Black Saddle," "Wyatt Earp," "Wanted: Dead or Alive," and "Gunsmoke." No wonder that realistic medical episodes were viewed with intensity.

After the demise of "Medic," no immediate medical successor appeared. During the 1960s, however, the Kennedy presidency provided a backdrop for a different perspective on the healing arts. In 1961, "Dr. Kildare" and "Ben Casey" appeared and created two significant cultural heroes. Both shows seemed intent upon capturing the efficiency, alertness, and dedication of youth, through the performances of Richard Chamberlain as Kildare and Vincent Edwards as Casey. Yet, both series also included the tempering influence of elder statesmen in the profession, portrayed by Raymond Massey (Dr. Gillespie) and Sam Jaffe (Dr. Zorba). A central theme seems to have been the "passing of the torch." The reasoned caution and compromise of the older generation were contrasted with the idealism of young surgeons, anxious to try new methods or champion unpopular causes. The setting of a metropolitan hospital for "Dr.

Kildare" provided the necessary variety of cases, most requiring surgery, even though the show's producer, David Victor, admits that a surgeon is not really involved daily in the lives of patients.

Since both series survived for five years and became immensely popular and lucrative for advertisers, some comparisons are in order. I have noticed in many hours of viewing over these past several years that ABC seems to be characterized by a certain coarseness of production which contrasts dramatically with the smoothness of NBC. For some curious reason that same comparison applies to the two characters, Casey and Kildare.

ABC's Casey was jarring, aggressive, a believer in justice. He consistently expressed anger, at times violently, and he "made waves." His sense of justice transcended the protocol of his profession. He was impatient. He quite often drew a line between the hard, long, underpaid hours of the hospital staff and profitable private practice. And, even as he was teaching doctors, he felt that dedication to principle (an important attribute to the younger generation in 1963) could force one to forego the pleasures of the medical good life.

NBC's Dr. Kildare, in contrast to Ben Casey, was cultured and refined. His education showed. He was respectful of authority. There was just the touch of piety in his demeanor not present in the abrupt righteousness of Casey. Yet, like Casey, Kildare often found just causes more important than surgical techniques and he was willing to challenge authority for such causes. Casey was an established professional and, as such, the writers tended to treat him as a static character with no ambition for advancement. Kildare, on the other hand, went from first year intern to chief resident, and thus exhibited growth incorporated in the plot. When Kildare's progress led producer David Victor to attempt to move him into private practice, NBC was not interested, because the network wished to retain a hospital setting. According to Victor, Marcus Welby "takes up a Dr. Kildare figure in the later years."[3]

The two programs inaugurated the idea of a plot in search of a disease. While "Medic" had focused upon the discipline of medicine, Kildare and Casey dwelt upon its practice. These two doctors, caught up in predictable dramatic structure, were heroic as they combatted the evils of death and ignorance. Since the adversary was inevitably impersonal, the pristine reputation of the medical practitioner was in no danger of becoming tarnished. The doctor/surgeon achieved heroic status for his participation in human conflicts through his expertise in the profession of medicine. The viewer identified this expertise by the use in the dialogue of technical jargon, effective "medical music," and masked faces but knowing glances.

Little, if any, understanding about illness and health was imparted to the lay public. As far as medical ethics were concerned, these were normally reduced to simplistic issues such as whether to inform a terminal patient of his or her condition. Such issues as medical incompetence, excessive fees, medical school quotas, euthanasia, abortion, birth control, and death with dignity were seldom addressed; and when they were, it was with a gingerly touch. Moreover, these early medical shows did not enjoy the freedom of language that prevails today. A good example is an episode of "Ben Casey" concerning a patient who was impotent. The word "impotent" could not be used, however, and the patient only alluded to his condition by such phrases as "I am not a real man." Had the word "impotent" been allowable in 1963, the script would have diminished by half.

Despite these limitations, medical shows made earlier attempts than other types of shows, such as police and lawyer series, to deal with personal drama. The reason for this was probably that public interest in a weekly bout with disease was limited. The result was that Casey and Kildare also became counselors and distributors of justice. They directed attention to humanistic values. Right was defined as standing for a patient against the system, or fighting bureaucratic red tape. Dr. Zorba and Dr. Gillespie were reminders of a gentler age of medicine, but an age no less conspicuous for its human concerns. Since Kildare and Casey were almost devoid of professional errors, their positions became nearly invulnerable.

Reflecting on his work in "Dr. Kildare," producer David Victor says that he believes his television drama "made a definite impact on the image of medicine." Richard Levinson and William Link, the producers and writers who presently have responsibility for "Columbo" and "Ellery Queen," have a different view. They believe that "popular entertainment does not create social change," but rather reinforces already held attitudes. These two men wrote an early "Dr. Kildare" script condemning funeral practices, "but as to whether it helped even one individual avoid exploitation at a time of bereavement we couldn't say. . . .All we can realistically hope for is to touch people aesthetically every now and then, and possibly, over a period of years, add an infinitesimal something to the prevailing climate of opinion."[4]

While a discussion of this matter would consume a chapter in itself, as a professor in the humanities who taught throughout the sixties, I am inclined to agree with Victor's judgment. The quality of idealism and optimism which grasped such a large portion of college students during that period could easily be attracted by the likes of Casey and Kildare. It was not that doctors were seen as holy and incapable of error. Rather, their potential for human service and unselfish utilization of the tools of medicine made the two TV doctors believable, if not typical. Yet, in the bitter years of 1965 through 1968, such idealism melted under the white heat of Vietnam. Both series disappeared after 1966, and three years passed before there was renewal of medical shows.

In some ways "The Bold Ones" was an effort to recapture the optimism which characterized the beginning of the decade by seeking the elusive "relevance" so prized in that era. This 1969 anthology dealt alternately with a white cop and a black district attorney, three law partners, a crusading senator, and a group of doctors. The doctors' portion of "The Bold Ones" helped revive medicine on television and, in so doing, attempted to engage "substantive issues" objectively, while "not taking a shot at anybody."[5] It also made a greater effort than previous shows to inform the audience about diseases and medical problems being treated. David Hartman, as Dr. Hunter, became a kind of teacher, and he recently commented to me that the series undertook to "use television to educate and inform while entertaining." On the other hand, while humor had gained slight entry in "Ben Casey" and "Dr. Kildare," it now came into full flower in the exchanges between Drs. Hunter and Stewart, with a quite believable senior medical officer played by E. G. Marshall.

Unfortunately, this ambitious undertaking collapsed in 1972, but not before it set some high standards for its genre. As an example, a 1972 drama, *Quality of Fear*, humanely engaged the critical issue of psychological treatment for cancer patients. Only in the privacy of a home setting could such a drama have a substantial impact. No other entertainment forum offers the same ideal conditions leading to significant intimate response.

"Marcus Welby, M.D.," the second long-running and highly popular medical show produced by David Victor, is a significant departure from previous medical shows in that it examines the work of two family physicians, Welby and Kiley. Before casting, Welby was drawn as a middle-aged man. However, when Robert Young was signed to play the part, the hero evolved into a compassionate senior general practitioner who largely reflects the personality of the star. Welby is a doctor who cares, who visits in homes, who is involved in patients' lives. Victor admits that Welby is "fictionalized, over-sentimentalized," but he believes "there *are* some Welbys." Indeed, admittedly for a diminishing portion of Americans, there are still doctors who are concerned with medicine as a healing art rather than as a means to a high standard of living.

Because of the nature of any dramatic series on TV, medical shows often assume a plurality of functions for the hero that may tend to suggest invincibility or even deification. Certainly this was true in the cases of Dr. Casey and Dr. Kildare. And, commenting on a "Welby" episode, student Elizabeth Gay wrote: "The plot is a fantasy, where doctors have time to case the streets for a patient. Superhumans, they not only hold the talisman of medical knowledge but have untold powers of persuasion and marriage counseling. They are superhuman in their devotion to others, they are always right and always know it." There are many who feel this medical glorification has exceeded sound judgment.

In a highly critical article entitled "The Great American Swash-bucklers," Peter Schrag asserts that "the deification of Medicine goes right on," and "for all their demystification of doctors, the new TV medical shows fail utterly to convey the idea that real health depends on confidence in self-management and the ability to cope."[6] It may be true that TV has failed to convey this idea, but then it is proper to ask whether the idea is valid. It would appear that Schrag has under-estimated the depth of the prevailing, almost sacral character of medicine and healing which goes far beyond a simple and natural respect for a science that has helped to alleviate pain and suffering. From ancient times the medicine man has held a place of honor in society. Schrag's appeal to rationality alone overlooks the fact that, for most people today, medical science is still a very emotional and even mystic subject.

Yet medical shows are still basically vehicles for dramatic art—some good, some poor. They are part of the popular culture, utilizing the professions as artistic props. And the TV producer, because he lives in the realm of emotion as a script supervisor, usually desires to "deal with heroes not anti-heroes." His decision to have heroes de-termines the unrealistic, oversimplified issues and stereotypical characters often presented in these shows. Hopefully, as TV drama matures, other dimensions will find their way more often into new scripts.

The most moralistic TV doctor thus far has been Joe Gannon, the hero of "Medical Center," which was first aired in the same year as "Marcus Welby" and, like "Welby," is now in its sixth season. But, whereas Dr. Welby is a pragmatic traditionalist, Gannon is "hip." He is a modern matinee idol. Gannon is "cool." Teenagers, even younger children, make "Medical Center" a decided favorite in the Nielsen ratings.

Dr. Gannon champions causes in the name of openness. His is a "plea for tolerance of any deviation one can come up with"—for example, a friend who desires a transsexual operation. Actually, Gannon is a highly moral man who becomes angry when injustice appears in the plot. But his moral judgments are based on his acceptance of people as individuals and he resents those who seek to impose their own definitions on others.

Nevertheless, there are times when Gannon reveals that he has strong, predetermined attitudes about right and wrong, and, though he is less traditional than his rival, Dr. Welby, he is more doctrinaire. In an episode entitled *Aftershock*, Gannon remains committed to an absolute "pro-life" perspective and refuses to allow a terminal patient to die, even though the oxygen used by the dying man might deprive at least four healthy persons of the chance to survive. Gannon refuses, in his own words, to "play God." In some instances, Dr. Gannon seems to feel that it is murder not to employ every available means of life support. The notion that God decides upon the time of death is subtly woven into several scripts. Yet the fact that without modern technology and medicines, death would have occurred months or years earlier is apparently ignored. Gannon's perspective is not necessarily right, but proponents of alternate positions, such as "death with dignity," must still take his particular set of values into consideration.

In the 1969 episode *A Life In Waiting*, Gannon addresses the issue of abortion and expresses a profound belief in the "value of life." He moralizes heavily upon this theme as it relates to the unborn fetus and indicates that his students would laugh at his ideas. Yet, by the seventies, Gannon could champion the cause of a girl who wanted an abortion even when her parents were opposed to the idea. Obviously, a successful series must recognize cultural shifts and the need for change.[7]

In his capacity as producer for "Medical Center," Frank Glicksman looks for "subjects that are important, that have something to say." Now, after over 160 episodes of "Medical Center," he and his associate Don Brinkley feel that they are able to expose more of what is going on in the culture because America's youth are bringing more subjects to the surface. Special interest groups insist on being heard and, interestingly, Brinkley believes that pressure groups have forced the networks to deal with issues they would have previously buried under the rug.[8] As we noted with "Medic," pressure can operate both ways. However, the security against one point of view becoming dominant is the collaborative nature of the industry itself with its internal checks which tend to exclude excesses.

If the two current giants of the medical genre, "Marcus Welby, M.D." and "Medical Center," have a major common flaw, it may have to do with the neat, elegant, traditional, middle-class settings both present. If patients are from other than white middle- or upper-class environments their presence seems to require explanation. However, because the university setting of "Medical Center" is clearly upper middle-class, the clientele is certainly realistic. The same is true of Marcus Welby's practice. Perhaps Richard Levinson is right when he says that the "people who make TV only know upper-middle-class."

Women in these medical series are also represented in stereotyped ways. A recent content analysis of fifteen select shows found, at least in that limited sample, an overwhelming predominance of white male doctors and young white female nurses.[9] "Marcus Welby," for example, presents a rather traditional perspective on women. David Victor justifies this omission by pointing out that there was "no function for a wife in the series." Male dominance is presumed, reinforced by the receptionist Consuelo Lopez who carries the freight for the minority ethnic group while performing the "proper" womanly functions as a protective, emotional, and efficient employee. The current season has provided marriage for Dr. Kiley, a giant leap for TV physicians, but it has had little practical effect upon the plots.

The male dominance of the "Welby" program is gentle and paternalistic, but nevertheless, it is a clear-cut affirmation of the primary role of men in medicine. This is not to say that "Welby" is unusual in its treatment of women. Certainly, neither "Welby" nor "Medical Center" provide adequate professional models for women and girls who watch these shows. Even on the occasions when women are presented as full-fledged doctors, they have their special place.

In one memorable episode of "Ben Casey," Maggie, the female doctor, was portrayed as learning her place as a woman through counseling a patient:[10]

Female Patient: What can I do to help my husband?
Maggie: Let him [husband] make the decisions. Let him decide who your friends are.
Female Patient: That will change my whole way of life.
Maggie: Isn't that what getting married means?

Casey to Maggie concerning a date: What do you want to do?
Maggie: I'm not going to make that mistake. I'll do what you want to do.
Male doctor colleague: Who says doctors don't learn from their patients?

And it should also be noted that this treatment of women is not confined to television's medical programs. Women have little more than traditional roles on police and detective series. Angie Dickinson may be the star of "Police Woman," but she is essentially a weekly setup for male entrapment, a traditional female part. McMillan's wife is largely decorative; Columbo has an invisible but vocal Italian stereotype for a wife; Petrocelli's wife is a secretary. Most recently, "The Bionic Woman" has appeared as a "coequal" to "The Six Million Dollar Man," but she chooses to spend her time between adventures as—a schoolteacher!

At the same time, it is important to remember that this representation of women is a realistic one that does reflect things as they presently are. At a recent dental board hearing in Virginia (the entire State Board was male), a presentation in support of a controversial dental assistance program, nationally funded by the Department of Health, Education, and Welfare, included a slide presentation from HEW. The slides represented all dentists now and for the future as men, while most of the proposed dental assistants were women. Even HEW, when it is not thinking "women's rights," falls into long-held presumptions. In fact, Marcus Welby is more enlightened on this subject than many actual physicians seem to be. Though he resides in a traditional, picket fence world, he is a liberated man, accepting the new growth of independence and freedom for all persons.

But, does any of this really make any difference? Don't most people watch TV for entertainment and relaxation? Probably the answer is affirmative. Yet, as we are entertained, our minds do function. The reinforcement of values and principles in long-running shows surely must have impact. On this point, social scientists, network executives, writers, advertisers, producers, and humanists generally agree. Gannon and Welby, Casey and Kildare have reinforced some highly traditional values: honesty, trust, justice, freedom, tolerance, equality, education, family, hard work, discipline. Producer Richard Levinson, who would demur on any claim of permanent influence, does contend that conventional liberal attitudes have dominated television for the past fifteen years. Critic Michael Novak concurs: "We are lucky that the social class responsible for the creative side of television is not a reactionary and frankly illiberal class."[11] TV programs seem to conserve historically recognized, western ethical value structures within the context of "conventional" liberalism. For the present, given the oligopolistic capitalism in the three networks, and given our diverse political and religious affiliations, this may be a healthy compromise.

Of all the "values" considered by the medical programs, the question of trust may prove the most unsettling as it is portrayed in patient-doctor relationships. Patients are seldom represented as thinking rationally about their diseases. ("The Bold Ones" is an exception.) Instead, patients show irrational fear, misunderstanding, and resentment. No answer is provided to the question of how one may be assured that a particular doctor is worthy of trust. Pennsylvania Insurance Commissioner William Sheppard blamed " 'Marcus Welby' for causing the public to expect much more of doctors," and he claimed "the series might be one reason for an increase in malpractice suits."[12] Of course, being human, doctors do not measure up to their TV models, and the most recent forays into medical drama have attempted to cope with that matter.

NBC observed the marked success of its two competitors in the medical program field and decided to make two new entries into the 1975 ratings war. By the end of November, both "Medical Story" and "Doctors Hospital" were casualties of Nielsen. Despite critical acclaim, the former lost its place in the schedule.

In its first showing, NBC's "Medical Story" made a serious attempt to deal with malpractice and incompetence in the profession. In this episode, Dr. Ducker, an intern, struggles to prevent an operation by an established surgeon. He fails, as is illustrated in the following dialogue with the Chief Surgeon of Ducker's division in the hospital, a respected physician on the executive board:

Ducker: They are operating on Donnelly in the morning. (He explains the risks.)

Chief: What has this to do with me, Ducker?

Ducker: I'm going to ask you to put a call in to the Board.

Chief: It's not my case.

Ducker: But you verified my findings. I want you to call the Board.

Chief: You want me to call the Board or are you ordering me to?

Ducker: I'm sorry, sir. I don't know who to go to.

Chief: We can't have doctors interfering in other people's cases. It will cause chaos.

Ducker: I told you the symptoms, I told you what he [the surgeon] was doing. Are you saying you don't want to interfere because it would be bad form?

Chief: How do I know Dr. Nolan isn't right?

Ducker: I see. Yea! We are all members of the same club. There are certain things that we don't do even if a person's life is at stake.

Chief: I think you better go.

As it turns out, the operation does prove to be a mistake. The patient dies and the hospital Board has to admit that Dr. Nolan was wrong and Ducker was right. There follows a closing scene:

Chief: The Board is not going to renew your contract. It would cause too many tensions. . . .We are going to give you letters of recommendation. . . .This is an organization like anything else. Some things have to be sacrificed for larger things.

Ducker: What if I go to the papers? . . .the accrediting committee?

Chief: I wouldn't do that. You need your letters of recommendation. You'll find there is a tendency

> to close ranks within the medical profession. If
> you haven't learned anything else from this
> episode you should have learned that.
>
> Ducker: I learned that.
> Chief: . . .you can't win.
> Ducker: All right I'm fired, but I'm still going to be a
>   doctor. . .

This anthology continued to investigate, on a weekly basis, such issues as the meaning of death with dignity, the use of patients as objects of experimentation, abortion, industrial poisoning, malpractice, and sterilization. There were still heroes, but they did not necessarily find success within the system. It was ironic to see Vincent Edwards (playing a new doctor, but with his old Ben Casey posture still unchanged) handcuffed by police and taken into custody for performing an alleged illegal abortion. This episode ends with the surgeon in question saying he will leave the matter in the hands of the court. And, venturing even further into the uncharted television territory, this episode portrays a priest as a "heavy." The words of Cleveland Amory seem appropriate: "Imagine a doctor show without a pat or a happy ending. We tell you it's a medical millenium."[13] Well, not exactly. The program was not popular and "Medical Story" fell to sixtieth place by late October. Despite brave predictions from NBC executives, economics dictated cancellation.

"Doctors Hospital" was more traditional than "Medical Story," but it suffered the same fate. George Peppard as a neurosurgeon reminded us of "Ben Casey." Yet there was an update. Like "Medical Story," this series gave sympathetic treatment to the role of women in medicine. There were flirtations with serious professional issues. In one particular episode, a woman surgeon is faced with the ultimate questions of life that finally tear at the presumption of medical diety. Then, out of a plethora of philosophizing reminiscent of Ecclesiastes, there emerges an essentially nontheistic humanism: "All there is is life and all that you can do is celebrate it."

The answer to why "Welby" and "Medical Center" survived, while two new competing efforts have failed, is not easily discovered. Familiarity certainly played a part. Competition in the allotted time slots is also an important consideration. However, I am inclined to believe that the TV medical show is historically in a distinct category. At no time since 1950 have more than three medical programs been simultaneously and successfully sustained. Yet the success which the industry has found in spin-offs and copies of other types of shows may have led executives and producers to expect the same principles to apply in the medical shows. I doubt that they do.

It is probable that the public reaches a saturation point in this area very quickly. For one thing, there is a strong viewer identification with the principal doctor characters of medical shows. Many supporters of one series tend to ignore other series. Part of the reason for this phenomenon may be that few of us consistently has more than one or two doctors attending us. Moreover, healing is an art with which we have frequent contact. Hospital visits are as common for most of us as prison and police station visits are rare. This surfeit of medicine in our personal lives may cause us to reject too much medicine on TV.

Also, another important reason for the failure of such a series as "Medical Story" may be that the public simply does not wish to have its trust in doctors challenged so directly. Viewers still seem more satisfied with medical shows which present familiar perspectives in health care and which tend to reinforce the already positive image of the doctor in society. The public's medical hero is a model of integrity, good citizenship, professionalism, and human kindness. And, on top of all these virtues, he is a believer in the ethic of hard work.

Medical shows which promote such super-doctors might easily convince one that the field of medicine is almost totally populated with professionals whose only commitment is to service. The economic rewards of the profession are not questioned, and one would scarcely guess that there are vast numbers of citizens living in poverty and discovering that their level of existence does not entitle them to receive the medical services which their TV sets promise them.

However distorted this altogether positive image of medical professionals as a whole may be, it is easy to understand that it is an accurate reflection of society's *desires*. People still want to believe in their doctors. The vast majority of seriously ill patients still want to believe that, "if there is a cure," then their doctor will find the surgeons or other specialists to attack the disease. Because the ultimate concerns of these medical shows—the mysteries of life, sickness, and death—are profound, attitudes about them change slowly, and the history of the genre suggests that successful programs cannot differ greatly from the prevailing attitudes and beliefs of their audience.

Yet a few successful shows *have* given attention to the critical issues of medical ethics—malpractice, euthanasia, genetics, fee structures, hospital costs. During its brief tenure, "Medical Story" opened many of these issues for viewing and challenged the mythic image of doctors. For instance, "Medical Story" raised the suspicion that one's doctor might not know "the cure" and that, if he did, his personal character could affect the outcome of the case as significantly as the procedure he chose to use. Despite the fact that "Medical Story" met an untimely death, its presence on NBC for almost four months points to a qualitative leap in the treatment of medical drama.

Of course, the medical dramas intend to entertain, and it is within this frame of reference that discussion of impact must occur. But current medical dramas also show every intention of including moral and ethical comment as well—a motive which is certainly not antithetical to good entertainment. Although traditionalism remains a strong element in most medical series, there *are* messages being delivered. There are also challenges to modern medical practices, and a few more realistic medical models. This continuing struggle over humanistic values portrayed on the tube may have a salutary effect on viewers, and some producers in the television industry believe that there are still ways to develop greater maturity in TV medicine.

That there is a connection between television's medical shows and societal conditions seems clear. However, which has the greater influence on the other is less clear. Are we being conditioned, or are we merely viewing reflections of ourselves and our culture on TV? Probably there is some of both. Yet the public is showing increased interest in the issues of medical science, as the Quinlan euthanasia controversy verifies. And if it is true, as recent disclosures in nationally published inquiries suggest, that five percent of practicing physicians are incompetent,[14] then the possibility that doctor shows are causing more malpractice suits may be an encouraging sign. Hopefully, greater expectations will produce more responsible doctors. In any case, whether they are a cause or effect in society, television's medical shows are a unique and significant forum for public consideration of questions which literally are matters of life and death.

Chronology of Primetime Medical Programs

Medic Ben Casey					
Dr. Kildare The Bold Ones					
Marcus Welby, M.D.** Medical Center*					
Medical Story** Doctors' Hospital**					

1954 '55 '56 '57 '58 '59 '60 '61 '62 '63 '64 '65 '66 '67 '68 '69 '70 '71 '72 '73 '74 '75

* Continuing Shows
** Cancelled Shows

Footnotes

1. *New York Times*, September 15, 1954, 48:3.

2. *New York Times*, May 25, 1956, 47:5.

3. I wish to thank David Victor for an interview in July of 1975 and other assistance rendered by Norman Fox.

4. I express appreciation to Richard Levinson and William Link for a lengthy interview held in July, 1975. Quotations are from that session and from other materials supplied by them.

5. David Hartman kindly submitted to two interviews, July and December, 1975. He also made available a most useful tape and arranged several meetings for me while I was in Los Angeles.

6. Peter Schrag. "The Great American Swashbucklers," *More*, November, 1975.

7. By contrast, in a 1972 episode on abortion, Dr. Welby approaches this issue neither moralistically nor legalistically. For the pragmatic Marcus Welby, the welfare of his patient and her psychological state determines his decision. He can express respect for the attitudes of the girl's parents, while deploring "parental tyranny."

8. The help extended by Frank Glicksman has been useful and much appreciated. He and Don Brinkley spent the better part of one afternoon in July, 1975, discussing with me their work. In addition, I have received numerous "Medical Center" scripts for information purposes.

9. James M. McLaughlin. "Characteristics and Symbolic Functions of Fictional Televised Medical Professionals and Their Effect on Children," unpublished M.A. dissertation, The Annenberg School of Communications, The University of Pennsylvania, 1975, p. 10. (This research did not include the most recent programs, "Medical Center" and "Doctors Hospital.")

10. All dialogue contained in this essay was taken from programs at the time of airing.

11. Michael Novak. "Television Shapes the Soul," *Television as a Social Force: New Approaches to TV Criticism*, Praeger Publishers, N.Y., 1975, p. 21.

12. McLaughlin, *op. cit.*, p. 36.

13. Cleveland Amory. "Review," *TV Guide*, Vol. 23, No. 44, November 1, 1975, p. 20.

14. *New York Times*, January 26, 1976, 1:1.

Fact or Fiction—
Television Docudramas

Bill Davidson

I have long since reformed, but I began my career in journalism as a writer of lies for a sportscaster named Bill Stern, who, in renown at least, was the Howard Cosell of his day. Every week, another writer and I—on Stern's direction—would unabashedly make up so-called true sports stories, mostly about historical characters who were dead and could not protest. One of my classics was about Abraham Lincoln, who, having been assassinated at Ford's Theater in Washington, regained consciousness just long enough to say to Secretary of War Stanton, "Tell General Abner Doubleday not to let baseball die." After that whopper, NBC ordered Stern to label his dramatizations "sports *legends*," but his weekly radio show continued to prosper.

Now, with the age of "docudrama," "actuality drama," or whatever it may be called, the broadcasting industry seems to have come full cycle. There it was again, the word "legend," as in "The Legend of Valentino" on ABC-TV last fall. Rudolph Valentino was introduced as a starving house burglar (actually he began as a fairly successful hustler and movie bit player); his benefactress, June

Mathis, was portrayed as a beautiful minor writer who went back to obscurity in Brooklyn to suffer her unrequited love for Valentino (actually she was fat and ugly, one of the most powerful screenwriters in the history of the movies, and much more influential than Valentino); etc., etc., etc.

But ABC at least had the good grace and honesty to label its Valentino picture "a romantic fiction." The problem is that too many other blockbuster network docudramas *also* are tainted with romantic fiction, but, just as with Bill Stern's tall tales, they are presented to the public as essentially true stories.

Last November, for example, NBC gave us "Eric," about a real-life young man who died after a courageous struggle against leukemia. The two-hour film began with the flat-out statement that "this is a true story," yet the boy's name was changed, the locale of his battle for life was transposed from Connecticut and New York to the State of Washington, chronology was altered, the unpleasant but most inspiring facts of Eric's ordeal were excised, his athletic prowess as a soccer player was blatantly exaggerated in a scene just before his death, and—most inexcusable of all—there was a tender love story between Eric and a nurse named Mary Lou, which according to the boy's mother, Doris Lund, didn't happen as it was portrayed.

Earlier came "I Will Fight No More Forever" on ABC, which at first viewing seemed to be a noble, historically accurate look at the persecution of Chief Joseph and the Nez Percé Indians by the U.S. Army in the late 1870s. The show's sponsor, the Xerox Corporation, even sent out printed classroom guides for use by schoolchildren throughout the country. But then the historians were heard from. They complained that not only were there incorrect juxtapositions of time and place in the docudrama, but that even attitudes and recorded events had been distorted. For one thing, Chief Joseph's pursuer, General Oliver O. Howard, was shown as a liberal in his thinking toward Indians; but actually, at the time of the events depicted, he was one of the Army's hardliners, dedicated to the use of all means to defeat the Nez Percé. Another typical historian's complaint: the show opened with the murder of an Indian by a white settler, who later was killed in an act of vengeance by the Indian's son. Historically, a Nez Percé Indian *was* murdered, but his son's revenge was exacted not on the actual malefactor but on 19 other innocent settlers in the area.

How about "Babe" on CBS, the "true story" of the great woman athlete Babe Didrikson and her valiant losing fight against cancer with the help of her wrestler husband, George Zaharias? As CBS vice president Steve Mills told me, "We frankly set out to make this a warm, idyllic, unusual love story, from the facts as supplied by Zaharias himself. I guess he can't be blamed for remembering only the good things of the marriage." Unfortunately, too many sportswriters were witness to the frequent storminess of the Didrikson-Zaharias relationship and they complained, in effect, that Hollywood had made a sugar-coated Disneyized version of what essentially was an "All in the Family" conflict, with tragic overtones.

Similar accusations of truth-bending have been leveled against nearly all of this season's docudramas, among them "The Silence," "Fear on Trial," "Foster and Laurie," "The Deadly Tower," "Collision Course," and "Guilty or Innocent: The Sam Sheppard Murder Case." Swipes have been taken in advance at "Helter Skelter" (the dramatization of Vincent Bugliosi's book about the Charles Manson murders) and "Return to Earth" (the story of astronaut Buzz Aldrin's emotional breakdown after walking on the moon) and "Farewell to Manzanar" (a personal reminiscence of our controversial concentration camps for Japanese-American citizens during World War II).

Does this mean that the docudrama is more drama than docu? Probably yes.

Are facts sometimes distorted to make a better story? Probably yes.

Is the American public deliberately being misled by representations that these films are in fact true stories? Probably yes.

My answers to all three questions are qualified because there are some extenuating circumstances in what is an ages-old conflict between hard fact and dramatic license in all forms of theater, dating back to William Shakespeare and beyond. There are no better illustrations of this problem than the two most challenged docudramas of the season: "Fear on Trial" and "Guilty or Innocent: The Sam Sheppard Murder Case," which, incidentally, has the highest Nielsen rating of any TV movie so far this season.

"Fear on Trial," you will recall, was CBS's *mea culpa* about how it contributed to the anti-communist blacklisting of radio-TV personality John Henry Faulk in 1956, and his long court fight for vindication. The show, though generally praised, has been accused of selective condensation to the point where important CBS witnesses against Faulk (and on the side of the blacklisters) were eliminated. Also, there has been considerable criticism of the not-quite-accurate handling, in the docudrama, of Faulk's estranged wife, who drops out of sight midway through the script, whereas she was in fact in the courtroom for at least part of the trial.

David Rintels is the writer of "Fear on Trial." He also is the respected president of the Writers Guild West. Rintels told me, "It's been a bitter, galling experience for me to be accused of falsifying facts. I had to tell a story condensing six or seven years into a little less than two hours, which means I could just barely hit the major highlights. I did what I think all writers should do—present the *essence* of the facts and capture the truth of the general story. As it was, CBS didn't come out looking too good, even though I couldn't include all the details. Attorney Louis Nizer's summation to the jury took more than 12 hours. I had to do it in three minutes.

"As for Faulk's wife, the divorce was so messy that I made the judgment call that it would be better to eliminate her from the latter stages of the story, rather than dredge up painful problems for a lot of people. I stuck to the record, except in intimate scenes for which there was no record—and that's what writers are paid to do. I'll go to my grave believing I dealt honestly with the overall facts."

The defenders of NBC's Sam Sheppard docudrama also claimed the right to winnow out the truth as they saw it, in the interests of necessarily compressed storytelling. The main beef against the film was that it overexaggerated newsmen's outrageous behavior in the courtroom *during* the trial, whereas the U.S. Supreme Court's landmark Sheppard decision had also cited "massive pretrial publicity" as an important factor bearing on the inability of the defendant to get a fair trial.

To Louis Rudolph (who wrote the story and developed the project), it made more sense dramatically to play up visible courtroom disturbances by the press rather than concentrating on the difficult-to-photograph pretrial transgressions by late columnist Bob Considine and others. "It all amounts to the same thing," he told me, "and every word we used in the disturbance sequences came out of the transcript of the trial." He admitted some exaggeration for dramatic effect, and executive producer Harve Bennett added, "We *did* select only certain scenes from the transcript for emphasis—but they were all true."

The truth. There indeed are varying versions of it, as writer Ernest Kinoy found when he wrote the script of ABC's "Collision Course," in which Henry Fonda plays Douglas MacArthur and E. G. Marshall is a credible Harry Truman. Kinoy says he faithfully followed both the MacArthur and Truman memoirs in depicting the events before and after the fateful meeting of the General and the President on Wake Island at the height of the Korean War. "But then," said Kinoy before the program was telecast, "I was faced with the meeting itself, which took place inside a Quonset hut on the island with absolutely no one else present, not even a military secretary. I made up that intrinsic key scene, based on what I knew had happened afterwards when Truman fired MacArthur. The Truman partisans have one idea of the truth of that meeting in the Quonset hut and the MacArthur admirers have their version—so undoubtedly I'll be slammed by both." He was, and apparently with good reason, because the version of the meeting that Truman developed later strayed a good distance from the facts.

John Henry Faulk loved "Fear on Trial." After all, it was his version of what had happened. Astronaut Edwin (Buzz) Aldrin isn't quite so sure about ABC's interpretation of his inability to cope with life after leaving the space program, even though the film "Return to Earth" is a dramatization of his own book and he served as consultant to the TV project. (The movie has not yet been shown on TV.) Aldrin said, "On the whole, I'm satisfied with the picture, but condensation sometimes alters the truth. For example, you're left at the end thinking I'm still a mixed-up guy emotionally, when by now I'm actually recovered and coping quite well. Also, there's a romantic scene at the end in which I'm walking down a beach hand in hand with my ex-wife. It never happened that way. I'd already told her I wanted a divorce and was going to marry someone else."

Brandon Stoddard, vice president in charge of TV movies at ABC, has his own version of the facts in the Aldrin docudrama. He told me, "In normal film structure, we'd show a man slowly falling apart, destroying his family, but fighting back and recovering. But we didn't do it that way because it didn't happen that way at that time. Aldrin then was a man suffering deep depression and I felt we *had* to show a depressive as he actually is. It doesn't help the film but it is accurate."

Of all the docudrama experts I spoke with, Stoddard made the most sense. He frankly admitted that his network does "actuality" movies because they're easier to sell to a potential audience during pre-broadcast promotion "if there are actual names and events that are familiar to people to begin with." He said, "We should not be held to the absolute truth of pure documentaries, because we're in the business of making *movies,* and audiences watch movies to be moved, to get involved with characters who live and breathe and whom you like and don't like. I'm not a reporter. If it's pure documentary you're looking for, the news department does it better. Docudramas get much higher ratings. I consider them to be historical fiction as opposed to history—and historical fiction always far outsells history at the bookstores."

Stoddard added, "On the other hand, we are very aware of the terrible danger and responsibility involved in doing our kind of historical fiction. By using dramatic license, we can take a point of view that could affect the attitudes of millions of people. For example, we have '21 Hours at Munich' in development. It's about the massacre of the Israeli athletes by Arab terrorists at the 1972 Olympics. Since we have to tell at least part of the story from the point of view of one of the Arabs, we can't create sympathy for him. We *must* get the message across that with acts of terrorism, no one wins in the end. I'm not sure it will work, and if it doesn't, we'll yank it as a docudrama."

The problem is that, given the success of the docudramas, no one in the industry is ready yet to openly label their product "historical fiction"—except possibly in the rare case of a "Legend of Valentino," in which the truth was *so* distorted that to do otherwise would have been ridiculous. Thus, CBS's "Helter Skelter" (an upcoming film about the Charles Manson murders) begins with actor George DiCenzo saying, "You are about to see a dramatization of actual facts in which certain names have been changed. But the story is true." The story is *not* all true. At the very least, because of pending lawsuits, certain fictional adjustments had to be made.

What with possible docudramas coming up on Senator Joseph McCarthy, the Attica prison riots and Martin Luther King, Jr., television experts in the academic community are justifiably disturbed. One such expert is psychologist Dr. Victor B. Cline of the University of Utah, who pioneered in studies of the effect of TV violence on children. Dr. Cline told me, "The very real danger of these docudrama films is that people take it for granted that they're true and—unlike similar fictionalized history in movies and the theater—they are seen on a medium which also presents straight news. No matter how much they call these movies 'drama,' they're really advocacy journalism. They can't help reflecting the point of view of the writer or the studio or the network. I think they should carry a disclaimer to the effect that the story is not totally true but based on some of the *elements* of what actually occurred."

But, as we learned from Orson Welles' panicking the country with his radio version of "War of the Worlds" in 1938 (and recently done in semifictional docudrama form on ABC-TV), even that won't prevent people from believing what they see on television.

An Englishman's Castle— The State of the Art

David Chamberlin

In any discussion of the television medium, and particularly of television programming, there is inevitably the question of whether the medium can produce narrative works that attain the level of art. Indeed, there are many who think that "television aesthetics" is a contradiction in terms. Film, too, was once dismissed as mere popular entertainment, but who now would dispute the artistry of such films as *Citizen Kane, The Rules of the Game,* or *8½?* Ultimately, I believe, selected works from the television medium will also come to be recognized as art, and the three-part BBC drama *An Englishman's Castle* may well be among those works.

Before I begin to discuss *An Englishman's Castle*—and to demonstrate the state of television art—I should identify my criteria for successful works of narrative art:

First, such works manage to balance conflicting emotional responses rather than relying entirely on a simple pattern of good vs. bad, hero vs. villain, "us" vs. "them."

Second, these works become more rewarding with repeated exposure, mostly because we as an audience see or feel increasing symbolism in the characters and images.

Third, these works utilize the specific properties of their medium. (This is why none of the greatest novels have produced great films; and conversely, why most of the greatest films, like the three mentioned above, were conceived originally for the medium of film.)

An Englishman's Castle was written for television by Philip Mackie, who is also responsible for the much acclaimed television adaptation of Quentin Crisp's autobiography, *The Naked Civil Servant*. Originally shown in England in 1978 as a mini-series of three one-hour segments, *An Englishman's Castle* is a difficult work to classify. In a recent public television showing it was announced as a "BBC suspense drama," and the script certainly provides enough twists and turns to justify that label. But the drama also goes beyond the plot level to show a medium commenting upon itself, examining the role of television in the lives of both the people who create for the medium and the mass audience who view it.

The central character is Peter Ingram, the writer and producer of a soapy BBC series called "An Englishman's Castle."* Shown Monday through Friday at 7:30, the series follows the lives of a typical middle-class English family during World War II. The series is in its third year and is the most popular show on British television. The author, Peter Ingram, has reaped the rewards of success: a luxurious home, a sleek new car, membership in an exclusive social club, and a succession of extramarital affairs—the latest with the beautiful young heroine of his series. At age 58, Peter is obviously pleased by what he has achieved and is happily absorbed in the demanding daily routine

---

*A problem of terminology is created by the fact that "An Englishman's Castle" is the title of both the television drama I am discussing and a daily television series which is being written, produced, or performed by the central characters in the drama. In order to clear up the confusion, I have chosen to italicize the title of the drama and to use quotation marks for the series. I have also used the terms *drama* and *series* throughout as in the preceding two sentences. The term *story* always refers to the plot and actions in the drama.

of writing and production. His comfortable home life includes a devoted and undemanding wife and two bright and handsome sons in their twenties.

The first major surprise in the drama is the political situation. After several minutes, the viewer becomes aware that the England in which Peter Ingram lives is under German rule. The premise is that Hitler had avoided the mistake of breaking his 1939 nonaggression pact with Stalin and that, instead of invading Russia, he had concentrated on the western front, invading and conquering England. Following the conquest, Hitler had set up a puppet regime on the model of Vichy France. Churchill had been unwilling to play the role of Marshal Pétain and was executed on "Black Friday," after which a general amnesty was declared and most remaining resistance fighters returned from the hills of Scotland and Wales. All Jews and "colored races" have been systematically exterminated. The United States "has so completely turned its face toward Asia" that it is ruled out as a market for Peter's series. After a violent uprising in 1947, the occupied British nation has remained relatively stable and is in fact prospering economically in the 1970s. However, a shadowy anti-fascist underground is becoming increasingly active and is preparing for a new uprising, which they hope will launch a revolution.

The political situation gives the lie to both the title and the standard opening image (a fortress-like English castle) of Peter Ingram's series. In the England of Peter Ingram, a man's home is definitely not his castle, as Peter discovers anew when the Special Police invade and search his home and arrest his son Mark. In similar fashion, the progression of the drama continues to draw back the camera focused on Peter's "ordinary" life in order to reveal the larger framework of societal oppression. As viewers, we are made to share the characters' increasingly claustrophobic sense of being caught between the unseen German authority on the one side and the terrorist freedom fighters on the other.

Peter's series, a sentimental depiction of "the Worth family" living through the German conquest in the summer of 1940, is welcomed by the German authorities as a valuable pacifier for the mass audience. Ingram has captured the pulse of the nation by glorifying British heroism during the war, while at the same time subtly stressing the futility of resistance in the present, the need to accept the inevitable and "get on with the business of living."

The series is based on Peter's own life, which has been a perfect model for this attitude. Peter splits himself into the Worths' two sons, Frank and Bert, who represent respectively the heroic and rational sides of his character. (This split is reflected in Peter's own two sons: Mark is a terrorist, hotheaded and idealistic; Henry is an aspiring TV director, ambitious, cerebral, and "lacking heart," in Peter's own words.) Frank, Peter's "idealistic self," is killed in the war, while Bert escapes the draft through bad eyesight. Sally, based on Peter's wife, breaks her engagement with Bert in favor of the heroic Frank. After Frank's death, Bert is inspired to join the resistance, which is as far as we follow the story. Mr. and Mrs. Worth are pleasant stoical British stereotypes, serving tea in the middle of Sally's traumatic switch of allegiance from Bert to Frank.

As this synopsis of the series suggests, the newscaster who calls Ingram's stuff "terrible crap" is not entirely unfair. Ingram's son Mark actively despises the series, and even Peter's mistress Jill, who plays Sally in the series, tells him that the only justification for a series like his is to give steady employment to those actors and technicians who are breadwinners.

The dutiful and efficient director of the series refers routinely and without sarcasm to the "moral" in each episode: Mrs. Worth's "patch it up, like the French are doing"; Mr. Worth extolling survival after having experienced World War I and the Depression; one of Frank's fellow soldiers refusing to fight tanks with rifles (i.e., don't wage a hopeless struggle); and a weary resistance fighter who quotes Dr. Johnson's assertion, "Sir, it does not matter a half guinea to the average individual what form of government he lives under."

The moral of the drama *An Englishman's Castle,* and the basis of its suspense, is quite different. It is stated in the opening scene by Harmer, the BBC Program Controller (meaning censor), as he and Peter discuss an episode of the series that they (and we) have just been watching. Harmer has guessed that the seemingly cowardly Bert will turn out to be a hero, and he explains, "People are never quite what they appear to be—the opposite is always closer to the truth."

Contradictions between appearance and reality keep coming up throughout the drama: Jill, who in her role as Sally is a convincingly all-English ingenue, turns out to be Jewish and a member of the underground. She has been assigned by the underground to recruit Peter, whose task will be to insert the signal phrase for the uprising, "Britons strike home," into one of his scripts for "An Englishman's Castle." The actor playing Frank, whose manly appearance matches his role perfectly on and off the set, ends up throwing a tantrum when he learns that Frank will be killed off in the story. The actor playing Bert, who always looks mousey, even when seen as a resistance fighter in the series, turns out also to be a member of the underground. (We learn this when, during a rehearsal for the series, a brief reaction shot shows him recognizing the signal phrase for the uprising. It is a powerful shot which succeeds in reversing an image built up for almost the entire three-part drama.)

The most deceptive character, however, is Harmer himself. As Program Controller, Harmer constantly preaches cooperation with the German authorities. He calls the British surrender "a victory—for common sense." He tells a newscaster to play down a reshuffling of the German government, as if it won't affect England much, though they both know it will mean a tougher policy toward dissidents. He is always poised and impeccably dressed, adding to the calculated tone of most of his lines. He is an authority figure and a manipulator (he keeps Peter waiting each time they have a meeting, and he often stands while Peter is sitting, emphasizing his height). Even his name seems deliberately chosen. Yet Harmer also turns out to be a member of the underground—and a hero in the story.

The character of Harmer and his role in the plot remind us that the social setting of *An Englishman's Castle* is a special one—that of a subject nation. The parallel to the Vichy government in France is important, partly because it includes the theme of broadcasting's role in a repressive society. One of the most pervasive facts of everyday life in Vichy France was the radio, constantly urging support for the "New Alliance" with Germany, broadcasting frequent speeches by Marshal Pétain, whose prestige in France in 1940 approached that of Eisenhower in the United States in 1950.

In the British Vichy of the drama, television represents an even more powerful means of encouraging public acceptance of the status quo. "An Englishman's Castle" is effective specifically because it uses the characteristic format of the medium—the serial—to reinforce the social values of a Nazi-occupied Britain. The compromised entertainment Peter creates with the series might be called "bourgeois propaganda." Indeed, Peter quotes Lenin as saying, "England is the only country in the world not only with a bourgeois aristocracy, but also a bourgeois proletariat." "An Englishman's Castle" domesticates ideology by placing it in the same living room setting inhabited by its viewers.

The power of television is the one topic on which all the major characters agree. Mark Ingram is angered enough by "An Englishman's Castle" to hate his father solely on account of it. Harmer gets

Mark away from the Special Police by threatening to do a television program on them. Jill is contemptuous of "An Englishman's Castle" for preaching submission; but once she has fully enlisted Peter into the underground, she starts echoing Harmer in urging him not to glorify the resistance. The series must be kept on the air in order to launch the uprising effectively.

The interpretive power of the medium is demonstrated throughout the story by the glimpses we get of the various stages of production of "An Englishman's Castle." Each of the drama's three hour-long segments begins in a control room with a shot of the series director and his two assistants counting down to the final taping session of an episode of "An Englishman's Castle." They are watching a panel of at least ten television screens which show different shots of the action (and which remind us of the selection and arrangement that shape the way television viewers will perceive the action). We then zoom into the central monitor screen to watch the episode, including the opening credits.

Each of these series episodes starts with the exterior shot of a castle, accompanied by a Handellian overture, then moves into the Worths' living room, where we see the captions June, July, and August 1940. Because the drama is structured in this way, each of its one-hour segments can be viewed as an ironic comment on the series episode that begins it. The progression of each segment of the drama is from the idealized past of the series to a climactic revelation about the troubled reality of the present: Jill's "I'm Jewish" at the end of Part I; Harmer's statement at the end of Part II that revolution is imminent; and the sounds of the uprising at the end of Part III.

This parallel structure is reinforced by the music, which is used sparingly but effectively. The rousing overture for the series episode that begins each segment of the drama is answered by a subdued and ominous theme which closes each segment, swelling at the moment of revelation in the last scene and continuing under the closing credits. The latter is a simple classical melody played first by violins alone, then accompanied by a soft drum beat. The theme is introduced when Peter is first alone with Jill in her apartment and she unexpectedly insists on postponing sleeping with him because "It's too important"—the first complication in the plot of the drama. After that, the theme appears only in the three closing scenes. It is virtually the only background music in the program.

The complications and revelations of the plot gradually change Peter's relationship to his series. At first, "An Englishman's Castle" was entirely rewarding for Peter. It not only earned him fame and fortune, but gave him the satisfaction of recounting his life through rose-colored lenses to an appreciative audience. As the story unfolds, however, Jill's taunts, Harmer's censorship, and the arrest of Mark Ingram force Peter to view himself as a coward, aiding the forces of repression. In his attempt to redeem his life, he turns to the ideals of his script, and when Peter actually interrupts an episode of his series to put himself on screen and signal the uprising, his life has overtaken and merged with his series. Just as Peter changes from expressing himself through fiction to expressing himself directly, the role of the television medium changes abruptly from reinforcing to attacking the social order.

Peter's progression from author to hero is carefully developed. When Jill tells Peter "I'm going to go to bed with you tonight," her announcement immediately follows an episode in the series in which Sally (played by Jill) decides to go to bed with Frank (the young Peter's alter ego). Peter can't resist asking Jill if she was influenced by Sally's character and behavior. As they undress in Jill's apartment, Peter looks at himself in her large mirror and is depressed by the image of his 58 years and innumerable compromises. When Jill embraces and consoles him, tongue-in-cheek as always, the camera remains fixed on Peter's image in the mirror. From this point on, Peter seems to seek an escape from the literal truth of the mirror image in the more compliant image of the television screen.

He identifies increasingly with his characters. In the first of the series episodes that open the drama, Frank echoes Churchill's vow that they will fight "to the last man." When Peter talks to his agent about challenging Harmer's censorship, he speaks incongruously of fighting "to the last man," and the agent recognizes the quote from the series. Peter also begins to identify with Mr. Worth, who concedes his wife's point that he is 58 years old, Peter's age, but still wishes he could go with Bert to join the resistance. After Peter does make the heroic gesture that Mr. Worth is unable to make, he clutches himself in pain, recalling Mr. Worth's heart attack. He seems to see Frank and Bert as what he was, and Mr. Worth as what he now is. In the same way, Sally is what his wife was, while Mrs. Worth (who like Mrs. Ingram is constantly knitting) represents what she has become—"Kinder, Küche, Kirche," as Jill says.

When Henry Ingram (Peter's second son) is killed by the Resistance, Peter's wife tells him "Your Mrs. Worth didn't cry when they told her that Frank was dead. I shall not behave any worse than any of your fictional imaginings." After Peter allows the Special Police to pressure him into betraying Harmer, Jill tries to convince him that he only did what anyone else in his place would have done. "Then," replies Peter, "I must try to do better."

"Like a character in your show?" she asks.

"Yes," he says, and repeats to her what his wife said to him. Again, when the Special Police contingent in the corridor shoot their way into Peter's office after his announcement of the uprising, Peter looks up and speaks the closing line of the program: "I shall not behave worse than one of my fictional imaginings."

We can understand Peter's withdrawal into the world of his series because we ourselves get emotionally involved in just the brief portions of the few episodes we see. Even as we follow the drama's cynical running commentary about the superficiality of the series, the series demonstrates the power of its conventions by absorbing us, at least temporarily, into its mass audience. Though the program begins with a shot of studio activity, we immediately accept the scene in the Worths' living room as the primary narrative level, and we resent the studio interruptions until we come to realize that the studio action is the "real" story.

As an audience, we generally don't like to have our faith in the screen image betrayed. Nor do we like to have our emotions toyed with this way. Part of the difficulty, particularly for television, is that we are so conditioned to trust the small-screen image. Most Americans get the news from television and consider that news more accurate and unbiased than the print media. In addition, the medium retains its aura of immediacy from the early, "live" years of television, even though it is now generally pieced together as artificially as film. One expects illusion and artifice in the movie theater, but not in the living room.

Peter's climactic appearance on the television screen needs particularly careful attention if we are to judge the ambition and the success of *An Englishman's Castle*. The viewer who regards Peter's act only as one of heroism will have seen a good suspense drama. But the viewer who also regards Peter as a victim of his own "fictional imaginings" has seen a more complex work. With the outbreak of revolution, Peter's series, and therefore his "importance," would end, which I think is the point of his final walk past the deserted sets in the studio. When Peter puts himself on camera, he turns to the monitoring screen at his left and sees the image of himself turning to the left. This placement of the screen is significant, because it means that

Peter cannot see the image of himself looking boldly forward and heroically exhorting his audience.

Thus, the idealized self-image that has eluded Peter throughout the drama continues to elude him as he stiffly repeats "Britons strike home" for the camera. He will never join Jill in victory, if there is one, and there is no assurance that she will miss him. Only the anonymous guards in the corridor hear his "fictional imaginings" line borrowed from his wife. Reality for Peter now, whatever the outcome of the fighting, will be "death, prison, concentration camp" (Jill's words when she told Peter she was Jewish). He has become a victim of the grand illusion of heroism that provides the title for Renoir's film masterpiece.

This does not mean that Peter's action isn't admirable, particularly in that he did it partly to protect the woman he loves. What seems sad, though, is that Peter has been the only really human character in a world of politicized grotesques. In contrast to Harmer and Jill, the chief supporting roles in the drama, Peter is consistently open and honest, naive and vulnerable, patient and loving. All this is expressed in the wonderful face of Kenneth More, which on the visual level is the real subject of the program. The face seems scarred by experience, particularly the lines that droop from the sides of his mouth, and the right eyelid that sometimes half-closes in resignation. If the natural function of the television screen is to serve as a frame for the human face, as has often been suggested, then this story of Peter's (and Kenneth More's) face is ideally suited to the medium.

Harmer and Jill are victims of the underground code; as Jill explains, its members must appear to cooperate with the German authorities "at whatever cost to your personal relationships"—or, she might have added, to your own humanity. Jill herself is the best example of that cost. We see her entirely through her relationship with Peter, in which she is at first flirtatious and teasing, then critical and nagging, but above all dominant. She often stands over Peter, like Harmer and the Special Police chief. She manipulates him throughout, always with a kind of smug one-upmanship.

Though she says early in their relationship that she loves him, she does nothing to confirm this. When he asks her if she went to bed with him for love or politics, she only replies "it doesn't matter" and tells him to "answer with your brains" about joining the underground. But this is hypocritical, because she has deliberately short-circuited his brain by exploiting his desire for her. When she tells him she is Jewish, for example, it is when they are about to make love for the first time—hardly the moment for a rational assessment of the dangers involved.

If my treatment of Jill seems harsh, so, I would argue, is the author's and director's. She wears excessively heavy make-up throughout, which seems intended to transform her face into a mask. When she and Peter are driving to her apartment after the murder of Henry, both faces are disembodied against the dark background. But his face is tearful, while hers is rigid as she reminds him that Henry, as an informer, was also a murderer.

Jill is the key to the complexity of the drama. We can admire her role as a freedom fighter and explain her coldness as a defense developed during her struggle to survive under the "racial purity" laws. At the same time, it is difficult to like a character so purged of all emotions except hatred—and so calculating in her relationship with a man who loves her. When she says "I'm dead three times under their laws," there is more irony than she realizes, because her humanity has indeed been killed. And so Peter's climactic sacrifice for her sake leaves us with a divided feeling of admiration and regret.

This divided feeling for the viewer is the first characteristic of narrative art—the balancing of conflicting emotional responses. None of the main characters in *An Englishman's Castle* evokes an unmixed response. Peter's goodness is qualified by the fact that he is unfaithful and even indifferent to his wife. Henry, who is the worst character morally, is the most likable on the surface, the son who never made his mother worry. The subtleties of the script, which continually undercut our natural tendency to stereotype the characters, reveal themselves increasingly with each viewing—the second of our characteristics of narrative art.

The third characteristic, the feeling that a work belongs uniquely to its medium, is the hardest to identify in a television narrative. The medium obviously borrows heavily from the older narrative forms of theater and film. But *An Englishman's Castle,* with its forty-odd scenes, would be chaotic on stage. And since the shots are primarily close-ups, they would become cloying on a large screen, even though the close-ups are varied and expressive portrayals by fine actors. *An Englishman's Castle* demonstrates that the phrase "talking heads," often applied to television drama, does not have to be negative.

Above all, *An Englishman's Castle* seems to belong on television because it is about television, just as Fellini's fine work *8½* is a film about film and film-making. Fellini's alter ego Guido is unable to shape his fantasies into a coherent story, but Fellini takes advantage of the visual power of the large screen and darkened theater to make those fantasies the real subject of his film. *An Englishman's Castle,* on the other hand, is as mundane visually as *8½* is extravagant. It shows an increasingly claustrophobic world of people in rooms: restaurants, offices, a studio, an apartment, and a home. Even Peter's series never moves outside the Worths' home, except for a few brief shots of soldiers talking in the countryside.

In *8½,* there is virtually no setting where we could picture a television set. In *An Englishman's Castle,* nearly all the settings could reasonably include a television set, and most of them do. Philip Mackie shows us the visual world we normally inhabit, and uses the ubiquitous television screen of that world to play a new variation on the underlying theme of all narrative art—appearance vs. reality.

TV Advertising—
The Subtle Sell

Richard P. Adler

The purpose of advertising, according to the Federal Trade Commission, is to "provide consumers with the information they need to make rational decisions in the marketplace." But what information is being communicated in the following commercial?

The opening sequence: a weekend afternoon game of touch football in a city park. The players are in their late twenties and early thirties, probably in professions. The game is good-natured but intense. A balding, nimble jock catches a pass and scores the winning touchdown. The game breaks up, the men gather around a cooler, toast themselves with cans of Schlitz beer, and the theme music rises. The end.

The style of this ad is typical of many currently on television. It makes no explicit claims for the product, nor does it offer any verbal description of Schlitz beer or its attributes. On one level, the commercial simply seems to present the product in a casual and attractive setting. On another level, however, the images suggest that Schlitz is an essential ingredient in the celebration of male camaraderie and virility.

Such use of imagery is hardly new. Advertisers have been using pictures to sell products for a long time. In fact, images began to play an important role in advertising as early as the 1920s, when advertising campaigns were affected by improvements in photographic reproduction techniques and color printing processes. Even before the technology of television was perfected, advertisers were aware of the persuasive potential of the new medium. Writing in 1931, for example, adman Edgar Felix foresaw some of the possibilities: "The cigar advertiser who appeals to young men can actually demonstrate that cigar smoking will make any young man look like a major executive. . . . A reproduction of a luscious strawberry short-cake [will be] much more effective in creating an appetite than any word-of-mouth description." Television, because of its ability to illustrate and dramatize an advertiser's message, was destined to become, Felix wrote, "the most powerful medium for sales stimulation."

What Felix prophesied came to pass. Television became the nation's dominant medium of communication, and advertising played a vital role in its growth. Today, the country's three networks and seven-hundred commercial television stations receive more than $7 billion a year in advertising revenues.

Carefully conceived and endlessly repeated, television advertising thoroughly exploits the audiovisual resources of the medium to produce the maximum impact in a minimal amount of time. Considering that many commercials are produced with budgets of $2,000 or more *per second,* it is not surprising that they are often more lively and entertaining than the programs they surround. According to the author of *The Best Thing on TV: Commercials,* Jonathan Price, commercials are "the closest thing to video art on television."

Most viewers, whose responses to television commercials range from mild amusement to mild annoyance, accept advertising as a reasonable price to pay for "free" television. But to the Federal Trade Commission, the techniques and strategies used in commercials are a more serious matter.

Several key staff members of the FTC have expressed concern that the agency has failed to keep up with the realities of how advertising actually works. They argue that by concentrating on the literal truth or falsity of advertising claims, the FTC has virtually ignored what has become the most important component of advertising—its visual imagery. In the words of one FTC staff member, the commission has persisted in attempting to regulate advertising by applying "Gutenbergian solutions" to "Marconian problems."

The first public expression of FTC interest in advertising imagery came in a speech given in October 1977 by Albert Kramer, director of the commission's Bureau of Consumer Protection. Quoting Marshall McLuhan, Kramer declared that "the unconscious depth messages of ads are never attacked by the literate because of their incapacity to notice or discuss nonverbal forms of arrangement and meaning. They have not the art to argue with pictures."

Kramer, an attorney with a background in public-interest law, made it clear that he believes the FTC had better learn "to argue with pictures." While regulators remain tied to the written word, he asserted, "the media have left the written word behind in a cloud of dust and have created a new environment of multisensory experience of which the written word is a minor part." Kramer did not reveal what specific steps the FTC should take to catch up with the media. But he said a thorough reexamination of the agency's mandate was needed to determine how it might be extended to take into account the "total sensory experience of an ad."

Ironically, the Federal Trade Commission is itself partly responsible for making words less important in advertising: Over the past forty years, the FTC has successfully gone after advertisers whose claims it judged to be false, deceptive, or misleading. Thanks to the FTC, for example, Carter's Little Liver Pills can no longer use the word "liver"; STP can no longer claim to improve the performance of a car's engine; Wonder bread can no longer state that it "helps build strong bodies twelve ways"; and Geritol can no longer claim to be a cure for "tired blood."

There have also been instances in which the Federal Trade Commission has acted against "pictorial deception" in ads. But these have generally been cases involving the use of specific images which could be "translated" more or less directly into specific product claims. Thus, the FTC ruled that a rayon and cotton fabric called Duro-Persian could not use a picture of a lamb on its trademark because of the obvious—but false—implication that the fabric contained wool. Similarly, a mattress advertisement in a magazine, which showed a mattress and a man in a white coat writing a prescription, was deceptive, the FTC said, because it implied the mattress carried a special medical endorsement. (Since then, the practice of using "men in white coats" in ads has generally been discontinued.)

One of the most significant cases of pictorial deception involved the "sandpaper" television commerical for Palmolive Rapid-Shave. This 1959 commercial began by showing a football player who, according to an announcer, had "a beard as tough as sandpaper . . . a beard that needs Palmolive Rapid-Shave." Rapid-Shave lather was then spread on a piece of sandpaper as the announcer explained, "To prove Rapid-Shave's supermoisturizing power, we put it right from the can onto this tough, dry sandpaper." As a hand holding a razor was shown easily cutting a swath through the sandpaper, the announcer exclaimed: "It was apply . . . soak . . . off in a stroke!

Shortly after the commercial was first broadcast, the FTC began receiving complaints from irate viewers who had tried and failed to duplicate the demonstration in the commercial. The FTC launched an inquiry and discovered that the "sandpaper" in the ad was not sandpaper at all, but a sheet of Plexiglas to which grains of sand had been glued. The commission rejected the company's defense that "technical limitations" of the television medium had required the substitution and issued a "cease and desist" order. The defendants carried the case all the way to the Supreme Court, which, in its first case involving a television commercial, upheld the FTC's decision that the ad was deceptive.

As a result of the FTC's vigor in prosecuting false or deceptive advertising claims, sponsors are now aware that they must be prepared to provide documentation to support any claim they wish to make about a product's performance or qualities. So, many ads now make *no* explicit claims at all: Geritol commercials feature handsome middle-aged men proclaiming their affection for their attractive wives, who take Geritol; STP commercials associate its additive with tough guys like Johnny Cash and Robert Blake.

Tracy Westen, the deputy director of the FTC's Bureau of Consumer Protection, notes that noncognitive, nonrational appeals of this kind are not necessarily deceptive. First the FTC would have to determine what the imagery of these ads is "saying," then decide whether that message should be judged legally deceptive. Westen has begun by attempting to interpret the images appearing in print advertising for cigarettes. While the visual techniques used in print and television are often similar, print ads are generally simpler to analyze than the multi-image, multisensory television commercials. And cigarette advertising raises some special concerns: The accumulated scientific evidence about the health risks of smoking have made it increasingly difficult to make a "rational appeal" for smoking. As a result, Westen believes, cigarette ads strive to "bypass the cognitive decision-making process altogether, making it difficult or impossible for consumers to make a decision on a rational level."

Westen, in a speech last year, reported the results of an "informal, highly unscientific" experiment he conducted to determine the message that was being communicated by the picture in a magazine ad. The ad for Vantage cigarettes shows a handsome man, dressed in suit and tie and holding a cigarette, who says, "Smoking. Here's what I'm doing about it." Westen reported that when he showed the ad to twelve people picked at random and asked them a series of questions about the picture, the answers he received were surprisingly consistent: Nearly all agreed, for example, that the man was a college graduate, something of a playboy, made more than $30,000 a year, and lived in an expensive apartment.

Using his little survey as a basis, Westen speculated that the message of this ad might be something like: "Smoke Vantage and you, too, can be (or be like) this single, attractive, self-confident business executive who earns up to $40,000 a year, drives a sports car, and lives in an expensive high-rise condominium" Or: "Vantage is the choice of successful, intelligent executives because it is 'safe.' " Westen noted that if a cigarette advertiser attempted to make this sort of claim verbally, the FTC "would be all over him in five minutes." If the claim is made visually, however, it is far more difficult to document.

When Westen turns his attention to television advertising, he will find some equally questionable messages being communicated visually. One interesting example is the recent commercial for Sanka decaffeinated coffee that features actor Robert Young. This thirty-second drama opens as a couple, with Young, enter their house. The husband slams the door, muttering angrily about the traffic he has just encountered. The following dialogue ensues:

Young: Why get so upset, Roger?
Wife: His doctor says that caffeine makes him tense.
Young: Oh! You should try Sanka.

Roger is skeptical ("I like *real* coffee"), but gives Sanka a try. Of course, he is pleasantly surprised ("Hey, this *is* real coffee"). A fast fade brings us to scene 2 ("a few weeks later"), in which Young encounters a newly serene Roger who pledges his allegiance to Sanka.

While there is nothing apparently deceptive about the images in the ad, one of the most important elements in the commercial is unspoken: Robert Young, let us recall, spent seven years on prime-time television in "Marcus Welby, M.D." "Men in white coats" may have been banned by the FTC, but the folks who sell Sanka have found an ingenious visual equivalent.

Equally ingenious is the commercial which, by showing a Volkswagen against a background of the U.S. Capitol (the excuse is that its driver, a congressman, is being interviewed by reporters), is able to imply that buying a German car is an act of patriotism. Or the McDonald's commercial which portrays a harried secretary working in a cold, impersonal office, then fighting her way through a crowd until she reaches the haven of her local McDonald's. The friendly greeting she receives and the bliss of her Big Mac imply that McDonald's not only sells hamburgers but provides a refuge of sustenance and personal caring ("We do it all for you!") in an otherwise indifferent world.

To the critics of the FTC, its concern about advertising imagery represents just one more irresponsible effort by federal bureaucrats to intrude into an area in which they are neither wanted nor needed. Columnist George F. Will characterized Tracy Westen's speech as "another example of the lengths to which government agencies [will] go to concoct excuses for expanding their powers." According to Will, Westen and his colleagues must assume that consumers are "feeble creatures . . . easily tricked into zany delusions." On this assumption, Will concluded, is based "the theory of government as nanny."

Which brings us to the question that lies at the heart of this controversy: How powerful are "mere" pictures? Are they more powerful than words because they are less rational and, therefore, better able to evade our critical defenses? Or are they less potent because they lack the precise, agreed-on meanings of the written and spoken word? Another way of putting the question: To what extent are we rational beings who act on the basis of objective fact, and to what extent are we vulnerable to irrational, emotional appeals?

There are no simple answers to these questions. Several years ago, psychologist Erich Fromm was asked to comment on the impact of television commercials. He began by noting that many television commercials employ fantasy images to suggest that products will satisfy our emotional needs. These fantasies play on our fears and desires ("Take Geritol and your husband will love you"); they promise to perform miracles ("Come to McDonald's and be renewed"). But, Fromm was asked, do people really believe these obviously outrageous claims? He replied, "Well, it seems to me the answer is yes and no: They know that the claims of the drugs and the foods and the pills and the cigarettes are all nonsense. But at the same time they would like to wish, they would like to hope, that there might be something to [them]. And so, they have an experience which does not clearly differentiate between fantasy and reality, but fantasy and reality become mixed up." Fromm added that these emotional appeals may be highly effective but that "they don't operate much on a conscious level."

If Fromm is right, the FTC will have its work cut out for it: In moving from words to images, the commission will be leaving the relatively familiar, well-lighted arena of objective truth and falsity to plunge into the murky depths of the subconscious. While psychologists and psychiatrists may be at home in this realm, it is uncharted territory for lawyers and regulators.

The FTC staff members are well aware that they are attempting to break new ground. Westen acknowledges that the FTC's traditional remedies may prove inappropriate for dealing with the problems of pictorial deception. Instead of attempting to decode and evaluate the messages of individual ads, Westen suggests, the commission might require all ads for certain products to include specific pieces of information. Or it might call for creation of "counter ads" to provide important information not being supplied by current advertising.

Clearly, the regulation of visual imagery in advertising is in a primitive state compared to the regulation of verbal claims. As a result, advertisers are able to communicate images in pictures which would be deemed false if stated in words. But how much persuasive impact the visual images really have, as well as what sort of remedies are needed for dealing with visual deception, is much less clear.

So far, the FTC staff members have found more questions than answers. But they have already come under fire just for asking the questions, and they are certain to encounter even more heated opposition if they attempt to move further. Still, the staff does not seem inclined to let the issue drop. But no matter how it turns out, their undertaking will be worth watching: It could well provide the most revealing inquiry to date into how television images communicate and how advertising really works.

Part 4.
News

News programming occupies only a small portion of the total broadcast schedule. Yet more has probably been written about television news than about any other aspect of the medium. Since news purports to describe events in the real world, there are always questions to be asked about the accuracy, objectivity, and completeness of its reporting. However, the authors of the essays in this section focus on a different issue: the ways in which TV news shapes its reporting to conform to audience expectations, traditions of storytelling, and the imperatives of the medium itself.

Paul Weaver looks at the aesthetics of TV news by comparing its structure to print news. He comes to the surprising conclusion that television is the more subjective medium. Sharon Sperry argues that the kinds of stories told by television reporters can be best understood by the use of narrative theory. Finally, Michael Robinson combines political and formal analysis to demonstrate that the ultimate effect of TV news on its audience may be quite different from what we usually assume.

TV News and Newspaper News

Paul Weaver

The American newspaper as we know it today has been an established and essentially unchanging institution for upwards of 70 years. The same can hardly be said of television. As recently as 30 years ago it was nothing but a gleam in the entrepreneurial eye, and over the intervening decades it has passed fitfully through its infancy and adolescence. Today, however, television can fairly be said to have attained its majority and entered adulthood. Fully mature it obviously isn't, but adult it most certainly is; what was once a congeries of open-ended possibilities is now a settled and distinctive reality.

The fact that television is now a full-fledged institution and mode of communication implies, among other things, that it has finally become a fit subject for serious scholarship. For the humanist, television provides a settled *genre*, or family of *genres*, for study and criticism. These may not be high forms, but they are forms nevertheless and as such are presumably worthy of attention. For the social scientist, the institution of television itself, and its impact on other institutions and social processes, is at last something that can be looked at without fear that tomorrow everything will suddenly be different. And for everyone's scrutiny there is the central reality of television as a settled and powerful force in American civilization, actively at work affecting our culture, politics, economy, and individual lives.

What difference has the advent of television made to American society? Nobody really knows, of course; it is still too early to tell, and until recently critics and scholars have generally dismissed TV out of hand, calling it "chewing gum for the eyes" or some other expression of thoughtless contempt. In these pages I would nevertheless like to offer a few tentative thoughts about the nature, assumptions, and political consequences of one element of modern television, the nightly network news program. It is clear to me that, in comparison to newspaper news, television news is not just "more of the same." Despite their many shared characteristics, newspapers and telelvision differ in several fundamental respects and consequently tend to shape public perceptions and opinions in different ways.

I.

It is more or less impossible to think coherently about the comparison between newspaper news and television news until one grasps a simple but all-important truth: that news is a *genre,* a distinctive mode of writing and of depicting experience, and that any comparisons between newspapers and television must at least begin by analyzing the variant of this *genre* that each represents. Economic, technological, legal, and social considerations may be explored later, but to begin with what one is talking about are two related but not identical modes of expression and vision. And since expression and vision are so heavily influenced by culture, one cannot for the most part think coherently about such modes in the abstract—one must look at journalism *in a given place* and *at a stated time.* National and historical differences within journalism are extremely large. In what follows, I shall be concerned solely with American newspapers and American TV as they exist today.

In order to discourage anyone from entertaining an exaggerated notion of how different these two media are, and with the hope of putting their real differences in some perspective, let me begin by sketching what seem to me to be their most important common characteristics. Many of the vices and virtues that people attribute to television or newspapers are in fact not unique to the medium in question but are instead characteristics of news as such.

First, newspaper news and television news are alike in being varieties of journalism, which means that both consist of a current account of current events. ("Criticism of the moment at the moment," was James's useful formulation.) This two-fold contemporaneity—the present as a subject matter, and the present as the perspective in time from which it is described—is what accounts for the intense and universal appeal of journalism, and also for the extraordinary difficulty journalism encounters in achieving a depiction of events which experience and criticism affirm to be coherent, balanced, and reliable. This difficulty, it should be emphasized, is an inherent one for which there can be no solution; the best one can hope for is a recognition of the difficulty, an earnest effort to cope with it, and a general scaling down of claims and expectations all around. However that may be, television and newspapers share the appeal and the difficulty of contemporaneity more or less equally. The familiar criticism that TV is under greater time pressure, and therefore is less thoughtful, is essentially false. The criticism applies to both media.

Second, newspaper news and television news are alike in "covering" current events by means of reportage, i.e., factual description of what an on-the-scene observer of the event in question saw and heard. Thus news in America has long possessed all the distinctive advantages of reportage—concreteness, immediacy, and faithfulness to the particularity of events. But by the same token it has also been prone to the special weaknesses of reportage, chief of which are a relative inability to depict complexity and ambiguity and a powerful disinclination to pursue the meta-observational questions which illuminate complexity and ambiguity. A further shortcoming of reportage is that it increases the likelihood that the newsman, in the course of gathering information about a given event by being on the scene, will alter the event. This "Heisenberg effect" is an everyday occurrence in modern journalism and can be seen in the omnipresence of "pseudo-events" (happenings engineered by sources for the purpose of being reported), in the common practice of "milking the news," and in the much rarer instances of deliberate "staging" of events by newsmen desperate for a good story to report. Newspapers and TV are equally prone to these pathologies.

Third, newspaper news and television news are alike in being accounts of events that are vocationally-produced by special-purpose organizations. News is gathered and written by persons whose full-time occupation is to gather and write news. Thus newsmen may be said to be specialists—members of a distinct occupational community that has its distinctive traditions, concerns, and ways of doing things. Inevitably, news reflects the specialized ethos of the journalistic community and is shaped by its structure and processes, even though the intention of news is to speak to, and embody, the general concerns of the average citizen.

Fourth, newspaper and television news are alike in being essentially melodramatic accounts of current events. Partly by virtue of their focus on "events" and partly as a result of the traditions which define the ethos of the newsman and the structure of the news story, both newspapers and television depict events as actions that carry forward an implicit and usually extremely simplistic line of dramatic action. Thus events derive their journalistic identity in no small measure from the dramatistic fictions which newsmen and sources spin around them. One consequence of this practice is that news has historically defined the present as a period of transition—as an outgrowth of the past and a prefiguration of the future, yet different from both; as a time of discontinuity rather than continuity, of instability rather than stability, and of danger, crisis, struggle, and adventure rather than the reverse. Another consequence is the way in which the decisions of news organizations about the newsworthiness of a particular event quickly come to be self-fulfilling prophecies: what one prints today establishes a line of action which identifies related events tomorrow as being newsworthy, the printing of which both confirms the validity of the first day's decision and points to events still farther in the future as being worthy of coverage. So faddism and sensationalism are tendencies of both media.

Finally, newspaper news and television news in America are alike in using the same themes, formulas, and symbols in constructing the lines of melodramatic action which give meaning and identity to events. The two media, in other words, are cut from the same intellectual and rhetorical cloth. For instance, both newspapers and television typically report events associated with political campaigns in terms of a generalized image of politics as a horse race. Events associated with major changes in public policy, by contrast, are generally presented in terms of a model of policy-making as the under-taking of expert and well-intentioned leaders acting in the public interest. The failure of policy is ordinarily described according to a scenario in which existing policies are defended by officials and other interested parties for selfish motives against the opposition of an aroused public opinion indignantly demanding reform. These gen-eralized images are but a few of the many formulas that give con-crete expression to the two central themes that run, colliding with each other as they do so, throughout all newspaper and television journalism in America—the populist notion that the people should rule directly in their own felt interests, and the republican notion that established institutions should rule in behalf of the public inter-est under the scrutiny of the electorate.

II.

So much for similarities; now for some of the differences which make the advent of television journalism an event of no small mo-ment in American political history. Undoubtedly, the most obvious of these differences is a structural one. In comparison to newspaper news, television news is far more coherently organized and tightly unified, and this is true of the individual TV and newspaper news story as well as of the TV and newspaper news aggregate as a whole (the newspaper edition and the TV news program). This difference is associated with the fact that TV is organized and presented in time, whereas the newspaper edition is organized only in space.

The difference in structure becomes most apparent when one considers newspaper editions and TV news programs as wholes. Though both are limited in volume, the newspaper contains a vastly larger number of stories by a factor of something on the order of ten. This occurs because the newspaper, being organized in space, can feasibly publish many more stories, and much more text, than most readers care to read; its contents are thus an *a la carte* menu which the reader rapidly scans and from which he selects a "meal" accord-ing to his interests and time. Inevitably, therefore, the contents of the typical newspaper edition are chosen to be extremely diverse—are chosen, in fact, *not* to be read in their entirety by a single reader. There is, in consequence, a loose, open-ended, discursive quality to the contents and structure of the newspaper edition.

It is precisely the reverse with the television news program. Being organized in time, it cannot so easily present news *a la carte:* to "scan" all the possible stories, the viewer would have to see all of them in their entirety in the first place before choosing which ones to view—which is an absurdity. The television news program is thus a *table d'hote,* a collection of stories selected and arranged to be seen in their entirety by every viewer without reducing the size or interest of the audience as the program proceeds. The consequence is that the television news program contains many fewer stories and that the ones it does contain are chosen carefully for their interest and balance and are presented as a relatively coherent and integrated package.

Thus, whereas the contents of the newspaper make up a diverse, numerous, often inchoate aggregate, the elements of the television news program typically form a unified whole. They seldom if ever attain perfect unity, of course; the materials of the real world, though malleable in television journalism, are not *that* malleable. But almost invariably there are several stories in a given program that exhibit a common theme or mood, and frequently there are further stories designed to provide contrast, emphasis, or development. This does not happen by accident; it is intentional on the part of TV newsmen, and the fact that it is intentional is proof that the underlying goal of the television news program is to attain the condition of wholeness, to exhibit theme, structure, and unity.

One consequence of this is that the TV news program tends to present a single, unified interpretation of the day's events *as a whole* and to construe periods of time as having a single defining movement, action, or mood. To the extent that we think or speak of the day's events holistically as good, bad, hopeful, discouraging, dramatic, boring, or whatever—and of course we all do this constantly—we are thinking in the mode of television journalism. In newspapers, by contrast, the events of the day rarely have anywhere near so clear a thematic identity; the newspaper's day is always a comparative mishmash.

Though it is not widely recognized and is often actually denied, precisely the same general relationship exists between the television news story and the newspaper news story. We are used to thinking of the TV news story as a slight, weak, and unsophisticated expository instrument in comparison to the newspaper news story. TV, according to conventional wisdom, is essentially a "headline service" that must content itself with formulaic capsule summaries of the top "spot news" stories of the day; newspapers, by contrast, have the time, space, and capacity to produce long, meaty, analytic, more fully-realized accounts of what's going on. Yet the reality is exactly the reverse, as a glance at the scripts of just a few film news stories immediately demonstrates. Allowing for the fact that the newspaper news story *is* longer and does contain more raw data, the truth is that ordinarily it is the television news story which is more analytical, which more consistently and insistently goes beneath and beyond the surface of events to exhibit the larger trends and meanings of current affairs, which achieves the more integrated and coherent exposition of the reporter's findings, and which constitutes the more flexible and sophisticated reportorial instrumentality.

The standard newspaper news story is organized according to the principle of the "inverted pyramid."[1] Its subject and focus is a single, unitary event as defined in one or two sentences (the headline and the lead paragraph). Having stated in the simplest and most reductionist of terms the bare bones of the event (who, what, where, when, and so on), the newspaper news story—*every* newspaper news story—has already achieved a kind of completeness and can be terminated at that point without rendering it unintelligible; if it is published in this form we call it an "item" or "filler." (A significant proportion of the "filler items" published by our newspapers, interestingly enough, are in fact major stories from out-of-town and foreign newspapers which have been cut off after the second or third paragraph in precisely this way.) But the news story need not be, and characteristically is not, terminated at this point. Instead it goes on, in a quasi-random sequence of syntactically crude sentences and disjointed paragraphs, to adduce additional data that elaborate on this or that aspect of the story-, topic-, and event-defining headline and lead. In theory, these data are to be presented in descending order of importance, and to some extent they are—the objective here being to enable an editor to cut as much material as suits his purposes (he reads down the story until he has had enough). But for the most part the data are presented in a quasi-random order, for the simple reason that they are all roughly co-equal in importance—or rather in unimportance, since the fact remains that the story stands on its own with all but the first few paragraphs eliminated.

The television news story is radically different.[2] Unlike the newspaper news story, which is designed *not* to be read in its entirety while still achieving intelligibility, the television news story is a whole that is designed to be fully intelligible only when viewed in its entirety. Its focus is therefore upon a theme which runs throughout the story and which develops as the story moves from its beginning to its middle and then to its end. Information, narrative, sound, and pictures are selected and organized to illustrate the theme and to provide the necessary development.

Events in the newspaper sense of happenings that can be defined and comprehended in a single sentence are but the occasion of the television news story, not its *raison d'etre.* In fact, a surprisingly large proportion of TV news stories are not about events in any intelligible sense and do not pretend to be; and of those that do deal with events nearly all either dramatize or re-enact them, or treat them as incidental epiphenomena of the larger phenomena or ideas which are the true thematic focus. But whatever the case, the TV news story, structurally, is virtually incapable of limiting itself to the simple event-naming and embroidering function performed by the newspaper news story; inevitably it goes into, beneath, or beyond the ostensive event to fix upon something else—a process, mood, trend, condition, irony, relationship, or whatever else seems a suitable theme in the circumstances.

A number of conclusions follow from the structural differences between newspaper and television news. One, clearly, is that television news is a far more flexible and intellectually accommodating form than the newspaper variety: more "interpretive," less constrained by the daily flow of events, and less committed to the newspaper's narrow, one-day-only perspective in time. (Whether TV makes proper use of this ability, or squanders it, is another question, on which more later.) Second, it seems equally clear that, as regards the interpretation of current events, television is capable of being— and ordinarily is—far more monolithic than the newspaper. Just as a single idea or theme governs the selection and presentation of all the information in the TV news story to a far greater extent than in the looser, more discursive, less "disciplined" newspaper story, so can a single theme or mood come to determine the contents of an entire TV news program and thus minutely shape its depiction of current affairs as a whole—something that is essentially impossible in a newspaper edition. Finally, and in consequence, the structure of TV news renders its contents far more completely within the practical, day-to-day, discretionary control of the TV news executive than is the case with newspapers, the content of which is by comparison more powerfully influenced by events, sources, and other external or uncontrollable forces.

III.

A second major difference between the two media is associated with the fact that television is both visual and aural, while the newspaper is visual only. It thus becomes possible—and television, from the beginning, has chosen to exploit this possiblity—for TV news to rely on spoken narrative as against the written narrative of the newspaper. This in itself is a substantial difference, but its consequences are made all the more powerful by the distinctive ways in which the two media have chosen to execute their narrative functions.

Newspaper news adopts an intensely impersonal narrative voice. In part, this means that the reporter, in writing his story, never speaks in the first person, but the matter goes far beyond that. The reporter also never makes reference to his own actions in observing events and finding facts; there is never any explicit allusion to the reporter's own awareness of the motives of sources, the probable validity of quoted statements, the extent to which the story at hand confirms or falsifies previous stories, and so forth. Moreover, the news story is couched in the extremely narrow and stylized vocabulary which has become standard for all modern news writing; it too helps to expunge any intimation of the reporter's identity and consciousness. The almost random structure of the newspaper news story and the crude syntax of the prose have much the same effect, making it nearly impossible for the reporter to express his best personal understanding of the subject at hand and of the relationships and contexts of the data he adduces. In short, the form of the newspaper news story systematically obscures any trace of the actual person who is doing the writing, who has observed the event in question at first hand, and who presumably has developed a critical understanding of it. What remains in the story is only a residue of impersonal statements of unambiguously observable fact; the newspaper news story narrates the flow of current events in the rigorous and remote voice of the scientific paper.

This impersonal narrator endows newspaper journalism with a number of advantages and disadvantages. As for the advantages, there is first the fact that the newspaper's style tends to maximize the reader's belief in the truthfulness and dispassion of what the newspaper prints. It is a style which suggests an author who is so passionately scrupulous about facts that he will write literally nothing that an independent investigator could not verify as a fact. It suggests an author so rigorous in his positivism that he will not even imply relationships or nuances. And it suggests as well an author who is so dedicated to the ideal of objective neutrality in all things that he will make literally no reference, however modest or oblique, to his own person. The voice of the newspaper, in short, suggests an author who is a fact-machine, and nothing more.

Or rather almost nothing more: for the reality, of course, is that behind every newspaper news story there lurks a real, flesh-and-blood author who, being only human, does have real thoughts, real personal experience and knowledge, and real feelings. The disjointed, low-key, facts-only, simple-declarative-sentence prose this real person writes powerfully suggests a kind of deliberate repression of self and thus establishes within newspaper writing a distinct intensity, an undercurrent of taut emotion in the manner of Hemingway. Thus to the quasi-scientific authority of the fact-machine there is added the interest and drama inherent in the intensity radiated by this deliberately impersonal person.

There are also some disadvantages, however. The newspaper's laconic, facts-only voice prevents the reporter from conveying to the reader the substantial proportion of his knowledge and feel for the event at hand that cannot be formulated as statements of unambiguously observable fact. As a result, this information is simply denied to the reader. Moreover, interrelationships among the facts presented in the news story are rendered deeply ambiguous by the disjointedness of their exposition. The narrowness of the news story's vocabulary also obliterates complexity and nuance; events are effectively reduced to things that are fully described by their overt physical attributes and their legal-bureaucratic status. In the last analysis, then, this is a voice that does almost as much to make it hard for the reader to understand events as it does to help him—and this in turn calls into question the intentions of the real author, the reporter. What kind of person would present himself as a fact-machine—as a person who is not human and who exercises no judgment? What sort of person sometimes tells the reader less than he has reason to believe? Who would write things whose implication he knows to be false or misleading? The answer is easy: someone who at best is gravely confused and at worst is utterly dishonest with himself and his reader. He is a person who refuses to assume responsibility for the meaning of what he writes; who evades the obligations that are instantly created between author and reader the minute one sets pen to paper; and who cynically manipulates the reader's trust. The author of the news story, in sum, seems to want to bamboozle the reader as much as to inform him, and in this sense he is an unreliable narrator.

The narrative style of television news is the polar opposite of that embodied in the conventions of newspaper writing. It is, above all, a *personal* voice that tells the day's news on the tube. One actually hears the voice; one sees the face, body, and manner of the person who speaks. This individual is constantly on view, intruding his person and personality almost continuously into the narrative. If there is an interview with an important newsmaker, the story will depict the reporter, asking questions or listening and responding to answers, as well as the interviewee himself. Sometimes this personal narrator will make a passing reference to the process of covering the story. In fact, there is scarcely a moment in the television news story when the look, sound, manner, thought, and personality of the reporter-narrator is not visibly and audibly present. If the narrator of the newspaper story may be said to be a sort of disembodied zombie, then the narrator of television news is emphatically a real, flesh-and-blood person in all his uniqueness.

But not necessarily in all his fallible humanness. The television reporter, on camera, displays precious few weaknesses. His stance is easy and masterful, his voice commanding, his diction perfect; his lines are spoken flawlessly, his clothes wrinkle-free, custom-made, and color-coordinated, and his every hair is perfectly in (or out of, depending on the style) place. He may be a real person, but clearly he is playing a role, and in most cases (but not all: there is a measure of variety here) the posture he assumes is one of omniscience.

There is hardly an aspect of the scripting, casting, and staging of a television news program that is not designed to convey an impression of authority and omniscience. This can be seen most strikingly in the role of the anchorman—Walter Cronkite is the exemplar—who is positively god-like: he summons forth men, events, and images at will; he speaks in tones of utter certainty; he is the person with whom all things begin and end. But the omniscient pose is also adopted by reporters in the field. The "eyewitness" story format offers a particularly useful illustration: the reporter usually stands in front of the building or scene in question, his head and torso many times larger on the screen than the physical objects and persons involved in the actual events being reported. Throughout the report the actual occurrences are like putty in his masterful hands. He cuts from one shot to another; he stops the President in mid-sentence; he "voices over" images of kings, Congresses, wars, and citizens. At every point he conveys the subterranean but nonetheless powerful suggestion that the reporter is larger than life, that he literally as well as figuratively towers over the mere mortals whose doings and un-doings he so easily and unerringly grasps and whose pretenses he sees through in an instant. Newsmen protest that this isn't at all what they have in mind; their concern is just to make the news visually interesting and intellectually coherent. Maybe so. But it doesn't really matter why they do it; the important thing is that they do it—and that, intentionally or not, they convey these suggestions of the TV newsman's omniscience to the viewer.

But most of all the television newsman's omniscience is appar-ent in what he says and how he says it. He is hardly one to limit and discipline himself in the manner of the newspaper narrator; he does not say less than he knows, nor is he willing to suggest by his silences, omissions, or ambiguities that there are things he does not know or cannot say for certain. To the contrary, he speaks authoritatively and self-confidently about everything that comes into his field of vision: men, events, motives, intentions, meanings, significances, trends, threats, problems, solutions—all are evidently within his perfect understanding, and he pronounces on them without any ifs, ands, or buts. To be sure, there are exceptions to this pose—TV newsmen such as John Chancellor who have begun to assume a stance not of omniscience but of a kind of sober, honest, self-critical, *reflexive* authoritativeness, in which the newsman not only says what he does know, but also makes clear his doubts, uncertainties, and the like, as well. These exceptions are few, however; most newsmen still pat-tern themselves after the example set by Walter Cronkite, who, despite the palpable absurdity of the notion that a definitive account of events is possible in principle, let alone in a 22-minute time-slot, continues to pronounce, God-like, the epitaph, "And that's the way it is . . ." at the end of each installment of "The CBS Evening News with Walter Cronkite."

The personal and omniscient narrative of television journalism is noteworthy in a number of respects. It endows TV with an enor-mous added measure of moral, intellectual, and personal authority, as witness the fact that Walter Cronkite is among the nation's most admired and trusted men. It is hard to see how this narrative voice could be anything but a central cause of the enormous persuasive power of modern television. Yet it must also be said that the authoritativeness which TV newsmen pretend to is, in the end, a two-edged sword. For, omniscient or not, these newsmen are still identifiable on the screen as human beings, and it is therefore inevitable that, at some level, the audience is going to be aware that no one in real life ever knows so much or is so undoubting and intellectually self-assured, and that these television men are putting on a not entirely honest act. And when these men begin pronouncing *ex cathedra* on subjects about which the audience has strong feelings or substantial knowledge, the viewer is likely to be doubly irritated—first at the objectionable depiction of events, and second at the fraudulence and arrogance of the omniscient posture assumed by the man who conveys the objectionable depictions. Thus, ironically, each added increment of credibility which the omniscient narrator garners for television journalism automatically creates an equal increment of potential for "credibility gap" and public hostility toward television.

A second consequence arises out of this pose of omniscience as well: intellectual and political hubris. By the example its narrators set, by the "truths" they so confidently proclaim, and by the extraordinary power of the medium itself, television journalism encourages its viewers to entertain a badly inflated notion of how much it is possible to know and to do in the real world. By encouraging the sin of hubris, television journalism shows itself to be as unreliable, in the end, as the narrator of the newspaper news story, but for the opposite reason: not because it says less than it knows but because it says more.

IV.

Finally, television news differs from newspaper news in the vastly greater importance that TV attaches to spectacle. This is not so simply because television has such a large and sophisticated capacity for depicting the sights and sounds of events. At least as important is the fact that American television journalists have long since become institutionally committed to exploiting and emphasizing this special capability. They could—and in the early years of American television they did—follow, if only in a vague sort of way, the admirable model of the BBC and pay no more attention to the spectacular aspects of events than good newspapers do. But in American TV journalism today it is otherwise, to put it mildly. In almost any aspect of TV news that one might care to explore, one will find that considerations of pure spectacle count for much more than they do in newspaper journalism: in the choice of events to cover, in the allocation of resources among events, in the construction of events, in the choice of materials to illustrate stories, and perhaps above all in the television news organization's preoccupation with film, and especially with "good" film—i.e., film that clearly and dramatically depicts action, conflict, ritual, or color. Faced with a choice between two potentially newsworthy events, the American TV news organization will prefer, other things being equal, the one for which there is better film. What film they have for an event tentatively identified as newsworthy ordinarily guides, and in some instances may completely determine, the way the event is defined and the theme chosen for the story—a practice which can easily cause the story to misrepresent the situation as it really was. And in rare instances television news organizations have been known to "create" film, to stage spectacles for purposes of being filmed, in order to have something newsworthy to report. In newspapers, spectacle is but one of many competing and more completely coequal considerations, but in television it is a preoccupation. This preoccupation leads television journalism to give disproportionate coverage to events, or aspects of events, which are spectacular and spectacularly filmed.

This emphasis is noteworthy for a number of reasons. For one, it largely vitiates the unique flexibility and interpretive capabilities of the television news story, or rather it prevents their value from being fully realized. For under the influence of TV's passion for spectacle, the possibilities of the news story that could be used to counteract the inherent journalistic tendencies toward narrowness, literalness, short-sightedness, and the like, are instead exploited principally as a means of making news and events more visually interesting and emotionally stimulating than they are in real life. Second, the emphasis on spectacle tends to make TV journalism superficial in the literal sense of being fixated on the surface sights and sounds of events. Third, it powerfully reinforces the melodramatism inherent in American journalism, rendering television preeminently an instrument of symbolic politics. Fourth, the emphasis on spectacle lends additional forms of authority and interest to TV news: the interest and excitement which are characteristic of spectacle, and the largely specious but still quite real authority, or "credibility," of film as a mode of eyewitness observation. And finally the television emphasis on spec-tacle fixes the focus of TV journalism uniquely upon the ongoing drama of nationhood itself. Whereas newspapers focus on a diverse mass of specific events, television depicts something more directly thematic and melodramatic—the spectacle adorning the national dramas of the whole and the parts, of conflict and consensus, war and peace, danger and mastery, triumph and defeat, and so on.

V.

Though I don't pretend to know what all of them are, I am cer-tain that there are many other differences between newspaper news and television news; the three discussed here illuminate only a small part of what is obviously a large and complex relationship. Yet even these elementary distinctions of structure, voice, and content do seem to establish the importance of looking into the relationship more deeply. For if what I have said thus far is true, then clearly the introduction of television journalism deserves to be considered an event of major consequence for all aspects of American life, and per-haps especially for American politics. Toqueville showed how the American political system rests on an uneasy balance between equal-ity and liberty—or, as I would put it, between democracy and liberal-ism. On the analysis in these pages, the conclusion seems inescapable that whereas the effect of newspaper news is to sustain that balance, television news tends to upset it by reinforcing the egalitarian idea and by weakening liberalism.

Newspaper news tends to sustain the Tocquevillian balance by providing a great deal of precise information within a cognitive frame-work that is crude and nearly chaotic. It thus mobilizes public atten-tion to public affairs (thereby performing an egalitarian-democratic function), while preserving to a significant extent the ability of each reader to choose for himself what to read and what to make of the data he encounters (the liberal idea). Thus there is an activation of public opinion as a whole (the democratic idea), but in behalf of no particular vision or objective save perhaps the ideal of individualism itself (the liberal idea). Through the newspaper, a single organization communicates directly with the electorate (the democratic impulse), but in a manner which suggests that no single coherent vision of public affairs is legitimate or even possible (the liberal idea). The newspaper sustains the Tocquevillian balance between democracy and liberalism, then, by incorporating both of these antagonistic ideas into its very conception of news. This practice is not without its disadvantages, to be sure. The liberal idea in particular, associated as it is with impersonal narrative and chaotic cognitive structure, creates more than its share of confusion. Yet as Tocqueville showed, the institutionalization of both ideas is necessary to the stability and legitimacy of the American regime—and if a bit of confusion or inelegance is the price we must pay for having them institutionalized in our media of public information, it seems a worthwhile bargain.

Television news, by contrast, incorporates no such admirable ambivalence. It is almost uniquely an expression of the democratic-egalitarian impulse. Television news is like newspaper news in that both mobilize public attention to public affairs and disseminate information—but there the similarities end. For television news is all mobilization; it seems utterly to lack the liberal, privatizing characteristics of print journalism—the discontinuities, the randomness, the ambiguities, and the diversity which give the ideal of individualism real substance. The television news emphasis on spectacle, its reliance on the single omniscient observer, and its commitment to the notion of a unified, thematic depiction of events, all make TV an extraordinarily powerful mobilizer of public attention and public opinion. The mobilization is organized around a single vision of public affairs promulgated by a single journalistic organization. Thus television news gives credence to the idea that there exists in America a single, coherent national agenda which can be perceived as such by any reasonable and well-intentioned person. Television news consequently lends a distinctive power and authority to the denigration of differences among us; it asserts that on the most fundamental level—that of deciding what is important enough to merit public attention—all Americans are essentially agreed and that wise public decisions can be reached through plebiscitarian consensus rather than through a system of institutions designed to represent and mediate differences among Americans.

Television news, in other words, is perhaps the most powerful centralizing-democratizing machine ever let loose in American society, a machine which, in its commitment to social unity and intellectual coherence, can scarcely avoid riding roughshod over the historic aspirations of liberalism—pluralism, diversity, localism, privacy, individualism, and untrammeled freedom for what is personal and idiosyncratic. So it is hard to imagine that the advent of television journalism is without significance for American politics and it is equally hard to believe that, in its current form, it is something that Americans should welcome with untroubled hearts.

Footnotes

1. There are other modes of newspaper writing, of course: the column, the editorial, the feature story, the news analysis. Each of these has its own characteristics. Here I am analyzing only the standard news story.

2. I should emphasize that I am dealing here only with the filmed news story from a remote location. TV news programs also present "items" and "commentaries"—not many, usually, but some. These have their own characteristics and are not discussed in this paper.

Television News
as Narrative

Sharon Lynn Sperry

Network television is the primary source of news for more than half of the American public.[1] Moreover, the newsman, particularly the anchorman, is an object of special affection from that public. Walter Cronkite, for instance, has enjoyed a higher popularity rating than most contenders for public office and some incumbent Presidents. Television news itself continues to attract an increasingly loyal and trusting audience. Roper Research Associates' periodic studies of the various news media reveal that 51 percent of the respondents in 1974 thought television was the most believable of the news media. That figure represented a significant jump from 1959, when only 29 percent of the Roper sample stated their faith in TV news.[2] The 1974 survey also demonstrated, for the first time in the 15 years of the Roper poll, that a majority of college-educated respondents (56 percent) preferred television as their main source of news.

It is noteworthy that the believability of the TV news medium has grown in the very years when American institutions generally, and government particularly, have suffered from a much-cited credibility gap.[3] What is even more interesting is that journalism as a profession has come under serious and sustained attack during these years—and not merely from politicians and citizens' lobbies with self-serving motives. For every *public* voice attacking the credibility of journalists, we also hear, or at least sense, an uneasy choral response rippling through the country.

Certainly, TV newsmen feel that critics are lurking in every living room. Walter Cronkite cannot have been speaking only to the likes of Clay Whitehead or Spiro Agnew when, on returning from a Christmas vacation on January 6, 1975—a time when neither Whitehead nor Agnew was around to nettle him—he felt compelled to address these unseen critics:

> Good evening. Well, one can sail away through the islands of the Caribbean out of touch with daily newspapers, radio, and television and one can begin to believe as all the good news advocates keep pointing out to us that the world isn't in nearly as bad a shape as it appears through the news dispatches that cross this desk each night. And then you come back to the rude awakening. The news makers just won't cooperate. As long as they're making the decisions that affect our lives in this complex society, we'd better know what they're up to, unpleasant or not. We can bury our heads in the sand at our peril. There aren't many smart ostriches. So here goes today's report.

The situation resists easy explanation. Newsmen are under general attack, but television newsmen are nevertheless watched and believed by the greatest percentage of the population. Numerous articles and books take television to task for sensationalizing the news, for hyping conflict, for over-simplifying events, and skimming the surface. More bitter critics accuse the national news media, television included, of ideological bias. Television, particularly, is blamed for public apathy and voter cynicism.[4]

Some of those accusations can be answered satisfactorily. Some are valid and ought to lead to changed performance. But none have dealt adequately with the question of why television journalism, as we know it in the network evening news, has been able to build a large and loving audience in a decade when journalism generally is a suspect institution in the public mind.

It is my opinion that the explanation resides, not in the literal content of television news, but in the implicit content of its architecture. By examining the structure, the subtle internal form of the half-hour network news program, we really begin to see what it is that makes television news the most popular—and controversial—brand of journalism.

This examination must begin by recognizing that the national television news shows stand at the front of prime-time programming each evening, and that the networks expect the news to capture an early audience which will stay tuned for the rest of the evening's programs. Consequently, the networks pour their resources into the half-hour news shows with an eye to building an audience as well as to fulfilling their responsibilities for news coverage. This policy, in turn, sets the parameters for the form that the news assumes: half an hour's worth of news *stories*. Television news is a blend of traditional, objective journalism and a kind of quasi-fictional prime-time story-telling which frames events in reduced terms with simple, clear-cut values.

In other words, if the target audience for network news is that group of people who will tune in to "Kojak," or "Columbo," or "Baretta," it is natural to offer them news in a form congruent with their expectations for those later programs. Bound to report the day's events accurately, and prevented from creating convenient and attractive fictions, the network executives' only recourse is to adopt the same structure which the entertainment programs assume —namely, the telling of a story. Understanding this, we might usefully apply narrative theory to television in general, and television news in particular, in order to reveal the peculiar structure of television news and the reasons that these programs so attract their audiences.

Narrative Theory

Narrative theory, as it has been developed by literary critics, is the examination of the strategic and aesthetic devices which develop when someone tells a story to a reader or a listener. Narrative is a form as ancient as human speech. Man is a shape-maker, a metaphorist, an incorrigible imagist. To know and give order to the world he lives in, man has always devised and shared stories.

There are three elements in the narrative mixture: teller, tale, and listener. The two human elements act in concert to relay the tale, which can be fact or fiction, philosophical speculation or scientific definition or metaphorical explanation. When the narrative presumes to present fact—Truth—it is understood that that Truth is necessarily approximate; for it must be filtered through the point of view of the narrator. Like the fictional narrative, the non-fiction narrative must also be pruned and shaped by the narrator if it is to accomplish its goal; for that goal is not merely to provide information but also to affect the listener in some way: to persuade or change him, to evoke an emotional response, or simply to interest him.

The nonfiction narrative form demands these compromises of the Truth—a point of view and a shaping and simplification. And, by both tradition and necessity, the listener assents to these narrative necessities. There is a "willing suspension of disbelief" by the listener, and an agreement by the narrator to approximate reality as he has seen or heard it. This agreement by the two is based on an understanding that the narrator has struck the right compromise between Truth (the chaos of reality) and the listener's expectation of a coherent and effective (or affective) form.

The credibility of the narrator is the key to this understanding, and for this the teller must possess authority. Seeking authority—credibility—for the point of view is an indigenous narrative problem —a challenge to narrators as old as Homer and as recent as Walter Cronkite. It is this struggle for authority which marks the TV newsman most conspicuously as a member of the narrative clan.

The Anchorman as Narrator

In every narrative, the narrator—the authority who tells the story—is of primary importance, and this must be true for the television news program as for any other narrative. Consequently, the structural pattern for the half-hour program is directly tied to the function of the anchorman. He is the one who stands in the position of the author of the tale: the ultimate narrator.

Each news story, although relayed by individual correspondents, is framed by the presence of the anchorman. It is the anchorman who reads all the briefer reports and who introduces each filmed report with a line or two, indicating that he commands the substance of all the reports.

ABC NEWS. Tuesday, December 3, 1974. Harry Reasoner in New York introduces the first story with these words:

Representative Wilbur Mills, until recently perhaps the most powerful man in Congress, has been admitted to Bethesda Naval Hospital just outside Washington. A hospital spokesman said Mills entered the hospital in mid-afternoon but gave no other details. For some time Mills has reportedly suffered from ill health. Last year he was away from his office for an extended period with a back ailment. More recently the Congressman has had serious problems as a result of his association with a striptease dancer. Some of Mills' power in the House Ways and Means Committee has already been taken away by the Democratic Caucus in the House. Earlier, before Mills entered the hospital today, some of his close associates were even saying he might resign from Congress. ABC Capitol Hill correspondent Bob Clark has more.

That "more" will be the first story of the night, and though it may sometimes include a film, it will always have a narrative. By introducing these stories as he does, the anchorman implies that he has control over them. In reality, he may never have seen the film before, but his words still suggest absolute control. The anchorman is, in effect, a corporate creature, the human representative of the central monolith which is the single television screen. Whatever developing theme the half-hour assumes is pinned to his constant presence in the interspaces of the program. His words move the program along, linking story to story according to some larger pattern of meaning, as if the stories of the half-hour were thoughts from his single mind, ordered and moving in rational progression.

The anchorman is omnipresent and, standing in the center of the events he presents, his tone is omnipotent. Even when he disdains omnipotence and expresses tentative doubts, as John Chancellor sometimes does, he cannot escape the fact that he sits in New York, at the command desk, and marshals the evening's program. His audience necessarily perceives him as holding a position of superior knowledge. His function is to provide the only available effective model for action and answers, because he alone commands the whole body of problems, conflicts, and characters, and he alone provides the continuous thread of meaning. It is in this function that he derives the trust and admiration of the audience. He has ritualized the presentation of the news, and in that ritual, lies the audience's only security. It is a curious security, as we shall see.

The Hero Plot in TV News

Prime-time television entertainment is made up mainly of plotted hero stories—simple, evocative, and, therefore, effective narratives. Each story assumes a line of action which is built around a few regular characters. A number of lesser characters, usually bearing the problem that sets the plot in motion, appear for a single episode and then disappear at the end of that episode when their problem has been resolved by the regulars. The plot is always one of overt action. Thought, emotional growth, and cognitive recognition have never been a priority on television except as they assume the explicit shape of action. A problem arises and the main character, the protagonist, with the support of the few regulars who make up the continuing cast, jails the crook, or saves the fatally ill woman, or finally speaks his mind to the obstreperous neighbor. Most of these programs, whether dramatic or comic, are hero stories designed, in Richard Carpenter's words, to "celebrate the conquest over evil within a highly ritualized contest."

> Such a pattern, repeated night after night in dozens of versions all portraying the same basic theme, implies that the TV audience derives satisfaction from a ritual formalization of ingrained feelings that the evil in the world can be overcome by men working together under the guidance of a leader.[5]

The narrative plot of action for television programming taps the roots of man's simplest and most pervasive myth: Men muddle through life as best they can, but when tragedy strikes, they require and seek a leader, a single individual of superior worth and superior skill, who will meet the problem and conquer the evil. The story is told everywhere in every type of communicative form: *The Odyssey*, *Beowulf*, "Anthony and Cleopatra," "The Lone Ranger," "A Man for All Seasons," "Kojak."

As the keystone of each network's evening programming, television news attempts to build and hold its audience by lifting elements of that mythic formula which is the basis of its entertainment programs. Av Westin, former president of ABC News, says that he expects an audience to come to his news program asking "Is the world safe, and am I secure?"[6] There is clearly a link between that question and the answer provided by a news structure that plots events directly along the lines of the hero story:

> The world at peace is disrupted by some event (say, an act of terrorism). That event, which becomes the evil, is named and, if possible, analyzed and understood. It is then attacked by some leader, the hero figure, often a representative of the people. However, this leader, whether by choice or by the nature of his vocation, may not be able to meet the problem alone. So he gains allies, other leaders, and he also gains enemies—potential leaders who disagree with his plan of action, or rebels who align themselves with the evil. As these alignments become apparent, stories are then told of the effect of the problem on the average man. And, if the alignments become a matter more significant than the original event, we will also hear about the suffering of the average man as his appointed leaders fail to meet the problem. Eventually, the disruption is settled or forgotten, and the world returns to its original state of rest and security.

There is a primary problem with this structure of the news as hero story. The world and the world on television news are never really at rest or in security. The answer to Westin's question is inevitably, "No, the world is not secure, nor, perhaps, am I." Problems on television news do not end; they are only replaced on the agenda by new problems—Vietnam becomes Angola; one terrorist act becomes many successive acts; Charles Manson becomes Squeaky Fromme, who has taken the mantle of Lee Harvey Oswald.

Despite this incongruity, television news remains tied to the structure of a hero plot: A conflict involving a small cast of characters arises from the introduction of a problem. The problem is to be solved by some representative protagonist whose activity on behalf of the people is designed to ensure that good will prevail.

We can choose any night at random, on any of the networks, and observe the formula unfolding:

> September 19, 1974. CBS EVENING NEWS. Roger Mudd sits in for Walter Cronkite.
>
> Special prosecutor Jaworski wants to summon former President Nixon to testify in the Watergate trial in order to substantiate the state's use of the White House tapes as evidence.
>
> The figure of Fred Graham appears, standing in front of the federal courthouse. Graham tells us that if Nixon pleads ill health, Judge Sirica will probably send a court-appointed doctor to examine him. The pre-trial hearing is scheduled for Tuesday.

The first stories of every newscast are generally the tales of mighty figures in public life, and one such cast can be with us for a long time.[7] Like soap operas, news stories often involve a set of major characters whose activities continue for months and even years. You may miss several passages of the story and still remain familiar with the major characters and their problems. Here, the characters—Nixon, the Watergate defendants, Judge Sirica, and Leon Jaworski—have become "regulars" appearing many times throughout several weeks of the news program, each time in the context of a new problem that derives from their special relationship with one another.

In this particular story, the roles and principles are clear. In simple terms, Jaworski is the protagonist, representing the law of the land, who is striving to conquer the evil of lawlessness. Judge Sirica is his supporting ally, who is about to send a new character, a doctor, to California to examine Nixon. That doctor, like a secondary character in "Petrocelli," will appear once, do his job, and disappear, setting the stage for the solution to the problem. The minor plot of getting the White House tapes verified as trial evidence is easily enough resolved in a few installments; but the larger context of the drama, involving how these characters will work against each other through the many complications implicit in their roles, will take many weeks, perhaps months.

The story has an extended interest because one of the major characters, Nixon, has shifted from his one-time role as a protagonist—as President—to an antagonist, at odds with the workings of the protagonist and associated with the villains of the story, the Watergate defendants.* None of this is deliberately ideological. Ideology has no relevance here at all. If you tell the news as a story, and if the story form you have chosen is a heroic tale, then there must be a protagonist and an antagonist. It is not political favoritism but simply a formulaic understanding of how the world operates.

Each individual news story, then, is a small but distinct narrative, with a recognizable plot of action which sets character against character in a struggle to redeem the world. A larger pattern becomes visible as story follows story in the half-hour news show. The conflicts are staked in greater issues, become more abstract in nature, and are less available to direct action on the part of any one character or group of characters. There is evil afoot, but it cannot be clearly identified, and the usual channels for discovering it are bogging down. Action and resolution become increasingly difficult, yet action is the only alternative when the structure of the stories pits character against character.

Another story on the same CBS News program illustrates the problem:

> HEW, Mudd reports, has convened a conference of business leaders to discuss the economy and a special committee of Congress is also investigating the state of the economy. To report on the congressional investigation, Daniel Schorr appears.
>
> Senator Kennedy, a member of the committee, urges them to focus on the forgotten. He attacks Greenspan, who has come to testify, for penalizing the poor. Greenspan replies on film.
>
> All of us are suffering, he says, but the Wall Street brokers are hit the hardest. Laughter follows. Someone shouts "face facts" and there are cries from the audience in the chamber.

---

*I would submit that one of the reasons television was slower than the other news media to investigate Watergate was that the President, by nature, is a protagonist. Only when overwhelming evidence began to shift the weight of positive action to others—the courts, primarily—did Nixon's image as protagonist begin to diminish on television. Such a shift of characterization is nearly impossible in the dramatic format of nightly television, where the lines of force for good and evil are sharply rigid, and a story cleanly begins and ends with the roles of hero and villain intact.

In this story, the simple hero plot, in which evil and good are clear and the line of action is obvious, begins to turn on itself. The evil in this second story is an ambiguous force, the erratic economy, which is not an evil which can be readily analyzed or understood. It can be known only by its symptoms (the price of groceries, the loss of jobs, etc.), and even these symptoms do not lend themselves easily to the demands of film for action. Our constituted leader, the available protagonist, is a Senator. Yet the plot of the story limits this new protagonist's ability. The economic problem is a disembodied miasma. Kennedy can lead an investigation, but unlike Jaworski or Sirica, he cannot eventually resolve the problem, even after a whole series of news stories concerned with this "plot."

When complaints, investigations, and issued statements are the only actions, and when faces are continually present and continually talking at us or at each other but rarely acting, we know we are in the presence of an ineffective protagonist and failed narrative. Before our eyes, Kennedy has scored a point against Greenspan and is applauded by the audience in the chamber. But by structuring the story of the economic disruption in this way, the television newsmen have conveyed a faulty message. Implicit in their coverage, and in the customary expectations of the audience is the notion that Kennedy's simple act can settle the problem. The economic difficulties of the nation and the philosophical conflict between the two political parties are symbolized (and simplified) by this one-on-one televised confrontation. Yet, the contrary tones of ultimate failure and impotence in dealing with the real problem create an oxymoron: the semblance of action which has no force of action in it. Kennedy's —the protagonist's—action does not change the situation, does not redeem the actor or his community.

The Need for Action and News Perspectives in TV News

Both the Watergate story and the Kennedy committee hearings on the economy illustrate two other problems peculiar to news coverage on television. Filmed hearings or statements or news analyses are not the stuff of drama. The medium—the broadcast motion picture—requires movement, action, if it is to hold the attention and interest of its viewers. Thus, television news is frequently compelled to create action where none exists by "confronting" opposing leaders in a series of quick-cut statements, by developing a hero plot with the depiction of the "average man's" activities in coping with an intangible but newsworthy issue, and, most controversially, by selecting and focusing on a lesser but dramatizable moment from within a larger, more significant, but wholly undramatic context.

The other problem of TV news is freshness. In dealing with news stories which recur night after night, week after week—the Vietnam War, the Middle East crisis, the Watergate scandal—the network newsmen must contend with the probability of audience boredom. How often in the 1960s did we see a network correspondent, hunkered down in a steamy landscape, saying: "The bombs are falling on us here"? How inured did we all become to the bloodshed and tragedy shown nightly on our TV screens?

TV news programs seek viewer interest and loyalty, and they also accept a responsibility to *involve* the viewer, to help the American public understand and feel the issue at hand. Thus, the networks necessarily attempt to offer new perspectives and fresh insights in covering "old" but continuing news stories. One narrative device that they have adopted to solve this problem is the microcosmic and metaphoric feature story:

> Saturday, May 3, 1975. CBS EVENING NEWS. The last Americans left Vietnam 24 hours earlier. Morton Dean reports that a young Vietnam veteran who was once a hawk has begun to speak softly of the "wasted" deaths of his friends in a war that no longer has meaning for him. His own voice from the past chants a pro-war song as the film cuts to the contemporary scene: the subdued mumble in a Louisiana bar and his own bearded face.

It is not useful to discuss such a news story—and there are many like it—in terms of fact or fiction, truth or falsehood. Credibility here is not so much a matter of empiricism as of an understanding by the audience that the newscaster has struck the right compromise. The audience assents to the narrative assumptions. What are those assumptions? For one, we know that what Morton Dean has reported is both true and false. We know that America is dissatisfied, even angry with the Vietnamese adventure and depressed by its meaninglessness. We know that there are many other young men like this veteran. We also know that the issues and the changes in attitude toward the war are not as simple as this young man's transition from singing a war ballad to growing a beard. We know that all events are not so easily structured along novelistic lines—protagonist blind, protagonist awakened—that not all young men who grow dissatisfied can articulate the issue so economically and effectively.

Morton Dean created a metaphor, and as with every metaphor, it is both a real report on our world, and a false, oversimplified presentation of a much more politically and emotionally complex issue. The agreement between viewer and narrator is to admit the need to simplify in order to say something which is approximately true. In this case, granting Morton Dean's and CBS News' credibility, the audience agrees willingly to the metaphorical act.

Not every news story strikes as successful a balance as Dean's did:

> Friday, November 8, 1974. CBS EVENING NEWS. David Dick reports from Tennessee that the Tom Marlow family have been barely surviving on a monthly welfare check ever since Tom Marlow was injured in a mining accident eleven years earlier. Against the backdrop of the World Food Conference, Walter Cronkite reminds us that there is hunger in America.

The next Monday a follow-up is necessary because calls poured into the CBS Studio over the weekend and envelopes stuffed with money arrived at the Marlows'. David Dick and Walter Cronkite explain patiently that it had not been the intention of CBS to make a special plea for one family; others were worse off than Tom Marlow. The point of their story was that Americans should not lose sight of poverty at home as we listen to talk of hunger abroad.

Something went wrong in the original story, or else a follow-up—a correction of an error—would not have been necessary. Again, there is no way to analyze the failure in terms of truth or falsehood. The journalistic response to the problem would, I suspect, be a comment about the viewers only hearing and seeing what they want to hear and see—not an untrue statement, by any means, but not a very useful one. Once it has been said, what is to be made of it? Isn't it, rather, a bit more helpful to realize that the assumption at the base of David Dick's narrative construct is an invitation to the audience to respond emotionally—a response which has its roots in storymaking, in the narrative function?

Dick created not a factual presentation (the stock market report is a factual presentation and, therefore, the least interesting segment of any news program), but a humanly motivated story. A news narrative, as does any narrative, engages the imaginative—hence, inevitably, emotional—response of the viewer. Narrative asks what are they like, why do they act, how does it feel, and invites the attendant emotional, imaginative realization of those questions. To expect the American viewer to sit in cold contemplation as a hungry American family is singled out is as impossible as if Dickens had forbidden weeping at the death of Little Nell. One compacts certain terms with any audience in the act of narration, and to expect to go around or under or over those terms, to expect to check their consequence, is to fail to understand the rules of the game. It is—to borrow from Scholes and Kellogg[8]—to expect to have your empirical bread and eat your narrative cake.

Cognition, in such a case, is distant. The reality of the narrative is the viewer's emotional reaction, and emotional engagement is the trickiest of relationships to predict or understand. Aristotle was hard put to explain it, and nobody after him has managed to clarify whether emotions are purged or incited by narrative presentation. What TV newsmen *do* know is that stories given to the depiction of elemental human dilemmas will galvanize emotion, and they will attract and maintain an audience.

A Challenge for
New Forms in TV Newscasts

By structuring an event as a plotted story, involving all the drama of filmed confrontation (which is the preferred stock of television news) and the portrayal of complex matters in terms of simple conflict (which could be transferred without substantial change to an entertainment program), the television newsman deliberately invites his audience to respond to the news in the same way that it responds to entertainment programming. But news stories can never share the opening stasis and closing return to stasis of the heroic plot structure. The story (and the protagonist) is never able to achieve completion and never returns the world to a state of safe stability. We can vote the bums out of office, but each new set of leaders deals with nearly identical problems in the same ineffective ways. Not finding Jimmy Hoffa's body, or even a

concrete crime connected with his disappearance, is the characteristic shape which events assume on television. The problem is carefully presented and detailed by filmed interviews. The leaders are
seen working toward its solution. Then the story slowly fades away,
usually unresolved. Hoffa's body hasn't turned up and no crime
has been identified.

Not that the newsman should or could present a resolution
where none exists. But in introducing action and simplifying conflict in order to dramatize the news and attract an audience, the
television newsman can hardly escape the public frustration that
surfaces when he fails to close his drama in some way more satisfactory than "That's the way it is."

The newsman, and the anchorman in particular, also disap-
points the audience through his constant objectivity and dispassion. He should be a hero of action. He is the only character in the
drama who commands the information, the resources, and the un-
sullied stature to act. He brings together the events of the world,
summons the storytellers to relate their plots, and structures the
whole into a recognizable and ritualized pattern. If the audience
were able to accept the premise of his role—that knowing is the
only action possible—he would succeed. But the various plots which
constitute his knowledge and his story-telling are based on another
premise: that knowing is related to the ability to act and that plotted
action leads to resolution. As a result, the anchorman must forever
assume a role fragmented by his inability to resolve problems or
offer a concluding act. He is limited to telling the stories.

Changing the character of the anchorman—as John Chancellor
has tried—will not alter the situation. We know from earlier experience at the BBC that no matter how conscientiously the newsman tries to act as a neutral announcer within a structure which
casts him in a role as an authority, he will fail. British audiences
were, for a time, witness to newsmen who tried to erase all suggestive implications in their delivery, but the vocal mannerisms
which distinguish one human being from another inevitably emerged,
and the audience quickly seized on favorites. Characterization is
an element in narrative structure. Thus, as long as the TV news
structure forces a person to sit as the functional authority, his
character is manifested in that role.

One could say that television viewers ought to be capable of
distinguishing between the clear-cut, repetitive resolutions of prime-
time entertainment and the necessarily open-ended news stories of

a world forever in transition, forever becoming. One could say that, if we didn't see the news programs, night after night, structuring the news events as narrative stories. Certainly, we can understand the networks' concern with building an audience for their news shows. And, perhaps, on a rational level, television audiences realize that the news is, by nature, fragmentary—a cyclical, unending series of events. In a sense, there is a kind of agreement between the networks and newsmen who present the news and the audience who views it: The newsmen recognize the need to structure the news so as to make it entertaining, while the audience recognizes that this entertaining narrative structure does not actually reflect the real world.

Yet, the narrative structure of the news programs still lead us to *emotionally* expect the congruence to be found in traditional narratives. That is, although we may understand why TV news is structured as it is, and why that structure does not always work out, we still somehow expect the narrative promise of wholeness and completion. And because this promise is not fulfilled—can never be fulfilled—we may feel disappointed and even antagonistic toward news shows and newsmen.

Network news has pandered for too long to the formula which fills most of the night's programming. Rather than counter the fragmentary nature of the news by superimposing forms on it which promise wholeness, television news should seek methods which will allow the fragmentation of news content to find its own complementary form. What those forms might be are perhaps suggested in programs like "Washington Week in Review" on PBS.

Whereas the core meanings of commercial network news lie in filmed narratives, and the structure of those narratives put the newsman, and the anchorman in particular, into the authoritative, authorial role, "Washington Week in Review" derives its energy from human conversation. The attention is shifted directly to the newsman, the story is known only from his discussion of it. The result is an attention to the human act of interpretation. Paradoxically, the newsman's role as an authority is made less significant when we see him develop his story, rather informally, before our eyes. Each reporter is also subject to question and disagreement from colleagues sitting around the table, and the moderator, Paul Duke, is cast more as a convener than as an anchorman.

The solution seems to be, then, not to remove the newsman from our attention, not to place him or her behind the story, but to make the newsman as newsman a part of the story. Only Charles Kuralt achieves that role on network news. The distinction between his human interest reports and hard news is less in the lighter content of his reportage than in the manner of it. Kuralt appears as part of his stories and, by doing so, enforces our awareness that he alone interpreted these events and in that aloneness is subject to judgment.

Footnotes

1. Roper Research Associates report for the Television Information Office, released at the National Association of Broadcasters, April 1975. *Broadcasting*, 88 (April 14, 1975), pp. 48-50.

2. "If you got conflicting or different reports of the same news story from radio, television, the magazines and the newspapers, which of the four versions would you be most inclined to believe—the one on radio or television or magazines or newspapers?"

	12/59	11/61	11/64	11/68	11/72	11/74
	%	%	%	%	%	%
TV	29	39	41	44	48	51
Newsp.	32	24	23	21	21	20
Radio	12	12	8	8	8	8
Mag.	10	10	10	11	10	8
DK/NA	17	17	18	16	13	13

3. "In April 1974, *U.S. News and World Report* asked five hundred U.S. 'leaders' to rate organizations and institutions according to the amount of influence . . . for decisions or actions affecting the nation as a whole. TV came in first, with a score of 7.2 on a scale of 1 to 10. The White House tied the Supreme Court for second place, and newspapers came next. In Burns Roper's 1973 report on the information preferences of the nation, TV was still at the top, with 64 percent of the population.

   "In a special study done by Louis Harris for the Senate Subcommittee on Intergovernmental Relations, TV news was found to have made by far the greatest gains in public confidence since 1965—overtaking the military, organized religion, the Supreme Court, the U.S. Senate, the House of Representatives, and the executive branch of the federal government." — Marvin Barrett, ed., *Moments of Truth: The Fifth Alfred I. Dupont-Columbia University Survey of Broadcast Journalism.* New York: Thomas Y. Crowell Co., 1975, page 137.

4. See, for instance, Michael J. Robinson, "American Political Legitimacy in an Era of Electronic Journalism: Reflections on the Evening News," *Television as a Social Force: New Approaches to TV Criticism*, edited by Richard Adler. New York: Praeger Publishers, 1975.

5. Richard Carpenter, "Ritual, Aesthetics, and TV," *Journal of Popular Culture* (Fall, 1969); reprinted in *Mass Media and Mass Man*, edited by Alan Casty. New York: Holt, Rinehart and Winston, 1968.

6. Robert Daley, "We Deal With Emotional Facts," *New York Times Magazine* (December 15, 1974).

7. In an unpublished essay, Madonna Kolbenschlag of Notre Dame writes of the mirroring in television news of the hierarchy of story types established by Northrup Frye via Aristotle. First came the epics—superior characters in superior circumstances; then the hero tales—superior characters in ordinary circumstances; next, the melodramas—ordinary characters in ordinary circumstances; and finally, the low comedy—characters we can look down on who do not manage the everyday very well. Hughes Rudd is a genius at ending his morning news program on this last type.

8. Robert Scholes and Robert Kellogg, *The Nature of Narrative*. New York: Oxford University Press, 1966.

Reflections on the Nightly News

Michael J. Robinson

As long as the economy holds out, liberal democracies get by—with or without political legitimacy.[1] But legitimacy is always an essential reserve. In the long run, democratic systems do not—cannot—survive monetary or social crises with institutions that lack the public's trust and respect. Thus in 1975 the instability of our economy, the inadequacy of our energy reserves and the incredulousness still surrounding our near impeachment, together, have forced many of us to doubt our capacity to preserve the Social Order—strange as this thought may be for those who have never once considered ourselves members of the American Ruling Class.

But these nightmares about Watergate, inflation, and gas lines are in some respects at least ten years too late. In terms of our legitimacy, Watergate admittedly did us no favors. According to the Harris poll, the percentage of our adult population expressing confidence in the executive branch (not the President)—once our most legitimate branch—hit a new low of 19 percent in November, 1973.[2] Following the "Saturday Night Massacre," a full 66 percent of the nation felt that they could, at best, trust the government "only some of the time" to do what is right.[3] But despite the very recent and precipitous decline in public confidence in the executive, his office and his government, the fact is that our inflation, our shortages, even our Watergate, all represent a wave, not the tide, in American politics. In truth, the tide has been moving inexorably since the late fifties—always on the ebb.

Until the sixties, the legitimacy of the American system had been forever growing—at least since the Depression. As late as 1958, whites and blacks—even in the year of Little Rock—showed identical and overwhelming levels of commitment to and belief in our national political institutions.[4] But somewhere along the way, somewhere perhaps between the Kennedy and Johnson years, our political malaise began to emerge; it has abated only once since that time—during the first two "happy" years of the Nixon administration.[5]

Congress, the President and the Supreme Court have not been the only casualties of the sixties. As a nation we have also lost faith in ourselves as political entities. In fact, there is evidence to indicate that we came to doubt ourselves before coming to doubt our institutions; such was the depth of our loyalty. Since 1958 the proportion of Americans believing that they cannot even understand politics has virtually doubled.[6]

We have, in short, witnessed the slow and steady decline of two basic political commodities—belief in the worth and appropriateness of our governmental structures and belief in our own capacity to know and understand politics.

Not surprisingly, there are almost as many theories to explain this corrosion of spirit as there are theorists. There are theories of cyclical history—the Toynbee theme. There are theories based in Maslovian psychology. There are other, more straightforward theories too—theories which attribute our malaise to disconnected but dramatic events. But I suggest that there are now both data and logic which support a McLuhanist interpretation—that we are suffering from Videomalaise, that our doubts about ourselves and hostility toward our institutions would be far less severe were it not for the images we receive from the electronic media, more specifically, from network journalism.

In one respect this is an academic question. Our growing illegitimacy would not end tomorrow were we to shut down the networks in a fit of authoritarian pique. The effects may be so deeply embedded within the national psyche that daily choruses of the *Star-*

Spangled Banner and *My Country 'Tis of Thee* sung by David Brinkley and Dan Rather would produce no remission whatever in our symptoms. I don't believe, however, that our case is inevitably a terminal one. Our condition is chronic, not critical. And I believe that we can find the roots of our condition first in 1956, the year in which the Huntley-Brinkley "Report" began, and especially in 1963, the year in which the two major networks, in pursuit of the public interest, developed the thirty-minute news program and began a new era of electronic journalism.

In the first section of this essay I will look at this supposition—that our current political pathology is a function of our television news system. And, having worked to establish a meaningful connection, I will try in the sections that follow to explain it, evaluate it from a moral and political perspective and suggest methods for coping with it.

Theories and Findings

My beliefs about television and its impact on legitimacy came to me only recently. Years ago, my own library research and my personal intuitions had led me to believe that television news, with its "liberal" bias, simply and mechanistically moved the society toward the left. But during the last three years I have found in several independent bits of research that the principal effect is not political liberalization; it is, instead, political frustration—political malaise. Having conducted a series of social experiments in the early seventies using "The Selling of the Pentagon," I discovered that the general response to so controversial a program was neither a markedly increasing disdain for the military nor a markedly decreasing credibility for CBS, the parent of the program. The general response was an increasing belief that the viewer himself couldn't come to grips with the political issues involved.[7] After seeing "The Selling" my white, Christian, midwestern subjects left the viewing studio feeling frustrated and politically emasculated—politically impotent, so to speak. I found a similar reaction—a reaction based in frustration—among two groups of randomly-selected Oregonians, following their own voluntary exposure to the televised Watergate hearings.[8] Respondents came away

from that experience with an increasing hostility towards government and an increasing sense of personal perplexity.[9] But I use these
studies only as a backdrop. In this essay I prefer to focus upon other
work with which I have been most recently involved. These findings
are, I confess, only partly mine; the data belong to the Survey Research Center at the University of Michigan. Therefore, although the
calculations are all mine, the respondents are eternally theirs and I
thank them for the loan.

My recent work with television has forced me to build a yet
untested theory concerning the growth of political illegitimacy. I
have begun to envision a two-stage process in which television journalism, with its constant emphasis on social and political conflict,
its high credibility, its powerful audio-visual capabilities and its epi-
demicity, has caused the more vulnerable viewers first to doubt their
own understanding of their political system. (The major institutions
are, after all, too preciously regarded to disdain at first.) But once
these individuals have passed this initial stage they enter a second
phase in which personal denigration continues and in which a new
hostility toward politics and government also emerges. Having passed
through both stages of political cynicism, these uniquely susceptible
individuals pass their cynicism along to those who were, at the start,
less attuned to television messages and consequently less directly vulnerable to televisual malaise. (Public opinion polls may prove to be
the most effective carrier for those who are not directly connected to
or dependent upon TV news.)

All this is theory, of course. But the theory fits nicely with the
findings from the experimental work I have done in the past.[10] To
demonstrate that the theory fits with national survey data as well, I
offer the following set of findings from the 1968 election study, a
national survey conducted by the Michigan Survey Research Center,
in Ann Arbor.[11]

I divided all the respondents in this survey into three disctinct
groups. Those individuals who relied upon something other than television for their political information in 1968 were placed in Group A;
those who relied principally upon television were placed in Group B;
and those who followed politics *only* through television were placed
in Group C. Having constructed such a "variable"—a variable with
three distinct levels of television dependency—I checked to see if
those who were dependent upon television were different, politically
speaking, from those who were not.

If the theory of televisual malaise were to have any validity, one should have expected from all these operations to find, at a minimum, two things: (1) some correlation, however modest, between the level of television dependency and attitudes towards one's own political self-esteem, and (2) some correlation, presumably smaller than that above, between the level of dependency toward political institutions. (One might also expect to find, were there data from earlier elections, that the first set of correlations—correlations between the level of dependency and political self-esteem—would appear at an earlier point in time than would the others.)

Although the findings do not match perfectly with the theory, there is enough correspondence to merit further investigation, as well as an explanation. A more stringent test of the theory is in progress, and the explanation of the theory begins on page 322.

I have selected three items which in some ways tap some of the dimensions of public opinion which are relevant to any discussion of legitimacy. I have selected these three because they deal with the two stages on the road to illegitimacy—political self-doubt and political cynicism directed against our institutions. I have also chosen them because they tend to fit the theory rather well. But many of the items I checked which are not reported here fit the theory almost as well.

Two of the three items are of one type: Respondents were asked whether or not they agreed with a series of political statements. The statements were:

1. Sometimes politics and government seem so complicated that a person like me can't really understand what's going on.

2. Generally speaking, those we elect to Congress in Washington lose touch with the people pretty quickly.

The third statement was different in that it provided three possible choices:

3. Do you think that quite a few people running the government are a little crooked, not very many are, or do you think hardly any of them are at all?

The first item was specifically used to assess the individual's attitude toward himself as a political entity. The second item—about

Congress—was the one direct test of institutional responsiveness. The third item was a bridge, asking not about a specific institution but all the individuals involved, collectively, in the government.

The findings are presented in toto in tables 1, 2 and 3. In general, the pattern I had anticipated emerged. Even when examining respondents with similar levels of education, the greater the dependency upon television, the greater the personal confusion and estrangement from government. Those who rely upon television in following politics are more confused and more cynical than those who do not. And those who rely totally upon television are the most confused and cynical of all. The differences among the groups run generally between 10 percent and 15 percent. When looking at respondents with a similar level of education the differences diminish, but they do not disappear. Interestingly enough, the differences are greatest among those with a high school education—the middle-status Americans—a finding which fits well with the conventional wisdom concerning "the real America" during the last ten years.

There is one other bit of evidence which fits the theory. In general, there are greater differences between the groups on the items concerning personal political capacity than on items dealing with governmental institutions. Obviously, this does not prove that the process is, in fact, two-staged. But this finding is consistent with that interpretation.

In general, these findings do not "prove" anything. When two variables correlate, one cannot infer that one causes the other. In fact, some will undoubtedly argue that my findings show precisely the reverse of what I suggest—that those who are already frustrated are merely moved to watch television, instead of the other way around. (More on that later.) For now we should remember that these variables cannot tell us much about the sequence of events. Did personal frustration really precede frustration with the institutions? These data cannot give a definitive answer. Nor do these data speak unequivocally to the basic theory—that television produces political malaise. There are holes here. But we should remember too that the findings run in the right direction. The relationships, if weak, are as predicted in most cases, even with controls for other variables. And we should also remember that the TV variable we use is a very poor one—one which does not really convey the amount of exposure, only the comparative amount. Furthermore, there is no specific item about "network" television. But one has to use the data available to him or to her. As it stands now, I am planning my own research project to get at this question of television malaise more directly. But for the moment I hope that these findings will at least set the stage for the essay which follows.

TABLE 1
Respondent's opinion as to
whether or not he can understand politics

	GROUP A Those not relying on television	GROUP B Those relying on television	GROUP C Those relying *only* on television
Percentage who cannot *understand*	63% (417)	71% (693)	91% (130)

Controlling for education level of respondent

	GROUP A Those not relying on television	GROUP B Those relying on television	GROUP C Those relying *only* on television
Percentage who cannot *understand*			
Less than 8 grades	83% (23)	87% (67)	97% (30)
Grades 8 thru 11	82% (102)	84% (223)	96% (51)
Grade 12	62% (129)	70% (211)	82% (39)
Some college	51% (77)	60% (110)	71% (7)
College	54% (60)	38% (59)	100% (1)
College +	33% (27)	58% (24)	100% (2)

There are, however, two last points to be made in defense of this assumed tie between television exposure and prevailing political ethos. First, all these relationships exist not only in the 1968 data but in the 1964 data and the 1960 data as well. Before that time there was no relationship between television dependency and one's opinions about his or her political worth or the worth of our political institutions.[12] This dividing line between 1956 and 1960 is a fasci-

TABLE 2
Respondent's opinion as to
whether or not government leaders are crooked

	GROUP A Those not relying on television	**GROUP B** Those relying on television	**GROUP C** Those relying *only* on television
Percent believing *"quite a few"* *are crooked*	21% (401)	27% (676)	34% (115)

Controlling for educational level of respondent

	GROUP A Those not relying on television	**GROUP B** Those relying on television	**GROUP C** Those relying *only* on television
Percent believing *"quite a few"* *are crooked*			
Less than 8 grades	24% (21)	26% (65)	43% (21)
Grades 8 thru 11	26% (97)	29% (214)	35% (46)
Grade 12	22% (126)	29% (207)	32% (38)
Some college	20% (74)	29% (108)	14% (7)
College	17% (58)	19% (59)	*
College +	8% (25)	17% (23)	50% (2)

*No valid codes.

nating one, which suggests that the coming of the Huntley-Brinkley "Report" may have initiated the coming of a new era of political estrangement. It is at least an interesting point to consider.

TABLE 3
Respondent's view as to
whether or not Congressmen lose touch
with constituents after election

	GROUP A Those not relying on television	GROUP B Those relying on television	GROUP C Those relying *only* on television
Percent believing Congressman does lose touch with constituents	47% (402)	57% (675)	68% (122)

Controlling for educational level of respondent

	GROUP A Those not relying on television	GROUP B Those relying on television	GROUP C Those relying *only* on television
Percent believing Congressman does lose touch with constituents			
Less than 8 grades	71% (21)	75% (65)	76% (25)
Grades 8 thru 11	58% (97)	66% (216)	69% (48)
Grade 12	46% (127)	54% (217)	62% (39)
Some college	51% (76)	44% (108)	71% (7)
College	29% (56)	46% (56)	100% (1)
College +	32% (25)	30% (23)	50% (2)

The other point is more procedural than substantive. Agreed that the findings I offer here do not set the world on fire. When combined with findings from my other research they become a little more convincing. Even when these findings are taken alone, it is amazing that any of the differences between the three groups occur, given the inherent weakness of the procedures used to uncover them.

But, despite all the weaknesses and all the caveats, I hope that these findings will not be dismissed too facilely. Social scientists and journalists frequently discount theories such as mine—theories that even hint of a McLuhanist persuasion. Much of their skepticism is warranted, but at least some grows in the soil of an intellectual ethnocentrism. Social scientists may not see or admit the impact of television because they themselves are in its midst. Social scientists are especially vulnerable to this weakness—to deny an effect which may exist in them as well as in their subjects and respondents. But those who deny the possibility of any effects and plead their own sophistication as defense may in themselves prove to be the last to know what is happening around them. We have all had our perceptions of the world molded by television news, no matter how tightly we hold our copies of the *Times* or the *Post* to our breasts or our minds. I might even go so far as to suggest that the individuals who create the *Times* and the *Post* have even been affected by the images the networks provide.

So for the remainder of this piece I prefer to assume that the coincidence between the growth of television journalism and the growth in political illegitimacy is not coincidental. Nothing in these data, or in any data I have collected during the last four years, moves me very far from my convictions about television news and the state of our world. Therefore, I will suppose this hypothetical relationship between television and our political ethos to be real from this point on. And in the next three sections I will attempt to explain that relationship by analyzing (a) the audience for, (b) the contents within, and (c) the personnel of the network news system.

The Inadvertent Television News Audience

The enormity of the network news audience is undeniable. With virtually each passing year the audience for television journalism becomes larger and more television-dependent.

In 1973 ABC commissioned a Nielsen Survey and discovered that the three nightly news programs reached 50 million homes in the average month and 46 million homes in the average week—71 percent of all homes.[13] And these figures, although probably somewhat inflated, represented, respectively, a 7 percent and 9 percent increase from 1972, suggesting the imperiousness of television journalism.

Along with the absolute size of the news audience, dependency on TV news has also increased. The Roper poll has, with tedious regularity, demonstrated that television, year by year, strengthens its position as the most-preferred medium.[14] In my own research I find a clear majority (56 percent) following national politics principally through television and another 10 percent following only through television.[15]

However, the absolute size of the audience, in and of itself, is not the most important factor. The first crucial factor in understanding television's impact upon legitimacy is the abnormality of shape and composition of the television audience.

I begin with an assumption—that any increase in available political information within a society, especially a libertarian society, will probably increase, to some degree, the level of political frustration or disaffection. If this were not a high probability, one would expect much less concern with the once radical notion that the press should be essentially free—an idea that is, after all, rejected by the vast majority of the governments and, I dare say, people of our world. (CBS News itself discovered that as late as March, 1970, 55 percent of the American public felt that when our government believes national interest is involved it should be able to stop any and all news reports.[16])

Clearly, the potential effect of increasing information does not always materialize. During World War II, one guesses, our media expanded and presumably so did the availability of information. But under those extraordinary circumstances the increase in absolute level of information probably *decreased* the level of political disquiet. Information in a democracy need not always produce disaffection. Nonetheless, the increase of information in an open system of media carries with it a marked potential for creating political anxiety. And it appears as if the television news "system," which began in the mid-fifties, has helped to realize the potential anxiety. In fact, one might argue that public affairs television has so profoundly distorted the general historical pattern of informational expansion that the realization of that potential has become and is a certainty.

When Latin was translated into common tongues during the Renaissance, when print was invented, when the penny press emerged, there was an obvious expansion in the availability of information—political and otherwise. Generally, the expansion was downward through the social strata. But the increase in audience was biased in favor of the upper classes. Changing from Latin to English increased media exposure, but more for the nobles than the serfs. The adoption of print also increased the level of exposure for all groups, but the increase was greater among the social, economic and political elites. So it was always—at least until radio and television. But the electronic media have made the process of communication almost effortless. After all, it is easier to hear than to read, and easier to see than to hear. As a consequence, the electronic media—especially television—have produced an audience different from the Mass Audience of the eighteenth, nineteenth, or even early twentieth centuries; they have produced, instead, the Inadvertent Audience as well. The Inadvertent Audience is that large, amorphous portion within the Mass Audience, that portion which will *not read* the news of the day but which is willing *to listen to* or *watch* the news if the listening or watching is entertaining. Obviously, the Inadvertent Audience differs from the Mass Audience qualitatively as well. The new audience, unlike the old, receives its politically relevant information through a wholly passive process—one in which the viewer literally falls into the audience. Similar notions about accidental audiences must have tormented the German aristocrats when Gutenberg made possible not only the penny press but the pandering entrepreneur and yellow journalism as well. Every new medium is, after all, said to be the end—the ultimate disequilibriating social force; and I confess to my own temporocentric bias. But in some respects the audience for the pamphlets of Paine and the Manifesto by Marx were of a different—and far less inadvertent—character. All other things being equal, their audiences were even *less* volatile than those which television provides. Television, in essence, provides an audience which is the most likely of all to realize the potential political discord which accompanies an informational expansion.

Why should all this be true? Why is the Inadvertent Audience so vulnerable to the effects we have already documented? Why? Because television builds an audience with few of the self-regulating processes which the print media have always provided—self-regulating processes which have, until now, permitted government and free press to live together, even if the relationship were strained.

An early disciple of James Madison, writing in defense of a free press, would, no doubt, have looked beyond the inherent dangers of tabloidism by pointing to the most important internal check on the power of print—the direct relationship between class and propensity to read. At every other time, with every other medium, this relationship has served as a political filter. The aristocrat paid more attention to the written event than the farmer, the capitalist more than the worker. Information was obtained more frequently by those who could and would pay the price—in time, as well as in coin. John Robinson has shown how vibrant and how ironic the relationship between social status and exposure to the print media can be, even in the United States.

> *People with a college education, when compared to their countrymen with less than a high school education, are not only twenty times as likely to regularly read sophisticated commentary magazines and fifteen times as likely to read a general news magazine, they are also three times as likely to read a pictorial and general interest magazine . . . the best known of these magazines is often referred to as 'the magazine for those who can't think . . .'*[17]

But today the once immutable and universal law of exposure has been overturned. Not only are the less-educated no less likely to watch television journalism, they are more likely to do so! The data in Table 4, taken from a very recent study completed in Minneapolis and based upon diaries kept by viewers, show that the lowest educational stratum watches more television news than the highest—not only in terms of absolute minutes, but also in percent of total viewing time.[18] Neither William Randolph Hearst nor Henry Luce, at their best or at their worst, could achieve anything like this. Such is the nature of television's Inadvertent Audience.

An 18th century liberal would, one presumes, have based his case for maintaining both a free press and the social order upon the anticipated intellectual indolence of the rabble; the words to ignite the passions of the nonaristocratic population would never be read. This being a principal defense for freeing the press, the Inadvertent Audience must produce some serious anxieties for the Madisonian-based proponents of the First Amendment. Even for those who are more contemporary in their thinking, the Inadvertent Audience is still an unsettling reality.

Until the coming of the television news system, there was a second internal mechanism that could help reconcile press freedom with a commitment to preserve the social order. Had Madison had the chance to read Katz and Lazarsfeld he would have discovered that these two patently nonaristocratic sociologists had found another argument for allowing an independent media within a free society. Katz and Lazarsfeld realized that the mass audience was really two audiences in one, that political information did not pass from source to mass directly.[19] A wall of Opinion Leaders stood between them, Opinion Leaders who would invariably interpret the original message.

TABLE 4
*Actual TV viewing habits by level of education
in Minneapolis in 1970
(expressed in percentages of total minutes of TV watched)* *

EDUCATION

PROGRAM TYPE	0-8 yrs.	9-11 yrs.	12 yrs.	1-4 yrs. College
Comedy-variety.	27	25	27	23
Movies.	16	19	21	20
Action.	17	17	16	15
Sports.	6	9	8	13
Light music	11	11	10	8
Light drama	1	2	3	2
News.	20	15	14	17
Information and public affairs	2	2	2	2
Heavy drama	—	—	—	1
Religion.	1	1	—	—
Heavy music.	—	—	—	—
Base (Minutes): 100 percent =	41,535	39,540	163,150	73,740
N(number of viewers) =	(38)	(38)	(176)	(76)

*taken from Bower's *Television and the Public* (1973), p. 132.

While nobody could guarantee that the opinion leaders would be more sympathetic to and supportive of the prevailing institutions of the period, there was some evidence and some speculation to suggest that they were.[20] At the very least, the Opinion Leaders were a buffer between any disconcerting information and the potentially disconcerted reader or listener. Consequently, in most cases this two-step flow of communication between the media and the public could serve to militate against the types of effects that a free press might be expected to engender.

But in this instance as well, television journalism has reversed the traditional process of communication. The two-step flow has dried to a trickle.[21] Since the mid-fifites the networks have apparently managed to bypass the Opinion Leaders and deal directly with the Mass Audience and the Inadvertent Audience. By circumventing the Opinion Leaders, television has "subverted" another source of mediation between the source and the target, another self-regulating mechanism.

Both the obsolescence of the two-step model and the unique composition of the television Inadvertent Audience are, of course, the consequence of the tremendous pulling power of commercial television, a medium which manages to consume more than 30 percent of all our free time in America.[22] But there is still one more consequence of the magnetism of commercial television which is relevant to us in explaining the vulnerability of the network news audience.

Commercial television news has actually reduced the amount of contact with the other informational media (i.e., the competing news media). Having established itself as a serious journalistic enterprise, television journalism has managed to supplant other news media in popularity. Those who once read the news with less than complete dedication have begun to accept network journalism as an ample dosage of political information. The networks have become the only, as well as the first, source of information for millions of Americans. This is not a case for snobbishness; I have never believed that reading is, per se, the greater, purer good. But by unintentionally persuading viewers that they are informed by following television news—by narcoticizing viewers and unwittingly justifying their reliance upon one medium—the networks have undermined, to some degree, a third mediating factor in the communications process. The networks have, in the last ten years, undermined the tendency to supplement one medium with another. For much of the population—a growing percentage—the only supplementation of information is *among networks,* not between media. Given the subtle types of nonpolitical bias which exist at the networks (see the following section), this is a significant development in the process of political communication.

On the other hand, to some people in my audience—all those who have chosen to read this essay—these notions about the size, shape and composition of the Inadvertent Audience may seem a little boring, if not a little contrived. Despite the appearance of banality, however, these notions are fundamental. To understand the broad-based, denigrating effects of television news, one must remember that commercial television has produced a new system of political communication, a system in which some of the most important and self-contained mechanisms through which free media and political authority are reconciled have been jeopardized. Commercial television has not only produced an audience for television journalism which is unique in history; it has also produced an audience which is basic to all of us in trying to understand the flow of political information in the United States.

American television has, in short, assembled a national news audience that is at one and the same time disproportionately drawn from the lower end of the sociological spectrum, more likely to obtain its information directly from the source, and increasingly more willing to satisfy its total desire for information through only one medium. In fact, no one single factor helps explain television malaise more fundamentally than these unique, if relatively obvious, characteristics of the Inadvertent Audience. The Inadvertent Audience is a necessary condition for my theory.

But the uniqueness of the audience is just that—a necessary, not a sufficient condition for explaining the effects of network television upon our political institutions and our political ethos. If there were strict, authoritarian controls imposed upon news content, there would be no such effects. But given the content provided by the network news organizations, the effects are more readily understood.

The Nonpartisan Biases
of Television News

Given the general tenor of American journalism, if the actual content of television journalism were identical to that of the print media (i.e., if both used identical copy) we might expect television journalism to produce more political cynicism and estrangement than print—simply because television reaches more people. But the major media do not present the same copy. They each provide different emphases, different directions; each medium has its own inherent set of biases. Television journalism, in short, presents images of our society and our politics that are different from those of the print media or even radio, and these differences represent a type of bias.

Despite the conventional wisdom, the biases inherent in television news are not overwhelmingly, or even substantially, politically partisan. Edith Efron's assertions that the networks produce news that invariably supports the "Liberal-left Democratic Axis of opinion" is not so much wrong as ill-conceived and misinterpreted.

Political imbalance does exist within the press corps, both electronic and print. During my own limited experience with the press coverage of the impeachment process, for example, I witnessed an almost consensual expression of opinion favoring Nixon's impeachment among members of the corps. (Incidentally, that consensus preceded the Saturday Night Massacre.) One of the principal network correspondents assigned directly to the impeachment inquiry demonstrated, in private but audibly, a serious hostility to and a partisan contempt for then-President Nixon and his administration. However, very little of that political bias came through during this correspondent's nightly telecasts. (Indeed, in the one incident in which this particular correspondent was forced to choose between his own feelings about a successful impeachment and his personal commitment to report news as he had heard it, despite its implications for impeachment—the incident involved Peter Rodino's alleged prediction on the vote for impeachment within the Judiciary Committee—he chose the latter course, the professional course, albeit reluctantly.)

But, despite a relatively objective public performance on impeachment, the networks would be hard-pressed to make a case that there is no partisan imbalance within the minds and hearts of the press corps, even if the networks swear that the biases remain confined to the minds and hearts of their correspondents when the news is reported. In 1968, after interviewing the technical staff, executives and correspondents at NBC News, Edward Epstein concluded that the overwhelming majority of the correspondents at NBC thought of themselves as liberals or held positions on public issues which Epstein regarded as liberal.[23] Evidence that is perhaps more poignant comes from a *Playboy* interview with Walter Cronkite which took place as late as 1973. Knowing that his remarks in *Playboy* could boomerang,

Cronkite, when asked about the alleged left-of-center orientation of television newsmen, responded:

> ... *Well, certainly liberal, and possibly left of center as well. I would have to accept that. ... I think that being a liberal, in the true sense, is being nondoctrinaire, nondogmatic, noncommitted to a cause—but examining each case on its merits. Being left of center is another thing; it's a political position. I think most newspapermen by definition have to be liberal; if they're not liberal, by my definition of it, then they can hardly be good newspapermen. If they're preordained dogmatists for a cause, then they can't be very good journalists; that is, if they carry it into their journalism.*[24]

Cronkite's remarks point up two truths—that the television newsperson tends to be a liberal but that biases in reporting are not partisan liberal, or as Cronkite calls them, left of center. In fact, despite the overwhelming Democratic, "liberal" orientation among members of the network news corps, according to one still-unpublished analysis of the 1972 election, all three networks—ABC, CBS, NBC—reported the Nixon-Agnew candidacies more favorably (actually, less unfavorably) than the McGovern-Eagleton-Shriver candidacies.[25] This finding alone requires that we posit a more sophisticated interpretation of the type of content which network news organizations provide, an interpretation which transcends the relatively superficial conspiracy theories popularized by former Vice-President Agnew.

Basically, the images of television journalism are determined far more by the organizational needs of the networks and the organizational perceptions of the national audience than by the generally nonidealogical political opinions of the network journalists themselves. (Epstein says the correspondents are fundamentally nonpolitical in their thinking.)

Beyond their own commitment to reporting news, according to Epstein, the news organizations must do four things in order to maintain themselves and expand their budgets: (1) satisfy the corporation by cutting unnecessary news costs (Jack Schneider used to complain that fixed costs for news were reasonable but "unscheduled" news was hurting the CBS rate of return); (2) satisfy the parent organization by maintaining an audience, inadvertent or otherwise; (3) satisfy the affiliates by holding the audience and avoiding controversy over fundamentals; (4) keep the FCC away from the affiliates by presenting "balanced" news items and items which are of national interest. It is out of this rather cynical collection of obligations—not the liberal predispositions of the news departments—that the TV images of our society come, and have come, since the mid-fifties. It is their organizational needs which produce a content at ABC, NBC and CBS that is essentially the same—despite the varying political opinions of the people who run those three greatly similar organizations.

The Thematic Bias: The first characteristic which flows from the obligations of the organization is the thematic news report. More than any other major news source—except local TV news, a world unto itself—the networks have come to appreciate the Short Story. If one looks closely at the last 15 minutes of the evening news, one finds a virtual compendium of politically relevant essays. The Short Story is invaluable to the network news organization. It tends to hold the audience, especially the Inadvertent Audience (given the criteria for a successful news show, members of the Inadvertent Audience are just as valuable to the networks as any other).

The thematic Short Story has, however, become more than a simple pattern of evening news. The entire network news organization is geared to thematic presentation. In 1969 and 1973 I took the opportunity to quiz my undergraduate students about the then most-recent Democratic presidential primary in New Hampshire. The quiz was simple enough—who won? In both years the majority of the class was wrong, choosing McCarthy in 1968 and McGovern in 1972. Inevitably it was the networks which were the source of the misinformation. This is not to say that the networks ever gave the wrong information. They merely gave the wrong impression—thematically. The misrepresentation was inherent in the TV image of the New Hampshire campaign, not the campaign itself. Perhaps more than any other medium, network television was forced, because of obligations one and two, in both elections, to build a horse race, complete with a phantom winner. As the undisputed major source of information about the primaries, television was probably the most effective among all the media in convincing viewers and Democrats that losers were winners in New Hampshire, as well as in several other states.

But the theme of the dark horse does not tie us directly to television malaise. At best, it ties us to the crucial role the networks have played in confusing Democratic rank-and-file during the last two campaigns—a confusion that was far more serious than that produced by Dwight Chapin or Donald Segretti. But the same straining for story line has come to be the *sine qua non* of the evening news. Given the network perceptions of the news audience, themes must be simple and interesting: venality, social discord, bureaucratic bungling, and, especially, the good old days. This is the repertoire from which so much of the soft news is chosen. The hard news is usually allowed to take care of itself.

In one respect the theme of social discord is extraordinarily well-suited to television. It is a hook from which one can hang a good deal of sensational film footage. But, contrary to conventional wisdom, the networks do not include more violent news than the print media,[26] the reason being that most violence is unplanned and cannot be readily filmed.

When there is planned violence, or violence that takes place through an extended period of time, the networks can be expected to move enormous amounts of equipment to the staging area. The coverage of the battle of Wounded Knee was a finest hour—in terms of television needs. But, if there is nothing of that nature transpiring, nothing to meet the theme of social discord, the networks can shift to closely-related themes. Intragovernmental conflict is another theme that the networks continue to utilize. Senators fighting with businessmen, bureaucrats, each other, is a popular theme; so are governmental unresponsiveness and governmental laxity. David Brinkley, Hughes Rudd and Charles Kuralt have virtually built their television careers on the theme that our government functions badly and that it used to work far better than it does now.

The themes which the networks offer are predominantly negative.[27] That alone would suggest that our opinions about our government, our society and ourselves would tend not to be positive. But the more important aspect of thematic reporting is inherent conflict, either personal or organizational. My own experiments with viewers suggest that this personal and institutional conflict, so appropriate and essential to thematic reporting, is profoundly disturbing to the audience, especially the Inadvertent Audience. The news organization and the journalist may believe that conflict between Senators or business leaders or bureaucrats is good copy; perhaps it is. But among the inadvertent viewers I suggest that this copy takes on a different and more profound meaning. The general effects are, I surmise, not only sustained viewing but growing political estrangement and a desire to return to a bygone era of political purity and decency, an era which is undoubtedly overly-romanticized by the networks and all the mass media.

The Nonquantitative Bias: In their eagerness to provide palatable news, the networks not only construct thematic reports, they construct stories which are essentially qualitative bits of information taken from more substantial stories or items. The brief items may contain hard evidence—stock quotations, inflation statistics, unemployment figures, etc., but the longer stories do not.[28] My own experience with local television underscores the problem. Having spent three months on a study of the impact of the Watergate hearings on local public opinion, I made my findings available to the local newspaper and a local television station. The newspaperwoman I dealt with demanded to see my figures, checked my calculations and even asked about my sampling procedures. In the newspaper article which subsequently appeared all the information was there—the tables, the procedures, the conclusion. In stark contrast, the TV journalist who was assigned to the story asked me not to discuss the procedures or the findings—just my interpretations and the implications. So when I appeared I discussed everything but the facts of the case.

Ironically, both "stories" contained approximately the same number of words, but the TV report was clearly a story with less information. It was qualitative assessment, from start to finish. Not surprisingly, the television story was more dramatic, more unqualified. (I confess that I found myself straining to make my study sound more significant than I otherwise believed it was. The medium carries such temptations.)

The nonquantitative bias apparently exists at the network level as well. Again personal experience suggests that this bias has two roots—the widely-held belief that the audience does not want quantitative evidence and the self-realization that the journalist himself can't cope with data. I had the opportunity to present those same findings about the effects of the Senate Watergate hearings to a network correspondent who had actually covered the hearings for one of the networks. The correspondent showed interest in my work and asked that I send along a copy of the study. However, the correspondent, who possessed impressive academic credentials, also asked that I carefully explain the findings, because survey data presented in tabularized form were too hard to comprehend.

Obviously, television news cannot become a series of lectures based on quantitative data. Even the *New York Times* is, at base, a collection of anecdotes. But the nonquantitative bias—the antiquantitative bias—is more intense on the part of the networks than it is with the other prestigious news organizations. And, although we have come to take this particular form of bias for granted, almost as inevitable, this bias may have greater significance than many of the others in explaining the effects of television journalism.

As most radicals seem to recognize, qualitative stories characteristically paint the society more negatively than quantitative research does. Quantitative research generally offers a more optimistic picture—or, at the very least, a less vivid one. In the *Washington Post* in February, 1974, for example, we find a lengthy front-page summary of an OMB report on several social indicators in the United States.[29] The overwhelming majority of the indicators pointed upward during the last decade, indicating a continual improvement in the human condition. As well as can be ascertained, the report was not mentioned in any of the evening news programs at any time during the next week, despite its prominence in both the *Post* and its conspicuous inclusion in the *Times*.[30]

Edith Efron might argue that the report was not included in the network broadcast because it put the administration in a good light, at least indirectly. I suggest that this is not the reason at all. Neither the *Post* nor the *Times* has enthusiastically endorsed the Nixon or Ford administrations more frequently than the networks have. The report simply contained too much information, not too much positive information but too much tabularized—quantitative— information.

But looking beyond the motives which explain the cause for the omission, we need to face the more important question of the effects. Is it not possible that the networks, by developing a strong predilection for news which is nonquantitative, have produced a package of bizarre sensational anecdotes—anecdotes which themselves produce, as a by-product, a sense of political estrangement? George Gerbner and Larry Cross have already demonstrated that heavy reliance on all types of television programming is associated with distorted perceptions of social reality, in part because television provides such anecdotal and extraordinary images of society.[31] And it is hard to deny that the networks have a marked propensity for nonquantitative, anecdotal, image-based news. If one can suppose that the effect of this unwitting bias is a popular perception of society which is more imaginary than real, and more cynical than deserved, one can begin to comprehend at least one meaning to the McLuhanist dictum that the medium is the message.

The Bias of Artificial Balance: To ensure a cooperative relationship between themselves and their local affiliates, the networks must present news stories that are "balanced"—in other words, stories that do not violate the Fairness Doctrine. The doctrine requires that local broadcasters (affiliates) provide an opportunity for alternate points of view. Because the networks operate their own affiliates and because they must answer to the affiliates which they do not own, the networks abide by the provisions of the doctrine as scrupulously as the local stations. Ironically, this adds one more unique and disquieting dimension to the television news program—the bias of artificial balance.

To meet their obligation the journalists and producers always include "both" points of view (in the eyes of the FCC the world is always a dichotomy). While this procedure ensures that news will not persuade viewers to accept a point of view—the balanced story is, in most circumstances, the less effective story[32] —it also ensures the inevitable depiction of disputation and conflict. Sometimes the journalist is obliged to invent the second point of view, the conflicting point of view. But in either case this obligation to develop two sides to every story places legitimate organs of government or respectable segments of society at odds. The networks strain to find a credible "other side" and generally they do.

Under some circumstances the networks may omit the "opposing viewpoint." By 1972, for example, there was little network journalism that could be regarded as supportive of our continued involvement in Vietnam. And if we can accept the findings of Ernest Lefever's newest book (and in part I accept them), by 1973 there was very little indeed on the evening news to dispute the alleged advantages in Soviet-American detente.[33] But these are exceptional cases. The Fairness Factor is a way of life in network news.

The result of all this "fairness" is a mixed blessing. All the balance implies disputation. Under these provisions of fairness, programming may be less likely to persuade, but it is also more likely to confuse or irritate. For this reason the bias of artificial balance may explain why the people who rely on television are totally convinced that politics is not only venal but also indecipherable. And again the networks have produced, wholly inadvertently in this case, another source for Videomalaise.

The Federal Bias: The American communications system has been and remains remarkable decentralized. The United States has no national daily. The closest we come, ironically, is the *Wall Street Journal.* Consequently, until the advent of radio and television, national news was a pastiche of wire service reports and bureau copy.

But network television has changed both the tenor and pattern of news about national politics.

This predilection for monitoring life along the Potomac is easily explained. Central locating not only reduces the cost of news production, it also satisfies the local affiliates, who are themselves obliged to carry a proportion of national news. In early 1973, even before the impeachment process began, more than 40 percent of the network news items were out of Washington—four times the number out of New York.[34] This federal bias is, I suggest, much more significant than might first be apparent.

For one thing, the network national bias has totally re-routed the path toward the Presidency; what was once a regional or state process is now centered in D.C., thanks to the networks. Between 1900 and 1956 only 7% of those nominated to become President were Senators. But since 1956 only incumbent or former Senators have managed to run for President or Vice President, Agnew being the one exception.

More importantly, the federal bias has also contributed to our growing sense of political illegitimacy, again in an indirect and almost imperceptible way. I believe that there is an iron law of media exposure, a law no less deterministic—and no less dismal—in its implications than the iron laws of wages or population. The iron law of media requires that in nations where news is produced commercially and independently, the level (or branch) of government which receives the greatest emphasis will, in the long run, also experience the greatest public disdain. For several decades local government was the focal point for our localized, independent media, and it was local government which sustained the greatest public criticism. But network television has shifted the focus of daily news almost totally to national, to Washington, events. Again, given the types of messages provided by the networks, this focus has, in ten years, made national politics the most suspect. Stated as law, one ultimately finds that the locus of government which gains attention eventually gains opprobrium. This has been the case with our federal government since the late fifties. (See Table 5)

Interestingly enough, the new and intense focus on Washington has not caused a reduction in the absolute amount of local news coverage; television journalism has merely changed the proportions given to each type. One actually finds more coverage at all levels and, presumably, all branches of government than one found ten or even five years ago. And, as one would predict—were he or she to believe in the iron law of media exposure—public opinion concerning local government has, over the last few years, become more negative (Table 5). But, having received proportionally less attention, local governments have shown a slower rate of increase in public disdain.

It would not be difficult to demonstrate a final case for the iron law—to demonstrate that the coverage of state news has also increased with time, but at a rate slower than that of either local or national news, and to demonstrate that the increase in disapproval of state government has been, as expected, slower than that of the other two levels of government (again, Table 5). In short, television has increased its coverage of all three levels of government, and consequently all three levels of government have experienced an increase in public disapproval. The absolute increase in disapproval appears to be directly related to the absolute increase in the attention provided by the media.

All this implies that the federal bias, which is so severe and so intrinsic to network journalism, has, in one more paradoxical process, made the national government more visible, more salient, and, as a consequence, more disreputable in the public mind.

All told, the biases of television are subtle, generally unpremeditated, and nonpartisan. On one major political issue—American involvement in Vietnam—the bias was imperceptible at first.[36] (As late as 1968 there was virtually no relationship whatever between an individual's reliance on television and his or her opinions about Vietnam.[37]) But the nonpolitical or nonpartisan biases which are there—those which emerge as unpremeditated organizational by-products—are real and impacting. They are the ones which count.

The beneficiary of these biases is much more likely to be a George Wallace than an Edmund Muskie or even a Ted Kennedy, despite the wishes of the individuals who produce the news.[38] And in the end, as presently constituted, the images of television news seemingly do more to decrease our own sense of self-esteem and sense of political commitment than they do to liberalize our thoughts on inflation, pollution, shortages or housing issues—which the networks routinely address but rarely influence.

The TV Audience and the News: A Strange Mix

I have suggested that the messages provided by television news are in part responsible for some portion of our political dysphoria. I have also said that the audience which the commercial networks attract to their news programs is unusually important in understanding the effects of public affairs television. But in reality the two dimensions—the unique audience and the unique content—do not merely add together to create these effects; instead they serve to multiply each other.

The Inadvertent Audience, which slides into television information, is held tightly by the information it receives. Most viewers stay tuned; most viewers watch each item, early and late, with similar intensity.[39] The news program is prepared in such a way that the Inadvertent Audience will cling to it—or, at the very least, will not turn it off. In other words, we have an unholy relationship in which the networks create images which have theatrical appeal—enervating images by which those who are very likely to be unconcerned with political information receive the information. These viewers stay with the images and are, so to speak, subliminally affected; and they are affected largely because they are politically naive. This would appear to be the best interpretation of the correlation between television dependency and political estrangement that I have found during the last several years. However, in considering our findings and our notion of an explosive interaction between audience and content, there is one other interpretation which merits consideration.

TABLE 5

Confidence in local, state, and federal government today compared to 5 years ago*

	More confidence %	Less confidence %	About the same %	Not sure %
Local government total public	13	30	50	7
State government total public	14	26	53	7
Federal government total public	11	57	28	4

*Taken from Confidence and Concern, Louis Harris, 1973, op. cit., pp. 42-43.

I have heard time and again that the effects I have tried to document are pseudo-effects. Generally, this refutation is based on one premise: television journalism does not cause malcontentment; it attracts it.

Under this interpretation, relying upon television for information is but the consequence of the viewer's abnormality. But although this interpretation is a responsible one, I find it unconvincing in two respects. First, one who subscribes to this interpretation is almost forced to conclude that the two-thirds of the population which has come to depend upon television news is abnormal. (It would seem difficult to argue that two-thirds of the population is abnormal, although one could make a case.) But even if we accept the premise we are still left to explain the changing level in political frustration and distrust. If television attracted only the disaffected and did not produce disaffection itself, those who doubted our institutions before the coming of the television news system would doubt them now, and we would still need to explain the growth of disaffection.

To explain that growth, one might well combine these two seemingly discrepant interpretations concerning cause and effect, blend them, and accept the final premise that television journalism has activated a latent predisposition toward political disaffection that would not, under another media system, have been so acutely or so pandemically activated.

I suspect that television journalism attracts all kinds of viewers, that one can find every intellectual, social or psychological denomination among the Advertent and Inadvertent Audiences. Among those two audiences are, to be sure, the potentially malcontent and the potentially cynical. But I still maintain that television provides the images and themes which permit those predispositions to flourish.

In the United States we have our own special political culture, a culture in which cops and politicians are either all good or all bad, depending upon the circumstance. Never having resolved too well our philosophical contradictions concerning freedom and authority, the American potential for political frustration is enormous. Thus, once television irritates those predisposed toward malaise, they can in turn be expected to affect (a staunch conservative would say "infect," a liberal would choose "educate") the remainder of the population, whether or not the remainder is directly sensitive to television effects. Interestingly enough, the early sixties show the greatest difference in disaffection between those relying on television and those who do not—which is to say that the differences grow smaller as the estrangement becomes severe. So those sophisticated enough to re-process the end-product of television journalism have apparently been catching up with the inadvertently informed, as the polls and the media document the growing sense of disaffection.

Again, it is not just the content which produces these effects and not just the audience, it is the mix. And to those who work to preserve the viability of the system—whatever their motives—the mix seems to serve the interest of the inadvertent viewer and the national networks more than the interest of the public at large. From this perspective the mix certainly helps explain the nearly unabated increase in hostility toward the networks by the government, regardless of the party or individuals in charge, during the last twenty years. (The Nixon years were extraordinary by any standards, however.)

The struggle between the government and the television networks deserves our attention, and the last section of the essay will treat the issue directly and at length. For now, I move to the third basic aspect of the television news system—the television network news personnel and their characteristics—which provides insight into the impact of that news system.

Television News Personnel

TV networks have neither radicals nor reactionaries in their employ. Those who might have radical or reactionary inclinations leave them at home. There is no network conspiracy to undermine the American social, economic or political system. But individual network employees possess personal characteristics and predispositions which have some effect on the political ethos in which our government operates.

I have already outlined the four-part basic equation which motivates the networks—costs, ratings, the affiliates, and the FCC. I have suggested the by-products of these motives and calculations at the organizational level. Obviously, some of the motivations of the organization filter down to the individuals—the producers, the directors, the journalists themselves. But in this discussion we focus on the more personal needs and dimensions of the network personnel—especially the correspondents.

Unfortunately, we do not know a great deal about these individuals. At the network level Edward Epstein has done the most systematic work so far, focusing on the personnel at NBC in New York.[40] There are a few other studies dealing with the people at the networks and local affiliates, and a growing number of personal interviews with, or accounts by, some of the more famous of the television newspeople.[41] But in fact most of our knowledge of TV newspeople is as anecdotal and impressionistic as the reports the journalists provide. Nonetheless, there are some general tendencies worth noting.

Network journalism has moved through two generations and is working through a third. The first generation was almost frivolous. John Cameron Swayze has returned to commercial advertising, from whence he came. The very notion that NBC News would ever again accept the name "The Camel News Caravan" is patently absurd. The second generation of network newspeople began in 1956 with the beginning of the Huntley-Brinkley "Report" on NBC. When Walter Cronkite replaced Douglas Edwards at CBS, the second generation had come of age. The television journalist in this period was, as a rule, a former wire services pressman, one without terribly impressive credentials—at least by today's inflated standards. Among the three patriarchs of second-generation television news—Huntley, Brinkley and Cronkite—only one, Chet Huntley, graduated from college. None of the three founding fathers attended schools of overriding prestige.

Since 1964, the year television journalism was given its press commission—the year in which the newspaper and wire services asked that the networks help them report the election returns through News Election Service—network journalism has established a new genre. The patriarchal replacements and heirs-apparent bring with them more impressive social and educational credentials than their forebears. Roger Mudd and Dan Rather both hold college degrees and both have done post-graduate work. Tom Brokaw and Garrick Utley, the men who work directly behind John Chancellor, both have degrees; Chancellor does not. Even allowing for the inflation of credentials since World War II, when one speaks about the Brahmins and near-Brahmins of television journalism, 1975, one must acknowledge the substantial upgrading that has taken place during the last ten years.

At the next level within the TV news corps the same holds true. If one lists the correspondents by age, one finds that those between thirty and fifty are generally more impressive—at least on paper—than those who are older.

Stiffening the educational prerequisites for the newer generation of television news personnel is, of course, understandable and, to most of us, commendable. But once again an ostensibly harmless alteration—an upgrading of educational prerequisites—has an important consequence.

During the last four years three sociologists, William Bowman, John Johnstone and Edward Slawski, have thoroughly investigated the factors which lead to a more activist—"participant" is their word—orientation among newspeople. They have found that, among all factors, educational experience, both in duration and quality, is the best predictor of "participant orientation."[42]

Translated, this means simply that those who have had more schooling and who have gone to "better" schools come to journalism with a more activist and aggressive set of attitudes about journalism—the "New Journalism." Given the significant differences in schooling between this generation of television news personnel and the last, one can only expect that the new newspeople will be more aggressive and active than their predecessors, simply as a function of their training.

There is a second factor at work here. Over and above the trend toward better schooling there is an inconspicuous trend toward a younger network corps. The expansion of the networks over the last few years has produced a corps which is, on the average, younger than that which came before. And, according to Bowman, Slawski and Johnstone, "youth" is a principal cause of participant orientation in journalism. So, as a matter of chronology, the networks have, since 1963, offered a younger staff of newspeople and presumably, as a consequence, a tougher, more aggressive one.[43] As the growth of network news staff subsides, this process will be reversed. But in this essay, at any rate, we are trying to explain the last ten years, not the next.

All told, the age factor and the "school" factor do help explain the intra-medium difference between the new and old TV news corps. The same two factors may help explain the differences between the network corps and the press corps. The factors which make the new TV newsperson a little tougher than the old also tend to make the electronic news corps a little tougher than the prominent members of the local and established press corps. But one could make too much of differences. All journalists must strain to find good copy, to get a scoop, even under circumstances that do not warrant special treatment or exciting prose. But beyond that, television newspeople seem to offer news that, compared with other local or prestige newspapers, is more disestablishmentarian. Part of the explanation may be age and schooling. But one could make too much of that, too. However, if there are differences, then at least some of them may be attributable to the status of the network newspeople and their personal styles.

Television journalism has always provided status. Until the early sixties, however, that status was awarded by the public, not by peers of the profession. But Huntley, Brinkley and Cronkite brought professional stature, as well as notoriety. A serious student of journalism could consider television as a viable alternative to a career in print. Added to that new status was the extra incentive to avoid the sullying aspects of business, law, and government. (Government became especially sullying after the beginning of the war in Vietnam.) By joining the networks one could enjoy many of the old advantages of pressmanship—independence, freedom from routine, intellectual honesty—and also enjoy all the extra advantages of television—salaries, public notoriety and an indirect involvement in national politics, involvement that was publicly acknowledged. These advantages made network journalism an honorable and incredibly desirable profession. A quick check shows that the overwhelming majority of recent occupational transfers are from print to television, not vice versa. Even when we consider the *New York Times* or the *Washington Post*, the flow is toward, not away from, the networks (Fred Graham and Sally Quinn, for example). In short, television journalism draws from among the finest young journalistic talent around—journalists who possess background and experience which are generally associated with the anti-establishment, cynical proclivities that have become the hallmark of the New Journalism. And with respect to the values of the "New Journalist," it is interesting that two of the most common political themes—and stories?—running through the minds of the network correspondents are, according to Epstein, the universal venality of politicians and the universal political disposition to seek votes instead of facing issues.[44]

So the networks may choose from the cream. And the ability to choose from the cream means, in this era, choosing from among those who are oriented toward activist journalism and cynicism.

Recalling Walter Cronkite's discussion of the television newsperson, it is interesting to note that Cronkite actually tried to disclaim a propensity for leftist politics among the network corps by admitting to a general tendency toward disestablishmentarianism.

> *As far as the leftist thing is concerned, that I think is some-*
> *thing that comes from the nature of a journalist's work.*
> *Most newsmen have spent some time covering the seamier*
> *side of human endeavor; they cover police stations and*
> *courts and the infighting in politics.* And I think they
> come to feel very little allegiance to the established order.
> I think they're inclined to side with humanity rather than
> with authority and institutions. *And this sort of pushes*
> *them to the left. But I don't think there are many who are*
> *far left. I think a little left of center probably is correct.*[45]
> *(Emphasis is mine.)*

These cynical predispositions slip over into the news more easily than do the partisan, and with greater effect, I would surmise.

Finally, because network television has the capacity to attract virtually anyone, it has the opportunity to choose not only those who are intelligent and diligent, but those who will "fit." "Fit," of course, is hard to define; but it usually implies the ability to read copy, as well as write it, to look good, to have style. Sometimes "fit" is just a journalistic misfortune.

Recently I had the opportunity to speak with a program director for the NBC "Today" program in Washington. I asked if a decision had been reached about a replacement for Frank McGee. When I learned the matter was still unresolved, I asked if Edwin Newman had any chance whatever. Newman, in my opinion, is one of the best—well-trained, hard-working, articulate. I was told that Newman had, in fact, been considered and that he was held in highest esteem back at headquarters. But it was decided that he was "too good, too far above the audience—a liability in terms of ratings." No Newman this time around. Television is, after all, still television. But the pursuit and the prerequisite of "fit" have more serious implications than the Newman case suggests. The networks are looking for a theatrical quality, combined with journalistic skill. But theatre is still theatre. So the new journalists reflect the high-styled, high-toned, often egotistical pattern of behavior of the stage. In this, the news personnel add one more dimension to the news—self-assured, often sarcastic showmanship, a bizarre combination of Cambridge and Los Angeles. We get journalism that is young, urbane, chic, even if it is not literally Eastern-Establishment-liberal. (I suspect the revulsion for Nixon among TV reporters was rooted in style more than in conviction. It is well remembered that, before network journalists became "stylish," Nixon preferred them to print people.)

All this is not to defame the new generations of network correspondents and news personnel. They are good journalists in theory and practice, but they are also good, fashionable performers. They are becoming better and more fashionable as time goes by. A professorial-looking Paul Duke or a professorially-attired Bill Monroe is not drummed out of the business. But not too many more of their type have been invited into the TV corps. Performing has its own inevitable by-products; in this case the by-products are more cynicism, sarcasm, arrogance, sometimes hostility. And unlike print journalism, television journalism offers its nuances within the news reports. This is virtually inevitable in an audio-visual medium. The nuances blend subtly with the thematic reports that are the essence of television news. So we have an explosive concoction: thematic reports, most of which depict politics negatively, and forceful presentation, based upon theatrical skills which are themselves prone toward snippiness, if not pique. And, if Dan Rather is the archetypical case, he is certainly not the only one of his type. ABC and NBC have tried—and some say they have tried desperately hard—to emulate the Rather model by recruiting and quickly promoting Tom Jarriel and Tom Brokaw.

In summary, it appears that the very qualities which make up the contemporary network correspondent—youth, big-city life, a moderately prestigious background, theatrical skills—are the qualities which lead first of all to a pronounced affinity for activist journalism and secondly to a "modish" disaffection from conventional society and conventional politics. It would also appear that style, pique and hostility are keys to both success and effectiveness in network reporting. In any event, the combination of organizational needs of the network and the general make-up of the news staffs produce images which are most assuredly negative and are also very probably effective. Daniel Moynihan may have been wrong in assuming that the press corps is a frustrated elite. But he was probably right in implying that those who count in the press corps—which clearly implies the network press corps—act as if they were.[46]

What's more, the effectiveness of the network reporter is apparently enhanced by the high credibility of the journalists and the networks (popularity is a better term),[47] the comparative lack of control editors and producers can exert over their correspondents,[48] and the parasocial interaction which occurs between the journalist and his fans.[49] So we have an unconscious network news formula, based on impressions of politics and society and patterned upon the professional values and the personal styles of the most popular news people. This formula has been at the heart of television journalism for quite some time, long before the Watergate break-in or the advent of the war in Vietnam.

But one can carry on these criticisms too long. Given the unique demands and limitations placed upon them, the people of television journalism do a good job at much of what they do. It is not surprising, for example, that through network television the nation has appreciably increased its general awareness of politics, issues and politicians. But, given the unique demands and limitations placed upon them, it should not be surprising that the people of television journalism have also helped to produce a more disaffected, alienated and frustrated electorate.

The News as a Source of Political Indoctrination

Every society must teach iteself and its young that its basic values are good and its institutions are appropriate for achieving those values. In other words, each society, pluralistic or monolithic, must peddle legitimacy. It is this belief in and commitment to the values and institutions—it is legitimacy—that allows a nation to transcend brief crises or endure prolonged periods of deprivation. Consequently, every nation must teach, train, socialize and indoctrinate its own by conditioning them to believe. Authoritarian regimes seize control, directly or indirectly, of all the major sectors of society which can contribute to attitudes which are conducive to social sacrifice, patriotism, commitment. The sectors most important in socializing individuals are the family, the peers, the schools, the private social organizations, the government and the media. An anti-democratic regime wants to control them all and compel each to trumpet the same basic supportive themes. A democratic regime is less committed to control and, by choice, places the governmental sector at odds with itself—calling part the government and the remainder the opposition. This division, presumably, serves several societal interests, among them the preservation of individual liberty, which is preserved, hopefully, through a disunified and changing political authority. But to achieve one social value—liberty—implies sacrificing another—commitment to the regime. Democratic regimes consider the trade-off worthwhile—less indoctrination, more liberty.

Democratic regimes also permit a greater degree of freedom for their media, usually extending much greater freedom to the press than to electronic media. Again, this is done to ensure the preservation of one or more basic values—in this case the preferred values being truth, liberty, freedom of thought and the promotion of honesty in public or private life. But, once again, to achieve these values—to remove the media from direct political control—makes the basic process of political inculcation more difficult. And the more expansive the system of media, the more difficult the process. This relationship best explains the almost universal tendency for governments to refuse to allow television independence from political authority, even if the press is free. In this respect, American television is *sui generis,* being by far the most independent of all television systems on earth.

Before the development of modern television journalism in the United States, among the agencies which were responsible for fostering our basic political beliefs, there were four which had direct contact with the individual and which, in general, tended to support the political leaders of the moment, as well as the political system: family, peers, secondary social organizations, and the party controlling the government. With the exception of a miniscule intelligentsia, only the political opposition, working through the media, said that the nation was falling apart, moving backward, losing its purity or its way. But the opposition was always expected to provide this information. In that capacity the opposition had little credibility. Until television journalism changed this delicate balance, there was only one opposition at any one time. The President was, at that point, the strongest, most capable, hardest-working person in the entire world, to almost every American child.[50]

This balance has come unstuck. The network news organizations have become, in concert, a highly credible, never-tiring political opposition, a maverick third party which never need face the sobering experience of governing. Newspapers, to some extent, might long ago have achieved this same status; in fact they did, to a limited degree. But newspapers are faceless; they have no visible spokesmen. Their information is less vibrant and most often ignored by the bulk of the electorate. We must not forget that the vast majority of our citizens never read the newspapers, they glanced at them. It has always been the political sophisticate—the one less likely to succumb to media malaise from the start—who moves past page one.

If one accepts this behavioristic interpretation of political legitimacy which I am offering, one can regard television as a new and more compelling political opposition—an opposition which, by its political messages, causes the conditioned linkage between the public and the regime to grow less strong, less invincible. This would be especially true in the portions of the population which display a less sophisticated, less well-thought-out commitment to the society. Significantly, as we have seen, this happens to be the same segment of the population which receives the greatest amount of and exhibits the greatest dependence upon television journalism.

To state the theory more directly, television journalism has altered the long-established balance between *patriating* agencies— segments of society which generally portray our condition as favorable and preferable—and *dispatriating* agencies—those which generally portray our condition as wretched or becoming more so. One might say that even without the "New Journalism," the decline in belief in our institutions and ourselves was inevitable, given the change in ratio between patriating and dispatriating sources of information.

One might also say that this process is inexorable in a system which maintains a wholly free and competitive journalism. One might formulate another series of dismal laws: (1) As the amount of information from a free, competitive media increases, the ratio of patriating to dispatriating information decreases. (2) As the ratio of patriating to dispatriating information decreases, belief and support for political institutions decrease as well. In other words, the more information the population receives, the more politically estranged the population becomes, especially among that segment which has been given only a civics-book exposure to American politics.

While these laws may seem as bleak as they do reductionist, it is not terribly difficult to accept them, given the pattern of public opinion in the United States, especially since 1963, the year in which dispatriating information increased substantially on the heels of the 30-minute news format. (There was, perhaps, a much greater increase in "dispatriating" information than suggested by doubling the length of the news. The 15-minute program was perhaps 10 minutes of straight AP reportage with little vividly dispatriating information—

5 minutes at most. The 30-minute telecast contains the same 10 minutes of wire and 20 minutes of thematic information—potentially dispatriating information.)

There is one final point about the ratio of patriating and dispatriating information. If we accept the general behavioristic model, we might consider the specific ramifications of a shift in the ratio. In concrete terms, let us imagine that if all sources of opinion were controlled by the government the average citizen would feel 99 percent sure that his society and its political process were legitimate. But in pursuit of liberty we add an opposition party, a party which claims that things are bad and bound to get worse, etc. We find the same hypothetical citizen is now only 95 percent certain about his political system. Add free media and the change will not be 4 percent but, perhaps, as great as 8 percent. Add commercial, uncontrolled television to the system, and for our hypothetical citizen the loss may be, on the average, another 16 points. This is the general pattern that exists in psychological research when one changes the ratio of conditioning and extinguishing situations.[51] One discovers a geometric increase or decrease in conditioned response.

For those of you who find both this set of suppositions about public opinion and the analogy to Pavlovian psychology callous or without merit, I suggest that you reconsider before dismissing either premise. Virtually every authoritarian regime operates under these very suppositions, and so does every democratic regime, excluding, to some degree, the United States. After all, all of the western democracies except the United States allow newspapers to publish freely but stringently regulate or directly control their television networks.

Of course *neither the networks nor the opposition in the United States are unpatriotic because they are dispatriating!* The relationship between patriotism and patriatism is terribly difficult to sort out. I trust it is an insoluble problem. But, in any event, the networks, like the opposition, *are* dispatriating influences. And given our own sensitivity to any decrease in affection for our political institutions, even the relatively low level and watered-down quality of the dispatriating information offered by the opposition and the networks has had dramatic repercussions. And, of course, there have been decreases in our sense of self-confidence and our sense of institutional pride during the last decade. But before blowing the whistle on our dispatriating networks or our dispatriating opposition merely because they can dispatriate, we should put all our findings and all our interpretations into an empirical as well as a normative perspective.

Costs and Benefits
of Television Journalism:
Some Observations

Somehow, whenever I offer my opinions about television to students, journalists or colleagues, the ghost of Spiro T. Agnew seems to waft into the room. Frankly, I would like to have his ghost thrown out once and for all. I do not offer these thought with Agnewian vituperation or with an Agnewian sense of ulterior motive. I do believe, however, that there are serious issues to be raised concerning our most conspicuous medium.

Free media, just like free elections, represent a trade-off for any society—a trade-off from which is derived some "good" at the price of some "evil." On balance, I do not argue against free elections or a free press, or free television, for that matter. I suggest only that free television journalism has produced some effects which are socially "functional" and some which are "dysfunctional" (dysfunctional being the ultimate euphemism for that which is not supportive of the on-going regime) and that these effects must be considered together. In short, television journalism, like all free journalism, provides a classic case in cost-benefit analysis. On the plus side we get (1) a more widely-informed electorate; (2) a purer political process; and (3) a more responsive set of political institutions.

Television journalism has unquestionably increased the aggregate level of political information, i.e., politcally relevant facts, although information itself can sometimes be a cost. For example, a strong case can be made that without network television neither George McGovern nor Eugene McCarthy could have gained nearly enough political notoriety to pull their respective coups in the 1968 and 1972 Democratic primaries. (These two cases suggest both the power of television to make people aware of something as well as the difficulty one experiences in trying to decide if more information is always a benefit.)

Network journalism has also discouraged venality and corruption in those areas where television has been permitted to go and has wished to go. The national nominating convention is the prime example. There can be little question that the chair and the delegates behave more fairly and seriously than they did before the arrival of television. The enormous range of network journalism has triggered a new morality in political life. Watergate indiscretions notwithstanding, network television has made *overt* corruption in the White House, for instance, a contemporary impossibility.

The purity which television journalism brings is not itself directly relevant to policy. But there are implications for policy to be found here. The same process which produces institutional purity produces institutional responsiveness as well. In essence, network journalism makes the law of anticipated reaction much more binding on those individuals and institutions which receive coverage. Politicians and bureaucrats are virtually terrified of exposure by the networks. So strong is that terror that if one can make a patently legitimate case about some political (or economic) injustice through the networks, he or she can count on winning the case. In other words, the networks can compel responsiveness from bureaucrats or corporate executives, if conditions are right.

During the spring of 1974 thousands of the veterans who were eligible for education benefits and who were not receiving them— 6% of those eligible—sought redress from the Veterans Administration. This was an injustice, and a blatant one in terms of our national feelings about war veterans. The *New York Times* and the *Washington Post* had covered this story intermittently since the previous autumn, when the academic year began. But there had been little, if any, noticeable effect. Immediately following an expose on the NBC *Nightly News*—an expose based upon a lengthy story in the *Post,* it would appear—the President contacted the VA, demanded a quick response, and eventually requested that VA Director Johnson be retired.

This is just one instance in which the networks, by picking up a story from the larger, more investigative newspapers, stimulate a quick and decent response from the institution or individual having administrative jurisdiction. But there is another side to the ledger. Television journalism, unfettered and acting in a way which serves its organizational interests, does not always serve the public interest— whether one believes that the regime is blemishless or merely worth saving.

Television journalism can undermine our trust in our fellow man, increase racial hostility, and exacerbate the anti-democratic strain which has historically run through our culture.[52] But more relevant to us is the effect of television on our sense of legitimacy. This is, however, a more difficult issue to handle. Television may very well be undermining our national sense of legitimacy. But if one should accept the validity of that premise, one still faces a different but equally important issue: is our growing illegitimacy, in a word, legitimate?

Before addressing these questions, I offer two essential caveats: (1) that our crisis in legitimacy may be imaginary, and (2) that given a strictly behavioristic interpretation of legitimacy it is impossible to consider issues such as these.

The Crisis in Legitimacy: Strange as this may seem, I am not wholly convinced that we have a crisis in legitimacy. Part of the "crisis" is undoubtedly a mirage based on the survey items we use to measure change in attitude. While two out of three Americans may now believe that their government is untrustworthy, the vast majority still believes the basic governmental structure is worth saving and worth fighting for. Surveyors don't ask these questions too often, because the answers stay pretty much the same through time and surveyors want items that will demonstrate change—items that will justify continuing the surveys. One might argue that the "crisis" exists using only certain measures, or, on the other hand, that the crisis may be great in comparative terms but slight in absolute terms. In short, our notion that we are in a state of crisis may be an invalid one given us by our mass media, which love to reveal discomfiture, and our pollsters, who love to demonstrate change.

There is a second point which a commitment to intellectual honesty compels me to raise. Before discussing the legitimacy of growing illegitimacy, I must hedge on my behavioristic theory of legitimacy. If the level of legitimacy is, as I have argued, merely determined by the ratio of patriating to dispatriating sources of information, it is foolishness to speak about a justifiable level of support for the political system. The level of support is given, and that is that. But I cannot be so crassly deterministic. I believe that there is a grey area in interpreting legitimacy, one in which legitimacy is neither a totally behavioristic quotient nor a wholly evidential assessment of the system. In fact, I believe that, despite the caveats mentioned here, there *is* at least some erosion of political legitimacy in our society and that we can meaningfully discuss whether or not this erosion is justifiable, despite the generally behavioristic definition of legitimacy that has been posited.

As do most political scientists under thirty, I tend to believe that our growing illegitimacy is deserved. The American people have been, perhaps, too enamored with their political institutions for too long. The public has either ignored or remained unaware of serious contradictions and malfeasance within the political process. The public has been overly sanguine about our politics and our politicians. In this respect, the decline in legitimacy which television has fostered is justified.

But even if the general decline is defendable, the role which television has played in this affair has not been without blemish. The erosion in public trust and public confidence has been more the product of the imperatives of Madison Avenue than of an innocent pursuit of truth. And consequently the erosion in legitimacy has been relatively perverse, with the public rightly questioning their institutions but for the wrong reasons and in the wrong way. Specifically, the public has come to believe that things are worse than they *were*—that all this misery and misfortune is *new* to America and the world. The images of television have somehow persuaded the public that the society is coming apart, moving downward from where it once was. And this persuasion is as demonstrable as it is bizarre. As late as November, 1973, fifteen times as many adult Americans believed they as individuals were "doing well" as believed the country was doing well![53] In short, television's images are imbalanced and distorted. The effects of these images are distorted too, almost perversely. In that context, the impact of television on political perception is unjustified or, at least, criticizable.

Of course the networks are not responsible for most of the events which have been a necessary condition in our malaise. The networks did not invent the break-in at Watergate, inflate the dollar, authorize illegal bombings, arrange political assassinations, etc. Nor do the networks lie, although they've been known to cheat a little.[54]

But the networks speak to an audience which contains an enormous pool of politically unskilled individuals—those who rely on an eighth-grade civics curriculum to comprehend national politics. Their perceptions are not only limited, they are also naive. Television's focus is murderous for these people. It is in no way surprising that I have found that reliance upon television journalism is associated with greater support for George Wallace, especially among middle-status Americans.[55] These are the individuals who shifted first toward political cynicism and frustration, moving others along in time. And I suspect that the revelations about Watergate have hit this group particularly hard. These revelations will also, I suspect, tend to unleash the networks and compel them to provide even more of those images of society which so totally overwhelm middle-America. We may, in fact, be on the verge of a new era of television malaise, one that will begin now that impeachment and the fate of Richard Nixon have been resolved.

Recommendations

Given my criticisms of the networks, I feel obligated to say something about reform. Unfortunately, there is little to say. If one wishes to diminish the "dysfunctional" effects which television has brought with it, one faces a virtually insoluble dilemma: most of the changes that would work would be either antilibertarian, unconstitutional or unacceptable to the networks. We can never even consider limiting the audience; that would be patently unconstitutional. We cannot change the content very much without violating the Fairness Doctrine. We cannot expect networks to limit their coverage of Washington; that would be both antilibertarian and economically infeasible. In short, there is little to recommend that seems both plausible and meaningful. Nevertheless, I shall suggest three things which might render the networks less unsettling and would clearly render them less vulnerable to criticism.

One of the most conspicuous characteristics of television journalism is its search for the individual case which demonstrates some lesson, generally a lesson involving some social or political snafu. Given the need for thematic reports, this is a wholly understandable phenomenon. News executives believe that when a correspondent needs to examine the impact of public policy, the correspondent should find a case and film it. Unfortunately, when the networks follow the effects of policy in this way they are engaging in an especially "unfair" practice, one which I shall call the dilemma of the Lady-or-the-Tiger technique.

Imagine a hypothetical case. The networks do a film piece on a federally-sponsored welfare program in Chicago. The journalist points out that budgetary cuts have jeopardized this particular program, despite reasonable protest by the local black community. The implication is usually clear. When a community lacks middle-class credentials, there is nothing that anybody can do. The citizens are victims of their condition. They have no money, no skills, no status, no college training to parlay into political clout. The government fails the unfortunate.

Now imagine a governmental decision that has implications for our group in Chicago. Imagine that the government cuts defense spending and spending in related areas and increases HEW allotments for social services. What can we expect from the networks? We should not expect a piece on the program in Chicago which has managed to survive. Instead we should expect a feature about shipbuilders in Rhode Island who have been laid-off, who are victims of a government policy that has taken away their bread and butter. Once again, to accommodate, the government increases its appropriations for the Navy and decides to cut funds for developing supersonic aircraft. Now we can expect to find the networks in Seattle interviewing an aeronautical engineer whose future is jeopardized by the decision to stop funding for the SST. This time the implication is different. The government is not responsive to college-educated, skilled professionals. The government fails those who have worked hard and played by the rules.

Of course in some respects this story is contrived. The government is not quite so flexible; these events would take years, not months to transpire. But the cases are not hypothetical; I have seen them all, almost as a package. I do not doubt that each story is a true one, but I object to the method of presentation, which is without proper context and which, for the viewer, must certainly be an undeclared choice between the lady and the tiger. To cut defense spending directly implies unemployment at navy yards or air bases or somewhere. To decide to help the poor, low-status and unskilled becasue they are poor, low-status and unskilled is a fine goal for public policy. In the real world of budgeting, however, such a decision means that you would be giving less help to those who are not poor, not low-status, not unskilled.

If the networks must cover these types of cases in the human condition—and I, for one, think they should—they have a responsibility to put them into a meaningful context by making clear that unemployment in Seattle is the necessary, if sorry, outcome of deciding against the SST. But the networks generally do not place these types of stories in context; at best they append the edited and too-brief comments of an "opposing spokesman," who also serves as adversary and neglects to make plain the dilemmas of public policy.

By following this technique—by showing the negative consequences of policy A or policy not-A—the networks are not only promoting a perception of government policy that is unjustifiably dismal (especially when this particular theme is combined with the theme of "the good old days"), they are also behaving at least somewhat irresponsibly. If one must decry Seattle, one must "explain" Seattle and consider the difficulty in trying to achieve unspecified ends with specific policies. If there is a dilemma, point it out. It would probably be worth the added public confusion to educate viewers in the cruel world of economic and social trade-offs. The first recommendation must be to insist that studies dealing with the effects of government policy be treated more sophisticatedly and less dramatically, with greater appreciation of costs and benefits.

The second recommendation is more concrete than the first. I suggest that the networks make a concerted effort to include more stories based upon systematic and quantitative research, research that individuals or organizations outside the networks have conducted.

Ironically, with the exception of Dow Jones and a few statistics from the Department of Labor, the only systematic research that works its way regularly into the CBS News, generally regarded as the best of the three, is a four-city study in which food prices are checked month by month. The journalist in New York, Los Angeles, Chicago or Atlanta returns to the same store each month to buy the same items he or she bought the month before. Each shopper then displays his or her findings about the cost of a basket of food which in mid-1973 was exactly twenty dollars. I would guess that this on-going research was adopted when the news department was virtually convinced that prices would go up enough each month to justify this research as "news." (It will be interesting to see what CBS does should retail food prices ever stabilize. My intuition tells me that only inflationary increases can justify both the story as news and the cost of continuing the research.) In a word, systematic research is not the forte or even the concern of the networks.

But there is a need for and, I think, an obligation to include more stories which are not anecdotal or impressionistic, stories based in social science research. A five- or ten-minute segment given over to the social or financial or even the physical sciences would serve a necessary end. And once again, even if this suggested technique does not affect the ratings or the impact of the news, it will still increase the stature of the network news organizations and render them a more serious journalistic enterprise.

In 1972, CBS, seeking perhaps to enhance its own professional stature, attempted to do something similar to that which I have recommended. They offered on the evening news a lengthy (20-minute) evidential and sophisticated treatment of the large American wheat sale to the Soviet Union. Pleased with itself, CBS attempted a second feature, this time on Watergate. Due to political pressure the second feature was the last. But the shortcoming of this technique was a political one.[56] In general, I think that the addition of a research segment is well within the realm of the plausible, even given the realities of commercial television.

Finally, I think that there is a compelling need for the networks to reconsider the criteria used in selecting correspondents. The general trend has been toward bright, well-educated, highly-stylized reporters. But the most recent additions to the networks seem to suggest an even greater concern for style. I understand that this recommendation gets dangerously close to the heart of commercial television—that recruitment may be too fundamental an issue even to be seriously discussed by the laity, given the economic and political ground rules under which the networks operate. Nonetheless, I suggest that the networks might choose new correspondents who are no less energetic or hard-working but who are less adversarial and less hostile than some the networks have recently chosen. Zealousness is not new to American journalism, nor is zealousness necessarily a vice. But it would seem that the networks have shifted recently from essentially press people to essentially television people. This is, from my perspective, an unfortunate development, and I would prefer that the networks return to the newspaper people and move away from the recent genre, one in which the local affiliates have become the farm teams for network correspondents.

I should point out that these recommendations are not necessarily going to alter the effects attributed to network journalism. But these recommendations will make the networks look better and decrease their vulnerability to attack—attacks which would be far less sympathetic than mine or even those which have sprung up recently in *TV Guide*.

Even so, I am a realist. I recognize that the networks are sensitive to criticism and reluctant to change. They argue that my theory is either wrong—factually inaccurate—or that it is irrelevant to them because they are only reporting what goes on. One network producer suggested that my theory was correct once but that since Watergate, and especially since the network coverage of the House Judiciary hearings on impeachment, my theory has become "obsolete," that network journalism has increased our national sense of legitimacy. Perhaps so. But I gain the distinct impression that the networks may grow more the way they have been, almost as a consequence of their commendable role in the Watergate crisis. At any rate, I suspect that network journalism will continue to grow and that the public will become continually more dependent upon it. Under these circumstances, the theory of Videomalaise will, I fear, no longer be obsolete, inaccurate or irrelevant to any of us.

Finally, despite all my criticisms and anxieties I must conclude that, on balance, to this point the network system has been beneficial, perhaps more beneficial than the older system of communication. Of course, regardless of the beneficial balance there is little that we can do with our news system, one way or the other. Our present system will not be altered by the government; that would be politically unrealistic. Nor will the system be changed by the networks; that would be economically unrealistic. We are, so to speak, stuck with the potential and partially-realized effects. Until we, as a people, grow more sophisticated in understanding our own governmental process and our own communications process, these effects will not abate. So if reform seems so remote, one might ask, what's the point of all these interpretations and prescriptions?

The point is this: Americans consensually believe that despite its costs democracy is the best form of government. We also believe that despite its costs a free market is the best form of economy. And, as Americans, we have never doubted that a free press is the best form of communication. Network television has merely underscored the necessity to add, once again, that terribly important phrase: despite its costs. In the shadow of Vietnam and Watergate we sometimes forget.

Footnotes

1. For a thorough and interesting empirical test of this premise, see S. M. Lipset, *Political Man: The Social Bases of Politics* (Garden City, New York: Anchor, 1963), chapter 3.

2. *Confidence and Concern: Citizens View American Government,* U. S. Government Printing Office, 1973, p. 33.

3. Cited in *Washington Post,* January 8, 1974, p. 2.

4. Arthur Miller, Thad Brown, Alden Raine, "Social Conflict and Political Estrangement, 1958-72," paper presented at Midwest Political Science Association Convention, May, 1973, pp. 7-13.

5. There is some evidence that between 1968 and 1970 the decline in public trust and discontent abated. See Arthur Miller, "Political Issues and Trust in Government," paper presented at the American Political Science Association, September, 1972, also found in *The American Political Science Reivew,* Vol. 68, September, 1974, pp. 951-972.

6. *Ibid.*

7. Michael Robinson, "Public Affairs Television and the Growth of Political Malaise: The Case of the Selling of the Pentagon," unpublished, Ph.D. dissertation, University of Michigan, 1972; also forthcoming, with the same title, *American Political Science Review.*

8. Michael Robinson, "The Impact of the Televised Watergate Hearings," *Journal of Communication,* Vol. 24:2; Spring 74, 17-30.

9. *Ibid.,* pp. 28-29.

10. Michael Robinson, "Public Affairs Television . . . ," *op. cit.,* especially chapter 3 and conclusions.

11. I use the 1968 data because they are the most recent available with questions concerning the comparative reliance on all types of mass media. Unfortunately, from our perspective, the Survey Research Center in Ann Arbor chose *not* to use the very questions which would have permitted a similar analysis with the 1972 national election study.

12. Michael Robinson, "Public Affairs Television . . . ," *op. cit.,* p. 185.

13. Harvey Gersin, "The Dimension and Growth of Network Evening News," unpublished xerox, ABC News Research and Development, July 1973, pp. 1-3.

14. Burns Roper, *What People Think of Television and Other Mass Media, 1959-1972,* Television Information Office, New York, May, 1973.

15. See Michael Robinson and Clifford Zukin, "Television and the Wallace Vote in 1968: Are There Implications for 1976?", paper presented at American Association of Public Opinion Research Convention, Lake George, New York, May, 1974; also in *Public Opinion Quarterly,* Vol. 38, Fall, 1974, p. 445.

16. CBS News, telephone survey, March 20, 1970, reproduced in Hazel Erskine's "The Polls: Opinion of the News Media," in *Public Opinion Quarterly,* Vol. 34, Winter, 1970-71, p. 632.

17. John Robinson, "The Impact of Television on Mass Media Usage: A Cross-National Comparison," paper presented at 6th World Congress of Sociology, Evian, France, September, 1966, p. 2.

18. Robert Bower, *Television and the Public* (New York: Holt, 1973), p. 132.

19. Elihu Katz, "The Two-Step Flow of Communication: An Up-To-Date Report on an Hypothesis," *Public Opinion Quarterly,* Vol. 21, Spring, 1957, pp. 61-78.

20. Elihu Katz and Paul Lazarsfeld, *Personal Influence: The Part Played by People in the Flow of Mass Communications* (Glencoe: The Free Press, 1955).

21. Although nobody has systematically demonstrated the end of the two-step flow (nobody ever really demonstrated its existence), there is literature to suggest that process is no longer what it once was. See E. M. Rogers, *The Communication of Innovations* (New York: Free Press, 1972). The Roper data on sources of information also suggest that the links between the media and the public have become very direct. Burns Roper, *What People Think., op. cit.*

22. John Robinson, *op. cit.,* p. 1.

23. Edward Epstein, *News From Nowhere* (New York: Random House, 1973), pp. 211-212.

24. "Interview with Walter Cronkite: A Candid Conversation With America's Most Trusted Newsman," *Playboy,* June, 1973, p. 76.

25. This study, supported by the American Enterprise Institute in Washington, is currently being completed at Ohio State University. Publication of this monumental work will occur late this year.

26. Michael Robinson, "Public Affairs Television . . . ," *op. cit.,* pp. 169-170.

27. See Note 25. Most of these data show a pattern of neutrality. But there are far more negative items than positive.

28. For an interesting discussion of the network news format see Paul Weaver, "Is Television News Biased?" *Public Interest,* Winter, 1972, pp. 57-74.

29. *Washington Post,* Sunday, February 17, 1974, p. A1, p. A4.

30. It is impossible to determine, at this point, if any of the networks did include the story. The reports in the *Post* and *Times* came out on a Sunday. I watched both NBC and CBS that eve-

ning and saw no mention of the report. I checked the Vanderbilt *Index and Abstracts* and found no entries whatever for Sunday, February 17, 1974.

31. George Gerbner and Larry Gross, "Violence Profile 6: Trends in Network Television Drama and Viewer Conceptions of Social Reality, 1967-1973," mimeo, University of Pennsylvania, December, 1974.

32. Michael J. Robinson, "Public Affairs Television . . . ," *op. cit.,* especially chapter 3.

33. Ernest Lefever, *TV and National Defense: An Analysis of CBS News 1972-1973*, (Boston, Virginia: Institute for American Strategy, 1974), chapter 2.

34. Jeff Ring, "The Eastern and Urban Orientation of the National News," unpublished term paper, Eugene, Oregon, 1973, p. 11.

35. This point is disputed by Efron. But there is evidence to support a theory of balanced coverage of Vietnam in the early stages. See Frank Russo, "A Study of Bias in TV Coverage of the Vietnam War: 1969-1970," *Public Opinion Quarterly,* Vol. 35, 1972, pp. 539-543.

36. Although Lefever would probably dispute the premise that the early coverage of Vietnam was balanced, comparatively speaking, it is clear that Lefever has demonstrated that by 1972, the balance had been seriously eroded. E. Lefever, *TV and the National Defense, op. cit.,* especially chapter 5.

37. Michael Robinson, "Public Affairs Television . . . ," *op. cit.,* p. 148.

38. Michael Robinson, *et al.* "Television and the Wallace Vote . . . ," *op. cit.*

39. Russ Neuman, "Exploring the Impact of Television News," unpublished mimeo, Berkeley, 1972.

40. Edward Epstein, *News From Nowhere, op. cit.,* passim, especially chapter 7.

41. James Buckalew, "The Television News Editor as Gatekeeper," *Journal of Broadcasting,* Vol. 13, No. 1, 1968-1969, pp. 48-49; and "News Elements and Selection by Television News Editors," same journal, Winter, 1969-1970, pp. 47-53. Also see George Bailey and Lawrence Lichty, "Rough Justice on a Saigon Street," *Journalism Quarterly,* Vol. 49, Summer, 1972, pp. 221-238. Insiders include William Small, *To Kill a Messenger* (New York: Hastings House, 1972); Robert MacNeil (New York: Harper and Row, 1968); Fred Friendly, *Due To Circumstances Beyond Our Control* (New York: Random House, 1967).

42. John Johnstone, Edward Slawski, William Bowman, "The Professional Values of American Newsmen," *Public Opinion Quarterly,* Vol. 36, Winter, 1972-73, p. 259.

43. Age is negatively correlated with a participant orientation. John Johnstone, *et al, op. cit.,* p. 537.

44. Edward Epstein, *op. cit.,* pp. 215-219.

45. Walter Cronkite interview, *op. cit.,* p. 76.

46. Daniel P. Moynihan, "The President and the Press," *Commentary,* March, 1971.

47. Oliver Quayle discovered that Cronkite is the most credible person in the nation. The Harris poll shows that television news has, in the last year, increased its credibility more than any other social agency. See note 2 for citation.

48. William Small, *To Kill a Messenger* (New York: Hastings House, 1970), p. 280.

49. Leslie Sargent, "Communicator Image and News Reception," *Journal of Communication,* Vol. 42, pp. 35-42.

50. Among others, Fred Greenstein, "The Benevolent Leader: Children's Images of Political Authority," *American Political Science Review,* Vol. 54, 1960, 934-943.

51. Delos Wickens and Donald Meyer, *Psychology* (New York: Holt, 1960), chapter 3.

52. Michael Robinson, "Public Affairs Television . . . ," *op. cit.,* "Conclusions."

53. Cited in *Time* magazine, November 19, 1973, p. 25.

54. Following the broadcast of *The Selling of the Pentagon* there were several charges made: that CBS had, in that documentary, done unethical editing, that CBS had earlier on incorrectly attributed a child's death to malnutrition in *Hunger in America,* and that CBS had actually paid Haitian revolutionairies so that CBS camera crews might follow clandestine operations in the Caribbean. CBS has not denied these assertions. In fact, President Salant has tacitly admitted to the last two by stating that in one case the baby's cause of death was indeterminable, and in the second, that "no significant amount" of money was involved in the Haitian incident.

55. Michael Robinson, *et al.,* "Television and the Wallace Vote . . . ," *op. cit.*

56. Timothy Crouse, *The Boys on the Bus* (New York: Random House, 1973), pp. 173-175.

Part 5.
The Future

"It is difficult to make predictions," Hans Bethe has said, "especially about the future." Still, it is not particularly risky to predict that the future of television will be quite different from its past. The sort of programs currently provided by the three national commercial networks, which are the focus of most of the essays in this volume, are not likely to disappear. But it appears inevitable that a whole range of new technologies will expand and transform the role that television plays in our lives.

Cable and pay-TV services, videocassette recorders, and videodisc players have already begun providing viewers with a greater variety of program choices. Before long, more exotic technologies, such as direct broadcast satellites, videotext, and home computers, may turn the TV set from a source of entertainment into an interactive information center.

In the first essay in this section, Kas Kalba reviews the efforts of artists and documentarians to create new forms of programming through the use of such devices as the portapak and the video synthesizer. Next, a group of experts offer a "roundtable" on new technological developments. Finally, Martin Perlmutter looks ahead to the time when television may serve as the vehicle for development of a new visual language.

The Video Implosion

Kas Kalba

One field worker in the North left a camera with an Eskimo family for a winter. The camera was used freely, but when he returned he found that the resulting images which had been recorded by the Eskimos appeared strange to his eyes —very close-up shots of skin surfaces: elbows, arms, etc. While the recordings seemed meaningless to the observer, he could not help but notice a certain resemblance between the shots recorded on the tapes and the typical contoured styling of Eskimo sculpture. The observer further noted that, when played back to other Eskimos, the tape seemed to be enjoyed.—from "Using Videotechnology for Social Change," a report prepared by James R. Taylor and Elizabeth Van Every-Taylor, University of Montreal, 1973.

Innovation in television is commonplace. Contrary to some opinion, it occurs frequently and is offered relatively little resistance.

If anything, what is resisted is the passing of the old (for example, "Star Trek," "Lawrence Welk") rather than the coming of the new.

The *new* in television takes on many forms. It can pertain to technical breakthroughs, such as the advent of computerized, on-line editing or intercontinental satellite relay. It can be organizational in nature; for example, the pooling of network crews in the coverage of news events. It can verge on content—in both regular programming and commercials (the subjects treated by "All in the Family," the ads for feminine deodorants). Or it can result from political activism, such as the challenges rendered to specific programs or entire stations by the United Church of Christ, NAACP, Action for Children's Television and other organizations.

What is equally clear, however, is that these modes of innovation are incremental at best or are implemented incrementally. Because of costs and cultural differences, the satellite interconnect is used sparingly. Similarly, there are limits to what can be stated in "All in the Family," not to mention what can be shown. And even militant litigants chip away at complacency in local broadcasting only one license at a time. Because of competitive factors, a recent study of network news concludes, "the timing, length, content and cost of news becomes predictable."[2] Television, in short, has become an entire society within a society, the change of which involves a lengthy, complex adjustment process. Dramatic changes affect very small portions of the system; those involving its entirety are never dramatic.

There is, however, another level at which change is occurring in television today. At this other level, television is not seen as an industry—with its particular programming stock, regulatory structure, product sponsorships, hiring practices, etc.—but as a basic way of perceiving and communicating. It is seen as a daily staple of post-industrial living. Given this outlook, the change that is suggested is of an entirely different caliber: It is radical change, and this is the change in the medium with which this report will be concerned.

Introduction: Video Environments

The rhetoric of experimental television, or "video" as it is usually called by its participants and proponents, is not difficult to pinpoint. It speaks of "democratizing the media," of "raising electronic consciousness," of "two-way participation" and "feedback." The rhetoric continually suggests that the half-inch portapak, the video synthesizer or the access facility is the key to the achievement of communicative *nirvana*. The rhetoric, as even members of the video movement are increasingly willing to admit, gets carried away with itself.

Nonetheless, some basic steps have been achieved. They are perhaps best understood as aesthetic innovations, assuming that a broad enough concept of aesthetics is subsumed. If aesthetics is regarded as a set of relationships among the basic components (that is, form, content, medium, audience, subject, producer, etc.) of an artistic or communicative experience, then the video movement can be seen as dedicated to the restructuring, in one way or another, of the television aesthetic. Television, in this sense, is not only what we see, but also how we see it, where we see it, how it is produced, who gets to produce it, what we do with what we see, and so forth.

In conventional television, the underlying aesthetic structure of the medium—the mass audience, the copyright obligations, the set in the living room, the professional standards, etc.—is so taken for granted that the entire focus of development is on programming. Small variations in style or content keep the TV seasons flowing. In video, on the other hand, the emphasis is on re-inventing this underlying structure and consequently, the introduction of new aesthetic components, roles or relationships and the abandonment of prevailing ones is as important as the creation of individual videotapes.

In this respect, the portapak is only one but a very important example of a new aesthetic resource that the video movement has used to advantage. The relative inexpensiveness of the portapak technology reduces the ratio of producers to audience members. The unobtrusive nature of the portapak changes the relationship between producer and subject, making it more informal. Its portability expands the subject matter that can be covered and the manner in which that subject is covered. Its technical compactness collapses what is conventionally a matrix of professional roles (scripting, directing, sound, lighting, set design, processing, editing, etc.) into as few as one or two individuals. Nor should the effect of negative qualities on the shaping of the medium be overlooked. The technical inferiority (video, sound, editing) of the half-inch videotape drastically reduces audience viewing propensity. In this way, too, a new communications pattern is structured. Television becomes a small group instrument rather than a passive mass experience.

Not all of the aesthetic innovation being forged by the video movement is determined by the technology *per se.* It is based rather on imaginative uses of the technology. For example, the People's Video Theater in New York City developed a "video mediation" process, whereby two conflicting neighborhood groups would exchange videotaped messages before confronting each other in person; although control groups were not tested, it is possible that some cracked heads were avoided with this technique. Similarly, video artists have created special multi-monitor video environments in which the viewer becomes a part of the spectacle both in live and delayed time (Frank Gilette and Ira Schneider's *Wipe Cycle* at the Howard Wise Gallery in New York is an example). Another pair of video artists, the Vasulkas, have employed multi-monitor screenings for the presentation of a video performance based on documentary (but processed) images of natural settings. Or, with a different kind of viewer interaction in mind, the local cable TV system in Beloeil, Quebec, has encouraged viewers to call in requests for tapes they desire to be shown, with those most popular being cablecast.

Video is also beginning to be utilized in a variety of educational, consumer, professional and even research contexts. In high schools, "visual literacy" is taught through hands-on video production experience. Anthropologists, psychiatrists, architects and other professionals have also been using the medium for self-instruction, for recording behavior, or, in the case of one Ohio judge, for "editing out" prejudicial material in trials. Various practical uses of the medium have also been conceived in relation to tomorrow's channel-affluent cable TV systems. The provision of health and employment counseling, of consumer information and of interactive educational games could be featured as regularly on "service video" as today's serials, soaps and talk shows are on broadcast TV.[3] In sum, we might say that we are in the midst of a video "implosion."

Paying homage to Marshall McLuhan is not the only reason that "implosion" seems an appropriate way to describe today's experimental television activity. Admittedly, McLuhan was the first to point out the special properties of television as a communications medium. He specifically referred to an electronic implosion, epitomized by the cool, tactile, iconic image of television.[4] To McLuhan, the era of the printing press was psychologically explosive, fragmenting our senses and concepts, whereas the multi-linearity of television in today's world indicates an implosive process.

But there is a more specific reason for using the term "implo-

sion." While the activity of the video movement has been very intensive in the last three or four years, it has not been equally extensive.
If an opinion poll were taken today, only a small fraction of the
general public could reflect any knowledge of video developments;
and yet the energy being expended by the hundreds of video groups
across the country is truly astounding. Videotape upon videotape is
being produced; festivals are being held; communities are being
organized with the help of portapaks; art galleries are opening video
archives; proposals for funding programming projects are being
assembled; polemical battles as to favored production and organizational philosophies are being waged. Moreover, many of the elements
it will take to widen the implosion are coming into being, including
not only low-cost production equipment but also the emergence of
cable television and video-cassette programming outlets.

At the same time, a variety of practical difficulties limit video
development and may continue to do so. It is because of this fertile
moment of opportunities for expansion, matched by the many constraints on such expansion, that this report has been put together. It
will attempt to outline the evolution of video activity, the emerging
institutional approaches in the field, and the barriers that remain to
be surmounted. Finally, it will suggest some roles that government,
industry, foundations and community institutions might undertake
to overcome some of the obstacles.

Two more points need to be made about the subject matter of
this report. First, it is somewhat artificial to speak of all experimental
television as a single activity. As the accompanying list indicates (see
Figure 1), the influences on, and varieties of, video activity are many.
And to some degree, the pooling of various video approaches under
one rubric is a falsification of their diverse roots and objectives. For
example, conceptual video can be said to have more to do with conceptual art than with street video (which has more to do with community organizing).

Second, it is also artificial to draw boundaries between video
and local-origination programming on cable television, or between
video and independent film making. In each case, moving audio-
visual imagery—and often experimentation as well—is involved. Nonetheless, there are certain ways in which the activities covered by this
report exhibit commonalities while remaining distinct from outside
matter. On the one hand, the shared objective of video makers is to
radically change conventional television; on the other, there is an
overt concern not to imitate other media and art forms in making

Figure 1

**VIDEO
FORMS,
CONTEXTS
AND
INFLUENCES**

**(a two-dimensional
representation
of n-dimensions)**

happenings

underground press

call-in radio

commercial television

psychiatric video   video publishing

educational media

independent filmmaking

conceptual art

advocacy journalism   multi-media

video art

synthesized music

home movie-making

VIDEO

visual literacy   public access

service video

local origination   public television

citizens radio

video synthesizer   social research

cinema verite   telediagnosis

community organizing

guerilla theater   video training

video conferences

these changes (scripting, for example, is the basis of most film making, yet to most video makers it is anathema).

Finally, it should be asked why the video implosion of today is important? Why should attention be focused on it generally, and why should institutions consider its support? The first answer to this question is that clearly the video movement can be taken too seriously. While the portapak or the video synthesizer are marvelous inventions, they do not in themselves produce new communications messages or experiences. And yet video makers have sometimes been too dependent—perhaps "overwhelmed" is the better word—by these tools. A commentator in a recent issue of *Filmmakers Newsletter* put it well, although admittedly, he may have had a double interest in pointing out the shortcomings of video:

> Take a hammer away from a carpenter and he's still a carpenter; take the pen away from a poet and he's still a poet; but take the VTR away from a videofreak and he's just a freak with a head full of futuristic jargon.[5]

The commentator goes on to state that "The essence of any communication is conceptual, not technological, and no machine has yet formulated a concept nor had a vision." Simply recording events, he feels, is not a communicative act.

These statements contain some cinematic bias but also a measure of truth. Fortunately, an increasing number of video makers have begun to voice similar self-criticisms. The words of the editor of a parallel issue of *Radical Software* indicate a new degree of self-observation. "We have gone," she states, "through the freakout, self-indulgent, magic trip with the portapak, which for all of its excitement and stimulation, has left us somewhat cynical about our effectiveness."[6]

At the same time, the positive contribution of video can hardly be dismissed, even though it occurs in many distinct manifestations. In one instance, it helps a group become more sharply aware of a community issue. In another, it is a vehicle for a new form of artistic expression. It can educate the user in a new way of perceiving conventional television. It can report a crime as well as tell a story. More importantly, video is wrestling with the underlying information problems of the day: lack of "survival" information, multi-sensory environments, individual and social therapy, propaganda (as Jacques Ellul would define it), information overload, and the communication of group identity.

In relation to the problems they are confronting, what video makers have accomplished to date can at best be termed experiments or models. Indeed, to the city planner (as I am), the entire video experience can be compared to the starts and stops, the ideas and programs that have been recently witnessed in the rebuilding of our cities. While the new downtowns reflect each other systematically, like the disparate stations of the same broadcasting network, other areas less close to the mainstream are truly experimenting—for example, in inner-city recreational spaces, modular housing or personal rapid transit.

The video movement has been preoccupied with a less tangible, electronic community, and what remains unclear today is which of these cities—the tangible or intangible—needs rebuilding most. It is even less clear where one begins and the other ends. After all, the Yellow Pages are the "downtown" of Los Angeles as much as any physical center. Nashville and the weather occupy the radio spectrum. We meet on the residential telephone network as much as on the urban grid of streets and highways. Similarly, familiar televised images have replaced the institutions and relationships of the past: the eve-

ning news is our town square; the comedy serials are our neighborhood walk or porch stoop; the TV movies are today's theater district;
"Sesame Street" is kindergarten; the "Today Show" is a newspaper
stand or public library; the network logo is a statue in the park; and
grandmother's babysitting has been replaced by the children's evening TV special or early morning cartoons.[7]

It is in the context of this electronic community, these video
"new towns," that the experiments of today's video makers can best
be gauged. Some are building individual houses, monuments, cathe-
drals; some are reconceptualizing neighborhood plans and city-
neighborhood relations; some are recreating the little red schoolhouse
or designing models of entire new towns. We can see in these early
video experiments the shortcomings that accompany most fundamental undertakings—rhetorical excesses, technical deficiencies,
utopian escape, lack of organization and other limitations. But there
can be no doubt that what is being tinkered with are the root ingredients of contemporary living.

Evolution of the Video Medium

If there was one spark that gave birth to the video movement, it
resulted from a very peculiar collision during the middle and late
1960s. On the one hand, there was an emerging sense of what the old
television was doing to us. Almost poetic and mystical in character,
the vision of total TV impact given to us by a host of new media
visionaries, including Andy Warhol, Margaret Mead, Nicholas Johnson
and especially Marshall McLuhan. On the other hand, there was the
arrival from Japan (for export only?) of half-inch video technology.
To the artist or community organizer, this was as tangible a form as
television production had ever taken.

Yet the conditions of the video implosion were present even
before this synergistic collision occurred. They were certainly discerned by early video artists who, using existing television technology, attempted to create new forms and viewing experiences.

Experiments with Broadcast TV. Probably the first, and certainly the seminal artist to begin video experimentation was Nam
June Paik. As early as 1963, the Korean-born artist was prophetically
generating abstract visual images through television. At first, by

merely modifying the circuitry on old discarded TV sets and then passing a magnet before the screen, Paik was able to create visual explosions in which the transmitted image distorted and then dissolved into a rainbow of colors.

Yet without access to actual facilities, there was little that could be done by even the most imaginative artists. For the first 20 years of television, aspiring video artists were, in effect, denied both brush and palette by the commercial broadcast structure. In the late sixties, the institutions which first began to open up their control rooms to artists were three affiliates of PBS (then NET): KQED in San Francisco, WGBH in Boston, and WNET in New York. Motivated in part by an internal impetus from such innovative producers as Fred Barzyk, Brice Howard, John Coney and Paul Kaufman, and aided by a small influx of outside funding for experimental projects, these three affiliates became the broadcast pioneers of experimental television.

In 1967, KQED established the first experimental video workshop, which developed, two years later, into the National Center for Experiments in Television. Under Brice Howard and Paul Kaufman, a program was launched which continues to bring artists and technologists together to experiment. Support for the program has come from the Rockefeller Foundation, the National Endowment for the Arts, the Dilexi Foundation, and the Corporation for Public Broadcasting. Across the country in Boston, WGBH established "Artists in Television" to facilitate the production of experimental programs suitable for broadcast, by visiting artists. And in New York, WNET's Television Laboratory has provided video artists with the widest possible array of experimental television equipment since its creation in early 1972.

Previous to these early experiments, television had been imprisoned by a firmly entrenched and unimaginative set of engineering rules governing how production equipment should and should not be used. Designed to permit television to imitate film and perfectly reproduce the representational image, the rules held the medium in a straightjacket of conventionality. In a gradual but step-by-step fashion, the artists working in these experimental programs began to explore beyond the boundaries of this routine production work which, except for ads, continues to monopolize the commercial TV medium. For example, the effects of deliberately starving the camera's scanning beam of electrical current were tested. In so doing, they found that they could generate imagery with a new dimension, such as ghost images that seemed to stick eerily to the screen as the figure moved. With keying and chroma-keying (which had previously been used to separate images), new graphic designs were created through the blending of images.

These and other techniques established a linear imagery that invited a sensual and participatory perception on the part of the viewer. Much of the important early work was done at KQED. Terry Riley's "Music with Balls" synthesized sculpture, music and video into a color, sound and motion collage. In "Sorcery," Loren Sears utilized debeaming and keying to achieve images that disintegrated mystically into diaphanous lines and billowy clouds of light. In "West Pole," the first experimental piece broadcast by KQED, Robert Zagone initiated the TV audience with a harmonic fusion of electronic music plus visual electronic motion. Similarly, Joanne Kyger's "Descartes" brought a creative poetess to the medium through a unique synthesis of oral content and visual form.

In 1968, WGBH produced "The Medium Is the Medium," a compendium of a year's experimental work commissioned by the Public Broadcast Laboratory. Under the direction of Fred Barzyk, it included pieces by James Seawright, Aldo Tambellini and Nam June Paik. In "Capriccio for TV," Seawright violated all the well-defined rules of television production. He used chroma-keying to remove a background without replacing it. He also shot the piece in negative color. A renegade station engineer devised another totally unorthodox and unacceptable effect through tape delay. The result was an electronic ballet in which two dancers, performing the same action, appeared in four places in four colors at the same time. They moved effortlessly through an area suspended in space, without top or bottom, front or back. They sprouted graceful fans of detached human arms that encircled them like moving colored halos.

Tambellini's piece, "Black," was as different from Seawright's as Seawright's was from "The Ed Sullivan Show." Tambellini filled the studio with 30 black children, bombarded the studio space with a fusillade of 1,000 slides and 16-millimeter film, and used three cameras to record the action between the kids and the projected images.

Later that year at WGBH, Rick Hauser produced "City/Motion/Space/Game," the first broadcast attempt at stereovision. Two different but related images were broadcast simultaneously over two television channels, so that the viewer was presented with two continuous streams of images which alternately harmonized and counterpointed each other and forced the viewer to participate in the creative process by making constant decisions on which image to focus on.

Despite these and other early experiments, video artists were dependent on the beneficence of a few institutions and charitable broadcast stations. The cost of studio time (about $2,000 a day) and the inability of the TV establishment to recognize their work severely limited the number of experiments and participating artists. Video experimentation remained the province of the few and fortunate.

Portapaks and Synthesizers. In 1970, Nam June Paik bought the first half-inch videotape recorder sold to a consumer in New York. He taped scenes from his taxi on his way downtown, played back the tape at the Cafe Au Go Go in the Village, and proclaimed, "As collage technique replaced oil paint, so the cathode ray (television) tube will replace the canvas." The video movement was underway.

Clearly, the development of half-inch video was the spark which gave large numbers the opportunity to produce their own television. And like the new video consciousness, the new technology had its roots in television. Half-inch employed the same basic principles as broadcast technology, but on a smaller, less expensive scale. Indeed, broadcast videotape (two-inch quadraplex) was prohibitively expensive to all but large commercial stations. Even one-inch facilities, such as those employed in educational and industrial television, were generally inaccessible to the video artists, since these tapes were still much more expensive than half-inch by a factor of five or ten to one.

Thus, Japanese manufacturers, in developing half-inch (helical scan) technology, created a new television production tool which was portable, utilized re-usable tape, could be played back instantly, and was remarkably inexpensive. An entire recording unit cost less than $2,000. While the image quality and overall sophistication of half-inch were grossly inferior to the broadcast systems, these drawbacks were minor compared to the increased accessibility to and control over production that the new equipment accorded video experimenters.

In the early years of half-inch, Sony was the leading supplier of hardware. Its portapak, a portable video recorder (VTR) with camera, was easily the most functional and versatile unit in the half-inch arsenal. The VTR and camera weighed less than 25 pounds, was powered by a battery that could drive the unit for up to three hours, and was simple enough for a child to use. At the same time, half-inch hardware was not confined to the small portable unit. It also offered large, more sophisticated VTRs, studio cameras, editing facilities, and special-effects generators which could cheaply duplicate many of the functions of inaccessible broadcast hardware at a fraction of the cost.

At the same time that the portapak was beginning to be used in streets and in studios, another group of revolutionary techno-artists began to experiment with video as a tool to create electronic light imagery. They were drawn to video by its unique electronic light properties and sought to tap its potential for creating purer and more sophisticated electronic images. For these electronic visual artists, the coming of half-inch also introduced a new tool—electronic feedback —which is an electronic loop, a circular electronic process by which a camera, focusing on a monitor, simultaneously sees and also displays its own electronic image on that monitor. Through manipulation of the camera's position in relation to the monitor, a virtually limitless variety of complex electronic imagery can be produced. For the first time, artists could begin to generate purely electronic television art.

Although feedback was technically possible in the pre-half-inch era (David Atwood and Robert Zagone conducted early experiments), it was not practical because of the immobility of the heavy studio camera. However, given lightweight mobile cameras, video artists could experiment freely with this electronic kaleidoscope. By introducing other elements into the feedback process—additional cameras, time delays, reflective surfaces—and by feeding the image through a colorizer, the creation of even more elaborate imagery became possible. Stephen Beck, Nam June Paik, Bob Lewis and Jim Weisman are among the imagists who have been most responsible for advancing this technique as an art form.

But even more than video feedback, the innovation that has exponentially broadened the potential for the electronic artists has been the video synthesizer. Again, Paik was the initiator. In 1969, aided by design collaborator Shuya Abe, he built at WGBH the first video synthesizer. The synthesizer was intended by Paik to cheaply duplicate the effects possible in a color television studio, though Paik's synthesizer was built at a cost of less than $10,000. An "optical" synthesizer (that is, input signals must come directly from an external source), the Paik-Abe system consists of a cheap black and white camera and the synthesizer, into which the camera signal is fed, colorized and manipulated. With this synthesizer, any quantity and quality of color can be added to the black and white image; the image can be processed and manipulated in a limitless variety of ways; images can be abstracted entirely; and different video signal inputs can be used, including audio inputs to control the video input and make sound visible.

A similar type of video synthesizer was developed about the same time by Eric Seigel in New York. Then a year later, Stephen Beck built a video synthesizer which differs in many respects from the Paik-Abe. A result of his "search for a precise means of expressively controlling light," Beck's synthesizer is a "direct" video synthesizer; that is, it allows the artist to generate imagery and light from within the video system itself without external inputs. (It is also capable of optical synthesis and the integration of optical and direct synthesis.) In addition, Beck was able to increase the amount of control that the artist has over the image being generated. The Beck synthesizer is the ultimate tool in today's electronic video arsenal.

Directions in Video Art. The availability of various video processing tools has helped create one of the dominant forms of video art—namely, electronic video. But the technology has not been the only stimulant to this development; aesthetic concerns have also played a role. Many of the artists engaged in electronic video art see narrative and expository forms of art as limited in value—as forms which often distort reality by their insistence on ordering it and which inherently place the viewer outside the artistic process as a passive observer. The electronic imagists instead attempt to create an experience, not tell a story. They bypass linear reasoning and encourage the senses to perceive and integrate the material for themselves. What the video synthesizer has allowed these artists to do is to fulfill their aesthetic theories in unprecedented fashion.

This has occurred with stops as well as starts, of course. For instance, the Paik-Abe synthesizer was in mothballs for two years following Paik's departure from WGBH. But last year it was reactivated as the principal tool of WGBH's Music Image Workshop under the direction of Ron Hays. Six other Paik-Abe synthesizers are now in use around the country. In addition, several other techno-artists have attempted to build video synthesizers, but none of these have achieved public prominence. Despite the limited number of synthesizers and the difficulty that artists encounter in obtaining access to them, the synthesizer has been a watershed in the development of the electronic visual experience.

More recently, other media, such as computer graphics, have begun to be fused with video synthesis. Ed Emshwiller's brilliantly surreal and other-worldly "Scapemates," produced at WNET's Television Laboratory, is a fusion of these two media that produces an overwhelming perceptual experience of a dimension which has yet to be equaled through any other media. Motivated by the desire to allow an inexpensive integration of these two media, Bill Etra, in collaboration with Walter Wright, has recently constructed yet another synthesizer which enables video-synthesis and computer graphics to be generated and fused by a single piece of hardware.

Besides electronic or "abstract" video, two other genres of video activity are clearly evident in the art world. With respect to one of these, conceptual art, artists have been interested in using video as another tool to explore relationships between the individual and his environment. In "Noise," Linda Benglis chose video to examine the visual and audio-tactile space that surrounds us. Joan Jonas, in "Mirror Check" and "Left Side Right Side," has used the camera to effect an intense and highly personal exploration of the self. William Wegman uses video to create a series of brilliant dialogues with himself through which he mercilessly exposes the absurdity of not only the TV dinner but our TV existence in general.

To the uninitiated viewer, conceptual video art (as is often the case with other forms of conceptual art) can appear excessively redundant, trivial and boring. Yet, banality or "vulgarization" is a tool of the conceptual artist, whose objective it is "to tire out every eye that stakes all on the satisfaction of a retinal (aesthetic) shock, however slight." For it is only "Once the dwindling form/imprint/ gesture has been rendered impotent/invisible, [that] the proposition has/will have some chance to become dazzling."[8] In short, banality is consciously employed to go beyond the art object to the underlying proposition (or concept), to reach the "software" so often hidden by the hardware of art.

In this sense, it is also evident that artistic, psychological and even scientific uses of video have started to merge. For example, video has been used to pose questions about the medium itself: What is the relationship between the viewer and the videospace created by television? How does television foster a process-level experience in which *how* one sees is more important than *what* one sees? In "TV In TV Out," Keith Sonnier creates an electronic mix of two images which illustrate the illusions of depth, space and color that television induces. In "Participation TV" and "TV Chair," Nam June Paik showed the potentially participatory relationship between the TV artist and TV viewer by inviting the audience to join him as a partner in the creative process. "Please Superimpose Please," by Paul Haley and others, researches electronic love-making by means of a two-way video situation. And in "Beyond Sesame Street," Mike Mills poignantly explores the psychology of interpersonal relationships through video by having a small girl and her father relate to each other via closed circuit television.

Still other conceptual video art utilizes video in performance as well as on tape. Artists have set up exhibits in which spectators become both participants and objects as they see their own images on live monitors. Bruce Nauman in "Come Piece," Frank Gillette and Ira Schneider in "Wipe Cycle," Les Levine in "Contact" and "Iris," and Peter Campus in "Interface" have used video to persuade and cajole the viewer into examining and re-examining his self-image and his relationship to his environment.

A final area of experimentation by artists has been the use of video to extend and deepen the traditional representational form in which television functions. The relatively small group of representational video artists has been, in effect, reacting against the output of commercial television and suggesting that traditional techniques can be used in ways that are truer to both the properties of the medium and the world in which we live. Specifically, they have attempted to make tapes that utilize the potentially intimate relationship between the viewer and the image on the screen, tapes that draw the viewer into the relationship as an involved participant, tapes that convey the sense of reality that the television implies but rarely delivers.

Representational artists have been a smaller force in video than conceptual and electronic artists, perhaps because the latter two forms offer vehicles of expression that depart more radically from the conventional uses of the medium. Nevertheless, several pieces of enormous value have been produced and have significantly advanced the grammar of conventional television. "Recycle," by the Videofreex, contrasts the potential reality of video with the deliberate deceptiveness of commercial television. Frank Gillette's "Homage to Beach and Clouds" evokes the rhythm, the visuality, and almost the scent of the ocean. Linda Benglis' "Home Tape" conveys with quiet intimacy the range and intensity of emotion experienced in a visit home after a long absence. Grassroots Video's "The Edge of Ajax" is a parody of the afternoon soap opera with local (Aspen, Colorado) referents. Perhaps the most well-known is Video Free America's "The Continuing Story of Carol and Ferd," a video novel of epic proportions which utilizes several monitors to explore the bizarre yet flighty relationship between two people against the backdrop of their twentieth-century media environment. Preceding WNET's "An American Family" in time, many video enthusiasts would also argue that "Carol and Ferd" supersedes the public television series in achievement.

An additional area of experimentation is the recent introduction of video as an element of live theatre and dance. Most notable is the work of the creators of "Carol and Ferd." First in Heathcoate Williams' "AC-DC," then in Allen Ginsberg's "Kaddish," and most recently in "Kaspar," Art Ginsberg and Video Free America have interfaced video with theatre in a way that has deepened the dimensions of both media. In the same genre, Hippo Video's "Mother Wednesday" has been running for nearly a year in Los Angeles. And "Hamms," another such interface based loosely on *Waiting for Godot,* was recently staged in Cambridge, Massachusetts, by Vince Canzoneri.

Impact on Communications. In seeking background material for this report, I visited a performing arts institution that also housed a video group. Because of the live performing arts orientation of the other groups at this institution, one role of the video group was to provide video support for rehearsal purposes. However, conflict between this institutional role and the other objectives of the video group was apparent during a brief encounter between one of the video-makers and a professional dancer. The dancer wanted the video-maker to tape a rehearsal of hers so that she could observe her own performance and thereby improve on it. The video-maker, on the other hand, was primarily interested in electronically processing dance tapes as a form of video art. In effect, both the dancer and the video-maker perceived each other as objects, one of many inputs to their particular expressionistic activities, dancing in one case and image-processing in the other. The encounter was hardly communicative.

One of the risks of video's diffusion throughout society is, as the above example suggests, that it may become a mundane tool, which each group applies to its own utilitarian purpose. On the other hand, video can also spread in a way that fosters self-learning by the video-maker, the participating institution, and even the outside observer. This is what happened, for example, when Open Channel videotaped a black Baptist church ceremony in Bedford-Stuyvesant, utilizing modest equipment. The video group, the celebrants, and subsequent viewers of the tape each gained a new awareness of this particular religious service. Moreover, a conventional highly edited news coverage of the same event could have never achieved the same effect.

The development of video can also have a significant impact on the communications industry. The low-cost production techniques, new programming formats, processing experiments, and alternative concepts of programming content that video introduces will gradually infiltrate video publishing, educational television and cable origination. In particular, the opportunity of the cable industry to assimilate many of these video innovations needs to be emphasized, since without a new identity as an alternative to the over-the-air broadcasting, cable television is not likely to advance its own cause. Nor should the possibility that video will change broadcast television be entirely dismissed. UHF stations in particular may be influenced by some of the new programming concepts. And some of today's video-makers may yet become the network producers of tomorrow.

There is, finally, another perspective that can be cast on the video implosion. It has been expressed recently by Douglas Davis, a video-maker as well as art editor of *Newsweek* magazine, who sees video within the context of our society's emerging post-industrial status. "The world," he writes, "is no longer interested in our Fords; it wants instead our ideas, and our dreams . . ." In short, the output of our civilization is no longer manufactured products but innovation in its many manifestations: science, technological R & D, social change, new life styles and services, space research, professional and managerial problem-solving approaches, etc. Art is also one of these, the one that Davis examines most closely. He points out that whereas America has previously acted as the principal procurer of art, it is now the principal producer. More specifically, the outside world, states Davis, is "attracted to the most adventurous work we do—not to the traditional but to post-pop painting, conceptual art, and the new experimentation in video and film."[27]

Neither work nor play, video—and the social patterns it engenders—may well be a progenitor of post-industrial living. Its development can be a way in which we surpass ourselves as individuals, as institutions, as a culture. And cultural change, as McLuhan has so succinctly reminded us, is our ultimate business.

Footnotes

1. I would like to acknowledge the indispensable assistance of Fred Simon, project associate, who initially drafted the second section of this report, and Wendie Barron, my research assistant. Preparation of the report has also benefited from the various inputs of Richard Adler, Walter Baer, Red Burns, Dotty Chiesa, Forrest Chisman, Herbert Dordick, Brigitte Kenny, Gerald O'Grady, David Othmer, Michael Shamberg, Thea Sklover, Elizabeth and James R. Taylor, Carol Lynn Yellin, as well as the numerous video makers that I have had the opportunity to visit or talk to during the past year. In addition, a number of individuals have been helpful in reviewing and commenting on a draft version of this report, among them Fred Barzyk, Skip Blumberg, Carroll Bowen, David Cort, Richard Kletter, David Loxton, Robert Sample and Jon Shafer. Finally, project assistants Peter Hankin and Penny Moorhead contributed to the report by helping me assemble and interpret a sample of experimental videotapes.

2. Edward Jay Epstein, *News from Nowhere: Television and the News* (Random House, 1973), p. 259.

3. For a fuller description of "service video," see Kas Kalba, "Today's TV Headed for Showdown in '80s with New, Experimental Concepts," *Variety* (Sept. 13, 1972), p. 40.

4. See Marshall McLuhan, *Understanding Media: The Extensions of Man* (McGraw-Hill, 1964).

5. Samuel B. Earlywine, "Don't Switch That Dial Around:—I'm Here to Save You," *Filmmakers Newsletter* (March 1973), p. 53.

6. *Radical Software* (Vol. 2, No. 4), opening page.

7. I have elaborated on this communications vision of communities in "Telecommunications for Future Human Settlements: A Planning Framework for Minnesota Experimental City," *Ekistics* (Vol. 35, No. 211, June 1973), pp. 329-336.

8. Daniel Buren, "Beware:", in Ursula Meyer, *Conceptual Art* (E. P. Dutton, 1972), p. 72.

9. Douglas Davis, "My Turn: The Soft Sell," *Newsweek* (July 23, 1973).

Television in the Eighties

Emmy Roundtable

WALTER S. BAER is a senior physical scientist at The Rand Corporation. Since 1970 his research has focused on the effects of government regulation and technological change in the communications and energy fields. Dr. Baer is the author of Cable Television: A Handbook for Decisionmaking *and coauthor and editor of several books in Rand's cable-television series. He formerly served on the Office of Science and Technology staff in the executive office of the president; was a member of the technical staff at the Bell Telephone Laboratories; and served on the advisory committee to the Aspen Program on Communications and Society, and the cable-television advisory committee of the Federal Communications Commission. Dr. Baer is currently a member of the faculty of the Rand Graduate Institute.*

RICHARD L. GINGRAS is director, office of planning and corporate development at KCET. His responsibilities include development of program production and distribution activities in cable television, exploring information technologies such as broadcast teletext and examining potential uses of videodiscs. Before joining KCET in May 1979, Gingras worked as a consultant for the National Telecommunications and Information Administration in Washington where he analyzed administration policies relating to public broadcasting. From 1974 to 1976 he was associated with the Corporation for Public Broadcasting; an aide to the president for the development of satellite utilization policies; and manager of special studies.

JEFFREY A. ROCHLIS is president of Mattel Electronics, a company formed as a result of Rochlis's role as director of new business development for Mattel Toys. The three-year-old electronics division develops such products as electronic games, entertainment devices and home computers. Rochlis was formerly associated with Aurora Products Corporation, a subsidiary of Nabisco, Inc., where he served as vice president of marketing, director of marketing and advertising manager. Prior to that Rochlis was associated with McCann-Erickson and held the position of account supervisor and account executive and was involved in advertising campaigns for Sears, L'Oréal and CPC International. Rochlis has also served as account executive for Benton & Bowles advertising agency.

ROBERT STROCK, marketing manager of Theta Cable, is responsible for advertising, marketing and program development for Theta Cable and the "Z" Channel. Most recently involved in corporate marketing for the Coca-Cola Bottling Company of Los Angeles, Strock also served for 12 years as vice president of marketing for a division of American Machine and Foundry. In addition, Strock has held the position of president for his own marketing company, Marketing/70 Inc. A graduate of the University of California at Los Angeles, Strock has a broad range of interests in advertising and marketing development, specializing in the areas of product development, pay television and corporate acquisitions.

EMMY: How much impact do you think cable, pay TV, satellites, et cetera, will have on the three commercial networks?

BAER: The networks and broadcasting in general should continue to do quite well in the Eighties despite what we see as the rapid growth of cable and pay television. Based on new data, my colleague Ed Park just completed an analysis of the expected impact of cable on broadcasting. If, for instance, the FCC opens the floodgates and allows cable to take in any signals it wants, there would be some measurable impact but not all that much. Park's figures suggest a maximum effect of perhaps a 7 percent loss of audience among network stations in the top 100 markets and possibly twice that amount in the smaller markets. But that's not enough of a diversion to affect the industry significantly.

EMMY: The networks are predicting a 10 percent loss of audience. You agree, then, that that's an accurate estimate?

BAER: Based on the work that Ed Park has done that certainly seems to be in the right range.

GINGRAS: It's difficult to make any kind of accurate prediction. The key factor, of course, is the number of homes that will be on cable in the Eighties. Some are predicting that by 1990 the penetration will be 70 percent. Although I don't agree with that figure— I think it will reach 35 to 50 percent—that will obviously affect the total network share. No doubt it is going to go down. In Los Angeles, for instance, where the penetration of cable is not very high, the combined network share is 80 percent, and that's a result of the competition of 14 other broadcast stations.

STROCK: But, you know, an interesting thing is happening. I was with Theta Cable when it started the "Z" Channel about four years ago. Pay TV had been turned down by the electorate in California, and we had to decide whether or not to gamble on it. Basically cable television is a ho-hum industry—if people need cable for reception they get it, and that's that—so you had no great area of growth. We needed more dollars coming in so we decided, "Let's take a gamble on pay TV"—and it really was a gamble. A lot of people in our industry and within our own company said, "Hey, don't do that." But we went ahead, and pretty soon we had first-run movies on television.

The interesting thing is that, in our franchise area, approximately 25 to 30 percent of our subscribers are in the entertainment business. You notice that now, of course, theatrical movies appear on the networks much faster, and I think that pay TV on the "Z" Channel helped speed that up. All of a sudden the free-television consumer was seeing first-run movies a lot faster, and I think that if pay TV had not come on the scene that would not have happened.

EMMY: I'm sure you've noticed in the advertisements in *TV Guide* for several of their movies that ABC has included the line "Another Outstanding Movie on Free Television."

STROCK: Yes. They used to say, "first time on television" and now they say, "first time on network television." Richard, you mentioned tht much of Los Angeles isn't cabled. But now you've got Six Star and other operations coming in and buying up every franchise they can. They're bidding now for the Valley, mid-L.A. In about three years all of Los Angeles will be cabled. Now, I don't think that will happen in Chicago and other areas, but I think it's beginning to happen on a national level. Three years ago there was a total of about 5 million people on cable. Today there are 14 million —plus, with 5 million subscribing to pay TV. All of a sudden this industry is taking off.

GINGRAS: Well, what will be interesting will be the data obtained from studying the level of viewing among pay-television households in a city such as Los Angeles—and I don't just mean cable pay-television but subscription television as well. ON TV is already up to 250,000 subscribers. Nielsen did a study of 5,000 pay-television households which showed that on numerous occasions—and not only for their top-line films but for some of the lesser films as well—Home Box Office not only did well against the network competition but actually outpointed them. And this was during a sweeps week when the networks aired "Roots" and "The Sound of Music" against, I think, HBO's "Looking for Mr. Goodbar." "Goodbar" got a share of something like 27 percent, "Roots" got 25 percent, and the other two commercial shows did far worse. I thought that was amazing. You know, you would expect, since so many of pay-TV's offerings are repeated during the week, that on an hour-by-hour basis it really couldn't compete with the networks. But it's incredible that in so many instances it beats out the network competition.

STROCK: But I wonder how much of that has to do with the fact that this year network programming is not all that exciting and that viewers are looking for an alternative. I watch "60 Minutes" and the eleven o'clock news, and that's about all. I don't race home any more to see certain shows. I remember that years ago there were certain programs you always saw, and I've talked to a lot of people who feel that way. They say, "Gee, there's nothing on this year" and then read in the paper that a show has been canceled they've never even bothered to see once.

ROCHLIS: I think another factor that will enter into this, too, is that cable and the over-the-air systems will also be a means for transmitting information. In the near term I think that one of the things cable operators will be looking at—if they've got a system that was essentially laid for reception—will be ways to increase their monthly revenue streams because the percentage of subscribers-per-home-passed is fairly high. The company that has laid cable primarily for the paid portion of the service has gone to the same expense of laying cable and laying plant, but its density on homes-passed is fairly low. The company needs to get a good percentage of the rest of the homes-passed to subscribe to the system.

Now, through an interface with a home terminal, that television set can become a display medium for informational and interactive systems, be they entertainment in the form of a game, self-education in terms of learning a foreign language or financial services that compute your taxes. And even the one-way cable systems that are utilized today will efficiently transmit that kind of interactive software.

GINGRAS: For that matter, that same concept may very likely eventually be true for broadcasting, too. We think of broadcast teletext in somewhat the same way, as having a potential beyond simply presenting information like flight guides and weather maps. We hope to interface it with information technologies, home personal computers and games and then use our data stream to essentially dump software into those technologies.

ROCHLIS: Well, as you may or may not know, Mattel has formed a joint venture with Jerrold Electronics, a wholly owned subsidiary of General Instruments. Jerrold is the largest hardware supplier in the cable industry, providing about 70 percent of the head-end computers' adapter boxes, and it lays a lot of plant on a subcontractive basis. In February that joint venture will be marketed on a test basis in five markets. These services will interface with our home terminals, and we will down a cable and very rapidly transmit on a continual basis, on a single one-way channel, up to a hundred and some programs every thirty seconds which the computer grabs off the line and stores in its memory banks and which the consumer has complete interaction with.

BAER: And don't forget that the telephone lines can also be used to bring information into the home. Technically, what's fascinating is the potential competition among broadcast television, cable television and the telephone lines, each bringing some of the same kinds of information into the home for display on a television screen or to interact with the home computer or any of the other devices that would be in the home.

ROCHLIS: And there are several manifestations of the phone relationship. Even though the established commercial data banks are essentially serving only the industrial community, they can provide certain economic advantages to consumers in terms of software interaction. And when you get into Viewdata, the economics can be even more favorable. I think there will be a number of parallel, coexisting transmission mediums, and the common element for all of this is that television screen—it's the display medium. And when people spend time using that medium for either passive or interactive services that are other than the typical broadcast offerings, then you will have a degree of competition.

GINGRAS: But one should not assume—and I don't think you mean this—that simply because the television screen already exists in the home that the set itself will necessarily play that large a role in all of these information networks. I suspect that AT&T has ideas up its sleeve. From what I gather, AT&T has a small prototype terminal, no larger than a secretary's phone console, with a phone, touch-tone buttons for the phone and a small five-inch-square CRT with access buttons around it so you can use it as an information-access device.

It will be intersting to see how these transmission mediums develop. Each one has, I suppose, certain advantages over the others. For instance, we like to think of Teletext, broadcast Teletext, as simply an added dimension to the programming service.

STROCK: But in the television industry I think the challenge will be in the area of creativity. A lot of these things we're talking about now are data- and library-source-type things. But in the pure entertainment area—on all the channels—it's hard to find good programs. Even on public television, the range of new creativity is there, but you still don't fill all the hours. It's hard to find programming.

GINGRAS: It's hard to find money . . .

STROCK: Even with pay TV offering all these other channels and services the question remains: What do you put on it? That's really important. If you just put on data it's as boring as the dickens. You can't watch figures all the time. The entertainment challenge is just tremendous.

BAER: What we don't know is what the home subscriber wants and is willing to pay for in terms of information services. We don't know if people will be interested in dialing up the telephone and getting some kind of financial information or if the market is basically an entertainment one. We just don't know how it will all sort out in the next decade.

ROCHLIS: The more mundane transactional and static-information services are not going to be the catalysts to launch these systems as major competitive industries. It's going to be interactive, and it's going to be entertaining. And even though it may be service- or education-oriented, it's going to be enveloped in a fun-involving format that people are going to want to interact with. It's a new kind of entertainment, if you will.

GINGRAS: It may get to the point where essentially computer

programming and television programming begin to come together.

ROCHLIS: The computer is an interesting device because of what it is technically. It makes possible things that were not possible heretofore.

EMMY: How do you plan to market this new technology, particularly the information services that interface with some type of computer hookup? While most kids today seem quite at home with calculators and video games, many adults still have a basic fear of computers. How do you plan to reach them, and what will you do to spark their interest?

GINGRAS: Well, that gets into the whole question of the man/ machine interface. It will be interesting to follow the product development. For example, by looking at the home personal computer you can see how the product has changed in just the last year. At first there was the Radio Shack model, which is really just a smaller version of a basic computer. It has a keyboard that you use for programming. But the newer models that, for instance, Texas Instruments and Mattel are marketing are beginning to look less and, essentially, act less like computers. You don't have to know a computer language because you just simply talk to it.

ROCHLIS: Well, you're right about the current adult population. It has a negative mind-set. Computers came after they grew up so they're intimidated and a little bit naive about them. The perception is that computers threaten people's jobs. And you're also right in the sense that the intitial products offered were a bit shortsighted because they were nothing more than translations of larger-scale business computers. But they just sat there; they were pieces of hardware. But hardware is not an end unto itself, it's merely a means unto an end.

Computers are a software-dependent business just like the broadcasting industry is. We're not talking about selling television sets—we're talking about selling leisure-time occupation. And the products that are coming out now don't require anyone to go through a hundred-page manual to learn basic computer language. Nor do they require a consumer to sit down for three hours a night for three months to get the thing to do something. That belies the inherent concept of what a computer should do.

You are also right, I think, that children today are growing up with calculators. There's not a high school in the country that doesn't offer computer programming, at least as an optional course. But that population won't be adults for another 10 or 15 years.

During the interim, the most important thing is to have the right product, to have enough insight to understand what the home market will need in price and benefits in order to begin to respond. It will be an evolutionary educational process, and it will not come on like gangbusters tomorrow. Mattel, Atari and Texas Instruments, the companies that will manufacture the next generations of home computers, will sell hundreds of thousands but not millions.

BAER: It will be a slow developmental growth throughout the decade. Certainly, if you go into one of the computer stores today and look at who is playing with the terminals, you'll find that it's in large part 12-, 13- and 14-year-old kids who are developing their own programs. Within 10 years they'll be buying their own machines, and this generation, that not only uses calculators but also gets hooked on electronic games, is going to carry that through when they're purchasing products of their own.

GINGRAS: To get back to your interim generation, I think a lot of adults will begin to lose that intimidation unwittingly once they begin to use tools and appliances that make various jobs easier. They won't ever realize that they're using computers because these products won't even be called computers necessarily. I think anyone who buys a car five years from now, for instance, will be operating an automobile that is fairly well computer-assisted.

ROCHLIS: What you mentioned about computers is interesting. We don't even call our product a computer at this point in time. Right now our promotion and merchandising programs are geared to elicit a response from what I call a prime-tryer or a novelty or nut group. Three years from now we'll be talking very differently to the consumer. We may call it a computer then.

EMMY: It would appear that during the next decade the consumer/viewer will be offered many alternatives to network commercial broadcast. But where will the programs—the software—for these new distribution systems come from?

STROCK: I think the challenge, at least from a cable standpoint, is how to form an alliance of filmmakers and television people to create movies and programming for cable.

ROCHLIS: You know, with fiber optics coming into the industry, instead of 32 channels we're going to have 100. And what's interesting is that those 32 channels—with the exception of the regular broadcast replicated on one channel and the movie channel—are being wasted. The demand is going to be for software, for programming.

BAER: There is a proliferation of software for networking, and it's certainly going to continue. Satellites have created an abundance of technical network possibilities rather than the shortage we've had before, and we're already seeing some syndication of children's programming as well as special programming such as the televising of the House of Representatives. There's going to be a black network, there's Ted Turner's cable-TV news network, plus at least three religious-program networks, not to mention the sports and pay TV. So you are really seeing the proliferation of program possibilities.

STROCK: But the thing that is so crazy is that one of the "opportunities" you have—which isn't all that exciting—is that you can see "I Love Lucy" coming from Atlanta. So they're doing what the stations have done before—they're all relying on reruns and sports. It's cheap, easy programming.

GINGRAS: We're already hearing some people's criticism of this tremendous distribution system. I guess the networks kind of like to say every now and then: "That's fine, but you've got to have the programs." And I suspect in the short term that there will be a problem with availability of programming and even more so with the availability of good programming. But I suspect that in the end the creative community will catch up.

The best comparison I've thought of relates to urban planning with regard to highways. It's what all urban planners refer to as "the highway effect." They build a highway with the notion that it will reduce traffic, but every time a highway is built they find that more people are driving more often. Motorists find more reasons to go more places and to buy second cars. And I suspect the same thing is true with television.

We will start to attract more people in the creative community, including some people who I think have been repelled in the last several years because they felt that, due to commercial broadcast television's structure, if offered very little creative opportunity. We know what the commercial networks want, and we know what they don't want. And you either write something for those formulas, for that narrow focus, or you don't do anything. A lot of very talented people simply walk away. It's either public television or nowhere, and when we don't have the money they get frustrated and walk away from us, too.

STROCK: But the gap I find kind of frightening is that I don't think the schools are letting college students know where this opportunity is.

BAER: There is a real creative community out there looking for opportunities . . .

STROCK: But students have got to know it's there.

BAER: Yes. They've got to know it's there, and we can only hope that additional productions will be possible so we don't end up with 30 satellite channels all broadcasting reruns.

GINGRAS: Hopefully, a diversity of program services will offer flexibility to the creative process. If someone is not interested in producing sitcoms for ABC, then maybe that person can find a way to produce more, say, sophisticated dramas on a program designed for the more sophisticated viewer—a cultural service, as some people might refer to it.

BAER: I also hope that in the Eighties we will find that viewers are more discriminating. With the diversification and proliferation of programs and technologies that will be available, you do expect that at least some percentage of viewers will not turn on the television set and watch what's happening for three or four hours at a time but will make positive selections, whether these selections are from cable television, pay TV, video cassettes or broadcast network television. I think it's too early to predict, but if this occurs it will be a substantial change.

ROCHLIS: It almost has to. It's like going into a restaurant where the menu is too large. You really have to work at it.

BAER: You don't think that the easiest thing to do will be to just take that first item and stick with it?

ROCHLIS: No. You really have got to consider that it may become discriminatory.

GINGRAS: To be perfectly frank, I'm waiting for the cable systems to do a better job of letting me know what's on and when. They seem to find it very difficult at this stage—for certain logistical reasons—to put out a guide that tells you everything that's available on their full menu of programs. I'm left pushing the buttons on my decoder, and invariably I've missed part of something because I've tuned in midway.

STROCK: Well, we're experiencing growing pains in that area. All of a sudden, cable systems are obliged to send a lot of programs, but there are problems getting them out. I can't get some of the programs fast enough to even get a computer readout on the screen. But, again, it's just the growth of the system.

EMMY: What do the cable systems plan to do to avoid falling into the same programming trap that the networks have of just trying to fill the time?

STROCK: We're being offered an awful lot of new programming—sports, Galavision, Nickelodeon. As a system we are not out creating new things, but we're being offered a lot. Some of the larger systems, such as HBO and others, are creating films for pay TV, films that will probably be released theatrically. We're basically trying to offer a mixture of the best that's available, so we're not jumping at every single thing that comes along. Nor are we buying all the programs available on satellites. I'm sure that a small cable system in mid-America that has 5,000 or 10,000 subscribers is just going wild with their earth station and all those great programs. But it's a different ball game in Los Angeles where we have 13 television stations to choose from.

GINGRAS: Has Theta Cable felt the effect of over-the-air subscription television in Los Angeles?

STROCK: Yes, but in some very positive ways. Interestingly enough, when we introduced the "Z" Channel the common sales pitch was that this is what pay television is, these are the movies and the cable channels. Now, because of the tremendous amount of advertising that ON TV and SelecTV have done—I think ON TV is spending about $2 million a year, and SelecTV about $1 million—people call up and say, "Hey, what's the difference between 'Z,' ON and Select." That's been a beneficial effect. People in Los Angeles accept over-the-air pay TV—the awareness is there—but they don't really understand the difference. But we've not felt a sales effect within our prime cable area because, again, our franchise is set up primarily for people who can't get regular television reception. And if they can't get regular television reception over the air, they can't pick up ON or Select—they have to take the cable.

EMMY: How does Theta plan to reach those viewers who don't need cable for reception and therefore don't have access to the "Z" Channel? How do you plan to compete with ON TV and SelecTV?

STROCK: We've signed agreements with American TransVideo and Media Point, and we now offer the "Z" Channel over the air by microwave to Los Angeles and Orange counties. In those two non-cable franchise areas, we're head to head with ON and Select.

GINGRAS: But microwave, like ON TV, is limited in that it doesn't offer the multi-channel capacity that cable does. One of the key factors right now with regard to program development is simply that the penetration isn't high enough to generate enough revenue to produce quality programming. But, eventually, of course, as that penetration increases, as cable increases to 30 million households rather than the current 14½ million—and that's not an unreasonable estimate in 10 years or so—then you can target in on smaller audience groups. For that matter you could provide a service for the sophisticated viewer right now. All you need to generate enough revenue to produce a quality service is for 10 percent of those 40 million households to subscribe at a rate of $10 a month.

STROCK: The areas in which I think we will experience the most growth nationally are advertising and marketing. In this industry these areas are way behind, particularly in sophistication. There's so much coming down the line, but I haven't got enough of a budget to advertise it. I think it's going to mean spending a lot more dollars nationally to help the cable systems get more sophisticated as far as marketing and advertising are concerned.

ROCHLIS: Another important point: The rate of media inflation has been absolutely astronomical over the last few years. In fact, with the elections and the Olympics this year, we're going to establish a new norm, another 18 to 20 percent above last year. Plus, we have certain areas of broadcast, such as children's programming, where we're going to be squeezed, and the number of commercial minutes available is inevitably going to come down. That's sold-out time in 24 hours, and whatever we had last year is what we'll get. Cable may be a forced alternative we'll get into, and it will take advertising revenue away from the networks.

STROCK: The big thing is that you just don't know who's watching.

GINGRAS: Well, eventually you will. I mean, it's simply a matter of time before Nielsen develops that market.

ROCHLIS: Someone will when it makes economic sense to do it.

GINGRAS: But that's still a while off. I suspect there's been a lot of talk about advertising on cable. Bill Donnelly [vice president, Young & Rubicam], of course, made his great pronouncement a year or so ago that when the market reaches 30-percent penetration then advertising will be viable. I think that's actually a very optimistic statement because when you compare that to commercial television—which reached 30 percent in the Fifties—the audience was only divided among essentially two or, at the most, three offerings. Now, when you reach 30-percent penetration your audience will be divided up 16, 20 ways, so you're still talking about a miniscule audience. At this stage, and probably for the next three years or so, it's not worth an advertiser's effort to make the buy because the rate of penetration is so low. Not to mention the fact that in larger metropolitan areas there are so many cable systems that are uncoordinated and unnetworked that they can't sell the market. You can't buy the market of Los Angeles through cable; you can buy Theta in the hills.

STROCK: We wrestled with that the other day. We were talking about taking out an ad in the *Times* and using an 800 number, but we figured that with six cable and three over-the-air systems there'd be no way an operator could explain to a consumer who just wanted the service how he could get it. There's just no common denominator.

EMMY: It's been said that the independent and local stations must establish markets within the next few years or they will lose their audiences. What do KCET and the other PBS stations plan to do to stay competitive?

GINGRAS: Our business is changing just like everyone else's. Essentially my job is planning. Until a few years ago there weren't many planners at television stations or even in large companies, but I think if you compare commercial television to other businesses in this country you'll find few businesses that have been as consistent in both structure and performance over the past 25-year period.

In terms of public television the local stations are clearly going to have to find different roles because we suspect, at least to a degree, that many who are now prime supporters of public television will find satisfaction through some of these other delivery modes—particularly if in the next 10 years cable systems offer more than simply movies and sports. If the cable, subscription and satellite services do indeed begin to offer high-quality program services designed for the upscale viewer, that's clearly going to hurt us in terms of revenue. But we know there's a problem.

There's also a political factor, one that's as much perception as it is reality. With all the great expectations people have of cable—and a lot of people believe it's true before it's happened—the perception among some legislators may be that public broadcasting is less important because of these new delivery mechanisms and therefore less in need of federal support. Don't get me wrong, I hope these new delivery mechanisms offer something better. Public broadcasting's role is an alternative, so it should change as the commercial sector changes.

It may mean, in a sense, going back to some of the original things we were created for: instructional education, public affairs—such as the coverage of local hearings—and in-depth analysis of the news. I think we're probably moving into a Hearstian age of video journalism due to the need to fill the dial. And I suspect there's a need for us there.

Working in the area we call public telecommunications, I'd like to work with Theta Cable to provide additional channels for these local hearings or to offer adult education during prime time when more people can take advantage of it. Without being self-serving, I think KCET has been one of the leaders in redefining the role of alternative broadcasters. We strongly believe that there is still a public-sector need.

We are a slightly different organization than most because we're not simply a local public-television station but a national production company as well. So in that regard this new television marketplace presents opportunities to us. For instance, we can take the programs we now produce, like "Cosmos," and not only disseminate them through public broadcasting but through other delivery mechanisms as well.

Our main concern with this national programming effort is to produce quality product, get it out to as many people as possible and then, hopefully, use that revenue to support the local operations.

BAER: The key is certainly in services and not in owning a particular television channel. I think that the more the public-television stations look at their role as one of producer, coordinator and distributor of interesting alternative programming via a host of technical means—broadcasting, cable, video cassette—the more they will be really providing very useful services. And you see the major stations, like KCET, beginning to move in that direction.

STROCK: I think it's interesting that KCET seems to have the support of community leaders whereas the regular stations, by their very nature, do not necessarily have this backing. Maybe it's because everyone you've ever heard of shows up for your fund-raising drives.

GINGRAS: I really have to give credit for that to my boss, Dr. Loper, who has done an excellent job of building strong community support and of keeping the station well-financed during the 14 years it's been in existence. He's also had the foresight to make the people on staff aware of how the business is changing and to start moving us in some new directions. Our desire to develop new services is the major reason we get involved with things like broadcast teletext. We believe it has a far larger role in the public sector than it does in the commercial sector, at least in the short term. I suspect the commercial broadcasters will shy away from it for a while because, first, they can't quite find the legitimate uses that will return them a dollar on their investment, and because, second, quite basically what they'd be offering is an alternative to watching their own channel, and they're not terribly excited about doing that sort of thing. We, of course, see it as a way to strengthen our service as well as to add a new dimension such as providing a better service to the hearing-impaired with captioning or offering additional language translations, particularly in a market like Los Angeles.

STROCK: One of the things that we should get back to, though, is the fact that if the networks provide the programming they're not going to lose the audience.

GINGRAS: Well, I expect that the networks are going to have to find new ways of developing programs, perhaps even get away from all this sophisticated research that's so demographically oriented it ends up totally washing out creative input.

EMMY: Ralph Baruch, the president of Viacom, has speculated that the networks will take on the capacity that PBS now has to transmit several programs at once.

GINGRAS: I was in Washington when public broadcasting was developing its satellite system, and part of my job was to go out and hold seminars to explain the system to station personnel. One of the first questions asked was: "If this is such a great idea, why haven't the commercial networks used it first?" And the response, as you know, is really quite simple: The networks are strong and powerful because essentially they have one link to the affiliates and want to keep that network strong and viable. So it's: "What we give you is what you use when we want you to use it." They're not interested in letting the stations get away from that. I suspect they will only offer other choices to the affiliates when the broadcast stations are tied in to satellite networks. When the stations have their own dishes and are being offered choices from others then the commercial networks will also begin to offer choices. That's when the role of the networks will change. They will offer more to try to keep their affiliates. But, then again, maybe the whole idea of an affiliate relationship will disappear.

BAER: Well, it certainly will change. I think first you'll see the independents coming in with satellites, and then you'll see a lot more do-it-yourself networking. I think that eventually the existing networks will have to go along, but they won't be the leaders.

EMMY: How do you view the satellite systems from both a programming and a consumer-interest point of view?

BAER: Now that the FCC has dropped its licensing restriction, the price of earth terminals for television stations will go down and probably be under $10,000 before too long. When you look at what it will take to go directly into the home . . . although you might not have to pay the $36,000 that Neiman-Marcus charges . . .

ROCHLIS: There's at least a 50-percent markup there . . .

BAER: . . . you'll still be paying several thousand dollars. Scientific Atlanta and other manufacturers hope they can get that price down by mass-marketing the system. The figures that we've seen suggest that the price could perhaps be as low as $200, but one guesses that it will be somewhat above that. And we have to ask ourselves, if a terminal on the roof is going to cost, say, $250 or $300 and receive six or maybe eight channels, will it attract subscribers in the big cities? It will be attractive to people in rural areas, in very low-population areas—certainly in Alaska—but, given the fact that a cable system can be installed for about that same cost, what is going to be the economic attraction of having a satellite terminal on the roof?

GINGRAS: And it's not a simple installation. For one thing, who's going to install it? There's been talk about hooking up with some major company that's already in existence, but it's a tricky thing to install. I mean, that thing's got to be fairly accurately pointed at that little satellite way up there 22,000 miles away, and it's got to be securely based so that some night when it's windy the dish doesn't take an eighth of an inch, or, for that matter, a two-foot turn to the left, which would put it totally out of sync with the network.

BAER: You also have to look at the competition in the major markets with broadcast and cable. While there's a clear market in the rural countries, it's not at all clear that there's a market here. You certainly can see the prospects for direct-broadcast satellites in countries with low densities—Indonesia, Brazil, the Soviet Union, China, Australia, Canada. Clearly there's a market in countries that have less of a communications intrastructure than we do.

EMMY: What is Comsat's proposal, and how likely is it to actually come about?

GINGRAS: Well, essentially their proposal will be, I think, a maximum six-channel service, two national services and some regional services. At least one of the two national services will be Home Box Office—type fare . . .

EMMY: But not Home Box Office . . .

GINGRAS: Not Home Box Office. In fact, I would suspect that Home Box Office will be one of their prime opponents. What Comsat may do, because its market is not the same as the cable market, is take that HBO-type service and sell it to cable operators, in competition with HBO.

STROCK: Of course, the key to all this is what the movie companies will decide to do with their product.

GINGRAS: They obviously aren't too happy with HBO so I suppose they may go in and support Comsat if only to bring in more major suppliers to bid for their product.

EMMY: Are there any political hurdles still to be cleared, or is Comsat free to go ahead and offer that service?

GINGRAS: Well, I don't know. There are great questions there. I mean, how strong is the broadcast lobby today? I think we've kind of seen that it's not as strong as it used to be, but they're probably going to put together a pretty big effort. Also, how strong is the point of view that Comsat, if it's perceived to be a quasi-federal corporation—though essentially it is not—how strong will the feelings be that Comsat should pay a public dividend of some kind? Then again, I suppose it might end up in the courts. If the FCC says no, it's going to be interesting to see what rationale they will use and whether or not it will hold up legally.

BAER: The whole trend, I think, is toward less regulation and more competition, and I think it's a very healthy trend. I think the notion of allowing more competition among broadcasting, cable, video cassettes, videodiscs and any other form is certainly going to benefit the consumer.

EMMY: Yes, but at the same time the governmental agencies seem to be coming down harder on the networks, especially in the area of children's programming. Are these two trends related?

BAER: No. There's clearly been an ambivalence not just among the regulators but, I think, even more so in Congress, as to what and how to regulate and how strongly. In some sense, part of the regulation we've seen on children's programming has to do with the notion that you really do have to see that certain standards are upheld when you're dealing with audiences as sensitive as children. The other point of view, though, and the one I think you are now seeing in these economic decisions, is that the way to regulate is essentially through government intervention. If you set the right kind of ground rules then you can rely on the marketplace to by and large generate efficient solutions. That works from an economics standpoint although it doesn't necessarily work when you're concerned about the social effects of children's programs.

GINGRAS: One of the aspects that's changed, of course, is that six or eight years ago it was a question of the big, powerful networks against cable operators who were stealing their signals. Now you have huge financial corporations involved in every end of this business. The cable business is no longer the business of the small operator.

EMMY: How will all of these systems co-exist in the home? Will these products be component-based?

BAER: In time you will see the linkage of the television screen with the telephone as a way to provide both a communications link and a display.

ROCHLIS: And the nice thing about the telephone is that 70 million—plus homes have one, whereas only 14½ million have cable right now. This linkage does require the purchase or the leasing of an additional component called a phone modem which by next year should be down to around $150.

BAER: We're just now beginning to see television sets with input jacks that allow you to plug in home computers or calculators or TV games or whatever. You know, there's been talk through the years of looking ahead to the Eighties and finding people with great big home communications centers with high resolution, 3-D television screens, video recorders, computers and so forth. Well, although that's possible, I doubt it's going to happen. What I think you're going to see are video components being assembled, much as audio components are, so that they can be interconnected to create a modular system.

ROCHLIS: One thing that seems to be a common element in all this is the television screen—the display medium for it all. But that computer, no matter how powerful it may be, is limited to animation. We will never be able to create a film-quality image with computer animation alone. There's a hell of a lot less information, depth, richness, texture and realism in animation. Also, the jacks connect with the new television sets through the antenna system—you're not going directly into the gun—so they have a limited amount of resolution as compared to if you could just plug right into it.

GINGRAS: With so many new products coming along so fast, how much of a problem do you think will be caused by consumers waiting to see what's going to come along next that's better than what they can buy today?

ROCHLIS: Well, it's compounded by the fact that the electronic technology we're talking about will move faster in the next decade than technology as a whole has moved in the entire century. Now, that may be something that the Rand Corporation will argue with, but we happen to think that's probably a fairly accurate statement.

BAER: We'd agree that the hardware will move that way; it's not at all clear that the software will.

ROCHLIS: You're right. The hardware is not the key to this, and I've got to keep saying that over and over. Another key factor is that the technology introduction and obsolescence curves are in a different cycle than the marketplace curves. Technology would have us do a lot of things today that we're not doing and obsolete a lot of things that we are doing. And it's not just the technology but the application of the technology as well as the price/value relationship that are going to free up and turn on the mass market.

GINGRAS: And there are major political impacts. No one quite knows what might happen in that regard. I mean, who knows what the mood of the country will be like in five years when people start to feel more and more threatened because certain jobs are being eliminated as a result of the proliferation of these technologies.

BAER: Do you really think they will eliminate jobs? In the past, as many jobs have been created as eliminated. The jobs were redistributed, and you'd expect the same thing to happen today. I think people are concerned about a variety of other issues relating to the communications and information explosion, though—like privacy, for example. If cable systems become more interactive, how will you be able to keep the cable operator from knowing everything you're watching and buying and then, somehow, from putting that information together in a way that could adversely affect you. I think these are the kinds of issues that will come up. Certainly the home computer and its data-gathering ability will bring issues of privacy to the fore again, so I'm not sure that employment will be the key concern.

GRINGAS: When were the privacy laws written in this country? Was it in the Thirties? They really haven't been changed much since those very early days.

BAER: There is a new law that relates to data files the credit bureaus and the government keep on individuals. Those now come under some new legislative restrictions so that you can look at your credit files, see what's recorded about you and if there's wrong information do something to change it. Those kinds of problems and ways of dealing with them, I think, will simply be extended to encompass the new kinds of industries we're talking about here. As cable develops its interactive potential, as you get more interactive games and home-computer terminals, you're going to see the need to extend these same kinds of legal restraints into those areas as well.

There's also the question of how much people really want privacy and security and how much they're willing to pay for it. We know there are technical ways to make systems more resistant to wire-tapping or to somebody misusing the data in them, but they all cost money.

GINGRAS: You may be right, and I would believe you're right—let me put it that way—but I would suggest that the privacy issue may simply inhibit the development of some of these technologies. But even if this job is eliminated and that job created, it doesn't mean that the guy who lost this job is going to get that one.

BAER: Of course not. And when you have a political system in which those who lose jobs can keep things from happening then indeed you're going to have regulatory restrictions.

GINGRAS: We talk about a crisis of leadership in this country . . . I don't think there's a crisis of leadership. It's not a question of whether or not our leaders are any more mediocre than before but of our national decision-making process being such that special-interest groups—be they lobbies, unions or major corporations—have just as much power as the President of the United States.

BAER: Well, another tension exists between the communications industry, which has traditionally been regulated, and the information industry, which has not. Certainly we're not looking for a federal information administration to pass on the new games developed by Mattel and other manufacturers. But as soon as you hook these games into the telecommunications network through some kind of terminal, you're dealing with a regulated system. And when you have regulation the pace of change is a good deal slower than the pace of the technical explosion in computers has been.

GINGRAS: That also brings up the whole question of setting technical standards as the new technology is introduced, particularly in a medium like broadcast television that is and will continue to be regulated in many ways. What we hope is that the technical standards set for something like Teletext will be broad enough and flexible enough so that we can continue to explore and develop the technologies in these areas.

There are problems in Britain because the standards were set too low, and they eventually limited what could be done with the technology. The standards were set that way because the manufacturers wanted to get something into the marketplace quickly. And some of the same pressures will exist in this country. What we want is a wide standard so that we can develop and put into the marketplace the kind of component-based systems we were talking about earlier.

ROCHLIS: And the standard is a kind of key to any emerging industry. If the industry doesn't standardize—and it's never been willing to—there will be much less of a chance for success. Here we do have a definition of interdependency of hardware and software, of communications, broadcast and cable people involved with each other. And the government can play a positive role in establishing that standard.

BAER: A government and industry association. I don't think you want to put the whole thing on the government.

ROCHLIS: Right, no, no, certainly not. I'm just saying that's *a* role.

GINGRAS: It's an interesting process to follow. No one quite knows how it's going to turn out. I feel there will still be a substantial need for some type of public-sector effort in the business of telecommunications. The one fact that is painfully clear is that the impact television made in its 30 years of existence is minimal compared to what that impact will be 10, 15 years from now. Television will continue to play a larger and larger role in our lives, and that brings with it some negatives as well as positives. I mean, the average household already watches six hours and 45 minutes of television a day. And we know that as viewers are offered more programs these figures will go up somewhat. For instance, a survey done by Nielsen of 5,000 homes subscribing to a pay-TV service showed a higher sets-in-use figure than has ever been recorded in broadcast television. Eighty-five percent of the sets were in use in prime time, whereas they've never recorded a sets-in-use figure higher than 80 percent with only commercial networks.

STROCK: And I don't know if this was pointed out in their survey, but the people who were watching pay at that time were not subject to spot-commercial hypes for particular shows, and yet the programs still tested well.

GINGRAS: That shows that there is still enough interest for people to tune in and that there is still an appetite for video entertainment which has not yet been fully satiated. Now, why is that? What's the cause of heavy television viewing in our society? I suppose today one could say it's partially economic. Buying the "Z" Channel is very cheap entertainment over a month's use. You take the kids to the movie house one night, and if you've got four people going to the movies you've spent $16, $20 dollars with gas.

BAER: Yes, it's cheap, and it's comfortable, but I think that as you look toward more use of information or game-playing in the home you may see some erosion. What I really think you'll see is more of a differentiation of audiences; some will continue to watch as much if not more television as before, but others will probably be converted to these new activities.

GINGRAS: I think that's very true, but the question is, how different will viewing habits be? We're still talking about an increasing use of in-home electronic services, and the impact of that is yet to be seen. Are we moving toward becoming a nation of moles, spending tremendous amounts of time in our homes? For a lot of people, of course, that would be very comfortable; they don't want to go out into this cruel world, and the more time they stay in the less they'll want to go out. There are dangerous implications to all this. I just hope that we in the business keep one eye out for the downside of a lot of what we're doing. It's very easy to get tied up in this, to offer new services, more programs, more entertainment. I mean, everybody is sitting there happy, glassy eyed, watching the tube, and we think that's wonderful. And the profits are going up . . . I just love to see television executives get up there and say, "Gosh darn, we're not going to get hurt because people are going to watch more television than ever before. Isn't that great?" I find it hard to immediately jump on that bandwagon.

STROCK: That's what happened to the cable industry in the Sixties. They sold so much blue sky, then it never happened. The great classic program on cable—the special of the week—was a camera pointed at a fish bowl and FM music playing behind the shot. I think there's a danger in that now everyone is saying, "Hey, cable's the real answer." There may be a lot of people getting into the cable business because they think they can make a lot of money, and they promise city councils all those great things that they've read about, but they will never happen.

EMMY: Has Rand done any research to determine how this new technology will affect society?

BAER: Well, I won't even call it research although we have done some speculating as have many other groups. I think it's useful to focus on the kinds of trends that are coming and to suggest what might happen, but, as far as being able to predict the future, that's certainly well beyond what I'd be willing to admit to today. I think Jeff certainly mentioned some of the clearer trends in terms of hardware development rapidly outpacing software.

ROCHLIS: That means there is going to be a lot of false starts, and a lot of the tangents that we're talking about will get started and then fail. Then it will be several years before the industry, whoever the participants are, will get back together. We're talking about a redistribution of industry participants: People who were able to participate in their industry on a hardware-only basis will find themselves dependent on a software partner, or vice versa. And we're going to spawn whole new industries or groups of manufacturers as a result. It's all very, very complicated. I mean, what we've succeeded in doing here is putting a bowl of spaghetti on the table.

But your original question was how this is all going to impact the broadcasting industry. None of us really knows. But the technology will not stand still, and, if there is a business or commercial opportunity perceived to be there, there are people who are going to try to attack it. Hopefully that makes better competitors of us all, and hopefully the end beneficiary of all that good competition will be the consumer.

BAER: The problem is how to document any causal relationship between one event and another. We really don't know why people watch television, why certain people seem to watch a lot more television than others do or what happens to people after they watch television. Most of the research has been addressed to the connection between television watching and violence—particularly among children—and there are some strongly held views on that. But, overall, I think, we still have a relatively poor idea of how television watching has affected us.

EMMY: It seems as though these new products will require educating the public in how to watch television.

GINGRAS: Well, it's not enough to simply buy the statement that interactive television is going to be a tremendous success 10 years from now. If it's true that the potential for interactive television does exist, then the question is, how will it be used?

STROCK: We've had to educate the viewer in how to watch the "Z" Channel. We explain to people that pay television is a theater in the home, that there is a new movie every week which they can view at the time convenient for them. But we still have people who think we're commercial television, that every time they turn on the channel there'll be a new movie.

BAER: I think it's not going to be so much educating the adults about a new style of viewing as probably taking a whole new generation of people who have grown up familiar with calculators, electronic games and computer terminals and finding that they will just carry those habits on into adult life. I think, in terms of interactive television, that if, again, you find more kids participating in it that they'll just take the habit with them.

GINGRAS: Again, it depends on what kind of interaction you're talking about. One of the thoughts I've had—and it's also turned into one of my fears—is about the use of interactive television for things like voting and polling in a move toward what I suspect could eventually become an electronic participatory democracy.

STROCK: But right now we're voting for candidates who are packaged on commercials like they were soap.

BAER: Well, you're jumping way ahead. I don't think there have been serious discussions about voting via communications. What has been discussed is having more straw votes, more opinion polling, that sort of thing.

GINGRAS: I just raise the point because it's one of those potentially hairy areas. Once this type of product gets into enough homes—and I suspect that by the Nineties it will be in nearly everyone's home—I think that people will demand more and more of a say in what their government does. It directs that. One can see that it will eventually make the leap to a more participatory form of democracy. Now, politically, what impact that will have is anyone's guess. One person's populist ideal is another's tyranny by the majority.

BAER: Well, the question is, what do you want to do about it?

GINGRAS: What can you do about it?

EMMY: The people promoting these technological changes tend to focus on the benefits, but there are also people who can turn it to other ends.

GINGRAS: Yes, and I suppose that continuing to discuss the downside of all this is in itself a protection against some of these things occurring. But that's the kind of risk one takes, I suppose, with the development of any kind of technology. It's that element of risk that we see so well with nuclear energy. You can never quite tell exactly what the impact of something like that will be. One doesn't know exactly what the odds are of a major nuclear accident. We make our guesses, and eventually society decides whether or not to take the risk. I suppose the same is true of communications technology, also.

STROCK: But remember the other side: If someone isn't happy he can always turn the set off.

GINGRAS: I don't buy that. It's a terribly democratic thing— all you have to do is turn the set off. I mean, one could make the same comment about Librium in suburbia. Not everyone has to go get a prescription for it, but there are an awful lot of people out there who get it all the time and develop an addiction to it. I don't mean to say that television's an addiction, although some would suggest it is, but for a lot of people it's an automatic thing. When they come home they turn the set on. It's not a question of turning it on or off but of turning it from one channel to another.

GINGRAS: Well, there are tremendous positive aspects to all of this. And with regard to pay television, I think that for once the viewer will be treated as a consumer with a yes or no vote as to whether or not he wants these services. If you have enough people saying no you'll either change your service or go out of business. And it hasn't been that way with commercial television. They're just interested in getting those viewers and selling them to the advertisers. The viewer is not the consumer, he's the product.

EMMY: Now that we've taken a look at this decade, what are your predictions for television in the year 2000?

BAER: You'll probably see video screens in the home that will be used for information purposes as well as for entertainment. But, as we mentioned before, that's not going to supplant the home television set for entertainment. We're probably more likely to see additional video terminals, at least a second one, that will be used for these services and not necessarily to displace the primary entertainment medium.

GINGRAS: As we learn more and more every day, we know that just because a new technology is more efficient than an old technology doesn't mean that in terms of marketability or personal habit it's immediately going to take over that role.

STROCK: I think the selection of what people watch will be up to the person in the home rather than the television station that sends it.

GINGRAS: I think that's one possibility, whether it's 2000 or beyond. Again, a key to the things we've talked about is the development of new technologies and memory systems. Eventually the memories will become more sophisticated and cheaper, and better ways will be found to compress the data for that television image. For instance, instead of telling each dot on that screen what it has to be for each frame, you will simply tell it what it has to be when it changes. So much of it remains constant that you can compress the amount of information.

ROCHLIS: We've talked about the near-term generations and that this adult generation isn't ready to accept the technology we'd have it accept. To fully realize products like home computers and so forth we're going to have to wait until the kids who are now in high school become the adult purchasers.

GINGRAS: All technology is a tool, so you have to not only develop uses for it but uses that are practical and acceptable.

ROCHLIS: We've been talking about all these alternatives, all this marvelous hardware and all these transmission means, but the consumer doesn't care. It's all focused in terms of the television set, and the consumer really doesn't give a damn about where it comes from or how it gets there. Quite frankly, all he's interested in is what he gets for how much he has to pay.

The Language
of Television

Martin Perlmutter

"And the whole earth was of one language, and of one
speech."
> —The world before Babel, *Genesis.*

Many times, in many cultures, humans have dreamt of a universal language—a tongue of the heart and the mind, capable of reaching
across every boundary of breeding and history. Such a new language,
addressed to the eye with its appetite for the infinite, may now be
possible through television. This language will find its lexicon and its
grammar in the domain of dynamic visual expression.

Television teaches at the speed of light. Its messages need no
remembering, for they mobilize a part of the self as they are viewed
and are always available for evocation by association. Television
images are also manipulable. They can be interactively controlled by
the viewer. It is possible, for example, for a thinker to sculpt a visual

representation of his or her thoughts on a video display through the marriage of video and microelectronic computers.

The capabilities of image control hardware now approximate the limits of visual imagination. What will be done with this potential for externalizing the vision of the inner eye? Far beyond stone or scroll, interactive video beckons us to a new age of ideographic communication. Television offers thinkers the first dynamic visual medium for elaborating, and sharing, their concepts and their thinking processes.

From the West Coast of the United States to the Polytechnic Institute in Athens, efforts are underway to illustrate abstract ideas with visual displays. At the Paris Institute for Higher Scientific Studies, for instance, René Thom has conceived a significant if controversial new wrinkle in mathematics, *catastrophe theory*, which has been hailed by some as the most important development in mathematics since calculus. Catastrophe theory uses the visual and geometrical science of topology to describe phenomena that change abruptly from one form of behavior to another. The theory has applications in social and biological sciences as well as in physical science.

Catastrophe theory represents discontinuous events with a small number of topological forms. The folds, pleats, cusps, and slopes in these forms, or "catastrophe surfaces," provide insights into phenomena as diverse as a stock market crash, a prison riot, a cell's division, and a rainbow's genesis. Thom has identified seven elementary catastrophes in the world of three dimensions and time: (1) The *cusp catastrophe* can be used to study stock market behavior or the transition from calm to anxiety in man and animals. (2) The *fold catastrophe* helps explain the refraction of sunlight by raindrops to form a rainbow. (3) The *swallowtail catastrophe* has relevance to cell division in embryos. (4) The *butterfly catastrophe* can be used to predict certain kinds of behavior in human nervous disorders. (5) The *hyperbolic umbilic* can help analyze the collapse of bridges. (6) The *elliptic umbilic* provides a model for fluid flows. (7) The *parabolic umbilic* can serve as a model for solving certain problems in the field of linguistics.

The appeal of catastrophe theory lies partly in its applicability to the "soft" sciences of sociology, psychology, and biology. "Catastrophe theory is a major step toward making the inexact sciences exact," comments British mathematician E. Christopher Zeeman, one of its leading exponents. Thom's visual science has brought discontinuity and transformation into the ken of mathematics, as calculus never could. Released from the linearity of numbers, supplied with an image undergoing transformations, the mind can grasp a complex problem whole and then hunt creatively for solutions. Catastrophe theory demonstrates the power of geometrical and topological forms to convey abstract conceptual information.

In similar research efforts at MIT, educational technologists in political science have used moving, computergraphic images to explain concepts in game theory that are difficult to teach verbally. Calling their work *Concept Illustration by Image Manipulation,* the MIT experimenters have used a visual rather than a verbal mode to present the *Prisoner's Dilemma,* one of the more complex and paradoxical concepts of game theory. The numerical payoffs that describe the potential outcomes of the game have been symbolized by rectangular solids rising above and falling below a plane in a "landscape." Decision-makers can graphically assess the consequences of their choices and speedily grasp the lessons of the game.

Further research will attempt to display still more complex multivariate problems as "decision landscapes" in which a decision-maker may, by convention, "ski" downward toward "valleys" of less costly solutions, avoiding "peaks" of cost. We can imagine the evolution of such interactive graphic systems to assist government and business decision-makers in the visualization of problems and their solutions.

In another department at MIT, the ultimate in computer-graphics systems, the *architecture machine,* stands ready with all the capabilities required to display and interactively "massage" the most complex of mental landscapes. The architecture machine is a video painting system, similar to the New York Institute of Technology's Computergraphics Lab and the Ampex Video Arts system that is now penetrating broadcast television. An operator wields an electronic "brush" (called a *light pen*), thereby activating an extensive menu of operations (including color and shape control) which are wired into the control console and the system's programming.

Catastrophe theory and concept illustration signal the emergence of new forms of scientific notation. Visual systems will be used in a growing number of disciplines to describe and solve problems. These interactive visual problem-analyzing systems will be employed worldwide and will be designed to be virtually immune to differences in culture and spoken language. The display medium of these decison-and-control systems will be video. The content of the displays will be a language appropriate to the medium.

The "words" of video language will be patterns—images composed of tiny pixels (picture elements). Video ideographs will, like all symbols, be based upon the experience of the body and elemental natural forms. Some will be simply representational, perhaps derived from earlier media experience (e.g., imagery of nuclear explosions or the JFK funeral). Others will reflect consistencies observable in nature, in human interaction, or in the mind—archetypes roughly paralleling the psychic constructs envisioned by Carl Jung. There will also be pattern pictographs that embody kinesthetic experience (motion, mass, balance, transformation) or that reflect the shapes of nature (landscapes, seed-forms, wave-shapes). Some video-graphs will be abstract, perhaps mandalic. Others will be reminiscent of arcane Hermetic or Masonic symbols and will require learning to convey meaning. Many will be meaningful on first encounter and across cultures.

Mathematics may provide us with a Rosetta Stone for translating some concepts into images. Topology and projective geometry are visual mathematical sciences. Both are concerned with morphogenesis—the taking and changing of form. These formal systems, applied through innovative conceptual schema like catastrophe theory, may equip us to describe a range of natural and cognitive functions with clarity and impact.

Margaret Mead used the term "glyphs" for a proposed lexicon of cross-culturally meaningful graphic signs. I use the term *iconograms* for video symbols that embody concepts which derive their meaning from patterned display and motion on television ("icono-" since the content has a conventionalized and formalized style and archetypal content; "gram" in tribute to its electronic origins).

The grammar of video language will be embedded in rules and methods of image transformation. By reshaping one image into another, or by mixing two or more images in a particular way, we may describe the relationship between the referents: ideational, ontological, and/or temporal. I believe that iconogrammatic language is, in fact, native to television. That is, its range of meanings and uses will arise from the unique perceptual characteristics of the medium. It will require video display for this language to communicate its conceptual content.

Unhappily, and significantly, break-throughs in video language must await hard-science investigation of how television images are received and processed by the eye-brains of viewers. As McLuhan prophesized, the current medium has narcotized our senses, deadening them to conscious awareness. We don't know who discovered water, but it probably wasn't a fish. Similarly, television is pure mystification for us. While its contents progressively constitute the limits of the thinkable, knowledge of how video interacts with a viewer's eye and brain has advanced little since the earliest days of the medium.

The people who invented television were deeply concerned with how people saw. Using their knowledge of the eye-brain, they did no more than was necessary to fool the eye into seeing acceptably detailed and nonflickering images. From the beginning (1927) to Johnny Carson was but one small applications feat. From video vaudeville to brain research will entail a giant leap in human self-understanding.

How can we explain the fact that there are literally hundreds of studies of the social impact of television and not a single study of the perceptual dynamics of television? The nonexistent field of basic television research is a blind spot of historic proportions. Like the blind spot in our eyes, where the optic nerve exits to the brain and no light detection occurs, we are insensitive precisely at the locale of maximum importance to the seeing process.

Critical questions go unasked: Is there anything unique about the way video images enter our eyes and brains? Do we see television in the same way we see films? Do eye movements and neural behaviors change when the same visual information is presented in these different media? If we isolate differences, what then is the uniquely tele-visual aspect of viewing behavior? What does the eye-brain have to do to make sense of the dots and lines that comprise the television image? What does this tell us about the functioning of the brain?

It is easy to suppose that television is electric film. It is also probably wrong, and certainly unscientific, to simply assume so and make no further inquiry. There is serious, even urgent need for study of the differences in viewer eye movement and attending strategies for the same images on film and on television. The video image, for example, takes time to be scanned out. The whole picture appears to be present, just as in film, but it isn't. The television picture is constantly blurring and disappearing. McLuhan describes it as "a ceaselessly forming contour of things limned by the scanning-finger. The resulting plastic contour appears by light *through*, not light *on*, and the image so formed has the quality of sculpture and icon, rather than that of picture."

Thus, like human vision itself, video is a time-dependent process. "The TV image offers some three million dots per second to the viewer. From these he accepts only a few dozen each instant, from which to make an image," speculates McLuhan. At any instant, then, there's a blur of perhaps five square centimeters of fully illuminated picture available to view. Johnny Carson's familiar face is a pattern retrieved, compared, and "re-cognized" by his viewers. Yet we "see" Carson.

A fairer way to put it is to say that the "real" Johnny Carson is in your mind. In a sense, it is you who project his image onto your video screen. The television picture reminds you of—elicits from your infinite image memory—the image of Johnny Carson.

Television is as absorbing as it is because it surfs at the edge of our perceptual capabilities and engages us in solving a difficult visual puzzle. As patterns are detected, confirmed, and sorted by the brain, that miraculous organ has to do a great deal of short-term storage and filling-in of detail. Even the people inside network television have come to realize that viewers do not watch programming, they watch television. The technological device is almost ten times faster than the organic system that hastens to see its work. That makes the task of video viewing a challenge to the eye-brain. So we not only watch, in gladness or in terror; we are "mesmerized." As we view television, our brains are playing like dolphins in an electronic sea.

Soon, we may learn the rules of this game and video will be opened to a new level of analysis. If the operative perceptual "rules" of this medium do become known, the medium will, of course, be exposed to new levels of potential control and manipulation. On the other hand, the only protection against the mind-manipulating impact of media is a thorough understanding of how they work. The Faustian bargain has been made; we have no choice but to strive to understand this medium of television.

At the moment, unfortunately, there is not even a theory of the television-image perception process, nor is there support (governmental or private) to conduct this work. In the absence of a theory of television, empirical inquiry has been confined to the study of its effects—to investigations of behavioral responses to stimuli, with little attention as to how the stimuli interact with the visual system in the first place.

A hard-science neurophysiological inquiry into television viewing behavior will also be the first step toward video language. The process by which television pictures are recognized by the eye-brain may explain the basic methods used by the brain's visual system for all information-processing and patterns recognition.

In other words, with such research we will be seeking the language of the *whole* brain. The language of phonetics inhabits the left hemisphere. The right hemisphere is mute, but it has its order. A video-based visual language will address the right hemisphere, while embodying data meaningful to the verbally oriented left hemisphere. Video language will thereby address a level of consciousness more basic than grammar and vocabulary—it will resemble the "speech" of the mind itself.

Linguistic theorists have long posited the existence of some kind of "innate structure" in the brain, on which all languages, all grammars, are based. R. L. Gregory, world authority on perception, suggests that there may be a "grammar of vision," akin to the grammar of spoken language. To uncover the structure of this "grammar," a first step would be the study of how our eyes detect features and analyze images. Then, the research would move on to study what the inner eye is seeking as it encounters the world.

What imagery does the brain use as it hunts out features and rapidly compares them to some internal representation in order to "re-cognize" forms? How is it that higher animals are able to read even hidden features from retinal images and to predict their immediate future states? We seem "to classify objects according to an internal grammar, to read reality from (our) eyes," as Gregory puts it. There is every reason to suppose that learning behavior occurs "via modification of an already functional structural organization."

Television offers a means for experimentally investigating the inner structure of visual perception. Vision is physiologically interconnected with every sensory, affective, and cognitive system in the brain. Our effort to comprehend vision inevitably leads us to encounter the total structure and workings of the brain. Deep study of television may reveal the morphology of consciousness—the physiological and structural fundamentals of perception and cognition.

Humankind has always used its tools and its media as engines of evolution. We externalize our mysteries (the deepest of which are our senses) the better to grasp them. Tools and media are psychomotor irritants, driving us, enticing us, to grow as a species. The pebble tools found by the Leakeys at Olduvai Gorge taught a profound lesson: It was the tool that stretched the brain of its wielder.

So it is with television. Television was invented and has come to be the most common technological artifact found amongst our species because it externalizes so important a piece of our consciousness. Television is no less than our central nervous systems—our brains—turned inside out. Thus, television can lead us to know the "universal grammar" spoken of by psycholinguists, the grammar that, according to paleoneurologists, began in the visual mode and was later overlaid with the phonetic. Television will permit us to communicate at this bedrock level, conserving every nuance of sense and sensibility which activates the communicator. This new use of the medium will surely also allow us to think new thoughts, and to rapidly and interactively diffuse these thoughts to every culture.

The limits of the soul cannot be seen. God is not a mathematical design, as Blake chided. But television's synesthetic successors will clearly bring us closer to the godhead within ourselves. Wearing sensory stimulation and monitoring helmets, we will transmit and receive imagetic embodiments of our thoughts, and we will exult, "Behold, the people is one, and they have all one language . . . and now nothing will be restrained from them, which they have imagined to do."

Bibliography

Understanding Television: A Selected Reading List

Christopher H. Sterling

This annotated listing is a selected guide to the increasing amount of book-length literature on all aspects of TV programming, especially the commercial American product. All of these books should be either in print or in any good library. Those marked with an asterisk (*) are especially useful, while (P) means a paperbound version is available. The listing is somewhat arbitrarily divided into six sections: (1) television programming in general, (2) television drama, (3) TV comedy and game shows, (4) television journalism, (5) television commercials, and (6) criticism of television. Excluded are material on children's television and most government documents.

1. Television Programming in General

Baggaley, Jon, et al. *Psychology of the TV Image.* New York: Praeger, 1980. 190 pp. Highly technical analysis of impact of different kinds of TV visual and verbal images.

Barnouw, Erik. *Tube of Plenty: The Evolution of American Television.* New York: Oxford University Press, 1975. 518 pp. (P) A single-volume condensation of the television material contained in Barnouw's three-volume history, mainly from the third volume, *The Image Empire* (1970). Illustrated and brought up to date, but otherwise quite similar.

Berger, Arthur Asa. *The TV-Guided American.* New York: Walker, 1976. 194 pp. A popular culture approach to specific entertainment shows—and what each tells about its viewers.

Bower, Robert T. *Television and the Public.* New York: Holt, Rinehart & Winston, 1973. 205 pp. Results of a 1970 national audience survey on program preferences, viewing habits, and characteristics, providing comparisons with a 1960 survey (Steiner, *The People Look at Television,* 1963) and a good overview of TV's impact.

*Brooks, Tim, and Earle Marsh. *The Complete Directory to Prime Time Network TV Shows, 1946-Present.* New York: Ballantine Books, 1979. 850 pp. (P) Alphabetical listing with paragraph or two of description, cast list, and date and network details. Appendix has charts of each TV season's offerings. Excellent reference. Compare to McNeil and Terrace (below).

*Brown, Les. *New York Times Encyclopedia of Television.* New York: Times Books, 1977. Brief entries covering major programs, institutions, technical terms, and industry figures (on and behind the screen). Useful though not definitive.

*Brown, Les. *Televi$ion: The Business Behind the Box.* New York: Harcourt Brace Jovanovich, 1971. 374 pp. (P) A detailed, behind-the-scenes account of network program decision-making during 1970, concentrating on the factors behind the decisions and the people involved. One of the most revealing and readable books around.

*Cantor, Muriel G. *The Hollywood Television Producer: His Work and His Audience.* New York: Basic Books, 1971. 256 pp. Explores the job constraints and activities of prime-time program producers from a sociological perspective. See also the same author's later *Prime-Time Television: Content and Control* (Beverly Hills, Ca.: Sage Publications, 1980, 141 pp., P) for an updating of the research and a broadening of its applications.

Cole, Barry, ed. *Television Today: A Close Up View.* New York: Oxford University Press, 1981. 480 pp. (P) Major revision of the editor's 1970 compilation of the best serious writing from the pages of *TV Guide.* Includes about 70 articles, most from the past few years and dealing heavily with all kinds of programming.

*Comstock, George, et al. *Television and Human Behavior.* New York: Columbia University Press, 1978. 600 pp. (P) The best one-volume overview of research on both television content trends and the impact of television on its many audiences.

*Eastman, Susan Tyler, et al. *Broadcast Programming: Strategies for Winning Television and Radio Audiences.* Belmont, Ca.: Wadsworth, 1981. 384 pp. 17 chapters by industry leaders about what factors go into network and station level programming.

*Federal Communications Commission, Network Inquiry Special Staff. *An Analysis of Television Program Production, Acquisition and Distribution.* Washington: FCC, 1980. 567 pp. (P) Though copies may be hard to find, this is the best current analysis of how the network and syndication process works, covering prime time and daytime and all types of programs. It is essentially an economic analysis, updating FCC studies of two decades earlier.

*Head, Sydney W. *Broadcasting in America: A Survey of Television and Radio.* Boston: Houghton Mifflin, 1976 (3rd edition). 630 pp. Best single volume explaining American broadcasting, how it works, and how it got to be that way. Good starting point for those who lack background in the subject. Useful 50-page annotated bibliography as well. (Revised edition due late in 1981.)

*McNeil, Alex. *Total Television: A Comprehensive Guide to Programming from 1948 to 1980.* New York: Penguin Books, 1980. 1088 pp. (P) Includes daytime, syndicated, NET/PBS as well as prime-time network programs, with cast and credits and short paragraph of description on each. Compare to Terrace (below), and the more limited-scope Brooks-Marsh (above).

Michael, Paul. *The Emmy Awards: A Pictorial History.* New York: Crown, 1977 (2nd ed.). 382 pp. Some 12-18 pages per year of photos, brief text, and analysis. Gives a sense of top network entertainment and new programs of each season.

*Newcomb, Horace. *TV: The Most Popular Art.* New York: Doubleday Anchor Books, 1974. 272 pp. (P) Chapters divided along network program genre lines, covering both entertainment and information formats. Discusses content types and conventions with many examples from specific series and even specific episodes. While examples are dated, the analysis is useful.

Owen, Bruce M., Jack H. Beebe, and Willard G. Manning, Jr. *Television Economics.* Lexington, Mass.: Lexington Books, 1974. 219 pp. Title is misleading, as most of book deals with programming and how economic factors affect it. Includes a good deal of tabular reference material along the way.

Primeau, Ronald. *The Rhetoric of Television.* New York: Longman, 1979. 275 pp. (P) A work-text, this provides three major parts: an analysis of the major rhetorical theories applied to TV, the idea of television, and the third (longest) part devoted to sections on major TV program genres. Interesting format and some new ways of looking at familiar aspects of the tube.

Ravage, John W. *Television: The Director's Viewpoint.* Boulder, Colo.: Westview Press, 1978. 185 pp. An interview-based analysis of the role of the director in commercial (network level) television production compared to film. Compare to Cantor, above. For biographical and credit data on American TV directors, see Christopher Wicking and Tise Vahimagi's *The American Vein: Directors and Directions in American Television.* New York: Dutton, 1979. 261 pp. (P)

Stein, Ben. *The View From Sunset Boulevard.* New York: Basic Books, 1979. 156 pp. Short critical chapters on the content of Hollywood-produced entertainment series, seeking commonalities. Lots of interesting quotes.

Steinberg, Cobbett S. *TV Facts.* New York: Facts on File Inc., 1980. 541 pp. General reference with material on prime-time schedules, longest running series, cost of TV programs, ratings, advertisers, major award winners, networks and stations, etc.

Sterling, Christopher H., and John M. Kittross. *Stay Tuned: A Concise History of American Broadcasting.* Belmont, Ca.: Wadsworth, 1978. 562 pp. The last few chapters provide a broad contextual background for the development of television. Appendices include program statistics.

Tannenbaum, Percy H., Ed. *The Entertainment Functions of Television.* Hillsdale, N.J.: Laurence Erlbaum Assoc., 1980. 262 pp. Eight scholarly, original articles on news, drama, and comedy.

Terrace, Vincent. *The Complete Encyclopedia of Television Programs, 1947-1979.* Cranbury, N.J.: A.S. Barnes, 1979 (2nd ed.). 1211 pp. (P) Brief background data, cast and credit lists, some photos, running dates and times, network, for some 3,500 network and syndicated programs for all hours. Compare with McNeil (above).

TV-Season. Phoenix, Az.: Oryx Press, 1975-date (annual). ca 200 pp. Annual volume for each season with detailed credit listings for network (including PBS) and syndicated programming, along with appendices on awards, new and folding shows, etc. Nothing to read here, but useful updating reference.

Wilk, Max. *The Golden Age of Television.* New York: Delacorte Press, 1976. 274 pp. Unscholarly but informative account of the early days of live television. Based on extensive interviews with the people who made the shows. Chapters cover programs such as "Philco Playhouse," "Honeymooners," Milton Berle.

2. Television Drama

Edmondson, Madeleine, and David Rounds. *From Mary Noble to Mary Hartman—The Complete Soap Opera Book.* New York: Stein & Day, 1976, 256 pp. History of daytime serials on radio and TV, informal analysis, and useful behind-the-scenes information on production. (Revised and updated version of *The Soaps,* 1973).

*Gerrold, David. *The World of Star Trek* and *The Trouble with Tribbles.* New York: Ballantine Books, 1973. 278 and 275 pp. (P) Developed for the vast cult of believers in this network show. These two studies offer valuable views of the production process—the first volume looking at the whole program process, and the second volume reviewing a specific episode (Gerrold wrote the script).

Gianakos, Larry James. *Television Drama Series Programming: A Comprehensive Chronicle, 1959-1975.* Metuchen, N.J.: Scarecrow Press, 1978. 806 pp. Reference listing of episode titles and cast for network series, with data on date aired, a paragraph of description on each series, comparative network schedules, etc. A sequel covering earlier years (1947-1959) was issued by the same author/publisher in 1980.

Glut, Donald F., and Jim Harmon. *The Great Television Heroes.* New York: Doubleday, 1975. 245 pp. Short illustrated study written for the nostalgia market, and covering network programs up to about 1960. Discusses both children's and adult programs of various types, dealing with their characters and content trends.

Greenberg, Bradley S. *Life on Television: Content Analyses of U.S. TV Drama.* Norwood, N.J.: Ablex Publishing, 1980. 224 pp. A three-season analysis of programming with data on pro- and anti-social behavior, portrayal of minorities, family structure as seen on TV, and sex roles.

LaGuardia, Robert. *The Wonderful World of TV Soap Operas.* New York: Ballantine Books, 1974. 342 pp. (P) A light, fan-type book which offers some useful background and production information on the soaps, their characters, and creators as well as plot outlines.

*Stedman, Raymond William: *The Serials: Suspense and Drama by Installment.* Norman: University of Oklahoma Press, 1977 (2nd ed.). 514 pp. Scholarly yet eminently readable history of the serial form in film, radio, and television, the latter being one of the best available analyses of content and impact of this format.

*Whitfield, Stephen, and Gene Roddenberry. *The Making of Star Trek.* New York: Ballantine Books, 1968. 414 pp. (P) Probably the best study of a commercial network program ever published. Recommended even for those who did not care for the program, as it provides detail on early conception of the idea, character and actor development, sets and props, writer guidelines, pilot production, etc.

3. TV Comedy and Game Shows

*Adler, Richard P., ed. *All in the Family: A Critical Appraisal.* New York: Praeger, 1979. 320 pp. (P) A collection of scripts, early newspaper criticism, longer articles of analysis, research studies, photos, and a listing of 1971-79 episodes of the long-running top program.

Blumenthal, Norman. *The TV Game Shows.* New York: Pyramid Books, 1975. 272 pp. (P) Popular discussion of program types, operations and economics, personalities, and details on network shows. Useful for "behind-the-scenes" approach even though aimed mainly at quiz show viewers.

Brodhead, James E. *Inside Laugh-In.* New York: Signet Paperback T4059, 1969. 159 pp. (P) The only fairly serious published study of how this once-popular program developed and how a typical show was produced.

*Fabe, Maxines. *TV Game Shows*. New York: Doubleday/Dolphin, 1979. 332 pp. (P) The best book on the genre to date, this provides two major parts: an overview of the program type and how it operates today, followed by a chronological section with a few pages on each of the game shows that have aired on the networks from the beginning.

Fates, Gil. *What's My Line: The Inside Story of TV's Most Famous Panel Show*. Englewood Cliffs, N.J.: Prentice-Hall, 1978. 239 pp. A nostalgic review of the long-running format show, this study is of more interest than many similar works due to length of the show's run and because author deals with many background factors.

Metz, Robert. *The Today Show,* and *The Tonight Show*. New York: Harper & Row, 1976 and 1980. 300 and 350 pp. (P) Informal treatment of two of NBC's most successful shows, both dating to the 1950s—the morning talk/news program and the evening interview/entertainment/comedy show long starring Johnny Carson.

Mitz, Rick. *The Great TV Sitcom Book*. New York: Richard Marek Publishers, 1980. 350 pp. (P) Picture and text album covering all programs of the genre on the networks up to 1980, with cast and credit lists, bits of dialogue and other information.

Miller, Merle, and Evan Rhodes. *Only You, Dick Daring!* New York: Sloane, 1964. 350 pp. (P) Tongue-in-cheek, but an essentially true tale of an attempt to sell a program idea to then CBS Television President James Aubrey—and the reasons for this venture's failure. Useful analysis of program idea development problems.

Reiss, David. *M*A*S*H: The Warm, Intimate Story of TV's Most Popular Show*. New York: Bantam Books, 1980. 300 pp. (P) Photo-illustrated overview of the program, its development and dips into drama, the stars and its reasons for lasting in the top 10 for so many seasons. (This is a typical "fan book," increasingly evident in the literature on television.)

4. Television Journalism

*Adams, William, and Fay Schreibman, eds. *Television Network News: Issues in Content Research.* Washington: George Washington University TV News Study Program, 1978. 235 pp. (P) Unique guide both how to do such work and a review of some already done on different aspects of TV network news.

*Barrett, Marvin, and Zachary Sklar. *The Eye of the Storm: The Alfred I. duPont–Columbia University Survey of Broadcast Journalism.* New York: Lippincott & Crowell, 1980. 240 pp. (P) Seventh in a now biennial series of overviews of national and local radio-TV trends. Focuses on the good and bad points of each.

Epstein, Edward Jay. *News From Nowhere: Television and the News.* New York: Random House, 1973. 321 pp. (P) Detailed analysis of the process of gathering and reporting the evening network news during the 1968-69 season, with discussion of the people, restrictions, decision-making, and the final product. Critical, though dated (based on author's Ph.D. dissertation).

*Gans, Herbert J. *Deciding What's News: A Study of CBS Evening News, NBC Nightly News, Newsweek & Time.* New York: Pantheon, 1979. (P) 393 pp. Scholarly analysis based on participant observation of the television and magazine news production process compared, with examples from more than a decade of each. This is a critically acclaimed study.

Gates, Gary Paul. *Air Time: The Inside Story of CBS News.* New York: Harper & Row, 1978. 360 pp. (P) A sometimes gossipy history of the development of the personnel of first radio and then television network news at CBS, and the impact of the personnel on the product decisions.

Gitlin, Todd. *The Whole World is Watching: Mass Media in the Making and Unmaking of the New Left.* Berkeley: University of California Press, 1980. 330 pp. The role of TV and press in making media celebrities out of 1960's protesters and how this process affected protest movements.

Kraus, Sidney, ed. *The Great Debates: Carter vs Ford, 1976.* Bloomington: Indiana University Press, 1979. 550 pp. (P) Follow-up study to the editor's collection on the 1960 debates, this collection of original analytic articles and the transcripts of the debates themselves is one of several similar works focusing on TV's impact on national politics.

*Powers, Ron. *The Newscasters.* New York: St. Martin's Press, 1977. 250 pp. (P) Highly critical analysis, mainly of local television news shows, suggesting entertainment demands have taken over solid news content.

Tuchman, Gaye. *Making News: A Study in the Construction of Reality.* New York: Free Press, 1978. 275 pp. Serious sociological analysis of just what makes mediated news and the importance of such decisions to both the media (including television) and the nation.

Yellin, David. *Special: Fred Freed and the Television Documentary.* New York: Macmillan, 1972. 289 pp. Interesting study of a long-time CBS and NBC producer (who died shortly after the book appeared), made even more interesting by Freed's own descriptions of his work and the production process.

5. Television Commercials

*Arlen, Michael. *30 Seconds.* New York: Farrar Straus & Giroux, 1979. Traces the production of a single commercial from conception to airing. Arlen provides many details, few judgments.

*Barnouw, Erik. *The Sponsor: Notes on a Modern Potentate.* New York: Oxford University Press, 1978. 220 pp. Highly critical "history" of the development of advertiser roles in radio and then television, with the majority of the analysis dealing with the impact of sponsors in network and local television today.

Diamont, Lincoln. *The Anatomy of a Television Commercial.* New York: Hastings House, 1970. 190 pp. Illustrated album exploring all facets of production and use of a two-minute Kodak film ad.

*Price, Jonathan. *The Best Thing on Television: Commercials.* New York: Penguin Books, 1978. 184 pp. (P) An illustrated album of some of the better "mini-shows" with details on their production, the many types of commercials, concerns and controversies in TV advertising, and many sample "storyboards."

6. Criticism of Television

*Arlen, Michael. *The Living Room War,* New York: Viking, 1969; *The View from Highway 1: Essays on Television,* New York: Farrar Strauss & Giroux, 1976; *The Camera Age: Essays on Television,* New York: Farrar Strauss & Giroux, 1981. 242, 293 and unknown pp. (P) Collected television criticism by the highly respected TV critic for *The New Yorker,* heavily reflecting his concern over coverage of the Vietnam War. Many feel this is some of the best TV criticism written today.

Crosby, John. *Out of the Blue: A Book about Radio and Television.* New York: Simon and Schuster, 1952. 301 pp. The collected work of the critic for the old *New York Herald Tribune.*

Ellison, Harlan. *The Glass Teat,* and *The Other Glass Teat.* New York: ACC 1976; New York: Pyramid, 1975. 317 and 397 pp. (P) Collected anti-establishment (and somewhat predictable) television criticism of the *Los Angeles Free Press* critic.

Fiske, John, and John Hartley. *Reading Television.* New York: Methuen, 1979. 223 pp. (P) First attempt to combine a theory of the cultural role of television with a semiotic-based method of analysis whereby individual shows can be "read." British examples but broadly applicable analysis.

Hazard, Patrick D., ed. *TV as Art: Some Essays on Criticism.* Champaign, Ill.: National Council of Teachers of English, 1966. 160 pp. (P) Discussion of dramatic, musical, and other program formats in the arts.

*Newcomb, Horace, ed. *Television: The Critical View.* New York: Oxford University Press, 1979 (2nd ed.). 553 pp. (P) Essays dealing with specific programs, program genres, the role of TV in society, and the aesthetics of television compared to other media and art forms.

*Schwartz, Tony. *The Responsive Chord.* New York: Doubleday, 1973. 210 pp. (P) McLuhanesque discussion of the aesthetics of electronic communication (including TV sound), especially in commercial and political advertising. Emphasis is on the role of sound.

Seldes, Gilbert. *The Public Arts.* New York: Simon and Schuster, 1956. 303 pp. (P) The best statement on television programming by the one-time dean of media critics. For his earlier thinking on television, see *The Great Audience* (Viking, 1950).

Shayon, Robert Lewis, ed. *The Eighth Art: Twenty-Three Views of Television Today.* New York: Holt, Rinehart & Winston, 1962. 269 pp. Original essays on all aspects of television content. Originally assembled for a CBS quarterly that never appeared.

*Shayon, Robert Lewis. *Open to Criticism.* Boston: Little, Brown, 1971. 324 pp. Unique self-analysis of the then-critic for *Saturday Review.* Includes many of his columns, the background of their writing, and his later reaction to it all.

*Smith, Robert Rutherford. *Beyond the Wasteland: The Criticism of Broadcasting.* Annandale, Va.: Speech Communication Association, 1980 (rev. ed.). 112 pp. (P) The best current overview of the functions of broadcasting criticism with suggested approaches to the task, problems facing the critic, etc.

White, David Manning, and Richard Averson, eds. *Sight, Sound and Society: Motion Pictures and Television in America.* Boston: Beacon Press, 1968. 466 pp. Collected writings and articles, about half on television, with a strongly critical tone.

Index of Program Titles

A

W

About the Editor

RICHARD ADLER is a research associate with the Institute for the Future in Menlo Park, CA. He was formerly director of the Aspen Institute Workshop on Television and assistant director of the Aspen Program on Communications and Society. He has also been a research associate at the Harvard Graduate School of Education and taught at Oberlin College, UCLA, and Stanford University.

In addition to the two collections on which this volume is based, Mr. Adler has edited *All in the Family: A Critical Appraisal* (Praeger, 1979) and *The Electronic Box Office* (Praeger, 1974), and is co-author of *The Effects of Television Advertising on Children* (Lexington, 1980). He has also written a column of television criticism for *The Wall Street Journal* and contributed articles to many magazines.